Kant's Theory of Mental Activity

A COMMENTARY ON

THE TRANSCENDENTAL ANALYTIC

OF THE

CRITIQUE OF PURE REASON

Robert Paul Wolff received his Ph.D. from Harvard, where he taught for several years. He has published articles in scholarly journals as well as in a number of political weeklies. Mr. Wolff now teaches philosophy at the University of Chicago.

Kant's Theory

of

Mental Activity

A COMMENTARY ON

THE TRANSCENDENTAL ANALYTIC

OF THE

CRITIQUE OF PURE REASON

Robert Paul Wolff

HARVARD UNIVERSITY PRESS

CAMBRIDGE, MASSACHUSETTS

1963

Publication of this book has been aided by a grant from the Ford Foundation

Library of Congress Catalog Card Number 63-10877

Distributed in Great Britain by Oxford University Press, London

Printed in the United States of America

For Cindy, who laughed.

PREFACE

There are at present at least five commentaries in English devoted to Kant's *Critique of Pure Reason*. The earliest, by Norman Kemp Smith, is a masterful and comprehensive treatise whose accumulation of scholarship will not soon be equaled in a work of that sort. The others, while unable to achieve Kemp Smith's encyclopedic command of the text and its sources, are in varying degrees helpful as guides to Kant's philosophy. T. D. Weldon's short commentary in particular contains genuinely brilliant passages of philosophical explication. Taken all in all, the assorted commentaries and other books on Kant's philosophy offer more pages of explanation than even the most puzzled reader is likely to have a taste for. The question therefore naturally arises: why another commentary on the *Critique?* And why, indeed, a commentary so narrowly limited to just the Trancendental Analytic?

My answer must necessarily be personal, but I hope that it will achieve what Kant calls "subjective necessity" by discovering an echo in each of my readers. Briefly then, I found that even after a careful study of the existing commentaries, I was still completely unclear about the central arguments and doctrines of Kant's theory of knowledge. I had gained a certain grasp of the complexities of the text, to be sure, and in the study of Kant that is an indispensable preliminary to understanding. I had convinced myself, by a patient study of the Deduction, that the controversial "patchwork theory" of its composition was fundamentally sound as textual exegesis, however dubious as an actual history of the writing of the *Critique*. But when I tried to restate Kant's teaching in my own words, I discovered that I simply could not do so. Indeed, the very wealth of detail which I had gleaned from the secondary literature proved an embarrassment, for out of it emerged no single coherent doctrine. The Analytic, and in particular the Deduction, appeared to me a great tangle of insights and half-completed proofs. Each time I began to unravel it, I found myself enmeshed in still further loops and snarls. Where it began and where it ended I could not tell, nor was I sure that it would unwind into a single connected strand of argument.

In puzzling over this failure, it occurred to me that the problem might lie less in the complexity of the text than in the obscurity of certain of its key terms. While expending immense energy comparing proof texts and decomposing compound passages, the commentators had neglected to explain the meanings of the pivotal concepts on which Kant's analysis turned. In particular, I realized that I hadn't any clear idea of what Kant meant by "synthesis." Lacking this, I also could not explain to myself the concepts of synthetic unity, *a priori* synthesis, necessary connection of the manifold, transcendental unity of apperception, and so on. To be sure, I had various visual images of the meaning of "synthesis," based on the metaphorical descriptions of "running through and holding together" or "grasping" which Kant offers. But when I looked to the commentators for non-metaphorical equivalents, I found the same phrases repeated. I decided therefore to concentrate my attention on the only account of the process of *a priori* synthesis which Kant ever gives us — namely, the first edition Subjective Deduction — and to try to elicit from it a definition of the concept of "synthesis."

In order to do the job satisfactorily, I was forced to draw on hints and suggestions from many other parts of Kant's writings. The key to the puzzle proved to be Kant's rather cryptic assertion that "a concept is always, as regards its form, something universal which serves as a rule." This led to an analysis of rules and rule-directed activities, and to the recognition that for Kant, synthesis is a rule-directed mental activity. Once I had become clear about this, I could explain how synthesis conferred necessity upon a manifold of representations, and this in turn led to an understanding of the notion of the synthetic unity of the manifold. With these conceptual clarifications in hand, I returned to the text of the *Critique* and found that it now began to make some sense. It finally proved possible to exhibit the entire Analytic as a single connected argument, beginning with the premise that my consciousness has a necessary unity, and concluding with the validity of the causal maxim and the other Analogies. It turned out that Kant had known exactly what he was doing all along, and that when he claimed to have answered Hume's sceptical doubts, he was perfectly correct. The Analytic could now be seen as a proof of the law of causality. It did not assume the existence of knowledge merely in order to explain how such knowledge was possible, as many commentators have supposed. Instead, it offered a demonstration that from the mere fact of my being conscious, I could infer the validity of the highest principles of science.

The results of these investigations are embodied in this commentary. As my analysis sometimes extends rather far beyond the actual wording of the text, it seemed to me particularly important to present as much evidence as possible of its correctness as an interpretation. Consequently, I have cast this book in the form of a textual commentary. Save for an introductory section and some more general discussion of Kant's philosophy near the end, my chapters follow those of the Analytic in the usual manner of a commentary. At times I have found it necessary to descend to the level of sentence-by-sentence explication, and I have taken the liberty in those passages of assuming that the reader has the *Critique* open before him as he reads.

There are, of course, many persons to whom I owe thanks for their assistance and encouragement in the writing of this book. My debt to one man is of a very special nature, and it gives me great pleasure to have an opportunity to acknowledge it in print. As an undergraduate, I was privileged to attend Clarence Irving Lewis' lectures at Kant, during the last year of his long association with Harvard University. It was from him that I first acquired my interest in the *Critique*. None of us who took Lewis' course will ever forget the experience, I am sure. He demanded of us a weekly summary of the assigned reading, and somehow that paper always took as much time to prepare as all our other courses combined. Then, in his precise manner, he would proceed through the text, explaining difficult passages or pausing to demonstrate some point of logic. To me and to many of my fellow students, Lewis was the personification of philosophical commitment. There seemed to emanate from him a conviction that in the pursuit of truth, any less than one's best was morally reprehensible. We came away from that course not only with a magnificent introduction to Kant's philosophy, but also with an undying image of what it meant to *be* a philosopher. That same year, I took a course with Lewis on problems in the theory of knowledge. I submitted a rather superficial paper on Hume's theory of impressions and ideas, in which I did my best to pick apart some of Hume's statements, paying more attention to their wording than to the insights which they sought to convey. Lewis treated my effort very gently, and after remarking that "in this paper, it would be out of place to ask that [the points] should 'add up' to something in conclusion," he wrote: "I should hope that this general character of the paper is not a symptom of that type of mind, in philosophy, which can find the objection to everything but advance the solution to nothing." Those words express the spirit in which I undertook the study of the *Critique*.

I owe a very personal debt to a group of young philosophers with whom I studied as a graduate student in the Harvard Department. During the year 1955–56, Stephen Barker, Hubert Dreyfus, Samuel Todes, Charles Parsons, and I formed a small seminar to read Kant together. We met each Wednesday evening for four hours or more to pore over the *Critique* and argue out varying interpretations. In the years since, all of us have continued our study of Kant, and in endless conversations with the others I have sharpened my understanding of the *Critique*. In a sense, I have written with them always in mind.

Mrs. Ingrid Stadler, whose own philosophical studies have been in large measure devoted to Kant, has given the manuscript the most thorough reading that it will probably ever receive. I have made countless alterations, small and large, in response to her criticisms, which have ranged from the spotting of typographical errors to fundamental disagreement with certain of my central arguments.

Professor Lewis White Beck went through the final version of the manuscript with great care, and discovered several major, as well as numerous minor, errors or unclarities. My treatment of the transcendental object $= x$ in particular is influenced by his acute criticisms.

Mrs. Elizabeth Silbert took a lengthy and illegible first draft of the book and somehow managed to transform it into a legible typescript. Save for her heroic labors, it might still be a mass of blue-black scribbling.

Finally, I should like to thank the Henry P. Kendall Foundation for a grant which helped to finance the last stages of the writing and preparation of the manuscript.

Robert Paul Wolff

Chicago, October 1962

Contents

INTRODUCTION

COMMENTARY ON THE
TRANSCENDENTAL ANALYTIC

Introduction

All quotations from the *Critique of Pure Reason* are taken from Norman Kemp Smith's translation, unless otherwise noted. Works cited are listed in the bibliography. In order to reduce the number of footnotes, I have adopted the following conventions:

1. References to the *Critique of Pure Reason* are given in brackets in the text, with the customary "A" and "B" for the first and second editions, as in Kemp Smith's translation.
2. References to Hume's *Treatise of Human Nature* are included in the text in brackets, with the pagination of Selby-Bigge's edition.

CHAPTER I

THE HISTORICAL BACKGROUND
OF THE CRITIQUE

The *Critique of Pure Reason* is usually introduced to the student in one of two ways. The most direct method is simply to open the book and begin explaining the Prefaces and Introduction. Alternatively, the *Critique* can be set in its historical perspective, and the disputes among previous philosophers, as well as the progression of thought in Kant's own earlier works, briefly traced. If we choose the former, we run immediately into a very serious difficulty. Kant asserts in the Introduction [B 19] that his work is an attempt to answer the question, "How are synthetic judgments *a priori* possible?" In the *Prolegomena*, intended as a summary and introduction to the *Critique*, he repeats this formulation. Yet Kant gives the reader little or no explanation of the problem before plunging into the technicalities of the Transcendental Aesthetic. The key terms, "analytic," "synthetic," "a priori," and "a posteriori," are given the most cursory definition. Kant merely states, with no real demonstration, that there are synthetic judgments *a priori;* to the uninitiated reader it is exceedingly unclear why so long and difficult a book should have been devoted to the answering of so dubious a question. Indeed, it soon becomes clear that the question is a very inadequate representation of the subject of the *Critique*, for one of Kant's principal aims is to prove that all judgments, *a posteriori* as well as *a priori*, are in need of explanation and critique.

The inadequacies of the opening sections of the *Critique* are a consequence of the fact that Kant has more to say than can possibly be suggested in a Preface. To give an accurate picture of the subject of the book would have required the expenditure of many pages which could better be devoted to the doctrines themselves.

Nevertheless, Kant's choice of the problem of synthetic judgments *a priori* is neither arbitrary nor misleading when viewed in the context of the historical background of the *Critique*. Kant knew very well, what the unprepared reader cannot immediately recognize, that the problems leading up to the *Critique*, and the new doctrines emerging from it, find their focal point in the theory of *a priori* synthesis. Rather than dwell on the question of synthetic judgments *a priori*, therefore, I have chosen to begin this commentary with a brief summary of several of the lines of argument which come together in the *Critique*. When we have surveyed the problems which stimulated Kant to undertake the labors of the Critical Philosophy, and some of the early stages in the development of his thought, it will be clearer why he considered the existence of synthetic judgments *a priori* an appropriate starting point for the *Critique*.

LEIBNIZ AND NEWTON

As a convenient *terminus a quo* we may select the famous debate between the Leibnizians and the Newtonians over the foundations of the physical sciences. Mathematical, scientific, metaphysical, theological, and logical doctrines were intertwined in this conflict between the continental defenders of the Metaphysical Philosophy and the British proponents of the Mathematical Philosophy. At stake were fundamental substantive and methodological issues growing out of the new physics and mathematics, to which Leibniz and Newton had made notable contributions. The climax of the conflict was the exchange of letters between Leibniz and Samuel Clarke, a defender of Newton's philosophy. This correspondence, one of the most brilliant events in modern letters, was immediately published in English and French, and became the source of many future debates. Kant is known to have studied the letters carefully, and several of his early publications are attempts to advance the argument on one side or the other. Kant's *Inaugural Dissertation*, the most important of his works prior to the *Critique*, sought to work out a compromise position which would make a place for the truth which he felt each side possessed. It would require too much space to survey all the points of conflict between Leibniz and Newton, though many of them are directly relevant to Kant's thought. The present discussion is limited, therefore, to the problem which Kant made central to the argument of the *Dissertation:* the nature of space and time.

Leibniz on Space and Time

According to Leibniz, the universe consists of an infinitude of unique, simple, immaterial substances, which he calls "monads." Each monad possesses some degree of consciousness, and the succession of representations in its consciousness constitutes a complete point of view of the universe. There is no causal interaction between monads, although the internal perceptions of each monad seem to represent such interaction. Actually, says Leibniz, the causes of representations are to be found in preceding representations in the same consciousness, not in other substances. The cognitive validity of the perceptions of a monad is guaranteed by God, who makes the other monads as the perceptions seem to represent them to be. This pre-established harmony between representations and the objects they purport to represent provides Leibniz with solutions to the problems of substantial interaction, the relation of mind and body, and so forth.

Space is now defined as a set of relations of the monads to one another. It is "the order of co-existing things." Time becomes the relations of the successive states of consciousness of a single monad, or "the order of non-contemporaneous things." Bodies are explained as "colonies of monads," and since each monad is unextended, any body is endlessly divisible into bodies which are themselves infinite collections of monads. Mathematically, each monad is a point having no dimension, and spatial relations such as length or position can be represented as relations of monads. In this way, the order or interrelations of a plenum of distinct monads becomes a continuous system of mathematical points, which is to say space. The temporal order is analyzed in a similar manner, although the lack of a mathematics of time weakens the analogy to space. Time is one-dimensional, and the only temporal relations are succession and simultaneity. From the representations or perceptions in a monad it is therefore possible to construct a temporal order in which every element is either prior to, coeval with, or posterior to every other element (what mathematicians call a well-ordering).

Newton on Space and Time

Newton and his followers did not develop an elaborate metaphysical underpinning for his physical theories. Partly as a matter
of methodological principle he eschewed all "hypotheses." His
brief remarks on the nature of space and time, therefore, can be
viewed as answers to the question, what concepts of space and
time do we need for physics?, rather than as part of a general
theory of metaphysics.[1] Roughly speaking, Newton views space
and time as infinite and independent of objects. In two passages,
he describes space, by analogy to human perception, as God's
"boundless uniform sensorium," though the meaning of these
words is unclear. The two most important tenets of his theory
are, first, that there are absolute positions in space and time which
are not dependent on the objects which occupy them, and second,
that empty space or time is possible. The reasons for holding
these views are, as we shall see, primarily scientific in nature.
Newton was convinced that they were required by his theory of
motion.

Leibniz, on the other hand, denies both the existence of absolute
space-time and the possibility of a void. For if space and time are
relations of monads, then positions or dates can only be defined in
terms of the objects at those positions or dates, and where there
are no substances, there can be neither empty space nor empty
time.

The Clarke-Leibniz Debate

The two philosophies confronted one another in a series of ex-
changes during 1715 and 1716 between Leibniz himself and
Samuel Clarke, a defender of Newton.[2] The correspondence ran
to five increasingly lengthy papers and replies, in the course of
which all the most powerful arguments for each side were stated
and answered. The strengths and weaknesses of both positions are
clearly exhibited, and Kant could not have helped but recognize
the necessity for some intermediate position which would do
justice to each. What follows is a summary of the core of Leibniz's

[1] Cf. H. G. Alexander (ed.), *The Leibniz–Clarke Correspondence*, pp. xxxii ff.
[2] Alexander, *The Leibniz-Clarke Correspondence*.

attack on the Newtonian theory of space-time, and Clarke's responses.

Leibniz's Argument

In the course of the correspondence Leibniz developed three important arguments against Newton. The first[3] is directed against the Newtonian explanation of the nature of space.[4] Leibniz ridicules the notion that God needs a "sense organ" to perceive objects. As for the possibility that space is an "absolute reality," this would give to it "a greater reality than substances themselves. God [could not] destroy it, nor even change it in any respect."[5] These and other points show that Newton has no answer to the question, what is space? Metaphysically, the postulation of an infinite, subsistent non-substance (an "unthing" as Kant later called it) is simply a monstrosity.

The second argument attacks the concept of absolute space-time and the doctrine of the void. The two are linked together, for a void presupposes the independence of space, and conversely absolute space implies at least the possibility of a void. Leibniz summarizes his argument in the fifth paper:

> In order to prove that space, without bodies, is an absolute reality; the author [Clarke] objected, that a finite material universe might move forward in space. I answered, it does not appear reasonable that the material universe should be finite; and, though we should suppose it to be finite; yet 'tis unreasonable it should have motion any otherwise, than as its parts change their situation among themselves; because such a motion would produce no change that could be observed, and would be without design. 'Tis another thing, when its parts change their situation among themselves; for then there is a motion in space; but it consists in the order of relations which are changed. The author replies now, that the reality of motion does not depend upon being observed; and that a ship may go forward, and yet a man, who is in the ship, may not perceive it. I answer, motion does not indeed depend upon being observed; but it does depend upon being possible to be observed. There is no motion, when there is

---

[3] That is, the first which will be discussed here.

[4] And, by implication, time also. In all that follows time is rather the poor relation to space. This order of importance is reflected in Kant's *Dissertation* and in the Transcendental Aesthetic. Part of the difficulty in understanding the *Critique of Pure Reason* derives from the reversal in emphasis which takes place between the Aesthetic and the Analytic. In the former, problems of space are to the fore, while in the latter it is almost exclusively time which is discussed.

[5] Alexander, p. 37.

no change that can be observed. And when there is no change that can be observed, there is no change at all.[6]

There are two points in this passage which are particularly deserving of attention. First, Leibniz invokes the principle that any difference, in order to *be* a difference, must *make* a difference in the observable world. To say that God might have created the world a day earlier, or that He might have placed it in a different part of space, or that the entire physical universe might proceed through the void at some given rate of speed, is meaningless unless we can say what observable difference such states of affairs would make. Leibniz, of course, thinks they would make none at all. Second, it is a clear inference from Leibniz's argument that events or bodies find position in space-time only by their relations to other events or bodies. Time does not exist as an infinite line on which we can locate and date events. Rather, the time-series is constructed out of the relations of simultaneity and succession which events bear to one another. This doctrine, as we shall see, becomes of central importance to Kant's argument in the Analogies.

Leibniz's third argument invokes the famous principle of sufficient reason, and is also directed against the doctrine of absolute space. If space were absolute, Leibniz reasons, then in a preexisting void the pairs of concepts "right" and "left," "east" and "west," or "up" and "down" would have application. It would then be meaningful to inquire why God, in creating the world, ordered it in its present manner rather than as a mirror image. But two such counterparts would be characterized by all and only the same attributes — the same internal relations of distance and shape would exist among the bodies. Hence there would be no sufficient reason for God to choose to create one rather than the other, no mark of distinction on which a choice could be based. This, insists Leibniz, is impossible. His fullest statement of the argument occurs in the third paper:

Space is something absolutely uniform; and, without the things placed in it, one point of space does not absolutely differ in any respect whatsoever from another point of space. Now from hence it follows, (supposing space to be something in itself, besides the order of bodies among themselves,)

[6] Alexander, pp. 73–74.

that 'tis impossible there should be a reason, why God, preserving the same situations of bodies among themselves, should have placed them in space after one certain particular manner, and not otherwise; why every thing was not placed the quite contrary way, for instance, by changing East into West. But if space is nothing else, but that order or relation; and is nothing at all without bodies, but the possibility of placing them; then those two states, the one such as it now is, the other supposed to be the quite contrary way, would not at all differ from one another. Their difference therefore is only to be found in our chimerical supposition of the reality of space in itself. But in truth the one would exactly be the same thing as the other, they being absolutely indiscernible; and consequently there is no room to enquire after a reason of the preference of the one to the other.[7]

Clarke's Replies

Clarke attempts to meet all three of Leibniz's objections, but it is only against the second that he presents a coherent argument. In response to the first point, that it makes no sense to describe space as "God's sensorium," he offers the alternative characterization of space and time as "properties" or "necessary consequences" of God.[8] No further explanation of these terms is given, however.

Similarly, Clarke replies quite feebly to Leibniz's third argument, from the principle of sufficient reason. He says merely that God can perfectly well exercise His will to choose among identical alternatives. We see here an echo of the ancient theological debate over the relative supremacy of God's will and intellect. Leibniz follows the tradition that even God can act only rationally, for sufficient reason,[9] while Clarke adopts the alternative of voluntarism. The principal interest of this reply is that Clarke missed an excellent opportunity to employ the argument, later discovered by Kant, based on the paradox of incongruous counterparts.

When he turns to the second of Leibniz's arguments, however, Clarke mounts a very impressive defense. Drawing on Newton's laws of motion, and in particular on the concept of inertia, he argues that in fact there would be an observable difference if the entire universe were to begin to move, or were suddenly to stop, or if the heavens possessed the circular motion which Aristotle ascribed to them. He writes in his reply to Leibniz's fifth paper:

[7] Alexander, p. 26.
[8] Alexander, p. 47.
[9] Cf. *Monadology*, no. 46, in *Selections*, ed. by P. Wiener.

'Tis affirmed, that the motion of the material universe would produce no change at all; and yet no answer is given to the argument I alleged, that a sudden increase or stoppage of the motion of the whole, would give a sensible shock to all the parts: and 'tis as evident, that a circular motion of the whole, would produce a *vis centrifuga* in all the parts.[10]

And later in the same reply, he says with regard to the passage by Leibniz quoted above:

Neither is it sufficient barely to repeat his assertion, that the motion of a finite material universe would be nothing, and (for want of other bodies to compare it with) would produce no discoverable change: unless he could disprove the instance which I gave of a very great change that would happen; viz. that the parts would be sensibly shocked by a sudden acceleration, or stopping of the motion of the whole . . .[11]

The Outcome of the Debate

If we were to weigh up the arguments on either side and attempt to declare a winner, we should have to settle in the end for a split decision. On the one hand, Leibniz's account of the nature of space and time is far more lucid and reasonable than the Newtonian notion of a "sensorium" or a "property" of God. On the other hand, Clarke's arguments from the facts of acceleration and centrifugal force are scientifically correct, and Leibniz simply has no reply to them.[12] The Metaphysical Philosophy of Leibniz is superior in matters which are primarily metaphysical, such as the nature of space and time, while the Mathematical Philosophy of Newton is better able to account for the facts of physical science. The analysis of space as a set of relations gives to it an ontological status which is consistent with the rationalist metaphysics of the continent, but a doctrine of absolute space seems to be required for the new physics. This dilemma was the starting point for Kant's early studies in philosophy and science.

KANT'S EARLY WRITINGS: 1747–1768

Kant's writings fall naturally into three major periods. The first, 1747–1768, represents his early explorations into a number of prob-

---

[10] Alexander, p. 101.

[11] Alexander, pp. 104–105.

[12] Strictly speaking, a relativistic theory of space-time can be developed which allows for the phenomena of acceleration, but neither Leibniz nor Newton was aware of this possibility, nor indeed was Kant a half-century later. Cf. Alexander's discussion, pp. xlix–lv.

lems in metaphysics, logic, cosmology, physical geography, and other fields. It was during this time that he published the *Universal Natural History and Theory of the Heavens,* announcing the nebular hypothesis of the origin of the solar system which is known as the Kant-Laplace hypothesis. The second period, 1769–1780, includes the writing of the *Inaugural Dissertation* and the long years during which Kant struggled with the problems of the Deduction. The last period, ushered in by the publication of the *Critique of Pure Reason* in 1781, saw the systematic unfolding of the complete Critical Philosophy.

Kant received his philosophical training at the University of Königsberg under the direction of Martin Knutzen, Professor of Mathematics and Philosophy. Knutzen taught the version of Leibniz's metaphysics which had been made popular by the German philosopher, Christian Wolff. He was interested as well in the mathematical physics which had been developed by Newton, and he passed on to the young Kant all the puzzles, conflicts, and contradictions which existed between the two.

Shortly after leaving the University, Kant published his first work, *Thoughts on the True Estimation of Living Forces* (1747). The essay takes a Leibnizean standpoint, and attempts to account for the nature of space in terms of the causal interactions of unextended substances. Kant argues, in contrast to Leibniz's theory of pre-established harmony, that substances must really interact in order to be spatially related. Indeed, "If the substances had no force whereby they can act outside themselves, there would be no extension, and consequently no space." [13] He goes on to derive the three-dimensionality of space from the nature of the laws governing the interactions, but the attempt, as he himself confesses, is largely unsuccessful.

This and other writings during the early period reveal Kant trying to find a satisfactory version of Leibnizean metaphysics. At the end of this period Kant published an essay in which he adopted the Newtonian position, and argued against the relational theory of space. The piece, entitled *On the First Ground of the Distinction of Regions in Space,* makes devastating use of an argument which first appeared, unappreciated, in the Leibniz-Clarke

[13] *Kant's Inaugural Dissertation and Early Writings on Space,* trans. by John Handyside, p. 9.

correspondence. As quoted above, Leibniz had argued that if space were absolute, then mirror images would be distinguishable. But, he insists, they are perfect counterparts and therefore must be presumed to be literally identical. In response, Clarke merely asserted God's ability to choose between indistinguishable alternatives.

Kant, however, took up this argument and made a simple observation which decisively refuted Leibniz. Consider a pair of human hands, he suggested. They are perfect counterparts of one another, the relations of their parts completely parallel. And yet no twisting or turning can ever transform the left into the right. They are *incongruous*, like matching triangles in a two-dimensional surface, spherical triangles in three-dimensions, left-and-right-hand spirals, or even, as Kant points out, left-and-right-hand snail shells. From the incongruity of counterparts, it follows that the creation of a left hand would be, for God, a different act from the creation of a right hand. Although their spatial relations are identical, the two hands are spatially different, and consequently space cannot be simply the relations of parts of the universe to each other.

Should we, then, adopt the conception held by many modern philosophers, especially in Germany, that space consists only in the outer relations of the parts of matter existing alongside one another, in the case before us all actual space would be that which this hand occupies [it is assumed that God has created nothing but a single human hand]. But since, whether it be left or right, there is no difference in the relations of its parts to one another, the hand would in respect of this characteristic be absolutely indeterminate, i.e., it would fit either side of the human body, which is impossible.

Thus it is evident that instead of the determinations of space following from the positions of the parts of matter relatively to one another, these latter follow from the former. It is also clear that in the constitution of bodies differences are to be found which are real differences, and which are grounded solely in their relation to absolute, primary space. For, only through this relation is the relation of bodily things possible.[14]

With this essay, Kant came to the end of his attempts to find

----

[14] *Kant's Inaugural Dissertation*, p. 28. The assumption that God has created nothing but a single human hand is important, for otherwise it could be argued that its rightness or leftness derives from its relation to the surrounding parts of space. But if Leibniz is correct, then there is no space save where there is body, and consequently a universe consisting of one hand would contain only the space which the hand occupied.

a defensible version of rationalist metaphysics. In his next published work, the *Inaugural Dissertation* of 1770, he struck out in a radically new direction, and began the fundamental rethinking of philosophical issues which resulted in the *Critique of Pure Reason*.

THE INAUGURAL DISSERTATION OF 1770

The publication of the physical and cosmological works had earned for Kant a substantial reputation in Germany, and several times he was offered chairs at other universities. Wishing to remain at Königsberg, he continued in the laborious role of *privatdozent* until 1770, when he was appointed to the chair of Logic and Metaphysics. At the age of forty-six, he entered upon a twelve-year period of the most profound speculation. As was customary, the new professor submitted a dissertation at the occasion of his installation. The work was the first announcement of the revolution which its author was to carry out in the field of philosophy.

The *Dissertation* is too frequently ignored by students of Kant's philosophy, who find the *Critique of Pure Reason* labor enough to master. This is unfortunate, for the *Dissertation*, far better than the well-known *Prolegomena*, can serve as an introduction to the problems, terminology, insights, and turns of argument of the *Critique*. Many passages in the Analytic which baffle the reader by their cryptic phraseology and apparent contradiction with the surrounding text are made immediately comprehensible by a study of the *Dissertation*. In it can be found Kant's first attempt at resolving the conflicts between Leibniz and Newton, as well as several of the major philosophical innovations on which the Critical Philosophy is based. For this reason, I shall take the time to summarize the argument of the *Dissertation* in some detail and to comment on significant points. In what follows, I have concentrated attention on those parts of the *Dissertation* which are most relevant to the Transcendental Analytic.

The full title of the *Dissertation* is *On the Form and Principles of the Sensible and Intelligible World*. Its purpose, Kant states in the opening sentences, is to give an exposition of the concept of a world [*mundus*], by which he means a complex of substances. The problem about which the essay revolves is the paradox that it seems both necessary and impossible to form an adequate representation of such a world. Kant's resolution of this contradiction proceeds by way of a distinction between two sources, or modes, of representations — *sensibility* and *intelligence* — and the corresponding realms of being which they reveal. The essay is divided into five sections: (1) introduction and statement of the problem; (2) statement of the distinction between sensibility and intelligence; (3) analysis of sensibility; (4) analysis of intelligence; and (5) resolution of the problem by means of the material of sections 3 and 4, and general comments on the significance of the results.

Section I: On the Notion of a World in General

When the mind is presented with a complex of substances (by which Kant means a multitude of Leibnizean monads), it can seek either to analyze this complex until it reaches "a part which is not a whole, i.e., the *simple*," or else to aggregate or synthesize the parts until it reaches "a whole which is not a part," i.e. a *world*. In either case, we must distinguish between the mere conceiving of the simple or the whole, and the representing of it "in the concrete by distinct intuition." So far as the latter is concerned, we can never form a distinct intuition of a simple or of the totality of substances. For as the multitude of substances is both continuous and infinite, and as the intuitive analysis or synthesis must take place step by step, in time, it would require an infinite span of time to complete either process, and thereby to successfully "follow out" the concepts in intuition.

Accordingly, Kant says, "since the unrepresentable and the impossible are commonly regarded as meaning the same thing, and since representation of the concepts of continuity and infinitude in accordance with the laws of intuitive knowledge is clearly impossible, we see how it comes about that these concepts are usually rejected." Such a conclusion is unwarranted however, Kant asserts, revealing what is to be the key to his argument. For the difficulty of representing an infinite composition or decomposition in intuition merely demonstrates the disharmony of sensibility and intelligence.

The problem of the *Dissertation* is thus stated as an antinomy, namely, that if we attend to the conditions of sensitive representation, it seems impossible to employ the notion of an infinite whole, while considered from the standpoint of intelligence, such an employment seems legitimate and even necessary. Strictly speaking, Kant has not successfully framed an antinomy, for he gives no proof of the legitimacy or necessity of the intellectual concept of a whole. He says that the point is "easy to see," and then adds, in the closest he ever comes to a proof of it, that "when the mind is directed upon the conception of the complex . . . it demands and assumes, alike in abstract conception and in actual working out, limits in which it may find rest." In the Transcendental Dialectic of the *Critique*, Kant expands and revises his exposition of the antinomy in a far more successful manner. The conflict there turns upon the concept of the unconditioned, which appears in various forms as the concept of the infinite spatio-temporal universe (the unconditioned whole), the simple (the unconditioned part), the first cause (the unconditioned ground), and the necessary existant (the unconditioned being).

The inconclusive character of Kant's statement of the antinomy in the *Dissertation* results from the fact that his conception of philosophical questions is in process of changing. As I have tried to indicate elsewhere, Kant moved steadily toward the view that all philosophical investigations of the nature of being must be transformed into critical analyses of the nature of knowing.[15] At the writing of the *Dissertation*, he had completed this revolution only for questions concerning the sensible, or phenomenal, world. His statement of the negative side of the antinomy therefore is based on the subjective impossibility of generating a sensible representation of a particular sort — which is to say, it is an epistemological argument. But when he comes to the proof of the legitimacy of the (intellectual) representation of totality, he can give no reason why the mind must or may employ such a concept.

The section ends with a consideration of the "factors to be considered in the definition of a world," namely matter, form, and wholeness. Kant's principal concern is to define his position in the metaphysical debate concerning the interaction of substances. In his earliest essay, he had maintained against the Leibnizean philosophy that there must be a real physical interaction (*influxus physicus*) of monads rather than a merely virtual interaction coupled with a pre-established harmony between the internal

[15] See below, Concluding Remarks, pp. 319–326.

representations of each and the external relations of all monads. He repeats the doctrine here, employing an argument which in several forms turns up in the *Critique*. There must be real physical interaction because otherwise the multiplicity of monads would not form a genuine whole. Instead of a single world, there would be as many worlds as independent substances. For, Kant says, giving the argument a very important epistemological twist, "by embracing a plurality [in a representation] you may without difficulty make a *whole of representation*, but not, thereby, the *representation of a whole*." In the *Critique*, this becomes the argument that all objects of experience must stand in thoroughgoing community, since whatever cannot be connected with all the other contents of consciousness in a unity would simply not enter consciousness, and hence be as nothing to me.[16]

The section closes with a repetition of the clue to a solution of the antinomy: "Anyone who is seeking to escape from this thorny problem should note that the co-ordination of a plurality . . . does not concern the *intellectual* concept of a whole, but only the conditions of [its] *sensitive intuition;* and so, even if such totalities are not conceivable in sensitive terms, they do not thereby cease to be intellectual concepts." One would expect the sentence to end: even if such totalities are not conceivable in sensitive terms, they do not thereby cease to be *conceivable by means of* intellectual concepts. It was only several years later, as we shall see, that Kant realized the need for a critique of intellectual as well as sensitive representations.

Section II: On the Distinction of Sensibles and Intelligibles in General

Sensibility is the receptivity of the subject through which it is possible that its power of representation should be affected in a certain manner by the presence of some object. *Intelligence* (rationality) is the faculty of the subject through which it is able to represent things which cannot by their own characters act upon the senses. The object of sensibility is the sensible; that which contains nothing save what must be known through intelligence, is the intelligible. The former was called, in the schools of the ancients, phenomenon; the latter, noumenon. Knowledge, so far as it is subject to the laws of sensibility, is sensitive; so far as it is subject to the laws of intelligence, it is intellectual or rational.

[16] Cf. A 111, B 263, B 265 note a, B 273.

In this statement, which comprises the opening paragraph of the section, we see perfectly the stage in the Critical Philosophy at which Kant had arrived in 1770. The two independent sources of representations — sensibility and intelligence — have been discovered, and with them the two realms of objects of knowledge, *phenomena* and *noumena*. In the next paragraph, Kant formulates the difference between the two realms in the manner which has become famous: the former are "things *as they appear*," the latter "things *as they are*." This distinction between appearance and reality, which is the keystone of the Critical Philosophy, is derived, it will be noticed, from an epistemological distinction of faculties of representation.

With regard to intelligence, Kant now argues that there are two possible employments of this faculty.[17] It can be employed merely to order and compare concepts, whatever their origin, in systems of species and genera according to the laws of logic. Employed thus, intelligence deals indifferently with representations derived from the senses or elsewhere. Kant calls this its logical use. But intelligence is also capable of generating representations of objects or relations out of its own inner resources, thereby giving concepts to the mind. This is the real use of intelligence.[18]

Thus, the mind may draw its concepts from two sources: sensibility or intelligence. The former yields *empirical* concepts, such as the concepts of house, dog, and cow. The latter yields *pure* concepts, such as those of substance, cause, possibility, existence, and necessity.[19] In either case, by the logical use of intelligence, the mind can order and compare the concepts. For example, by abstracting the common marks of "horse," "dog," and "cow" we can form the concept "mammal." Similarly, we can classify substances as contingent or necessary.

The immediate purpose of distinguishing the real and logical uses of intelligence is to refute the Leibnizean doctrine that sensible representations are merely less clear than intellectual representa-

---

[17] "Intelligence," as used in the *Dissertation*, is a general term which covers the mental activities and capacities attributed to understanding and reason in the *Critique*.

[18] The distinction is preserved in a variety of ways in the *Critique*. For example, it grounds the division of logic into general and transcendental. Cf. B 74–82, especially B 80–82.

[19] This is the list actually given by Kant. It represents the earliest form of what was later to become the Table of Categories.

tions. According to this view, there is no difference in kind between the two, sensibility obscurely revealing the same (noumenal) reality which intelligence more adequately represents. In direct contradiction, Kant argues that although there is a difference between clear and confused representations, it pertains only to the logical use of intelligence, and hence does not serve to distinguish empirical from pure concepts. Somewhat sardonically, he says:

> For that matter, the sensitive may be very distinct, and the intellectual extremely confused. This is shown, on the one hand by geometry, the prototype of all sensitive knowledge, and on the other hand by metaphysics, the instrument in all things intellectual.

Kant has here struck at the heart of the rationalist tradition of Descartes, Leibniz, et al. Following the doctrine laid down in the Meditations and Discourse on Method, this school takes the quality of a concept (whether clear or confused, distinct or indistinct) as the measure of the reality of the *object* of that concept. Because Descartes has no clear and distinct idea of material objects, he doubts their reality. Conversely, the clarity of his idea of himself assures him of his own existence. Now it is apparent that once this way of thinking is adopted, it compels a choice between two opposed positions. Either one asserts that we can have clear and distinct ideas, in which case one claims that the objects of our knowledge are independent realities; or one denies that we can have clear and distinct ideas, and thereby retreats into an agnosticism about the existence of objects. The former Kant called Dogmatism, the latter Scepticism. Broadly speaking, he believed that they represented the dominant strains of continental rationalism and British empiricism.

In order to avoid these alternatives, which he considered equally unsatisfactory, Kant rejected the premise on which they are based. Not the degree of internal clarity of a concept but rather the nature of its origin became the measure of the reality of its object. Representations derived from sensibility reveal only appearance, no matter to what pitch of systematic order and distinctness they are brought by logic. Representations derived from intelligence, on the other hand, reveal things as they are in themselves, even if only dimly and with confusion.

Kant has hit upon an extremely clever way of composing the differences between the Mathematical and Metaphysical philoso-

phies. To the former he grants the validity of physics and geometry, but restricts their scope of application to appearances (phenomena). To the latter he grants the validity of the metaphysics of
monads, but denies that we have *sensitive* knowledge of such substances as they are in themselves. The key is the distinction between sensibility and intelligence, with all that follows from it.

Section III: On the Principles of the Form of the Sensible World

The problem of the *Dissertation* is the analysis of the concept
of a world, which is to say an interconnected community of substances. As there are two distinct orders of objects of knowledge,
phenomena and noumena, so there must be two principles which
"contain the ground of a universal connection, whereby all substances and their states belong to one and the same whole, that is,
to a world." The world of appearances is dependent upon the
conditions of sensibility and therefore the principle or law of
its form will be a merely subjective "law of the mind, on account
of which all things which can . . . be objects of the senses must
necessarily be presented as belonging to the same whole." The
principle of the world of noumena, on the other hand, will be an
objective "cause in virtue of which there is a connection between
things existing in themselves."

There are two sensible "laws of the mind," time and space.
Each is a mind-imposed order of phenomena which makes of the
objects of sense a whole, a world. In Kant's precise terms, space
and time are "schemata and conditions of all human knowledge
that is sensitive." Our concepts of space and time are not mere
innate ideas. Rather,

[they] are without doubt acquired, as abstracted, not indeed from the
sensing of objects (for sensation gives the matter, not the form, of human
apprehension), but from the action of the mind in co-ordinating its sensa
according to unchanging laws. . . . Nothing is here connate save the law
of the mind, according to which it combines in a fixed manner the sensa
produced in it by the presence of the object.

There is an interesting difference between this characterization of
the forms of sensibility and the later doctrine of the Transcendental
Aesthetic. Here sensibility is given the function of coordinating
the sensible material according to its own innate laws. Hence

physics as well as geometry derives from the forms of sensibility. In the *Critique*, on the other hand, space and time are passive forms of intuition, which merely presents a manifold or variety of sensuous material to the synthesizing understanding. Kant had not yet in the *Dissertation* arrived at the doctrine that all activity, as opposed to passivity, must be attributed to intelligence.

I have included this material from the *Dissertation*, despite the fact that it is more relevant to the Aesthetic than to the Analytic, because it throws light on the shifts in Kant's theory of mathematics. The Aesthetic embodies the *Dissertation* doctrine of space and time, virtually unchanged even to the particular arguments used in the Metaphysical and Transcendental Expositions.[20] It claims to account for the possibility of *a priori* mathematical knowledge solely by appeal to the subjective forms of sensibility. Now this is a feasible line of argument so long as one holds — as Kant did in the *Dissertation* — that sensibility itself contains laws for the coordination of a sensuous manifold. But when, in the *Critique*, he assigns the process of synthesis to understanding, it becomes impossible to maintain that any form of knowledge, whether mathematics or physics, can be adequately explained without reference to the contribution of intelligence. For this reason, Kant reverses himself in the Axioms of Intuition and grounds mathematics, as a knowledge of appearances, on the categories of quantity.

Most of Section III is devoted to the detailed analysis of time and space.[21] In terms of his new conception of *conditions of intuitive representation*, Kant can now find a *via media* between the Newtonian and Leibnizean theories of space and time. With the former, he agrees that space and time are absolute wholes in which the objects of physics find their location, but this is so because they are forms of sensibility lying ready in the mind, not independently subsisting containers or sensoria of God. With the latter, he agrees that space and time are the orders of contemporaneous things and successive states, but again this is so because they are conditions of intuitive representations of things, and not mere relations of independent substances.

In discussing space, Kant introduces a form of argument which

---

[20] Compare B 37–41, 46–48 with *Dissertation* §§ 14–15.
[21] Kant reverses the order in the *Critique*, dealing with space first.

grows increasingly more important in his philosophy. The Leibnizeans are wrong in describing space as a set of relations of existent
things, he says, for by so doing

they dash down geometry from the supreme height of certainty, reducing
it to the rank of those sciences whose principles are empirical. For if all
properties of space are borrowed only from external relations through
experience, geometrical axioms do not possess universality, but only that
comparative universality which is acquired through induction and holds
only so widely as it is observed . . .

This appeal to the conditions of the possibility of knowledge —
in this case geometry — turns Kant's investigations in a new direction. In the years following 1770 he came to realize that the
knowledge derived from the concepts of cause, substance, and the
other products of the real use of intelligence was in need of the
same grounding as that based upon the forms of space and time. The
Critique is in large measure the outcome of that realization.

Section IV: On the Principle of the Form
of the Intelligible World

This rather brief section is devoted to a defense of the metaphysical doctrine of *influxus physicus*. Its principal interest, curiously, is in what it fails to say rather than in what it says. The
discussion of sensibility was devoted almost entirely to the subjective characteristics of the mind whereby it generates sensible
representations and orders them according to the laws of space
and time. We would expect a parallel treatment of the real use
of intelligence, and an analysis of the concepts of substance, cause,
possibility, existence, and necessity. Instead, Kant defines intelligence briefly and negatively as the faculty which allows the subject "to represent things which *cannot* . . . act upon the senses"
[§ 3]. The pure concepts, he says, are not strictly connate to the
mind (i.e., lying fully formed in the mind prior to any experience),
but are "abstracted (by attention to its actions on the occasion of
experience) from laws inborn in the mind." [§ 8] Although Kant
leaves this notion unexplained, he apparently means that the mind,
when stimulated by the affection of its sensibility by noumena,
can discover from its own activities certain concepts which apply
to things in themselves, and not simply to appearances. In the
famous words of the Introduction to the *Critique,* though with a

considerably altered meaning: "All our knowledge begins with experience, [but] it does not follow that it all arises out of experience" [B 1].

The relation of the pure concepts to the world of appearances is not explored by Kant in the *Dissertation*. Cause, possibility, existence, and necessity are concepts which play a role in physics and mathematics, and possibly substance does as well. At this stage, Kant had not yet realized the importance of the problem of causation in the phenomenal world.

Section V: On the Method of Dealing with the Sensitive and the Intellectual in Metaphysics

In the preceding sections, Kant has dealt with the problems which, roughly speaking, correspond to the Aesthetic and Analytic of the *Critique*. Now he turns to the problem of the Dialectic: the origin and nature of error in metaphysics. Following an ancient tradition, Kant locates the failings of his predecessors — who "seem hitherto, with all the endless rolling of their Sisyphean stone, to have accomplished scarcely anything" — in the illegitimate extension of one faculty into the domain of another.[22] Metaphysical error, he asserts, arises from "*the contamination of intellectual knowledge by the sensitive.*" The principle to be followed, therefore, is "*carefully to prevent the principles proper to sensitive apprehension from passing their boundaries and meddling with the intellectual.*"

The point is that in any judgment, S is P, the predicate is asserted as the universal condition of the subject. In the somewhat psychological terms used by Kant, "the predicate is a condition without which the subject is asserted to be unthinkable." But if the predicate is a concept of sense, it will at most contain "a condition without which there is no possibility of sensitive knowledge of the given concept [i.e., the subject-term]." For example, in the judgment, "whatever is, is somewhere and somewhen," the predicate ("is somewhere and somewhen") is a sensitive concept involving space and time. Hence, it cannot legitimately be con-

---

[22] Compare Descartes' explanation of moral error as the extension of will beyond the bounds of intellect, or Hume's account of philosophical error as the extension of belief beyond the limits of perception.

sidered a universal condition of the possibility of the subject ("whatever is," i.e., all being). Rather, it is a condition only of the sensitive apprehension of the subject. To make the proposition valid we must revise it to state: "whatever is, *insofar as it is known as an appearance*, is somewhere and somewhen." On the other hand, the proposition "whatever is somewhere and somewhen, exists," is perfectly legitimate. Its predicate is intellectual and un-hindered by any subjective conditions of knowledge. Hence its sphere of applicability is universal, including among other things the realm of phenomena (i.e., the realm of what is somewhere and somewhen) [§ 24 n. 1].

From the above, it should be clear why Kant viewed sensibility as a limitation upon intelligence. In the *Dissertation*, of course, in-telligence is considered to have a valid use beyond the bounds of sensibility, but in the *Critique* Kant retreats to the position that knowledge and sensibility are coterminous. Nevertheless, some passages in the Analytic reflect the *Dissertation* doctrine, thereby causing a good deal of unnecessary confusion.[23]

Kant is the focal point of all modern philosophy. Into his works flow the main streams of seventeenth- and eighteenth-century thought, and from him arise the major schools of nineteenth-century English and Continental philosophy. From this point of view, the *Dissertation* is a more revealing document even than the *Critique*. By the time Kant had reached the latter, he had so transmuted the terms and problems of his predecessors that the modern reader must struggle to find in it a compromise between Continental rationalism and British empiricism. In the *Dissertation*, however, we catch Kant's thought in mid-flight.

The problem with which he begins is a metaphysical one: to discover a theory of the nature of space and time which will allow room for the legitimate claims of both the Newtonians and the Leibnizians. In this Kant succeeds quite deftly. The distinction between appearance and reality allows him to make a place for science and metaphysics, without denying to either the title of knowledge. His victory is achieved, however, only by setting in motion a train of argument which ends in the *Critique* by destroy-ing metaphysics and completely revolutionizing the conception of

[23] See, for example, § 13 of the Transcendental Deduction.

scientific knowledge. The turn from modes of being to ways of knowing is carried in the *Dissertation* only so far as the world of appearances. Nevertheless, once Kant had recognized the necessity of exploring the conditions of the possibility of sensitive knowledge, he could not long refrain from extending this critique to the knowledge of things in themselves. The result is a new kind of philosophical investigation, which Kant calls Transcendental Philosophy.

HUME AND THE REFORMULATION OF THE PROBLEM

The Letter to Herz

It is evident from the review just concluded that the *Dissertation*'s weakest point is the doctrine of the real use of intelligence as a source of knowledge of independent reality. The subjective forms of intuition are analyzed in detail, but when Kant passes to the pure concepts, he simply asserts that they are applicable to noumena. At the same time, these concepts "are given through the very nature of the intellect." [24] Consequently, Kant is still faced with the problem which had so much exercised Descartes and Leibniz: how can representations that have their origin in the mind nevertheless give us knowledge of independently existing substances? In Kant's terms, how can there be a *real* use of intelligence? Leibniz found the solution in a pre-established harmony of subjective representations with objective states, guaranteed by a benevolent Deity. Such a solution, however, is unacceptable, for if there is any problem at all of knowledge, it is how the knowing subject comes into contact with the object of knowledge. To answer that it does not is merely an admission of defeat.

Kant first recognized this unsolved problem in a lengthy letter to his friend, Marcus Herz, who had acted as respondent at the presentation of the *Dissertation*. The letter is dated 21 February, 1772. The following lengthy portion is quoted from Kemp Smith's *Commentary*:

Similarly, if that in us which is called a representation, were active in relation to the object, that is to say, if the object itself were produced by the representation (as on the view that the ideas in the Divine Mind are the archetypes of things), the conformity of representations with objects

---

[24] *Dissertation*, § 6,

:might be understood. We can thus render comprehensible at least the possibility of two kinds of intelligence — of an *intellectus archetypus*, on whose intuition the things themselves are grounded, and of an *intellectus ectypus* which derives the data of its logical procedure from the sensuous intuition of things. But our understanding (leaving moral ends out of account) is not the cause of the object through its representations, nor is the object the cause of its intellectual representations (*in sensu reali*). Hence, the pure concepts of the understanding cannot be abstracted from the data of the senses, nor do they express our capacity for receiving representations through the senses. But, whilst they have their sources in the nature of the soul, they originate there neither as the result of the action of the object upon it, nor as themselves producing the object. In the *Dissertation* I was content to explain the nature of these intellectual representations in a merely negative manner, viz. as not being modifications of the soul produced by the object. But I silently passed over the further question, how such representations, which refer to an object and yet are not the result of an affection due to that object, can be possible. I had maintained that the sense representations represent things as they appear, the intellectual representations things as they are. But how then are these things given to us, if not by the manner in which they affect us? And if such intellectual representations are due to our own inner activity, whence comes the agreement which they are supposed to have with objects, which yet are not their products? How comes it that the axioms of pure reason about these objects agree with the latter, when this agreement has not been in any way assisted by experience? In mathematics such procedure is legitimate, because its objects only *are* quantities for us, and can only be represented as quantities, in so far as we can generate their representation by repeating a unit a number of times. Hence the concepts of quantity can be self-producing, and their principles can therefore be determined *a priori*. But when we ask how the understanding can form to itself completely *a priori* concepts of things in their *qualitative* determination, with which these things must of necessity agree, or formulate in regard to their possibility principles which are independent of experience, but with which experience must exactly conform, — we raise a question, that of the origin of the agreement of our faculty of understanding with the things in themselves, over which obscurity still hangs.[25]

At this stage, the problem seems ripe for a solution along the lines developed for space and time: make the pure concepts applicable only to phenomena, deny that we have any knowledge at all of independent reality, and we can thereby eliminate the "obscurity" which hangs over the agreement between subject and object. In a sense, of course, this is the position at which Kant finally

[25] N. Kemp Smith, *A Commentary to Kant's 'Critique of Pure Reason,'* 2nd ed., pp. 219–220.

arrived, but the *Critique* would be a much shorter book if there had been no more to it than that. What happened instead is that a totally new element was added to Kant's investigations. David Hume entered the controversy.

Hume and the Problem of Causation

Kant's Knowledge of Hume's Philosophy

Kant's first opportunity to encounter Hume's philosophy was a four-volume translation, in 1752–1754, of Hume's essays. The second volume of this set contained the "philosophische Versuche über die Menschliche Erkenntnisse," the *Enquiry Concerning Human Understanding* and *Enquiry Concerning the Principles of Morals.*[26] Although Kant was acquainted with the *Enquiries* before writing the *Dissertation,* at the time of the letter to Herz the peculiar difficulties connected with the concept of causation had apparently still not struck him. It seems likely, therefore, that it was shortly after February 1772 that Kant experienced the awakening which he describes in the famous passage of the *Prolegomena:*

> I openly confess my recollection of David Hume was the very thing which many years ago first interrupted my dogmatic slumber and gave my investigations in the field of speculative philosophy a quite new direction.[27]

There is no direct evidence as to what produced this "recollection" (*Erinnerung*) of Hume, but the most probable cause was the publication in 1772 of a translation of James Beattie's *Essay on the Nature and Immutability of the Truth* (1770). Beattie, a member of the Common Sense school of Scottish philosophy, had undertaken to answer the "sceptics," among whom he numbered Descartes and Malebranche as well as Locke, Berkeley, and Hume. Fortunately, he quoted copiously from the works which he attacked, including the *Treatise* as well as the *Enquiry Concerning*

---

[26] There is good reason to suppose that Kant never was able to read English, and consequently was unfamiliar with Hume's *Treatise of Human Nature* prior to the writing of the *Critique.* The *Dialogues Concerning Natural Religion,* Hume's other major work, were known to Kant through a partial translation which Hamann showed to him in 1780. Kant made use of some of its arguments in the *Dialectic,* and later incorporated much of it into the *Critique of Teleological Judgment.* Cf. my "Kant's Debt to Hume via Beattie," *Journal of the History of Ideas,* 21:117–123 (January-March 1960).

[27] *Prolegomena,* trans. with introduction by L. W. Beck, p. 8.

Human Understanding. Through the translation of Beattie's book, Kant was therefore made aware of a number of arguments which had not been included by Hume in the *Enquiry*. Among these was the all-important criticism of the causal maxim.

The Sceptical Doctrine of the Treatise

Hume's sceptical attack on the validity of causal inference — and thereby on the possibility of all empirical knowledge — is contained in two very famous passages. The first is Part III of Book I of the *Treatise of Human Nature*, "Of Knowledge and Probability"; the second is Section IV of the *Enquiry Concerning Human Understanding*, "Sceptical Doubts Concerning the Operations of the Understanding." Although the latter work, together with its companion *Enquiry Concerning the Principles of Morals*, purports to be merely a briefer version of the *Treatise*, the two are in fact so different on many significant points that a comparison of them will be helpful. In particular, as we shall see, the *Enquiry* omits the criticism of the causal maxim, to which Hume devotes several pages in the *Treatise*.

The negative portion of the argument of the *Treatise* occupies the first three sections of Part III.[28] Hume begins by classing all philosophical relations under seven heads: resemblance, identity, relations of time and place, proportions in quantity or number, degrees in any quality, contrariety, and causation [*Treatise*, p. 69]. These in turn can be divided into two groups, according as they "depend entirely on the ideas, which we compare together," or alternatively "may be chang'd without any change in the ideas" [*Treatise*, p. 69]. In the former category fall resemblance, contrariety, degrees in quality, and proportions in quantity or number. When two ideas (or impressions) are presented to the mind for comparison, their resemblance or contrariety, their relative degrees of quality and proportions in quantity are quite independent of the temporal order in which they appear or the relative positions they

---

[28] Contrary to the common impression of students of philosophy, Hume gives far more space in the *Treatise* to his constructive theory of habits and mental propensities than to the better known sceptical arguments. A careful reading reveals that he conceives himself to be making a positive contribution to Moral Science, and hence can only be considered a sceptic in a quite narrow sense. See my "Hume's Theory of Mental Activity," *The Philosophical Review*, 69:289–310 (July 1960). *cf 144*

take up in the perceptual field. It matters not whether they appear alone or in company with other ideas, and no matter under what conditions they reappear, their relations in these four respects will remain unchanged.[29] Hence these four relations can serve as a secure "foundation of science" [*Treatise*, p. 73].

The other three philosophical relations — identity, situations in time and place, and causation — are quite another case altogether. For each "depend[s] not upon the idea, and may be absent or present even while *that* remains the same" [*Treatise*, p. 73]. We can easily imagine two objects in a variety of spatio-temporal relations while yet their characteristics remain unchanged. So, too, we may judge two impressions to be identical (i.e., the impressions of a single, identical object), or merely the impressions of resembling objects, depending upon the conditions under which they appear. Finally, as Hume goes on to argue, causation is inseparable from spatial contiguity and temporal succession of cause and effect; consequently the relation can be destroyed merely by varying the manner of appearance without altering the ideas themselves. For example, if one billiard ball rolls up to a second, which thereupon begins to move, I judge the two motions to be causally connected; whereas if they are spatially remote from another, or are separated by a span of time, I judge the very same motions to be unrelated.

The four relations which rest solely upon the nature of the given ideas cannot serve to carry us beyond our present experience to a knowledge of "the real existence or relations of objects," nor can the relations of identity or time and place. Hence the burden of our empirical knowledge falls upon the relation of cause and effect. It is to this subject that Hume devotes the remainder of Part III.

It is important to note first, however, that the distinction which Hume has drawn between the two classes of philosophical relations must *not* be confused with the distinction between what Kant labels analytic and synthetic judgments. The judgment that the early compositions of Mozart sound like (resemble) those of Haydn, for example, would belong to the first category of relations of ideas, although it would never be called analytic. Hume's

[29] Quite obviously, Hume was unaware of the phenomena of background and context on which Gestalt psychology is based.

criteria are psychological rather than logical, and as they are based on a now-discarded theory of conscious experience, they do not correspond to any modern system of classification. In the *Enquiry*, a new distinction is introduced, between relations of ideas and matters of fact, which comes quite close to the Kantian division of propositions. Nevertheless, despite its confusion of logic with psychology, the *Treatise* approach has some advantages over the *Enquiry* revision which will become clearer when we consider the significance of Hume's arguments for Kant's philosophical development.

Besides contiguity and succession, Hume discovers a third relation of cause to effect which "is of much greater importance, than any of the other two" [*Treatise*, p. 77]. This is *necessary connexion*, which distinguishes true causal influence from mere adventitious concomitance. *Necessary connexion* is an essential ingredient of causation, for otherwise every *post hoc* would entail a *propter hoc*. When Hume casts his eye upon particular causes and effects, however, he finds no such third relation beyond the mere contiguity and succession of the two. He therefore proposes to undertake an investigation of two questions, the answers to which will yield an analysis of the concept of causation. The questions are:

> First, For what reason we pronounce it *necessary*, that every thing whose existence has a beginning, shou'd also have a cause?
> Secondly, Why we conclude, that such particular causes must *necessarily* have such particular effects; and what is the nature of that *inference* we draw from the one to the other, and of the *belief* we repose in it?
>
> [*Treatise*, p. 78]

The first question concerns the so-called causal maxim; the second deals with particular attributions of causal influence, such as that fire causes heat. When we examine the text of the *Treatise*, we discover that it deals with them in very different fashions. Strictly speaking, it never succeeds in answering the first question at all. Though Hume argues very persuasively against the validity of the causal maxim, he fails to explain why we ever come to believe it. By contrast, while he devotes very little space to criticism of the rationalist defense of particular causal inferences, he deals at length with the mental propensities which produce our belief in them. In the *Enquiry*, all mention of the causal maxim is omitted, and if Beattie had not paraphrased the *Treatise* argument in his *Essay*, Kant might have been entirely unaware of it. Kant himself rarely discusses the problem of particular causal judgments. Since he denies a purely formal status to physics, he must allow for the role of experiment and observation in the discovery of scientific truths. But how we bridge the gap between the *a priori* propositions of Transcendental Philosophy and the empirical knowledge of science is totally unclear from the *Critique*.

The criticism of the causal maxim is contained in Section 3, "Why a cause is always necessary." Hume relies upon two philosophical principles which had been laid down in the opening pages of the *Treatise*. The first of these is that the mind is perfectly free to rearrange its impressions in any way which strikes the fancy, for no two distinct and distinguishable impressions are incapable of being separated, one from the other, in imagination. "Where-ever the imagination perceives a difference among ideas, it can easily produce a separation" [*Treatise*, p. 10]. But, secondly, *"whatever the mind clearly conceives includes the idea of possible existence"* [*Treatise*, p. 32]. This two-step attack — first the separability of distinguishable impressions, then the possibility of the conceivable — suffices to destroy the pretensions of the causal maxim.

All distinct ideas are separable from each other, and as the ideas of cause and effect are evidently distinct, 'twill be easy for us to conceive any object to be non-existent this moment, and existent the next, without conjoining to it the distinct idea of a cause or productive principle. The separation, therefore, of the idea of a cause from that of a beginning of existence, is plainly possible for the imagination; and consequently the actual separation of these objects is so far possible, that it implies no contradiction nor absurdity; and is therefore incapable of being refuted by any reasoning from mere ideas; without which 'tis impossible to demonstrate the necessity of a cause. [*Treatise*, pp. 79–80]

Hume also gives a refutation based upon his classification of relations of ideas. It appears in Beattie's *Essay* in slightly altered form:

All certainty arises from the comparison of ideas, and from the discovery of such relations as are unalterable so long as the ideas remain the same: but the only relations of this kind are resemblance, proportions in quantity and number, degrees of any quality, and contrariety; none of which is implied in the maxim, *Whatever begins to exist, proceeds from some cause:* — that maxim therefore is not intuitively certain.[30]

The same arguments are used by Hume to refute the claims of particular causal propositions. As one can imagine fire without heat, or collision of bodies without transfer of motion, it is at least possible that they so occur. Hence, no *deductive demonstration* of their connection can ever be given.

The Enquiry Concerning Human Understanding

Hume alters the direction of his argument in the section of the *Enquiry* which corresponds to Part III of Book I of the *Treatise*. As we have seen, the *Treatise* dealt with both the causal maxim itself and with particular causal judgments. The *Enquiry* treats only the latter, the reason very probably being Hume's inability to give an adequate psychological explanation of our belief in the maxim. The argument proceeds in two stages, corresponding to the two parts of the Section. In Part I it is shown that particular causal inferences are not *a priori* or deductive in character, and hence lack the necessity which the rationalists ascribe to them.

In Part II, it is further shown that "even after we have experience of the operations of cause and effect, our conclusions from that experience are *not* founded on reasoning, or any process of the understanding." [31] The argument turns on the question of the validity of the maxim of the uniformity of nature. Hume shows that it is not *a priori* valid, and cannot be established by an appeal to experience without circularity.

The section opens with a new and extremely important distinction between *relations of ideas* and *matters of fact*. Relations of ideas are described as "affirmations which [are] either intuitively or demonstratively certain . . . discoverable by the mere operation of thought, without dependence on what is anywhere existent in the universe." [32] As examples, Hume offers the Pythagorean

---

[30] Beattie, *Essay on Truth*, pp. 103–104; *Treatise*, p. 79.

[31] *Enquiry*, ed. by Selby-Bigge, p. 32.

[32] *Ibid.*, p. 25. Hume, like other philosophers of his day, was lamentably loose in his use of "idea," "proposition," "relation," and the like. We should never wish to say that a relation of ideas *is* an affirmation, though we might affirm the existence of a relation. This lack of precision makes it very difficult to compare the statements of the *Enquiry* with Kant's definitions of "analytic" and "synthetic." Such distinctions are also essential in the *Critique* when Kant comes to reject the traditional view that judgments are compounded of previously formed concepts (ideas), and instead asserts that the act of judging is the basic mental

theorem and a law of arithmetic. This represents a departure from the *Treatise*, where geometry is treated as an empirical and approximating science.

Matters of fact, on the other hand, are neither intuitively nor demonstratively certain. The following sentence indicates clearly the shift in Hume's analysis toward logical criteria:

The contrary of every matter of fact is still possible; because it can never imply a contradiction, and is conceived by the mind with the same facility and distinctness, as if ever so conformable to reality.[33]

The reference to the mind's power of conception remains, but the emphasis on contradictions and the omission of the list of philosophical relations makes the whole sound much more like Kant's discussion of analytic and synthetic judgments.

"All reasonings concerning matters of fact," says Hume, are "founded on the relation of *Cause and Effect*." But it is clear that no examination of the qualities of a particular object will ever enable us to deduce the nature of its effects. "Adam, though his rational faculties be supposed, at the very first, entirely perfect, could not have inferred from the fluidity and transparency of water that it would suffocate him."[34] Consequently, our knowledge of matters of fact is never based upon *a priori* reasoning. This, it is frequently said, is the challenge which Hume issued and which Kant answered. But Hume is here denying the *a priori* character only of individual causal judgments. Kant never supposed that one could infer the warmth of fire from its light, or the edibility of bread from its color and texture. He claimed only to demonstrate the general proposition that whatever begins to be presupposes something on which it follows according to a rule [A 189]. Thus if we are to view the *Critique* as Kant's answer to Hume, it would better be to the *Treatise* than to the *Enquiry*.

The Challenge to Kant

It is now evident why the re-encounter with Hume in 1772 produced so great an effect upon Kant. At the time of the letter to Herz, he was beginning to recognize the serious problems which

---

function. Without a clear distinction between ideas (concepts) and affirmations (judgments) this shift cannot even be stated.

[33] *Ibid.,* p. 25.

[34] *Ibid.,* p. 27.

were still to be solved in the doctrine of the *Dissertation*. The weak point was the real use of intelligence — the production of pure concepts which derive nothing from experience and yet apply with universal validity to independent reality. The most natural solution was perhaps simply to limit the pure concepts to phenomena and give up the claim to knowledge of noumena. But Hume's attack on causal inference undermined even this drastic retrenchment, for physics as well as metaphysics employed the concept of causation. Hence Kant was made to realize the need for a general critique of the functions of understanding and *a priori* knowledge. The statement of the argument in the *Enquiry*, although concerned with particular causal inferences rather than the causal maxim, suggested the problem of synthetic judgments *a priori*, for Kant wished to show that causal inference was both *a priori* and concerned with matters of fact.

In a much deeper way, Hume's sceptical arguments altered the character of Kant's philosophical enterprise. The *Dissertation* had separated sensibility from intelligence, restricting the first to phenomena and extending the second to things in themselves. The relation between the two — between intuitions and pure concepts — had been treated only negatively in connection with the "fallacy of subreption" and with regard to Leibniz's account of perceptions as confused ideas. The limitation of pure concepts to the world of phenomena left Kant with a theory of two independent and co-equal "conditions of the possibility of experience," sensibility and understanding. Neither conditioned the other and either could generate representations by itself, although both were required for knowledge. This relatively simple version of the critical teaching actually appears in some of the passages of the *Critique* such as the introductory section of the Transcendental Deduction. Hume's arguments, however, forced Kant to examine much more closely the relation between sensibility and understanding. The key to Hume's attack is the dictum of the separability of distinguishables. But the only true invariable relations between causes and effects are spatial contiguity and temporal succession. Since objects in different parts of space or time are distinguishable, it follows that they are separable in the imagination, and consequently that the one can at least possibly occur without the other. In other words, Hume's analysis revealed that it was not causation *in addition to* space and time, but rather causation *as based on* space and time, which required a defense. The working out of this intimate relation between pure concepts of understanding and *a priori* forms of intuition cost Kant a great deal of labor in the years before 1781. The results of his efforts are to be found in the Deduction and Analogies, where the problem is solved by the recognition that the pure concepts are actually rules for the synthesis of a manifold of intuition.

CHAPTER II

THE ROLE OF THE ANALYTIC IN KANT'S PHILOSOPHY

The series of philosophical works which Kant wrote in the two decades after 1781 is commonly referred to as the Critical Philosophy. It deals with epistemology, metaphysics, logic, ethics, physics, mathematics, psychology, aesthetics, and theology. To an extent which is remarkable even for a period of philosophical systems, these writings depend upon one another and can only fully be understood in their reciprocal relations. The outlines of the *Critiques* of *Pure Reason, Practical Reason,* and *Judgment,* and the *Metaphysics of Morals* and *Metaphysical Foundations of Natural Science* were conceived by Kant before he published the first *Critique* in 1781. The result is that no single passage can be successfully interpreted without considering its place in the entire critical edifice. In particular, the *Critique of Pure Reason* must always be read with an eye to the ethical and religious doctrines for which Kant is preparing the way.

For example, the question frequently arises in the Transcendental Analytic whether the pure concepts of understanding have any sort of application — even a merely possible one — beyond the realm of spatio-temporal intuition. As the argument of the *Critique* advances, it points more and more to the conclusion that they do not, for as rules for the synthesis of a manifold of sensuous intuition they cannot even be imagined to apply to things in themselves. Nevertheless, time and time again, Kant retreats from this consequence to the stock formula that the categories can problematically extend to the realm of noumena.[1] The reader who seeks an explanation for this inflexibility in the *Critique* itself will find nothing more than dogmatic and unsupported assertions concerning the

[1] See, for example, B 309–10, in the chapter on Phenomena and Noumena.

nature of concepts, assertions furthermore which have been contradicted by Kant's own arguments. But as soon as the matter is viewed in the context of the entire Critical Philosophy, this unwillingness to revise the theory becomes entirely understandable. Kant is looking forward to the unfolding of his ethical philosophy, where it will be essential to maintain that we can form an (empty) concept of the freely acting self in itself.

Because of this organic character of Kant's work, it may help to devote a few pages to a general picture of the Critical Philosophy, and then to indicate the place of the Transcendental Analytic in it. The reader should be warned, however, that he will almost always find the argument of the Analytic more worthwhile when it departs from, than when it adheres to, Kant's grand plan.

THE PLAN OF A CRITICAL PHILOSOPHY

Philosophy, Kant tells us in the Introduction to the *Critique of Judgment*, "contain[s] the principles of the rational cognition that concepts afford us of things." [2] It deals with that element or aspect of our cognition which the mind possesses *a priori*, and whose marks are necessity and universality. Hence it owes nothing to contingent observation or subjective sensation, though it may of course treat of their nature and limits. In past ages, philosophy, under the title of Metaphysics, has claimed to extend our knowledge beyond the limits of experience itself, to reveal the existence of God, the immortality of the human soul, and the inward nature of independent substances. But always there has been a dissension among metaphysicians which betrayed the unclarity of their concepts and the uncertainty of their principles. Each age has proclaimed new proofs with which to settle the debates, and each in turn has been succeeded by still newer refutations. In the clamor of this unceasing battle, the combatants have forgotten the teaching of the first great philosopher, Socrates, for whom the key to wisdom was a reflective examination of thought itself. Criticism of the canons of reasoning and the premises of argument, rather than endless novelty of expression, would alone reveal what and how man knows. So Socrates took as the motto of his life's endeavors the oracular command, Know Thyself.

Kant sees his age as an age of criticism, to which "religion

[2] *Critique of Judgement*, trans. by J. C. Meredith, p. 8.

through its sanctity, and law-giving through its majesty" must submit. The spirit of criticism, he asserts, is "a call to reason to undertake anew the most difficult of all its tasks, namely, that of self-knowledge" [A xi]. The outcome of this self-criticism is to be a new kind of discipline to which Kant gives the name "Transcendental Philosophy." This discipline does not yield knowledge about the objects of the several sciences, but rather concerns itself with the methods, limits, sources, and nature of all branches of human inquiry:

I entitle *transcendental* all knowledge which is occupied not so much with objects as with the mode of our knowledge of objects in so far as this mode of knowledge is to be possible *a priori*.[3]

Transcendental Philosophy is a self-reflective, second-level investigation whose purpose is to test and pass judgment upon the claims of reason in all its manifestations. Hence it presumably should not issue in substantive propositions of physics or ethics. This fact, as we shall see, is of great importance in interpreting the results of the Transcendental Analytic as well as the other parts of Kant's writings.

All knowledge, or knowing, involves both an object and a subject. As the student of knowledge — the transcendental philosopher — is himself a knowing subject, he cannot place these two elements on an equal footing, but must instead make the subject primary and the object secondary. In other words, before he can investigate the nature of objects, he must determine the powers and limits of the subject. Thus, Transcendental or Critical Philosophy can be viewed as a systematic inventory of the possessions of the human mind, a catalogue of the functions, capacities, modes of representation, passions, and actions of the self, all with an end to establishing the validity or invalidity of their cognitive claims.

In keeping with the practice of his time, Kant employs a faculty psychology to perform this task of classification. Nevertheless, the reader should not be misled into supposing that a rejection of eighteenth-century psychology necessarily carries with it the re-

[3] B 25. Kant elsewhere contrasts transcendental with *transcendent*, which he takes to mean *going beyond the limits of experience*. Thus, a correct use of the two terms would be in the sentence, "Transcendental philosophy demonstrates the impossibility of transcendent philosophy." Unfortunately, Kant almost never uses *transcendent* as an adjective, making do with *transcendental* for both meanings. The reader must therefore infer from the context which sense is intended.

pudiation of the Critical Philosophy, for in the *Critique of Pure Reason*, and to varying degrees in the other works as well, the language of mental faculties can be replaced by a more modern vocabulary of mental functions. When Kant discovers a clear distinction between two activities of the mind, he embodies it in a corresponding distinction of faculties. Thus the undifferentiated intelligence of the *Dissertation* becomes the three separate faculties of understanding, imagination, and reason in the *Critique*. The argument always runs from function to faculty, however, and Kant rarely attempts to infer any substantive fact about mental operations from some unverifiable premise concerning faculties.[4]

Because Kant changes his classifications from time to time, it is impossible to give a single definitive outline of his theory of mental faculties, although one could without difficulty give three or four. The basis of the three great critical works — the *Critiques* of *Pure Reason, Practical Reason,* and *Judgment* — is the division of cognitive faculties into understanding, reason, and judgment,[5] or alternatively theoretical reason, practical reason, and judgment, or again, cognition, volition, and feeling. The *First Critique* in turn is organized on the triad sensibility (Aesthetic), understanding (Analytic), and reason (Dialectic). In all Kant's triads the third faculty is conceived as mediating between the first and second, which are opposed as thesis to antithesis. For example, the gulf between theoretical reason (which deals with the realms of the conditioned = phenomena) and practical reason (which deals with the realm of the unconditioned = noumena) is bridged in the *Third Critique* by aesthetic judgment ("the beautiful is the symbol of the morally good"). In the *First Critique*, imagination mediates between sensibility and understanding by bringing pure concepts into relation to a manifold of intuition. Kant defends his reliance on the triad against the all-too-natural scepticism of his audience:

It has been thought somewhat suspicious that my divisions in pure philosophy should almost always come out threefold. But it is due to the nature of the case. If a division is to be *a priori* it must be either analytic, according to the law of contradiction — and then it is always two-fold (quodlibet ens est aut A aut non A) — or else it is *synthetic*. If it is to be derived in the latter case from *a priori* concepts (not, as in mathematics,

---

[4] The one important instance of such a fallacy is the Metaphysical Deduction of the Categories.

[5] See *Critique of Judgement*, Introduction, pp. 17–18.

from the *a priori* intuition corresponding to the concept,) then, to meet the requirements of synthetic unity in general, namely (1) a condition, (2) a conditioned, (3) the concept arising from the union of the conditioned with its condition, the division must of necessity be trichotomous.[6]

The whole articulated system rises on a framework which is referred to as the *architectonic*. This model of neatness, with a place for everything and everything in its place, is a sort of topology of the mind. It simultaneously reveals the structure of the mind's cognitive faculties and organizes the divisions of Transcendental Philosophy. Kant's fondness for his system was unbounded, and he frequently permitted his arguments to be twisted half out of shape to fit its demands. Nevertheless, it performed the indispensable function of molding together in some sort of order his innumerable insights into every branch of learning. When reflecting on Kant's adherence to outmoded forms in the second edition of the *Critique*, for example, the reader must remember what a labor it would have been for him, at the age of 63, to revise the entire skeleton of his philosophy in conformity with the revolutionary discoveries of the Deduction. At each stage in the unfolding of the Critical Philosophy, retroactive readjustments seem called for. The Analytic alters the doctrine of the Aesthetic, as the Dialectic does that of the Analytic; the *Third Critique* profoundly affects the significance of the *First* and *Second*. It is difficult to tell whether a consistent version of it all is possible, but the reader must at least attempt to grasp the whole if he is to understand Kant's intention.

The aim of the Transcendental Philosophy is critical rather than merely classificatory, and as Kant has formed a new conception of the nature of philosophy, so he presents a new mode of philosophical argument: the *deduction*. The idea of the deduction is first stated in the *Critique of Pure Reason*.

Jurists, when speaking of rights and claims, distinguish in a legal action the question of right (*quid juris*) from the question of fact (*quid facti*); and they demand that both be proved. Proof of the former, which has to state the right or the legal claim, they entitle the *deduction* . . . Now among the manifold concepts which form the highly complicated web of human knowledge, there are some which are marked out for pure

[6] *Ibid.*, p. 39, note 1.

a priori employment, in complete independence of all experience; and their right to be so employed always demands a deduction . . . The explanation of the manner in which concepts can thus relate *a priori* to objects I entitle their transcendental deduction. [B 116–117.]

In the strict sense defined here, a deduction is a proof that a certain mental faculty or mode of representation is capable of yielding synthetic judgments *a priori*, or can "relate *a priori* to objects." Thus conceived, a deduction is possible only for the pure concepts of understanding (categories), the rest of the Critical Philosophy being devoted to refuting the claims of other pretenders to *a priori* knowledge. However, as the first sentence of the above passage indicates, the deduction can be more broadly interpreted as an establishment of the precise limits of the legitimate employment of a faculty. Every division of Transcendental Philosophy will then have its deduction, although only the *Critique of Pure Reason* will yield a proof of the possibility of *a priori knowledge.*

This is in fact what we find when we examine the other parts of the critical writings. Kant exhibits a firmly anti-reductionist spirit with regard to ethics, aesthetics, or religion. The mind has many functions besides knowing, and each must be analyzed, criticized, its *a priori* element discovered and its boundaries clearly marked off. So Kant offers us deductions of the ideas of reason (in the Dialectic), the supreme principle of purposiveness or teleology (*Critique of Judgment*), and the judgments of taste (*Critique of Aesthetic Judgment*). None of these qualifies as knowledge, but each has a proper role to play in the life of the mind.

The ingenuity which Kant displays in distinguishing various cognitive statuses between knowledge and nonsense is best exemplified by the deduction of the judgment of taste. The problem is to find some way of attributing to aesthetic judgments a greater validity than sheer arbitrary preference while at the same time denying to them the objective validity of knowledge. The precise nature of the difficulty is clearly stated by Kant in the following passage:

The obligation to furnish a Deduction, i.e. a guarantee of the legitimacy of judgements of a particular kind, only arises where the judgement lays claim to necessity. This is the case even where it requires subjective universality, i.e. the concurrence of every one, albeit the judgement is not a cognitive judgement, but only one of pleasure or displeasure in a given object. . . . Now if this universal validity is not to be based on a collection of votes and interrogation of others as to what sort of sensations they experience, but is to rest, as it were, upon an autonomy of the Subject passing judgement on the feeling of pleasure . . . then it follows that such a judgement . . . has a double and also logical peculiarity. For, *first*, it has universal validity *a priori*, yet without having a logical universality according to concepts, but only the universality of a singular judgement. *Secondly*, it has a necessity, (which must invariably rest upon *a priori* grounds,) but one which depends upon no *a priori* proofs by the representation of which it would be competent to enforce the assent which the judgement of taste demands of every one.[7]

The solution is found by way of the concept of subjective, or *de facto*, universality. The beauty of an object of taste, says Kant, is that fittingness of its form which serves to harmonize the cognitive faculties of the perceiver. The pleasure which we take in it derives from this feeling of internal harmony, and hence the aesthetic judgment is subjective. At the same time, so long as it attends only to the form of the object rather than to its particular qualities (which may vary from perceiver to perceiver), the aesthetic response may be attributed to every human, for the cognitive faculties are identical in all men. Thus, by separating the criteria of universality and (objective) necessity, Kant finds place for a modified *apriority* appropriate to aesthetic judgment.

It would be entirely contrary to Kant's intention to attribute to him either the view that aesthetic judgment is knowledge just like science or the view that it is mere expression of preference. If a contemporary comparison may be permitted, Kant is akin to the school of linguistic analysis with its insistence on a plurality of "modes of discourse," while he is also like the positivists in his destructive critique of metaphysics and emphasis on the centrality of scientific knowledge. More accurately, perhaps, he is the forefather of both styles of philosophy.

THE PLACE OF THE ANALYTIC IN THE CRITIQUE

The *Critique of Pure Reason* as a whole is conceived as a system of Transcendental Philosophy designed to exhibit the existence and the limitations of knowledge. The work is divided first into a Transcendental Doctrine of Elements and a Transcendental Doctrine of Method. The latter is slightly over one hundred pages in

[7] *Critique of Judgement*, pp. 135–136.

length, and is of interest mainly for some passages on mathematics and a brief preview of the material to which the later critical writings are devoted. The *Critique* therefore is essentially the Doctrine of Elements.[8] Following the teaching of the *Dissertation*, Kant asserts that all knowledge involves both *intuitions* and *concepts*. Consequently, the Doctrine of Elements has two parts, a Transcendental Aesthetic and a Transcendental Logic. Of these two, again, the Aesthetic is quite short and contains little which had not already been worked out in the *Dissertation*. The Logic, on the other hand, contains the fruits of Kant's years of labor from 1770 to 1781.

There are several independent principles of organization at work in the Logic simultaneously, almost as if, in recognition of its importance, Kant lavished his architectonic attention on this passage. The major division is based upon the distinction between a *logic of truth* and a *logic of illusion*. As Kant has a great deal to say about the errors and confusions of preceding metaphysicians, he assigns a separate section to the subject, entitled Transcendental Dialectic. The logic of truth appears in the section to which this commentary is devoted, the Transcendental Analytic.

A second overlapping division is provided by the traditional logic on which Kant draws so heavily for his architectonic. Traditional logic customarily dealt with three elements of cognition — concepts, judgments, and inferences — and their corresponding cognitive faculties, understanding, judgment, and reason. So Kant divides his Transcendental Logic into the Analytic of Concepts, the Analytic of Principles (i.e., judgments), and the Dialectical Inferences of Pure Reason. This system conflicts with the first, however, for quite obviously reason and inference have perfectly proper employments in a logic of truth. What is more, dialectical illusion arises from other sources than fallacious inference, and Kant is therefore forced to introduce a chapter into the Dialectic on the Concepts of Pure Reason.

Finally, the entire Transcendental Logic — indeed, the whole of the Critical Philosophy — is fitted to the plan of the Table of Categories which appears at the beginning of the Analytic. The basic motif of four groups of three is repeated in the division of the Analytic of Principles into Axioms of Intuition, Anticipations of

_____

[8] *I.e.*, elements of knowledge.

Perception, Analogies of Experience, and Postulates of Empirical Thought, and is mirrored in the four Antinomies of the Dialectic.

Although Kant sets great store by all this systematic fretwork, it does not really assist the reader in understanding the argument of the *Critique*. Drawn as it is from a variety of pre-Critical sources, the architectonic is bound to reflect more of the philosophy which Kant is overthrowing than the new discoveries he has to offer. However, there is yet another principle which, while it is not emphasized as strongly by Kant, tells us a great deal more about the theoretical advance of the *Critique* beyond the *Dissertation* doctrine.

In the *Dissertation*, Kant had distinguished between the real and the merely logical uses of intelligence. The question which he had been unable to answer was how the products of the real use of intelligence — the pure concepts — could have *a priori* application to unconditioned reality. It was in response to this problem, as we saw, that Kant set out upon the path to the Transcendental Philosophy. In the *Critique* the distinction between real and logical use has been retained, but the faculty of intelligence has been split into understanding and reason. To each corresponds a real and logical use, and the question of the *Dissertation* becomes, What is the status of the real uses of understanding and reason? The term "pure concepts" is reserved for the products of understanding and Plato's "Idea" is introduced to designate the representations which reason generates out of its inner resources. Kant now asserts that the pure concepts have a legitimate *a priori* application to objects *so long as we recognize that those objects are mere appearances.* The Ideas, on the other hand, do not yield *a priori* knowledge of any sort, for no intuition adequate to them can ever be given.

This method of conceiving the subject matter of Transcendental Logic finds expression in some of the section headings of the Analytic and Dialectic. In the Analytic, the Table of Judgments appears in the section entitled "The Logical Function of the Understanding in Judgments," and this is followed by the Table of Categories, where the pure concepts of understanding are tabulated. In the Dialectic we find, in the Introduction, "The Logical Employment of Reason" and "The Pure Employment of Reason." The Transcendental Analytic can thus best be viewed as Kant's solution to the problem of the real employment of intelligence.

THE TWO LEVELS OF KANT'S THOUGHT

The Transcendental Analytic is an extraordinarily difficult piece of philosophical writing to understand. Despite the appearance of great order and structure, the text is filled with repetitions, contradictions, and not a few sentences which seem utterly incomprehensible. Although it is probably impossible to sort out the argument so perfectly that every sentence falls into place — and certainly impossible to explain away all the inconsistencies — still the effort must be made to clear up major difficulties, if only so that they do not stand in the way of the underlying argument. The principal source of difficulty is the fact that Kant's mind operates at two semi-distinct levels. Much of the discontinuity in the argument of the *Critique*, as well as the fluctuation in terminology and schemes of classification, owes itself to his unceasing effort to bring those levels into relation with one another.

The first level of Kant's thought is the level of the architectonic — the grand master plan for the entire Critical Philosophy, which I have described above. This is the uppermost level of Kant's philosophy, and if there were nothing more, he would be a major figure in Western thought. But time after time Kant delves beneath the surface of his system and grapples with the problems which lie there. As he pushes the argument deeper and deeper he makes discoveries which, if their consequences be accepted, require the reshaping of the entire philosophical enterprise. Not simply new answers, but new questions, a new vocabulary, a totally new orientation, are demanded. And Kant, in order to preserve his grip on a system too vast even for him to control, could not carry through that revision. So it is that after the profound speculations of the Deduction, Kant continues to use a system of organization which his own argument completely undercuts. We have seen, for example, that the Transcendental Logic is based on the traditional classification of concepts, judgments, and inferences (syllogisms). But one of the most important results of the Analytic is the recognition that the act of judgment is fundamental to cognition, so that concepts can only be defined by reference to judgments, rather than the other way around. Nevertheless, Kant goes right on using the old system of organization, with very unfortunate consequences for the clarity of the Metaphysical Deduction and other passages.

Kant's adherence to the architectonic continues in the *Prolegomena*, which are written entirely at the superficial level. Thus, having demonstrated in the section of the *Critique* entitled Axioms of Intuition that mathematics depends upon an *a priori* synthesis of imagination, Kant reverts in the *Prolegomena* to the assertion that the Aesthetic alone explains the possibility of pure mathematics.

It is not necessary, in accounting for this inconstancy on Kant's part, to introduce elaborate rearrangements of the sections of the *Critique* in allegedly chronological order. As the evidence of the *Prolegomena* demonstrates, the two levels of Kant's thought are not related as earlier to later. When he was thinking with all his might on some fundamental problem, Kant followed the thrust of the argument with little heed for its agreement with the other parts of his system. When he was finished, he did his best to adjust it to the rest of his philosophy, and then relaxed back into the architectonic.

In the portion of the *Critique* to which this commentary is devoted there are three important passages whose comprehensibility is threatened by the strictures of the architectonic. The first of these is the Metaphysical Deduction of the Categories, with which the Analytic begins. The unsatisfactory character of its argument will become apparent only gradually, as the deeper implications of the Deduction are revealed. It will therefore be treated rather briefly, and discussion of the issues which it raises will mostly be postponed until later. The Schematism is the second problematic passage, and the Refutation of Idealism is the third. In the case of the Refutation, only the position in the text is awkward, but with the Schematism the difficulty lies close to the core of the argument. If the interpretation which I have adopted here is correct, the entire section is unnecessary, and its presence merely obscures the connection between the Deduction and the Principles of Pure Understanding. However, Kant has managed to include in passing in this section some of the most important insights of the entire Critical Philosophy.

CHAPTER III

THE STRUCTURE AND METHOD OF
THE ANALYTIC

It is a remarkable fact that after nearly two centuries of intensive criticism and study, commentators have not come to an agreement about the precise nature of Kant's argument in the Transcendental Analytic. This disagreement, so far from concerning its truth or significance or deeper meaning, is over such straightforward matters as what Kant was trying to prove, what he assumed as premises, and what the steps were by which he connected the two. Clearly the Analytic, and thereby the entire Critical Philosophy, must remain an enigma until these questions are answered.

The confusion has its origin in the sheer difficulty of Kant's reasoning. It is greatly multiplied by his unceasing effort to weave together several more or less incompatible strands of argument, representing the demands of different parts of the Critical Philosophy. And in the first edition the whole suffers from the haste with which Kant put down on paper ideas which he was still thinking through. But there is another obstacle to understanding the Analytic, one for which Kant is himself to blame. It is his failure to make absolutely clear the distinction between the two methods of exposition which he employs in the Critical writings.

In the *Prolegomena*, he tells us that there are two modes of argument by which a theory may be set forth:

The analytical method, so far as it is opposed to the synthetical, is very different from one that consists of analytical propositions; it signifies only that we start from what is sought, as if it were given, and ascend to the only conditions under which it is possible. In this method we often use nothing but synthetical propositions, as in mathematical analysis, and it were better to term it the *regressive* method, in contradistinction to the synthetic or *progressive*.[1]

[1] *Prolegomena*, trans. with intro. by L. W. Beck, p. 23 note.

An example of the regressive method would be an analysis which takes as given and unquestioned the validity of our *a priori* mathematical knowledge — namely Euclidean geometry — and performs a regress on this given to the condition that space is an *a priori* form of pure intuition. In other words, a regressive analysis seeks out the presuppositions of a given proposition or body of knowledge. Such an exposition, needless to say, does not prove the validity of geometry. It merely shows *how geometry is possible*, by exhibiting in systematic form a set of conditions *from which* geometry can be deduced. In order actually to prove that Euclidean geometry is, as it claims, a body of *a priori* knowledge, we should have to provide an independent proof of those conditions or presuppositions. The regressive, or analytic, method is therefore strictly explicative rather than demonstrative.

The synthetic or progressive method, on the other hand, is simply the familiar deduction of conclusions from premises. It proceeds according to the canons of logic, which in Kant's day meant the laws of the syllogism. It is the progressive method which yields the apodictic certainty demanded by philosophy. A progressive argument for the validity of geometry might begin from the (independently established) fact that space is a subjective condition of the possibility of experience. From this would then be deduced the existence of an *a priori* science of space — presumably Euclidean geometry. Assuming that the individual steps of the argument were valid, the conclusion would, as in all deductive proofs, possess as much certainty as the premises.[2]

The distinction between the two methods can be illustrated simply by the classic example of the syllogism in Barbara:

> Major: All animals are mortal
> Minor: All men are animals
> Conclusion: All men are mortal [3]

A regressive analysis would begin by assuming that all men are mortal, and would then search about for premises from which this conclusion followed deductively. When the major and minor

[2] As it happens, Kant nowhere in the *Critique* presents a demonstration of the validity of Euclidean geometry *as such*. What he does attempt to prove in the Aesthetic and again in the Axioms of Intuition is that there *must be some body of synthetic propositions a priori* which has space as its object.
[3] The syllogism proving the mortality of Socrates is, as it happens, not a standard Barbara, since its minor term is singular.

premises had been found, the analysis would be complete. A progressive argument, by contrast, would begin with the major and the minor, and descend to the conclusion, that all men are mortal. Now it should be obvious that *unless you have some independent justification for the two premises,* a regressive analysis will not increase the credibility of the conclusion. After all, given any proposition, it is always possible to discover two other propositions from which it can be deduced. If the desired conclusion is "The moon is made of green cheese," for instance, we can deduce it from "All heavenly bodies are made of green cheese" and "The moon is a heavenly body."

But it must also be clearly recognized that *even if you are certain of the truth of the conclusion, a regressive argument does not increase the credibility of the premises.* It is a commonplace of logic that the truth of a conclusion does not guarantee the truth of the premises, although the reverse is of course true. With a little ingenuity, one can construct many pairs of premises from which "All men are mortal" follows. In addition to the pair cited above, we could use: All men are fish and all fish are mortal; All men are numbers and all numbers are mortal; etc. We need simply insert a middle term (animal, fish, number). In general, for any proposition, true or false, we can find an unlimited variety of premises, true or false, from which it can be deduced according to strict laws of logic. This means that a regressive argument, even if it assumes the validity of the proposition from which it starts, does NOT constitute a proof of the "presuppositions" to which it ascends.

In the *Prolegomena,* Kant leaves no doubt as to the nature of his method:

In the *Critique of Pure Reason* I have treated this question [viz. "Is Metaphysics at all possible?"] synthetically, by making inquiries into pure reason itself and endeavoring in this source to determine the elements as well as the laws of its pure use according to principles. . . . The *Prolegomena,* however, are designed for preparatory exercises; they are intended to point out what we have to do in order to make a science actual if it is possible, rather than to propound it. The *Prolegomena* must therefore rest upon something already known as trustworthy, from which we can set out with confidence and ascend to sources as yet unknown, the discovery of which will not only explain to us what we knew but exhibit a sphere of many cognitions which all spring from the same sources. The method of prolegomena, especially of those designed as a preparation for future metaphysics, is consequently analytical.[4]

In the next section, Kant propounds the famous four questions: (1) How is pure mathematics possible? (2) How is pure natural science possible? (3) How is metaphysics in general possible? and (4) How is metaphysics as a science possible? [5] From the passage just quoted, and the comments above concerning regressive (analytic) and progressive (synthetic) methods, we can determine how these questions are to be understood. To show that a science is possible, we assume it as given and then perform a regress to some premise or set of premises from which its existence can be deduced. But we have not yet "made the science actual." For that, we must provide an independent demonstration of the premises which we have discovered. Thus the regressive argument of the *Prolegomena* sets us a task, namely, to prove the premises from which mathematics and science have been shown to follow. This proof is provided by the *Critique of Pure Reason*.

The relation of the *Prolegomena* to the *Critique* can be represented in the following catechism:

Question: How are mathematics and natural science possible? (or, Under what conditions are . . . possible?)

Answer: Mathematics and natural science are possible if the validity of their concepts (space, time, cause, substance, etc.) is a necessary condition of consciousness in general.

Question: Is the validity of the concepts of mathematics and natural science a necessary condition of consciousness in general?

Answer: Yes, as the argument of the Transcendental Analytic proves.

The first question and answer summarize the results of the *Prolegomena;* the second question and answer summarize the results of the *Critique*. In brief, the *Prolegomena* asks, Is *a priori* knowledge possible? and the *Critique* asks, is *a priori* knowledge actual?

All of this would seem to be so clear as to allow for no uncertainty. But unfortunately, Kant muddled the matter thoroughly when he came to revise the *Critique* for the second edition. Into the text of the Introduction he inserted a ten-page passage adapted from the *Prolegomena*[6] which states the problem in *Prolegomena*

[4] *Prolegomena* (tr. Beck), pp. 21–22.

[5] In the Introduction to the *Critique*, the third question is altered to read: How is metaphysics, as natural disposition, possible?

[6] Sections V and VI in the second edition, B 14–24.

fashion as: How are *a priori* synthetic judgments possible? [B 19].
He then asserts flatly:

> Since these sciences [mathematics and physics] actually exist, it is quite
> proper to ask *how* they are possible; for that they must be possible is
> proved by the fact that they exist [B 20].

Things are now hopelessly confused, for the actuality of these
sciences is precisely what the *Critique* is supposed to demonstrate.
If Kant is going to begin by assuming the validity of mathematics
and physics, then his entire enterprise will be a mere begging of
the question.

The difficulty of the *Critique*, coupled with this ambiguity about
the structure of its basic argument, has given rise to a continuing
debate about just what — if anything — Kant has proved in the
Analytic. Lewis White Beck, in the introduction to his translation
of the *Prolegomena,* has this to say about the controversy:

> It has been indefatigably argued, with an acerbity unusual even in Kant-
> scholarship, which is notorious for the bitterness of its polemics, that Kant
> did *not* answer Hume but simply assumed what Hume doubted — for
> example, the validity of the causal law — and then "rationalized" his
> assumption . . . The *Critique of Pure Reason* is not guilty of this appear-
> ance of circularity, for its synthetical method does not assume science and
> mathematics but rather establishes, by a general epistemological inquiry,
> principles from which they can be derived.[7]

Thus far, Beck is quite clear, and he encourages us to think that
the *Critique* is indeed synthetic in method, "establish[ing] . . .
principles from which [science and mathematics] can be derived."
But the vision clouds as he goes on:

> [T]he justification of the principles is not merely that they produce the
> kind of knowledge Hume doubted; rather, they are, Kant argued, the
> necessary conditions also of *any* connected experience in time, of the
> distinction between the even apparently objective and the subjective, and
> of the distinction between perceptual truth and perceptual illusion which
> any sane man, including Hume, would have to grant. It may be that Kant
> fails to prove this, but he was certainly not guilty of a sophomoric *petitio
> principii.*[8]

What precisely does Beck mean? From the use of the words
"not merely" and "also," he would seem to be imputing to Kant

[7] Pages xviii–xix, note.
[8] *Ibid.*

an argument something like this: "A regressive analysis beginning from mathematics and science will not refute Hume, for mathematics and science is precisely what Hume professes to doubt. But if the very same principles (premises) which produce (imply) science and mathematics also imply the distinction between the even apparently objective and the subjective, etc., etc., then Hume will have been convincingly answered, for not even he can deny them."

If this is what Beck means, then he has relapsed into the same old confusion about the regressive method. I pointed out above that in a regressive or analytic exposition, the premises are not proved *even if the truth of the conclusion is assumed*. Therefore, it will not help any for Kant to show that the premises of the science and mathematics which Hume rejects are also premises of some distinctions which he can be presumed to accept. Neither fact in the slightest coerces Hume to grant the validity of the premises.

The first step in clarifying this matter is to examine the term *condition* and its variants. In a sense, the entire *Critique* can be summed up as a study of the modes of conditionality. The Aesthetic exhibits the sensuous conditions of the possibility of experience. The Analytic similarly exhibits the intellectual conditions of the possibility of experience. The Dialectic exposes reason's unwarranted attempt to go beyond phenomena, the conditioned, to noumena, the unconditioned. The word "condition" is Kant's broadest term for any relation of subordination or dependence. Analogous forms of conditionality turn up in all branches of inquiry: the cause is condition of the event; God is condition of the world, and is Himself unconditioned; the genus is condition of the species, which in turn is condition of the subspecies; the premises of a syllogism are the conditions of the conclusion.

The relation of conditionality is hierarchical, with each condition having its conditions in turn, and each conditioned playing the role of condition to some subordinate. For example, in the chain of causes, every cause is the effect of a predecessor, and every effect is the cause of some successor.[9] The model of a series of conditions is the syllogistic chain called a *ratiocinatio poly-*

---

[9] In the realm of phenomena, says Kant, we never come upon the unconditioned. There are no first causes or indivisible substances. Cf. the Antinomies.

syllogistica. This is a series of interlocking syllogisms in which the conclusion of the first is the major premise of the second, and so on.

In these terms, regressive argument can be described as ascending the series of conditions, and progressive argument as descending. The *Prolegomena*, for example, begin with geometry and physics as given, and then ascend to the *a priori* conditions of the possibility of these disciplines. What now are we to say of the *Critique?* According to Kant, its method of exposition is synthetic or progressive. But the Transcendental Deduction is supposedly a search for the "*a priori* conditions of the possibility of experience," and hence must be regressive.

Kemp Smith has suggested that in fact Kant employs a combination of the two methods, with the difference, however, that the starting point of the regress is ordinary experience rather than geometry and physics. According to this interpretation, the argument of the *Critique* proceeds in two stages, corresponding to the two Books of the Analytic. In the first stage, Kant assumes as given the facts of ordinary unreflective consciousness, and *ascends* to their conditions or premises, namely the whole machinery of categories and syntheses and forms of intuition. Then in the second stage, he begins with that transcendental machinery, and deductively *descends* to the validity of physics and mathematics. As Kemp Smith puts it:

By a preliminary regress upon the conditions of our *de facto* consciousness it acquires data from which it is enabled to advance by a synthetic, progressive or deductive procedure to the establishment of the validity of synthetic *a priori* judgments.[10]

This ascending and descending or "retreat and advance," which Kemp Smith calls the transcendental method, is roughly the same as that described by Beck in the passage quoted above. And like Beck, Kemp Smith suffers from a fundamental confusion concerning the nature of regressive argument. A regressive argument lends no weight whatsoever to the premises to which it ascends. In Kant's language, it merely shows them to be "possible." Hence a regress "upon the conditions of our *de facto* consciousness" will yield, not "data" as Kemp Smith says, but mere unsupported hypotheses. The subsequent "advance" to science and mathematics will not

---

[10] Kemp Smith, *Commentary*, p. 44.

add an iota of additional support to them. Even if Hume grants the facts of *de facto* consciousness, and grants also every step of the retreat and advance, it will still be open to him to reject science and mathematics as unproved.

At the risk of exhausting the reader's patience, I will try to make the matter absolutely clear by means of a simple example from syllogistic logic. If I seem to linger too long on this, I can only plead in defense that it seems to be a point which has thus far eluded some other Kant-commentators. Let us imagine, then, that Hume had disputed the proposition that All men are mortal, contending instead that there might for all we know be a man now alive who was immortal.[11] Now, if Kant had followed the pattern described by Kemp Smith and Beck, his answer might have run something like this:

1. You, Hume, will surely grant, as any sane man must, that

        a. No angels are animals
  and b. No angels are men.

2. Now, performing a regress upon the conditions of these two undisputed propositions, we find that they are implied by a set of three premises, viz:

        α. All animals are mortal
        β. No angels are mortal
        γ. All men are animals.

This is seen from the two syllogisms:

    A. All animals are mortal
       No angels are mortal
    ∴. No angels are animals (a)

  and B. No angels are animals
        All men are animals
    ∴. No angels are men. (b)

[handwritten marginal note: ∴ If all 'men' are mortal, any immortal 'man' would be non-animal, & an angel]

3. But from these very same premises, which we have acquired "as data" by this regress, we can deduce the disputed proposition, thus:

        All men are animals
        All animals are mortal
    ∴. All men are mortal.   Q.E.D.

Now it must be obvious that this is precisely the sort of "sophomoric *petitio principii*" which Beck assures us Kant has not com-

---

[11] This is not quite the customary direction in which Hume's scepticism ran, but that is not important for the example.

mitted. Only in this case (and in the argument of the *Critique*, supposedly), instead of assuming directly the proposition to be proved, Kant has assumed several premises from which it can be deduced. The preliminary regress represented by step 2 has no probative value whatsoever.

The key to all the difficulty, I think, is the meaning of the term "necessary condition" which recurs both in the text and in the analyses of the commentators. We shall therefore have to detour through the arid terrain of formal logic in order to clear up the confusion. On this point, I repeat, depends the success or failure of any interpretation of the *Critique*.

In logic it is customary to distinguish between necessary conditions and sufficient conditions. A necessary condition is a *conditio sine qua non*, which literally means "a condition without which not;" so, if we say that proposition Q is a necessary condition of proposition P, we are saying, without Q not P. In other words, If not Q then not P. But by a well-known equivalence of the propositional calculus,[12] this is the same as If P then Q. Thus, contrary to what one might expect, the *conclusion* of a proof is the necessary condition of the *premises*, not the other way around. Analogously, the effect is the necessary condition of the cause.

A sufficient condition is something that suffices for another. The premises of a syllogism suffice for the conclusion; therefore they are sufficient conditions of the conclusion. The cause is a sufficient condition of its effect. Thus if Q is the necessary condition of P, P will be a sufficient condition of Q. In the syllogism,

> All men are mortal
> Socrates is a man
> ∴ Socrates is mortal,

the mortality of men and the humanity of Socrates, taken together, are sufficient conditions of the mortality of Socrates. Correlatively, the mortality of Socrates is a necessary condition of the mortality of men together with the humanity of Socrates. To ring the changes yet again, if Socrates is not mortal, then either he is not a man, or else not all men are mortal.

From all this, certain important consequences follow:

[12] I.e., $\bar{q} \supset \bar{p} . \equiv . p \supset q$.

(1) If you wish to prove that Q is a necessary condition of P, *you must deduce Q from P and not the other way around.*

(2) From any proposition, P, it is possible to deduce an unending series of consequent propositions, all of which are necessary conditions of P. Therefore it is meaningless to talk about *the* necessary conditions of P, as if there were a finite set of them.

(3) Any proposition P can be deduced from an indefinitely large number of alternative possible premises, each of which is a sufficient condition of P. Therefore it is meaningless to talk about *the* sufficient conditions of P.

When this is applied to the distinction between progressive and regressive argument, it is evident that Kant's description of them is extremely misleading. First of all, if the regressive method is identified with *ascending* a series of conditions, as from the conclusion to the premises of a proof, then it is clearly a search for sufficient conditions. In like manner a progressive argument, which *descends* the series of conditions, discovers necessary conditions.[13] In short, the image of "ascending to necessary conditions" is completely inappropriate, for in the *ratiocinatio polysyllogistica* (chain of syllogisms) the necessary conditions lie farther down the chain.[14]

Kant actually leaves himself a way out of this mistake in the passage from the *Prolegomena* which I quoted at the beginning of this chapter. He describes the analytical method as "start[ing] from what is sought, as if it were given, and ascend[ing] to the *only* conditions under which it is possible." [15] As an ascent in the series of conditions, this method arrives at sufficient conditions. But if, as Kant says, these are the *only* such conditions, then in fact

---

[13] Again, it is the conclusions of the progressive argument which are necessary conditions of its premises.

[14] This suggests that the parallelism between causal chain and syllogistic chain, which was often asserted by rationalists, is a meretricious one. God may be a necessary being and first cause, but the assertion of His existence, while the highest proposition of metaphysics, is a sufficient and not a necessary condition of the contingent propositions which flow from it. Another way of putting this, which reveals one of the fundamental insights of Kant's theory of knowledge, is that the order of knowing is the reverse of the order of being. The first premises of our reasoning concern the most immediate — and most conditioned — facts. The farther we carry our inferences, the *higher* we ascend in the order of conditions. A more modern way of stating this is that the first principles of a science depend upon the observed data, not *vice versa*. Compare Aristotle's distinction between things more knowable to us and things more knowable by nature. *Physics* 184ᵃ 16–18.

[15] *Prolegomena*, p. 23 note, emphasis added.

they will also be necessary, for it is true that a condition which is the only sufficient condition is a necessary and sufficient condition. However, despite this loophole, Kant's characterization of the methods remains ambiguous.

There are really two and only two plausible interpretations of the argument of the *Critique*. Either Kant begins by assuming the validity of mathematics and natural science, and then works backwards by an analytic exposition to the *a priori sufficient* conditions of their validity. Or else he begins with some premise which is universally granted, and works forward by a synthetic deductive proof to the validity of mathematics and natural science.

The clearest statement of these alternatives is given by T. D. Weldon in the second edition of his commentary to the *Critique*.[16] Weldon begins by distinguishing the analytic and synthetic methods, and reports that Kant himself claimed the *Critique* to be synthetic. He then comments:

> Formally this claim is valid. He does begin with logical axioms in the *Metaphysical Deduction* and with what he claims as indubitable facts of consciousness in the *Subjective Deduction;* and he does proceed from these through the *Schematism* and the *Principles* to M[etaphysische] A[nfangs-gründe der] N[aturwissenschaft]. But his proofs are never rigid (they could not be since he is not engaged in formal logic or geometry, i.e. in manipulating a postulational system) and sometimes they just break down.
>
> A good instance is the main argument of the *Second Analogy*, which is circular. Kant's claim is that our recognition of the occurrence of a public time order proves that there is objective, necessary connexion between phenomena, i.e. causality in nature; but we have to recognize causality in nature as a condition of recognizing the possibility of a public time sequence.[17]

So Weldon suggests that it might be worth looking at the *Critique* — contrary to Kant's wishes — as a regressive or analytical exposition. Thus the argument (including its extension in the *Metaphysical First Principles of Natural Science*) becomes an answer to the *Prolegomena* question, How is pure physics as a science possible?, or alternatively in Weldon's version, What are the presuppositions of Newtonian Mechanics? On this reading of the Critical Philosophy, the entire *Critique* should be read *backwards;* begin with the *Metaphysical First Principles;* ascend to the Analytic

[16] *Kant's Critique of Pure Reason*, 2nd ed., pp. 172–179.
[17] Weldon, pp. 173–174.

of Principles, which contains the presuppositions of the *Metaphysical First Principles;* ascend further to the Schematism; and conclude with the highest presupposition, the Table of Categories (or perhaps the Transcendental Unity of Apperception). The resulting exposition is in no sense a proof either of the categories or of Newtonian mechanics. But nevertheless, Weldon asserts, it "has considerable force" and "has something to be said for it." [18]

Kant's insistence on the synthetic character of his proof stemmed, Weldon recognizes, from his conviction that nothing less would answer Hume and the other sceptical critics of *a priori* knowledge.

He wanted to derive [the categories] from pure formal logic and not to base them on scientific methodology. If this could be done . . . he would be able to claim that his doctrine was synthetically proved and not just analytically credible. He would have his unity of apperception as a unique kind of factual premise . . .[19]

But alas, "this is not a feasible project. Nothing, or anything, can be said to follow from the 'fact of self-consciousness.' " Weldon states the issue even more sharply several paragraphs later. The final question, he says, is whether it can "be proved that the validity of the pure concepts, especially 'space,' 'time,' 'substance,' and 'causality' is a necessary condition of the existence of self-consciousness as a fact, not just a 'presupposition' of it. I do not see how this could be proved." [20]

It is clear from the foregoing that if Kant is doing what Weldon suggests — if he is assuming the validity of Newtonian mechanics and arguing regressively to the categories — then he has not in any sense answered Hume. What is more, he has done nothing to increase the credibility either of Newtonian physics or of the Table of Categories. At most, such an argument performs the function described in the *Prolegomena* of showing Kant *what he would have to prove if he wished to answer Hume.* Now that would be a very impressive accomplishment for some minor eighteenth-century critic of Hume with an acute analytical mind and no particular creative powers. But Weldon and Kemp Smith and Beck and the

[18] Weldon, p. 178.
[19] Weldon, pp. 177–178.
[20] Weldon, p. 179.

others are asking us to believe that the man who is considered the greatest philosopher since Aristotle spent eleven years at the height of his powers searching for an argument (which Weldon assures us cannot be found) and then had not the wit to realize that he had failed. In short, they are saying that Kant did assume what Hume doubted, and hence that his entire philosophical enterprise does not even begin to do what he claimed for it.

This is the challenge which prompted me to write a commentary on the Transcendental Analytic: Can an argument be found in the *Critique* which, beginning with the fact of self-consciousness (*de facto* consciousness, as Kemp Smith puts it), advances by a rigorous deduction to the validity of the law of causation and the other principles of the Analogies? The answer, I believe, is yes. In the pages that follow I have exhibited such an argument. It is neither trivial nor circular nor at any point "regressive." If it is correct, then it completely answers Hume. But correct or not, it is an argument worthy of its author.

Commentary on the
Transcendental Analytic

SUPERFICIALLY, the argument of the Transcendental Analytic is quite straightforward, proceeding in three stages. First, in the passage ordinarily referred to as the Metaphysical Deduction (Chapter I of the Analytic of Concepts), Kant sets forth in systematic fashion the pure concepts of understanding, and presents an argument to show that the resulting Table of Categories is complete and correct. Second, in the Transcendental Deduction, it is proved that these pure concepts admit of an *a priori* employment, and are in fact the source of valid synthetic *a priori* judgments. Finally, in the Analytic of Principles, the foundation is laid for a system of such *a priori* knowledge, and its highest principles are demonstrated. The gap between the pure concepts and the system of principles is bridged by the Schematism (Chapter I of the Analytic of Principles), and the entire argument is followed by a chapter on Phenomena and Noumena which serves as a transition to the Dialectic.

When the argument is studied in detail, however, this simple picture is seen to be an inadequate representation of what Kant actually does. The opening passage is exceedingly arbitrary, and for the modern student especially, the list of Functions of Unity in Judgment seems to appear out of nowhere. The transition to the Table of Categories is artificial, both in the general line of argument and in the individual derivation of categories. The Deduction is hardly more satisfactory from the standpoint of the supposed line of argument. Leaving to one side its extreme difficulty, and the notorious incoherence of the first edition version, the Deduction puzzles the reader by never mentioning the particular categories which Kant has just finished tabulating. It is only in the Analytic of Principles that they once more make their appearance and are given detailed analyses.

Although these difficulties are undeniable, and must be faced before the Analytic can be understood, it is essential not to overemphasize their detrimental effect upon Kant's argument. The guiding motive of this commentary is the desire to exhibit the coherent and connected reasoning which is contained in the

Analytic, and I shall therefore treat confusions as obstacles to be got around, rather than as specimens to be dissected endlessly. In the present instance, the exposition of the Analytic could be brought more in line with its deeper argument by either of two relatively minor changes. The Metaphysical Deduction could be treated as an introduction in which a variety of concepts are explained and a summary given of certain results to be achieved (namely, the Table of Categories); or, alternatively, the entire opening chapter could be moved to the end of the Analytic, and presented as a systematic exposition of the conclusions of the Analytic of Principles.

This alteration is desirable because the real argument of the Analytic is rather different from the three-stage model described above. Roughly speaking, what actually happens is that Kant begins with the fact of the unity of consciousness. From the analysis of this fact he deduces that the mind produces the unity by an activity called "*a priori* synthesis." He then draws on analyses of the nature of synthesis and the temporal character of consciousness in order to deduce the particular forms which synthetic unity takes. These particular forms are, it turns out, the categories, which thus can be described as "modes of time-consciousness." In other words, the real argument *ends* with the Table of Categories instead of starting with it. The Deduction of the Categories is designed to prove only that *some categories or other* must be *a priori* valid of experience in general. The actual deduction of the individual categories takes place in the Analytic of Principles.

The source of the confusion is Kant's insistence on treating the categories as class concepts in the manner of traditional logic. Once they are considered in this way, it is natural to suppose that we can first discover them and summarize them in a table, and then apply them to derive certain *a priori* principles. If, on the other hand, we accept Kant's own description of the categories as "functions of synthesis," we are led to see that they are aspects of a mental activity, and that the characteristics of that activity are equally well expressed by a Table of Categories or a System of Principles.

CHAPTER I

THE CLUE TO THE DISCOVERY OF ALL PURE CONCEPTS OF THE UNDERSTANDING

Kant's purpose in this opening chapter is well expressed by the heading: to discover *all* the pure concepts of understanding. He rejects as inappropriate to Transcendental Philosophy the piecemeal discovery of categories which had characterized previous philosophy, and asserts instead that there must be a unifying principle which will guarantee the completeness of the list.[1] Kant sets great store by his table of categories and never tires of contrasting its self-evident completeness with the haphazard collections of other systems. Indeed, he announces himself prepared to stake his whole system on its success in any particular:

In this enquiry I have made completeness my chief aim, and I venture to assert that there is not a single metaphysical problem which has not been solved, or for the solution of which the key at least has not been supplied. Pure reason is, indeed, so perfect a unity that if its principle were insufficient for the solution of even a single one of all the questions to which it itself gives birth we should have no alternative but to reject the principle, since we should then no longer be able to place implicit reliance upon it in dealing with any one of the other questions. [A xiii]

In justification of so bold a claim, Kant argues that his system has to do only with the possessions of the mind itself, and makes no attempt to advance our knowledge of the universe [A xiv]. Such an inventory can, indeed must, be complete, for "what reason produces entirely out of itself cannot be concealed, but is brought to light by reason itself immediately the common principle has been discovered" [A xx]. So intimately interrelated are the several

[1] Kant has in mind Aristotle, from whom he takes the term "category." Cf. B 107.

portions of the system that "any attempt to change even the smallest part at once gives rise to contradictions" [B xxxviii].

It is difficult to know how the reader should view these repeated assertions of completeness and perfection. Judging simply by the frequency with which they appear in the *Critique*, Kant meant them to be taken with all seriousness, but no argument is ever given which satisfactorily demonstrates the completeness of the Table of Categories. Kant's own papers, in which he can be seen working up the doctrines of the Critical Philosophy, reveal that he tinkered endlessly with the lists of Judgments and Categories before hitting on the principle of four sets of three.[2] Furthermore, in contradistinction to the order of argument of the Metaphysical Deduction, Kant quite evidently adjusted the Table of Judgments so that it would yield the desired Table of Categories.

Under the circumstances, the best course is to take note of Kant's claims, clarify the Metaphysical Deduction as much as possible, and then move on to the Transcendental Deduction and the Analytic of Principles, where the real arguments are presented for the system of categories. Accordingly, I shall devote relatively little space to the opening sections of the Analytic of Concepts.

Kant's argument proceeds in three steps, to which correspond the three sections of the chapter: (1) The fundamental activity of the understanding is judging, which is the asserting of a unity or connection among representations. If we can tabulate the functions or modes of unity in judgment, therefore, we shall have obtained a complete catalogue of the powers of the understanding. (2) Traditional logic is familiar with such a Table of Functions of Unity in Judgment, and can quite easily provide us with a complete list. (3) But the introducing of synthetic connections into a given manifold or variety of sensibility is *also* a "unifying of representations." Consequently, the same basic mental powers must be employed, and the catalogue of functions of unity in judgment will provide the "clue to the discovery" of the functions of synthesis, which is to say, a Table of the Pure Concepts of Understanding. In short, judgment is the product of the *logical* use of understanding, and synthetic unity is the product of its *real use*. By tabulating the forms in which it performs the former activity, we will also discover the forms in which it performs the latter.

[2] Cf. Kemp Smith, pp. 186–194.

SECTION I. THE LOGICAL EMPLOYMENT OF THE UNDERSTANDING

In the Aesthetic, Kant has dealt with sensibility, the first of the two faculties of knowledge. Now he introduces the second, understanding. Despite the fact that Book I of the Analytic is entitled Analytic of Concepts, Kant almost at once moves to a discussion of judgments. This reveals what is to be one of the most important consequences of the Analytic, namely that judgment rather than conception is the fundamental activity of the mind.[3]

Concepts "rest on functions," and a function is "the unity of the act of bringing various representations under one common representation." This is a rather obscure way of speaking. What is the difference between saying that a concept "rests on" a function and saying that it *is* a function? Later on this will become somewhat clearer, although I cannot promise to remove the air of mystery entirely. Briefly, concepts turn out to be rules for the performance of mental activities, and according to Kant these rules are built upon certain underlying simple "functions." For example, the rule for counting is based upon the decade [B 104], the concept of cause and effect is based upon the temporal relation of succession, the concept of reciprocity is based upon the temporal relation of contemporaneity, and so forth. Kant now asserts that concepts can relate to objects only mediately, or indirectly. This marks a major break with the doctrine of the *Dissertation*, but it is stated so casually that the reader may pass over it entirely unless alerted. In the Aesthetic, Kant has stated that intuition is the means whereby the mind is in *immediate* relation to objects [B 33]. Put somewhat differently, intuition is that faculty through which "an object is *given* to us" [B 74]. A concept is general in nature. It unifies several representations by abstracting from their differences and attending only to their common characteristics. Hence, a concept is always at least at a single remove from its object. In Kant's terms, a judgment, which combines concepts, is "the representation of a representation" of an object [B 93]. We may make our concepts more concrete by including more notes in them. Thus, given the concept "man," we may specify it further as "adult man," "adult living man," "adult living American man," "adult living American unmarried man," and so forth. In no sense, however,

[3] Intuiting, it will be recalled, is passive rather than active.

have we moved any closer to the objects. Even an infinitely specific concept would still relate only mediately to an object by way of an intuition of it.

In the *Dissertation*, Kant claimed that pure concepts give us knowledge about things in themselves. But if all concepts by their very structure relate only indirectly to their objects, then it will not even be logically possible for a concept alone to yield knowledge of an object. The concept will always need the cooperation of an intuition by which the object is *given*. By this argument, Kant destroys the foundation of the *Dissertation* doctrine. Curiously, he also refutes one of his most cherished critical teachings, that the pure concepts have problematic application to things in themselves. This is now clearly impossible, for all knowledge demands relation to an object; intuition is the only means whereby relation to an object is given; and intuition is either *intellectual*, in which case concepts are unnecessary, or *sensible*, in which case knowledge is of appearances only. Here, as throughout the Analytic, Kant drives his analysis forward to conclusions which destroy the relatively simple assumptions of the architectonic framework.

SECTION 2. THE LOGICAL FUNCTION OF THE UNDERSTANDING
IN JUDGMENTS

The Table of Judgments can best be understood if we develop it step by step, indicating the meaning of each of the headings. Let us begin with a subject term S and a predicate term P, and the connecting word, or copula, "is." The basic framework for a judgment is then "S is P." In specifying this matrix, we can assert the predicate P of all the objects to which S refers, or only of a portion of them. This gives us the universal form of judgment, "All S are P," and the particular form, "Some S are P." Each of these forms, now, can be either asserted or denied, so there are two types of universal judgments and two types of particular judgments, namely: "All S are P," "It is not the case that all S are P," "Some S are P," "It is not the case that some S are P." The two clumsy negative judgments can be reworded, respectively, as "Some S are not P" (the negative of "All S are P") and "No S are P" (the negative of "Some S are P"). Finally, any one of these four forms of judgment can be asserted either problematically ("Possibly S is P"), assertorically ("S is P"), or apodeictically ("Necessarily S is P"). We thus have twelve forms of the categorical judgment matrix, "S is P."

To each of the first two pairs, Kant adds a third "function of unity in judgment." In addition to universal and particular judgments, he distinguishes singular judgments. These are judgments in which the subject-term is a proper name or singular description rather than a class term, as for example, "Socrates is mortal." In logic, singular judgments behave like universal judgments, for a proper name can be treated as denoting a class with only one member.[4] To affirmation and negation, the two modes of quality, Kant adds the infinite judgment, in which a positive assertion is made, but a negative predicate is employed, e.g., "Socrates is non-mortal."

Since each categorical judgment must have quantity and quality and must be asserted in some modality, it follows that there are twenty-seven possible forms. The following partial list should make this clear:

Universal affirmative problematic judgment:	"Possibly all men are mortal"
Universal affirmative assertoric judgment:	"All men are mortal"

   .
   .
     .

Particular negative apodeictic judgment:	"Necessarily some men are not mortal"
Particular infinite problematic judgment:	"Possibly some men are non-mortal"

   .
   .
   .

Singular negative assertoric judgment:	"Socrates is not mortal" [5]

Categorical judgments are the elements from which hypothetical and disjunctive judgments are built. A hypothetical judgment is composed of two categorical judgments, joined together by the connective "If . . . then," which asserts a relation of dependence or conditionality. For example, the hypothetical judgment, "If

---

[4] Cf. Kant, *Logic*, § 21, Anmerk. 1, in *Gesammelte Schriften*, IX, p. 102.

[5] Notice that the negative singular judgment follows the negative particular judgment, not the negative universal judgment. This is because there is no difference between the contrary and the contradictory of a singular judgment.

Socrates is a man then Socrates is mortal," is composed of two singular affirmative assertoric judgments. Similarly, a disjunctive judgment consists of a finite number of categorical judgments linked by repeated uses of the connective "or." [6]

It is fruitless to consider seriously Kant's professed reasons for adopting precisely this Table of Judgments. As Kemp Smith points out,[7] it does not correspond exactly to any textbook formulation of Kant's day, and the driving motives behind the alterations which he introduces are first, a desire for symmetry, and second, the demands of the Table of Categories which is to be derived from it. Nevertheless, some comment may be helpful, for the very failings of the Table are instructive from the point of view of the later passages of the Analytic.

The most important entries in the Table of Judgments are the functions of relation, categorical, hypothetical, and disjunctive. Kant bases on the first two the all-important categories of substance and causality. Now it is evident from our brief examination that the functions of relation are significantly different from the other three triads. They are not three different ways of specifying a judgment-matrix, but rather three different judgment-matrices. Even this way of putting the point is misleading, for the categorical judgment is of a totally different type from the hypothetical and disjunctive judgments. A categorical judgment connects two concepts (or, in Kant's more general terminology, two representations), the subject and the predicate. It thus creates a judgment out of elements which are not themselves judgments. But the hypothetical and disjunctive relations take complete judgments as their elements. In modern logical terminology, they are truth-functional connectives.[8] This difference between the first function of relation and the other two carries over into the categories of relation, and

---

[6] Needless to say, one can form hypothetical or disjunctive judgments whose elements are themselves hypothetical or disjunctive. Strictly speaking, the rules determining what counts as a judgment are as follows: (1) Every categorical judgment is a judgment; (2) Every hypothetical or disjunctive whose component elements are judgments is itself a judgment; (3) Every conjunction of judgments is a judgment.

[7] Kemp Smith, p. 192.

[8] Cf. B 141. It could be argued that they are not truth-functions, which belong to extensional logic, but rather intensional connectives. For a brilliant discussion of this problem in modern dress, see C. I. Lewis, *An Analysis of Knowledge and Valuation*, Chapter viii, and especially pp. 211–228.

in the Analogies of Experience produces a great deal of confusion. Kant there attempts to connect the categories of relation with three laws of physics: conservation of matter, the causal maxim, and the law of action and reaction. This is supposedly accomplished by identifying each of the categories, and thereby each of the functions of judgment, with a particular time-relation. But in fact, as Kant himself recognizes, there are only two time-relations, succession and simultaneity. Succession can be associated easily enough with the category of cause and effect (hypothetical judgment), and simultaneity with the category of community (disjunctive judgment). This leaves substance, which must be assigned the pseudo-time-relation, duration. Thus the logical difference between categorical judgments and hypothetical or disjunctive judgments reappears in the Analogies as the logical difference between duration and succession or simultaneity. The attempt to treat them all under the same heading in the Table of Categories reveals a pervasive unclarity in Kant's philosophy concerning the proper analysis of empirical objects. But this carries us beyond the present section of the *Critique*.[9]

SECTION 3. THE PURE CONCEPTS OF THE UNDERSTANDING, OR CATEGORIES

This section contains the heart of the Metaphysical Deduction. The opening portion, from the beginning to the Table of Categories, is the first really important passage of the Analytic. It introduces and provides a preliminary explanation of the central concept of the entire Critical Philosophy: *synthesis*. The complete analysis of the concept, which is one of the principal goals of this commentary, will involve considerations which only enter into the argument later in the Analytic, and therefore this discussion will serve merely as an introduction to the subject.

The section as a whole, including the two subsections added in the second edition [§§ 11, 12, B 109–116], divides into two parts, separated by the Table of Categories. The explanatory part which follows the Table is devoted principally to a justification of several of the more unfamiliar categories and requires no comment. The

[9] See below, pp. 246, 256–259

reader should pay particular attention to the distinction drawn between the mathematical and the dynamical categories [B 110] as it proves later to be quite important.

The opening part comprises seven paragraphs.[10] The first through fifth paragraphs introduce and discuss the concept of synthesis. The sixth and seventh then state the argument which links the Table of Categories to the Table of Judgments. I shall begin with a general consideration of the material contained in this passage, and then treat the argument paragraph by paragraph.

General Discussion

Much of our thinking consists in the analyzing of given representations, and the abstracting from them of common characters to form a class concept. For example, we examine various substances presented to our senses, and discover that certain among them have the characteristic of adjusting their shape smoothly to the surrounding container. By attending to this and other characteristics, we form the concept, *liquid*. We have produced what may be called an "analytic unity" of the representations of the several substances, by bringing them all together under a single concept. The bond which unites them is their partial identity — i.e., their possession of a common characteristic.

But all such thinking presupposes that the elements to be analyzed have already been combined. Before we can analyze the representations of Socrates and Plato in order to abstract from them the concept of "humanity," we must first have held together in one consciousness the manifold of perceptions which each representation contains. The representation of Socrates, for example, contains the perceptions of his wit, his snub nose, his arms and legs and organs, the sharpness of his tongue, and so forth. If it were not for the fact that we had already thought of these perceptions as a unity, there would be no representation of Socrates to analyze. Now, Hume had shown that such unities can never be *given* as such to the understanding. Consequently, the mind must create them by a spontaneous act of unifying, an act to which Kant gives the title, *synthesis*. The synthetic unity of a manifold of percep-

---

[10] The reader is very strongly urged to mark the paragraph numbers in his copy of the *Critique* whenever the textual analysis descends to that level of detail. It will make it much easier to follow the discussion.

tions is thus the necessary condition of the analytic unity of a concept, and indeed of all knowledge and experience.[11]

Analysis and synthesis are different in that the first merely organizes and rearranges what the second creates. But they are alike in that both create a unity out of a diversity. Analysis unites many different representations by bringing them *under* one concept (Socrates, Plato, etc., under the concept, man) while synthesis unites many different intuitions *in* one consciousness [B 104]. Now, asserts Kant, "The same function which gives unity to the various representations *in a judgment* also gives unity to the mere synthesis of various representations *in an intuition* [B 104-105]. Hence, to each function of unity in judgment, there will correspond a function of synthesis, or *category*. This is the "clue to the discovery of all pure concepts" from which the chapter takes its title.

Kant gives no proof at all for the assertion that analytic and synthetic unity arise from the same operations, and that the first can therefore be used as a key to the second. The argument, as Kant states it, depends on the claim that both kinds of unity are attributable to the same mental faculty, namely understanding, but Kant himself assigns synthesis to the imagination [B 103]. This destroys entirely any supposition that the two are parallel, and leaves the forms of synthesis to be deduced individually from the characteristics of time-consciousness. The Metaphysical Deduction is one of the few passages in the *Critique* which is at all dependent on a faculty psychology. Almost always, as I have mentioned, the argument can be couched in terms of the activities which understanding or reason or judgment is said to perform, but in the present instance, it is only by attributing analytic and synthetic unity to the same mental faculty that Kant can establish the isomorphism between the two Tables.

Kant's discovery of the problem of synthetic unity was part of

[11] The crucial step in this argument, of course, is the assertion that a synthetic unity of representations cannot be *given*, but must be produced by the mind. In a sense, this proposition is so basic to Kant's philosophy that he never attempts to prove it, but it is more accurate to say that the entire Analytic is a series of proofs of it. The easiest way to see the point is to recall, first, that all representations, as given, are spatio-temporal. Adding to this Hume's argument about the separability of distinguishables, we can conclude that there is no *necessary* connection among given representations. A deeper understanding of this important point must wait upon the discussion of the unity of consciousness.

the process of development beyond the *Dissertation* doctrine of real and merely logical employments of intelligence. In the *Dissertation*, the pure concepts produced by intelligence in its real use were considered by Kant to be class concepts, differing from empirical concepts only in their freedom from any admixture of sensation. They were presumed to apply to things-in-themselves in the way that all concepts applied to their objects — by a partial identity between the marks contained in the concept (rationality and animality, for "men") and the attributes of the object.

Now the original objections to the *Dissertation* do not demand a revision of the theory of pure concepts. What is needed, as the letter to Herz makes clear, is only that their sphere of applicability be limited as had already been done for the concepts of space and time. But Hume's sceptical dissolution of the causal nexus creates a wholly new problem for Kant. He must somehow account for, and prove the possibility of, a synthetic yet necessary connection among the disparate elements of a manifold (*mannigfaltige* = variety). To put the point somewhat differently, Hume has forced Kant's attention to turn from the nature of the pure concepts (that they are free of sensation and produced by the mind itself) to the nature of their object (a manifold of perceptions which must be given a unity).

Kant's response, as I have tried to show below, is to develop a theory of the forms of mental activity, which he groups under the title synthesis. Concepts for Kant cease to be *things* (mental contents, objects of consciousness) and become *ways of doing things* (rules, forms of mental activity). The revolution is completed for the pure concepts, and indeed is an essential part of the argument of the *Critique*. Empirical concepts are never fully treated by Kant, but his comments in the Schematism chapter indicate his awareness that they too are best analyzed as rules of mental activity.

Although the Dialectic does not come within the compass of this commentary, it might be worthwhile pointing out that this shift to a rule-analysis of concepts allows Kant to salvage a real use for reason as well as for understanding. In the section entitled The Regulative Employment of Reason, a theory of the constructive use of the Ideas is developed which interprets them as rules for guiding the understanding in the investigation of nature. Reason has a legitimate immanent employment, even though its transcendent employment leads only to dialectical illusion. Its product — the idea of the unconditioned in all its modes — serves as an ideal of unity, self-sufficiency, and completeness toward which the understanding strives to bring our knowledge of nature. Kant thus is able to say that it is the misuse of the product of reason, and not reason in itself, which leads to metaphysical illusions. Here, as elsewhere throughout the Critical Philosophy, Kant is guided by the extra-systematic belief in the purposiveness of nature. Every mental faculty, including reason, must have some genuine function to perform if only we can discover it.[12]

Detailed Analysis of B 102–105   Pure intuition

Paragraphs 1 and 2[13]

The opening sentence of the first paragraph echoes the distinction drawn in the *Dissertation* between the real and merely logical employment of understanding, as indeed does the entire chapter.[14] However, the situation has been altered by the appearance of the problem of synthetic unity, and this is reflected in a revised conception of the real use of understanding. According to the *Dissertation*, the understanding generates concepts which then apply *a priori* to independent reality. These concepts are "pure" because they contain no admixture of empirical — i.e., perceptual — elements, but they are otherwise ordinary class concepts. In the *Critique*, however, the pure concepts are seen as the forms of a distinct type of thinking, which consists in the unifying of a presented manifold of sensible intuition. As I have already had occasion to note, this newly discovered activity of synthesis is

---

[12] I have remarked above on the similarity between Kant's anti-reductionist search for a plurality of statuses for mental concepts and acts, and the contemporary linguistic philosopher's attempt to distinguish many different ways of speaking (the language of science, of ethics, of aesthetics, of politics, etc.) without insisting on any one as paradigmatic. The linguistic philosophers also tend to suppose that any way of speaking which has got itself firmly established must have a "logic" and be a *legitimate* way of speaking. Unfortunately, they sometimes do not recognize, as Kant always did, that criticism and a setting of the limits of thought (or discourse) is an indispensable part of conceptual (or linguistic) analysis.

[13] Whenever the text is dealt with in this detail, it will be assumed that the reader has the *Critique* open before him and is reading the passage as it is analyzed.

[14] See, for example, the title of Section 1, "The Logical Employment of the Understanding."

quite different from the analysis performed by the understanding in its logical use.

The explanation of synthesis which is given in these paragraphs is through and through metaphorical. Synthesis, says Kant, is the act whereby a manifold is "gone through in a certain way, taken up, and connected." It is a "putting [of] different representations together, and [a] grasping [of] what is manifold in them in one knowledge." [15] In the passages before us no literal content is given to the concept of synthesis. Precisely because synthesis is unlike analysis, the comparisons in the sixth and seventh paragraphs are unhelpful. As we shall see, the key to an understanding of the act of synthesis is to be found in the so-called Subjective Deduction in the first edition version of the Transcendental Deduction.

One final point can be raised in connection with these paragraphs: the meaning of the phrase, "a manifold of pure *a priori* intuition." The general problem of pure intuition cannot be discussed here, but some at least of the ambiguities in Kant's view should be brought to light. Intuition is defined in the first sentence of the Aesthetic as "that through which [a mode of knowledge] is in immediate relation to [objects]" [A 19]. The mind may be related to an object in either of two ways: immediately and individually, or mediately and discursively.

In the first case, which is that of intuition, the mind apprehends the object directly and as an individual. In the second case, the mind thinks the object indirectly by way of a characteristic which it shares with many other objects — i.e., the mind conceives the object. Concepts may be more or less general, may apply to more or fewer objects, but no matter how specific a concept is, it yet relates to a particular object only mediately, by way of the common characters which that object shares with other (possible) objects. So, for example, "man" is no less a concept than "animal" for being more specific.[16]

[15] Kemp Smith captures this metaphoric quality extremely well by translating "begriefen" as "grasping." The more prosaic, and equally correct, translation would be "conceiving." English, of course, gives the same conceptual interpretation to the verb, "to grasp." It might be well to point out that the word rendered in English as "manifold" is "Mannigfaltige," which is also translatable as "diversity" or "variety." Kant speaks so often of "*a* manifold" or "*the* manifold" that one can slip quite easily into thinking of precisely the opposite of a manifold, namely a homogeneous or unified entity.

[16] Given the shift in Kant from questions of being to questions of knowing, this doctrine can be considered the analogue of the Aristotelian view that it is *matter*

There are theoretically two ways in which a mind, or mode of knowledge, can be directly related to an object.[17] If the object depends upon the mind, then the mind is active with regard to it, and because of Kant's identification of the active or spontaneous with the intellectual, such relation is given the title "intellectual intuition." Alternatively, the mind may wait passively upon the object, and establish relation to it only in so far as it affects the mind. This capacity for being affected by objects is entitled "sensibility," and the product of such affection is "sensible intuition."

According to Kant, when an object affects the senses, there is produced a variety (manifold) of sensible intuitions, called perceptions. These perceptions are composed of two elements, material and formal. The material element, *which is purely subjective and cognitively valueless,* is sensation (colors, tastes, hardness, etc.). The formal and knowledge-giving element is the spatio-temporal ordering of the sensations. Now it is possible to take away from perceptions, at least in imagination, all that which belongs to sensation [B 35]. What remains is the pure form of intuition, devoid of all content. What remains, in short, is "pure intuition." Thus, after dividing representations into intuitions and concepts, and intuitions into the sensible and the intellectual, we can finally distinguish pure sensible intuitions from empirical sensible intuitions, or perceptions.

A great deal of the unclarity of the first half of the *Critique* derives from the ambiguity of the concept of pure intuition. In the introductory paragraphs of the Aesthetic, where the term is introduced, it appears to refer to what is left when all sensational content is "thought away" from perception. On this view, the mind imposes on sensation a spatio-temporal form. The only way to arrive at pure intuition would be by a process of abstraction, and "pure intuition" would thus exist "in the mind *a priori*" as a

---

which individuates a particular substance, not greater formal specificity. As it happens, many of the traditional problems which grow out of the form-matter distinction have their counterparts in Kant's distinction of concepts from intuitions. Compare Kant, *Logic,* § 1, Anmerk. 2, in *Gesammelte Schriften,* IX.

[17] "Mode of knowledge" is a rather unsatisfactory translation of "eine Erkenntnis," more literally "a knowledge." At times it means a judgment, or what is nowadays sometimes called a knowledge-claim. At other times it has more the meaning of "the mind, insofar as it has a [piece of] knowledge." Because Kant analyzes the mind solely in terms of its contents and the operations which it performs on them, statements about knowing and statements about knowledge tend to be interchangeable.

potentiality — in Kant's words, as a "mere form of sensibility" [B 35]. The implication of this passage is that the mind is presented with only the empirical manifold, all else being reached by an analysis of it.

But although this is the apparent sense of B 34–35, and though it seems the most sensible and defensible view, it is quite certainly *not* the view to which Kant adheres. In some passages Kant unambiguously asserts the existence of a totally separate manifold of pure intuition — a "manifold of *a priori* sensibility," as he puts it in the passage of the Metaphysical Deduction which we are now discussing [B 102]. In the second edition version of the Transcendental Deduction, Kant goes so far as to state that "space and time are represented *a priori* not merely as *forms* of sensible intuition, but as themselves *intuitions* which contain a manifold . . ." [B 160].[18] It is not clear to me what this means, and possibly Kant himself never clarified the concept to his own satisfaction. If the distinction between intuition and sensation is that of form and matter, then it is as hard to understand the idea of an actual intuition devoid of sensation as it is to conceive of being presented with a shape which is not the shape of something. Pure space is much like an uninterpreted logical system, in which the primitive predicates have not been given a meaning. Such a system would be a pure mathematics, and would become knowledge only when it had been applied to the world.

This analogy has a great deal to recommend it, for one of Kant's principal motives for adopting so difficult a view was the belief that it explained the possibility of pure, as opposed to applied, geometry. Pure mathematics, unlike even pure physics, does not depend for its possibility on experience. In order to develop a system of physics it is necessary to derive from experience the concepts of body, motion, and so forth [cf. B 58], but for a system of pure geometry no perceptions at all are required. Hence, or so Kant thought, pure intuition must exist as an actuality prior to experience, and not merely as a potentiality or form of possible experience. In a remarkable passage in the second edition Deduction, Kant recognizes the consequences for his analysis of pure mathematics of the theory which he has been expounding. In direct con

---

[18] See below, pp. 218–223.

tradiction to the Aesthetic, but in a manner suggestive of modern developments in the philosophy of mathematics, he writes:

Through the determination of pure intuition we can acquire *a priori* knowledge of objects, as in mathematics, but only in regard to their form, as appearances; whether there can be things which must be intuited in this form, is still left undecided. Mathematical concepts are not, therefore, by themselves knowledge, except on the supposition that there are things which allow of being presented to us only in accordance with the form of that pure sensible intuition. [B 147]

The doctrine of pure intuition is reenforced by Kant's belief that the transcendental synthesizing activity of imagination is performed on a pure manifold, not on an empirical manifold of perceptions. This further role of pure intuition will be discussed below in connection with the Deduction.

Paragraphs 3–5

In this passage Kant draws a distinction, which figures prominently in the first edition Deduction, between the synthesis of the manifold of intuitions and the unity of that synthesis. The activity of synthesis itself — the running through and holding together of the manifold — is assigned to the faculty of imagination. In a much-quoted sentence, Kant says of synthesis that it is "a blind but indispensable function of the soul, without which we should have no knowledge whatsoever, but of which we are scarcely ever conscious." This imaginative synthesis is given a *unity* by the faculty of understanding, which brings "[it] to concepts," and thereby to consciousness.[19] The distinction be-

[19] Kant never states explicitly that the act of bringing a synthesis to concepts is also the act of bringing it to consciousness, but this interpretation is strongly suggested by several passages. See, for example, A 103: "For the concept of the number is nothing but the consciousness of this unity of synthesis. . . . [T]his unitary consciousness is what combines the manifold, successively intuited, and thereupon also reproduced, into one representation." See also A 115: "*Sense* represents appearances empirically in *perception, imagination* in *association* (and reproduction), *apperception* in the *empirical consciousness* of the identity of the reproduced representations with the appearances whereby they were given, that is, in recognition." In both passages, Kant is describing the process of "recognition in a concept," which corresponds to the process of giving unity to a synthesis. Bound up with this point of interpretation is the question whether, on Kant's view, one can be conscious of the given manifold prior to synthesizing it. I have in several places indicated my reasons for believing that Kant eventually concluded that one cannot.

tween the synthesis and the unity of the synthesis, Kant suggests in paragraph 4, is illustrated by the operation of counting. When we count, particularly with numbers so large that we lose any feel for them, we perform a succession of operations whose unifying idea is the concept of the decimal system, or decade. That is to say, we order and grasp the synthesis of successive units by dividing them into groups of ten, groups of ten tens, groups of ten ten-tens, and so forth. "In terms of this concept [the decade]," says Kant, "the unity of the synthesis of the manifold is rendered necessary" [B 104].[20]

What are we to make of this division of labour between imagination and understanding? That it is forced seems obvious on the face of it. The activity of counting on the decimal system and the principle underlying that activity hardly seem capable of being separated in the manner that Kant desires. Can an activity be treated as a "function of the soul . . . of which we are scarcely ever conscious," while the rule or basis for it is a concept of which we are fully conscious? What is to be gained by such an unnatural distinction? The answer seems to be that Kant was unprepared to accept certain of the consequences of his own argument. As he moved away from the position of the *Dissertation*, he came finally to hold that not only scientific or mathematical knowledge, but sheer consciousness itself, depends upon certain synthesizing activities of the mind. Consequently these activities must be preconscious, and the rules or guides for them, although called "pure concepts," must be quite unlike the ordinary concepts which we consciously employ — hence the attempt to distinguish in synthetic activity a specifically conceptual element which can be attributed to understanding and characterized as conscious.

Kant developed this distinction in several passages of the first edition Deduction, and reiterated it in the second edition Deduction. There can be no doubt that it plays an important role in his mature position. Nevertheless, it leaves unanswered the difficult questions suggested above. The problem of pre-conscious concepts becomes particularly serious when Kant emphasizes the separation of the *a priori* manifold and its synthesis from the manifold of

[20] This last is a very dark utterance whose complete explanation will involve us in a host of difficult matters. Needless to say, nothing Kant has said to this point in the *Critique* is sufficient to make it clear.

perceptions and *its* synthesis. The farther Kant moves from the
familiar realm of ordinary conscious thought, the less clear becomes his use of such terms as "concept," "unity of apperception,"
and "synthesis."

Paragraphs 6–7

These two paragraphs contain the Metaphysical Deduction
proper, that is, the argument which links the Table of Judgments
of the preceding section with the Table of Categories which follows. As I have already noted, the argument is arbitrary in the
extreme. No proof is given for the key statement that "The same
function which gives unity to the various representations *in a
judgment* also gives unity to the mere synthesis of various representations *in an intuition* . . ." [B 104–5]. In fact, the distinction
between the contributions of imagination and understanding, which
is discussed above, destroys all the plausibility of this claim. If
synthesis is not even done by the faculty of judgment (understanding), then there is no reason to suppose that the unity underlying
it will bear any relation to the unity in judgment. This is probably
the weakest link in the entire argument of the Analytic. The appearance from nowhere of the Table of Judgments and the rather
flimsy argument to the Table of Categories are entirely unconvinc-
ing. The failings of the Metaphysical Deduction are not fatal, however, for in the Analytic of Principles Kant returns to the individual
categories and deduces them from the characteristics of time-
consciousness. The opening chapter of the Analytic of Concepts
is then revealed in its true role as an introductory exposition of
the results to be achieved in the rest of the Analytic.

CHAPTER II

THE DEDUCTION OF THE PURE CONCEPTS OF UNDERSTANDING IN THE FIRST EDITION

THE ORGANIZATION OF THE DEDUCTION

The Significance of the Deduction in A.

Kant says at one point in the *Critique of Teleological Judgment* that objects which exhibit a teleological organization must be founded on "the causality of an architectonic understanding" [1] which he elsewhere defines as an organization "in which every part is reciprocally both end and means." [2] The reader who attempts to unravel the *Critique of Pure Reason* may with some justice feel that he has come across a product of Kant's architectonic understanding, for like a living organism, the *Critique*'s every part is both end and means to every other. There is no section which does not presuppose a grasp of the doctrines of the rest. Ideally therefore the *Critique* should be read again and again until each sentence can be interpreted in the light of the entire book. Unfortunately, however, the commentator is not free to follow this course. Literary conventions and the restrictions of length make it impossible for him to tell the same story over and over, each time gaining in depth and meaning. So he must proceed in one order or another, knowing that wherever he begins, some things will be told last which should have been told first.

This problem is nowhere greater than in the section of the *Critique* to which we now turn: The Deduction of the Pure Concepts of Understanding. The Deduction, which constitutes the

---

[1] *Critique of Teleological Judgement*, p. 39.
[2] *Ibid.*, p. 24.

core of the Transcendental Analytic, is the most important passage in all of Kant's works, and one of the most difficult pieces of philosophical writing by any author. Its thirty pages contain Kant's deepest investigations into the nature and origin of knowledge; on the plausibility of its conclusions rests the entire Critical Philosophy.

The Deduction is one of the very few passages which Kant saw fit to rewrite from scratch in preparing the second edition. This fact alone might serve to warn us of obscurity and difficulty in the first version of the argument. When we actually examine the first edition text, our worst fears are realized. Contradictions abound, repetitions and digressions mar the exposition, paragraphs and sections seem to bear only the most external relation to their surrounding contexts, and the whole conveys no sense of a logical progression of argument. It is doubtful whether many readers, having worked their way through this section for the first time, could give a coherent summary of its structure or repeat in orderly sequence the steps of the argument. And yet the Deduction is no incidental chapter, hastily written to fill out the *Critique*. In the Preface to the first edition, Kant says that he knows "no enquiries which are more important for exploring the faculty which we entitle understanding . . . than those which I have instituted in the . . . *Deduction of the Pure Concepts of Understanding*" [A xvi]. These enquiries have "cost me the greatest labour," he adds, referring to the eight years and more between his first announcements in letters of the forthcoming *Critique* and its actual appearance. As a result of its obscurity, in the second edition the whole, excepting an introductory section, is completely recast. This time the argument is coherent and orderly, though of course still very difficult. Premises are laid down and their meaning discussed, conclusions are drawn, difficulties explained, and so forth.

In this commentary I shall follow the precedent of earlier works, devoting considerably more space to the first than to the second edition Deduction. Kemp Smith, for example, spends only twenty-five pages or so on the later version, out of a total of over one hundred pages on the Deduction as a whole. It may be well, therefore, to explain what appears to be sheer perversity. After all, Kant was satisfied with the revision, and it is clearly an improvement in clarity and coherence. Why then labor so long to sort out a passage which the author himself did not think worth preserving? And above all, why make it the center and focus of a commentary? Does the commentator, like the mountain-climber, grapple with a text simply because it is there?

The answer to this quite legitimate question is complicated and can only be completely stated after we have finished with the analysis of the entire Analytic. Briefly, the reasons for so close a study of the Deduction in A are three in number. First, the earlier version of the Deduction represents the culmination of a philosophical development which began twelve years before with the writing of the *Dissertation*. Preserved in its several sections are evidences of the succession of stages through which Kant's thought passed. As it is easier to understand a philosophical system by studying the systems which preceded it, and from which it developed, so in attempting to understand Kant's Critical Philosophy it is invaluable to trace its growth from the more easily comprehensible doctrine of the *Dissertation*.

Second, the rough and many-sided exposition of the Deduction in A preserves conflicts, ambiguities, indecisions which disappear from the polished revision of the second edition. To mention but one of these valuable glimpses into Kant's thought, the problem of the relation between transcendental and empirical mental activities is, as it were, debated in the first edition, but avoided in the second. Kant never resolved the contradictions which stem from this problem, and to understand his reasons for inclining first in one direction and then another we must study the Deduction in A.

Finally, and most important, the passage in the first edition called the Subjective Deduction, which Kant omitted entirely from the second edition, is the key to the interpretation of the entire *Critique*. With its help I will be able to explain the meaning of the term "synthesis," thereby clarifying the most difficult portions of the argument. In thus giving a central role to the Subjective Deduction, I must go against Kant's own assertion that it "does not form an essential part" of the enquiry [A xvii]. The justification for this procedure is the only possible one: that without the Subjective Deduction Kant's argument is incomprehensible, while by means of its suggestions, the argument becomes perfectly clear.

It might be added in defense of the Deduction in A, that an understanding of it will bring as well as understanding of all but one section of the Deduction in B. When the reader has finally mastered the first version, he will find, to paraphrase Kant, that "the reading of the second edition is a task which is rather an amusement than a labour" [A xxi].

The Patchwork Theory of the Deduction

The first edition Deduction is the subject of an extraordinarily complicated, subtle, conjectural, and at least superficially incredible theory, according to which it is a patchwork of passages, written by Kant during more than a decade and externally stitched together in the frantic months of the completion of the *Critique*. As I shall adopt a much modified version of this theory, a few words of justification and explanation may be in order.

The theory began with Erich Adickes, who argued that the *Critique* as a whole was an architectonic skeleton on which Kant had hung chapters, sections, or paragraphs written at various times during the period between the *Dissertation* and the publication of the *Critique*. Then Hans Vaihinger published a paper in which he analyzed the Deduction, breaking it down and re-assembling it in what he claimed to be the chronological order of the composition of its parts. Vaihinger found four major layers or strata of passages in the Deduction, put together for publication in an order bearing no relation to the chronology of their composition. Finally, Norman Kemp Smith, basing himself on Vaihinger's work and praising it unstintingly, undertook certain revisions based principally on an interpretation of Kant's doctrine of the "Transcendental object = x."

As presented by Kemp Smith,[3] the theory is that the first edition Deduction comprises passages expounding four stages in the development of Kant's thought. These are described by Kemp Smith as being (1) the doctrine of the *Dissertation*, which is distinctly pre-critical; (2) a semi-critical, or early, revision of this; (3) the mature, or Critical, doctrine, which reappears in the second edition; and (4) a super- or post-critical theory which Kant developed on the eve of the publication of the *Critique* and then dropped

---

[3] Kemp Smith, *Commentary*, pp. 202–284.

when he realized its incompatibility with the rest of his argument. This last layer is the so-called Subjective Deduction.

On the face of it, this theory is absurd beyond belief. Here is a man who is supposed to be one of the three or four greatest philosophers of all time. He has spent ten years doing very little else but thinking about the problems of this particular passage. When bringing it to completed form he is at the peak of his mental powers, about to embark on the crowning decade of his life. And yet, when he comes to the chapter which he himself rates as the most important in the history of philosophy, he composes it by tacking together some old manuscripts which contain manifestly incompatible arguments! H. J. Paton in his lengthy commentary on the first half of the *Critique*, has the following to say about the theory, which he completely rejects:

> No one need deny that Kant's mind, like that of other philosophers, worked on different levels; that he thought out some problems more fully than others; and that he was capable of solving one problem without at first realizing all its implications in relation to other problems. Nor need one deny that the notes which he had by him as he brought the *Kritik* into its final form were on different levels of reflexion, and may have influenced the *Kritik* as we have it today. . . . What I wish to protest against is the doctrine that Kant took isolated and contradictory notes, dating from different periods, and joined them together in a purely external manner.[4]

If we consider the patchwork theory solely as an historical or biographical reconstruction, recounting what is presumed to have been the actual sequence of events in which the *Critique* was composed, then Paton's criticism of it is eminently reasonable. Kant, we can be sure, did not intend the Deduction as a scrapbook collection of old pages. But if we concern ourselves rather with the interpretation of the Deduction as a piece of philosophical reasoning, we find one flaw in Paton's long and conscientious commentary which outweighs any measure of historical accuracy: he does not explain the text. He tells us *that* the several parts of the chapter are consistent, but he never shows us *how* they fit together. Repeatedly he asks us to believe, what I for one cannot, that Kant's meaning is clear and his exposition no more difficult than the material makes necessary.

But the patchwork theory is not an idle fancy, nor is it, save

[4] Paton, *Kant's Metaphysic of Experience*, I, 40.

perhaps in its more extreme versions, the result of too many German critics working on too little text. It grows out of the undeniable fact that the Subjective Deduction is at once the most profound and the most confused passage in the *Critique*. If we compare it with the revised Deduction of the second edition, or even with the Objective Deduction which occupies the last section in the first edition, the difference is more striking still. These latter are clearly all of a piece. They flow equably in rational order; the reader who has already an acquaintance with the *Critique* finds that the succession of paragraphs in them conforms to a comprehensible succession of ideas. At each point it is possible to say, "Now Kant will go on to mention — ," and then find that indeed he has done so. With the Subjective Deduction it is entirely otherwise. The exposition jerks and jumps, strange phrases abound which seem to contradict Kant's most cherished dogmas, problems are introduced which bear no relation to one another and solutions offered which do not hang together. It will not help to say that the Subjective Deduction is a provisional and regressive exposition, and hence merely a gathering of the materials for the genuine Deduction. For the most provocative and exciting suggestions of the Subjective Deduction do not reappear in ordered form in the Objective Deduction. To mention only the two most striking cases: neither the discussion of the concept of an object of knowledge nor the detailed analysis of the activity of synthesis is ever recapitulated in the supposedly progressive exposition of the Objective Deduction.

So I suggest that although as history the patchwork theory may be unbelievable, as a reconstruction of Kant's argument it, or a modified version such as I shall present, is eminently reasonable. The reader must of course be his own judge. I remind him that in this matter I am seeking, as Collingwood put it, to "rethink the thoughts" in Kant's mind. These thoughts may be well or ill represented by the words of the text, but I have in this task an invaluable aid which is denied the historian, namely the tools of logic. The *Critique*, as a philosophical work, must be presumed to have an "inner logic" in the quite literal sense of that often misused phrase. The sentences of the Deduction supposedly express a step-by-step argument, with premises, inferences, and conclusions. Where reason tells me that the argument has broken off or contradicted itself, I am justified in claiming a demarcation in the text. If the argument proceeds in step with the turning of the pages, so much the better, but if I must hunt back and forth for it, leaving it there and picking it up again here, still that will be all right so long only as the end result is a coherent argument. Any interpretation no matter how complex, which can discover such an argument in the text, is preferable to any alternative reading, however simple, which leaves the text opaque. In this we have to do not with evidence and historical remains but with logic and rational comprehension.

The Structure of the Deduction in A

Lest these rather ominous remarks convince the reader of the hopelessness of making any sense of the Deduction, let me hasten to state that I shall employ a much simplified form of the patchwork theory. This is possible because, as I have already indicated, my aim is philosophical clarity rather than historical accuracy. I make no claim that the passages I treat first were written earlier than those which I postpone until later. In one instance, indeed, the order of discussion of two passages is undetermined by their content, and for convenience' sake I merely take them in order of appearance in the text. Furthermore the patchwork theory, so far from finding contradictions which do not exist, will enable us to see why Kant contradicted himself and even why he might have allowed such contradictions to remain in the text. In this way the analysis presented below will, I hope, serve as a better defense of Kant than the sturdy insistence that the Deduction is perfectly consistent.[5]

In the first edition, the Deduction of the Pure Concepts of Understanding consists of three sections. The first section, entitled The Principles of Any Transcendental Deduction, was retained by Kant in the second edition. As we shall see, it constitutes a link between the *Critique* and the doctrine of the *Dissertation*, and

[5] My divergence from the original patchwork theory is so great that it might seem more accurate to drop the term altogether. I have retained it because my own interpretation grew so directly out of a study of Kemp Smith's discussion. Let me emphasize once more: the important question is not that of historical dating, but that of logical coherence. As one reader of this work has rather acutely put it, I do not believe the *Critique* was written as a patchwork, but only that it ought to be read as if it were.

therefore serves as a useful introduction for the eighteenth-century readers who knew Kant's philosophical views only from his earlier writings. The second section contains the collection of passages known as the Subjective Deduction, and the third section presents in orderly form the official objective Deduction of the Pure Concepts. Sections 1 and 3 are reasonably clear and straightforward; it is only Section 2 which can be called a "patchwork." In the second edition, Sections 2 and 3 were replaced by a new Objective Deduction which glosses over most of the problems dealt with in Section 2.

We begin, then, with Section 1 of the Deduction.

SECTION I. INTRODUCTION

Introductory Comment on Section 1 as a Whole

The first section of the chapter entitled "The Deduction of the Pure Concepts of Understanding" is an introduction to the problem of the Deduction. Its purpose is to explain what a Deduction is, and why one is needed for the pure concepts, or categories. It also offers a very brief sketch of the turn of argument by which this Deduction is to be proved. The section is divided into two subsections which we can conveniently refer to by the numbering which Kant introduced in the second edition: § 13 and § 14. Subsection 13, "The Principles of Any Transcendental Deduction," contains the statement of the problem of the Deduction — the problem which, better than that of the synthetic judgment *a priori*, defines the subject of the Critical Philosophy. Subsection 14, "Transition to the Transcendental Deduction of the Categories," states the outline of the solution of the problem.

Subsection 13 is a very difficult passage for the reader who has some prior knowledge of Kant's philosophy. Intermixed with familiar remarks about the difference between a deduction and a "physiological" or, as we would say, psychological explanation of the categories, are statements which seem the very contradiction of the Critical Philosophy. Kant appears to assert, for example, that the pure concepts apply to things-in-themselves and that we can be conscious of perceptions which are not subordinate to the categories — both views contrary to the central doctrine of the Analytic. In these and other ways, the opening paragraphs of the Deduction show themselves to embody an extremely early stage in Kant's thought, roughly corresponding to a period shortly after the letter to Herz of 1772.[6]

The second subsection of the introduction, § 14, offers a solution which carries the theory one step further. In this brief passage, Kant first introduces the concept of *conditions of the possibility of experience*. In so doing, he denies some of the assertions made in § 13, including the thoroughly unKantian claim that the categories apply to things-in-themselves.

Why should Kant have introduced the Deduction in this manner, using a terminology which he was about to alter, and making statements which he sought to disprove? And, what is puzzling even to the most extreme proponents of the patchwork theory, why should Kant have chosen to keep this section in the second edition, even when he had gone to the trouble of thoroughly rewriting the second and third sections? To answer these questions, we must recall the orientation of the audience for which Kant wrote. His readers had not grown up with the Kantian philosophy. They were utterly ignorant of the revolution which awaited them in the pages of the Deduction. Even if they were close students of Kant's writings, this could only mean that they had read the *Dissertation* of 1770. It was necessary for Kant to draw them into his new theory, showing how it grew out of the failings of the *Dissertation* doctrine, which in turn had sought to resolve the differences between the Leibnizeans and Newtonians. To the modern reader, it seems pointless labour to learn up the subtleties of the pre-critical philosophy simply in order that it may then be refuted. If Kant had thought his way past such things, then let

---

[6] Again, it should be emphasized that there is no attempt here to establish an historical proposition concerning the date of composition of this subsection. Whether Kant picked up a sheet of paper which had been on his desk for eight years, or whether he composed the passage in 1780, is irrelevant to an understanding of its meaning. What is not irrelevant, however, is the recognition that the language and argument employed by Kant here are those of the *Dissertation* and the letter to Herz, not those of the later sections of the Deduction or of the second edition Deduction. Historical speculations are in fact otiose, for any theory which makes it plausible that Kant would employ an eight-year-old draft, at the same time explains why he might sit down in 1780 to write a new draft taking the same line of argument. To deny this is to assert the utterly absurd proposition that Kant included passages in the central portions of the *Critique* without even bothering to read them. Actually, as we shall see, it is quite easy to understand Kant's inclusion of the subsection, and his decision to retain it in the second edition.

him scrap them and start afresh! But for Kant's readers these theories — obsolete now because of the very book which we are studying — were the intellectual milieu of the age. There could be no more natural starting point for Kant's exposition.

In effect, then, we can think of Kant as saying something roughly like this: "If you adopt the theory which I expounded in my last published work, my *Inaugural Dissertation*, you will find that a problem arises with regard to one of the elements of cognition, namely, the pure concepts of understanding [§ 13]. The resolution of this problem requires a far-reaching revision of the basic presupposition of the *Dissertation* position, which can in a rough preliminary way be summarized by saying that the pure concepts have validity only in so far as they are conditions of the possibility of experience [§ 14]." Once the reader has worked his way to the end of the Deduction, Kant leaves it to him to recognize the extent to which the very terms of the original problem have been altered. But the introduction remains as a guide post to the next reader who may venture that way.

Analysis of § 13

The Dissertation *Background*

In the *Dissertation*, it will be recalled, Kant attempted to resolve certain contradictions which grew out of the analysis of the concept of a world. More broadly, he sought to reconcile the rationalist metaphysics of the Leibnizean school with the natural science of the Newtonians. The key to Kant's argument was the distinction between the two sources from which the mind derives its representations of objects: sensibility and intelligence. From the affection of the sensitive capacity the mind receives perceptions; out of the activity of intelligence, it generates conceptions. Neither of these categories of representations can be reduced to, or explained in terms of, the other. Kant denies, in opposition to Leibniz, that a perception is merely a confused concept, a concept merely a clarified perception.

Kant then drew a second distinction, based on his first. Sensibility, he said, no matter to what heights of system and clarity it is raised, can give us knowledge only of objects *as they appear to us*. The subjective condition of the sensitive faculty is an unavoidable distorting medium. Intelligence, on the other hand, employing the pure concepts which, by its real employment, it has produced out of its inner sources,[7] gives us knowledge of things *as they are in themselves.* Thus is established the great division of the Kantian philosophy, between appearance and reality, or, in the terminology introduced in the *Dissertation,* between phenomena and noumena. Space and time, as the forms of our sensibility, give the most general characteristics of appearance. The physics and mathematics of bodies in space-time are valid, therefore, of phenomena. The metaphysical conceptions of substance, cause, necessity, and so forth, which first arise from the real use of intelligence, are on the other hand valid of independent reality, or noumena.

As we have seen, this ingenious theory is susceptible to attack from several directions. The doctrine of the real use of intelligence is undeveloped, and Kant consequently cannot explain how the pure concepts, produced by the mind independently of experience, can have valid application to things-in-themselves. What is more, the pivotal concept of causal influence is open to the devastating criticisms of Hume. Hence even the *Dissertation* account of knowledge of phenomena must be reconsidered, for Newtonian physics is built on the causal maxim.

Kant's recognition of the first difficulty — the status of the pure concepts — is expressed in the letter to Herz which has been quoted above. The Humean problem is not explicitly formulated by Kant until the publication of the Critique, which is of course devoted in large measure to resolving it. The passage which we are now considering states the subject-matter of the Deduction in terms of these two problems, with the terminology and from the viewpoint of the *Dissertation.* First the general line of the argument will be summarized, and then the text will be analyzed in detail.

The Argument of § 13

The entire subsection consists of eight paragraphs which divide naturally into three parts: paragraphs 1–4 form an introduction in which the concept of "deduction" is defined and explained; paragraphs 5–7 contain an argument to show that a deduction is needed of the pure concepts of understanding; paragraph 8 ex-

[7] See above, discussion of real and logical use of intelligence.

plains why Hume's associationism provides an inadequate account of the concept of causation.

Paragraphs 1–4. Most concepts need no justification for their use, since the objects or qualities to which they refer can be exhibited easily enough. Thus, to someone who doubts that such a thing as a horse is possible, it is only necessary to show him one [Par. 1]. Certain concepts, however, may be of such a sort that their employment assumes what no experience is sufficient to prove. They may, for example, involve normative or modal notions, such as "ought," "necessity," or "possibility" [Par. 2]. In fact, we already use concepts of just this kind, namely, the concepts of space and time, and the categories of understanding [Par. 3]. To be sure, we can give an account of how, in the course of experience, these concepts are first evoked by the stimulus of sensation and brought to consciousness. But such an account can never provide a justification for our employment of them *a priori* — the formulation, by their means, of propositions which go beyond what experience could ever teach. Hence, if deduction be the establishing of the credentials of a concept, it is a transcendental rather than an empirical deduction which these concepts require [Par. 4].

Paragraphs 5–7. The concepts of space and time do not appear to need further justification. They are sources of *a priori* knowledge, but knowledge only of appearances. Their validity is assured by limiting them to the sensible world. The pure concepts of understanding, however, are not thus limited. They abstract from all sensible conditions, and relate to objects universally [Par. 5]. Objects must conform to the conditions of intuition in order to be objects *for us*, or appearances [Par. 6], but there is not, on the face of it, any reason to suppose that they must also conform to the categories. They might perfectly well appear to us, so far as we know, without exhibiting any order and arrangement to which the categories could be applied. Hence we must explain "how *subjective conditions of thought* can have *objective validity*" [Par. 7].

Paragraph 8. It will not do to justify the categories — causation, for example — by appealing to experience. A cause is that from which something follows necessarily, and necessity can never be observed. The fallacy of *post hoc, ergo propter hoc* expresses exactly the difference between regularity and causation.

Although on superficial reading the section seems an adequate enough statement of the subject of the Deduction, closer examination reveals a series of obscurities and puzzles. What does Kant mean, for example, by the statement in paragraph 5 that the concept of space is employed "only in its reference to the outer sensible world," while the categories "relate to objects universally, that is, apart from all conditions of sensibility?" What does he mean, also, by the assertion that the categories tend to "employ the *concept of space* beyond the conditions of sensible intuition?" [Par. 5]. How can he assert, contrary to the most explicit statements of the Deduction itself, that we might possibly have perceptions to which the categories could not be applied? [Par. 7]. It is in the clarification of these obscurities that the patchwork theory finds its justification.

Detailed Analysis of the Text
   The Introductory Remarks, Paragraphs 1–4. (1) Paragraph 1. The entire Critical Philosophy, as I have indicated above, can be viewed as a systematic inventory of the possessions of the mind. Each mental content, be it perception, concept, idea, or feeling, is analyzed, its functions specified, and its place in the architectonic determined. The later works especially devote considerable attention to functions of the mind which, by the narrow criteria of the first *Critique,* are cognitively valueless. Broadly speaking, a deduction of a concept is this assignment of it to its appropriate niche. More strictly, a deduction is a demonstration of the objective validity of a concept — a proof, that is, that its employment yields knowledge. The question, however, is taken in a general sense, and it is considered whether the concept has a valid sphere of employment, not merely whether some particular application of it is correct. In the case cited by Kant, the problem is whether it is ever legitimate at all to speak of an event as fated, or due to fortune. Thus, a deduction seeks to establish the *possibility* of a concept, and Kant's new transcendental method consists in discovering the conditions, other than the merely logical, for the possibility of certain basic *a priori* concepts. To anticipate a bit, Kant concludes that the categories can have a legitimate employ-

ment *only* on the pre-supposition that they are conditions of the possibility of experience.[8]

(*2*) *Paragraphs 2–4*. The phrasing of these paragraphs raises, for the attentive reader, a problem which runs all through § 13 as well as other passages representing an early form of Kant's theory. Kant says, in paragraph 2, referring to concepts which have *a priori* employment, ". . . we are faced by the problem how these concepts can relate to objects which they yet do not obtain from any experience." At first reading, this might seem to mean that the *concepts* are not derived from experience, and in fact, in the very next paragraph, Kant says just that: "Their distinguishing feature consists just in this, that they relate to their objects without having borrowed from experience anything that can serve in the representation of these objects" [Par. 3]. But the wording, if examined closely, conveys quite a different meaning. It is the *objects* which are not obtained from experience, as well as the concepts. In other words, Kant here asserts that the pure concepts apply to things-in-themselves, or noumena.

The terseness of Kant's phrasing obscures a very important distinction between two quite different problems, both of which arise out of the *Dissertation* doctrine. The first is, How can concepts relate to, and yield knowledge of, objects which are never given in experience? The second is, How can concepts relate *a priori* to objects, yielding knowledge of a sort which no experience could ever adequately justify? These questions are not wholly independent, for if we have knowledge of non-experienced objects, it will necessarily be *a priori* knowledge. But the reverse is not at all the case, for we might quite well have *a priori* knowledge of objects of experience — physics and geometry are the examples Kant often cites.

The origin of this confusion should by now be evident. I have on several occasions remarked that the *Dissertation* is subject to two distinct criticisms, the first directed against the theory of the real use of intelligence, and the second, Hume's, directed against the notion of *a priori* knowledge in general. Now the first question

---

[8] The distinction between merely logical possibility and real possibility is of special importance for Kant, as it allows him to assign a positive status to those concepts, such as the Ideas of God, freedom, and immortality, which do not meet the conditions for empirical employment, but yet have a role to play in moral philosophy or religion.

— How can we have knowledge of objects not given in experience? — is obviously reflected in Kant's assertion that the pure concepts "relate to objects which they yet do not obtain from any experience" [Par. 2]. The second question — How can we have *a priori* knowledge? — is reflected in the slightly different statement of the third paragraph, that the pure concepts "relate to their objects without having borrowed from experience anything that can serve in the representation of these objects." Clearly the problem being alluded to in paragraph 2 is that of the real use of intelligence, expressed in the letter to Herz, while the third paragraph, on the other hand, alludes to the problem raised by Hume.

Of these two, it is the Humean problem of *a priori* knowledge which is central to the *Critique*, for Kant gave up the doctrine that we can know independent reality. Nevertheless, this pre-critical view finds expression in several parts of the first edition Deduction, including paragraphs 5–7 of the present section. The best explanation for these passages, in which Kant preserves a theory which he no longer holds, is that they express the problem of the *Critique* in language which its readers could be expected to understand.

The Statement of the Problem, Paragraphs 5–7.   In the central portion of the section, as in the introductory paragraphs, the two problems make their appearance. The objection to knowledge of independent reality is stated in paragraph 5, while the Humean problem of *a priori* knowledge of experience is stated in paragraphs 6 and 7. Kant still shows no awareness of the difference between the two problems. In particular, the passage gives no indication of the fact that he intends to *deny* the existence of knowledge of noumena, rather than explain how it is possible.

(*1*) *Paragraph 5.*   The argument makes it perfectly clear that the pure concepts are here considered to apply to things-in-themselves. The concept of space is applied "only in its reference to the outer sensible world," but with the pure concepts "it is quite otherwise." They "relate to objects universally, that is, apart from all conditions of sensibility." Knowledge of appearance is explained by the fact that we put into them what we take out again, namely, their spatio-temporal form. But this is not the case for knowledge of reality. That is knowledge of things as they are, *unconditioned* by any subjective forms of the mind. Hence the problem. In this context "universally" has the same force as "unconditionally," since any condition limits the sphere of the concept, and restricts it to less than universal applicability. Eventually, of course, Kant will solve his problem by denying the unconditionality of the pure concepts. They, like the forms of sensibility, have only a conditional universality. All events have causes, but events are only appearances, not reality.

Universal yet conditioned

The curious assertion is made by Kant that the pure concepts tend to "employ the *concept of space* beyond the conditions of sensible intuition," thereby throwing doubt upon both it and themselves. The statement derives from the *Dissertation*, where Kant develops an early form of dialectical illusion which he calls "the metaphysical fallacy of subreption." This is the fallacy of applying a sensitive predicate to an intellectual subject, as if the two applied to equally broad spheres. Consider, for example, the predicate-term "is somewhere" and the subject-term "existant," or "what exists." The first is a spatial predicate and the second an intellectual predicate. If we form the judgment, "whatever is, is somewhere," we make the mistake of treating the sensitive predicate, "somewhere," as applicable to things-in-themselves. The judgment is false, for noumena exist but are not somewhere (spatial position is a property only of phenomena). The converse, "whatever is somewhere, exists," is valid, as the realm of the predicate includes the realm of the subject. The fallacy consists in extending "the concept of space beyond the conditions of sensible intuition," as Kant puts it in the passage before us.[9]

(2) *Paragraphs 6–7.* In paragraph 5, the argument was that although space and time were valid only of appearance, the pure concepts applied to things-in-themselves and hence needed some sort of justification. Here the argument is that although space and time are conditions of the possibility of appearances and consequently have an *a priori* validity, the pure concepts are not at first sight conditions of experience, so that we must prove their *a priori* applicability to experience.

The crux of the argument is the assertion that appearances could be given in such a way that the pure concepts would find no ap-

[9] See above, pp. 20–21.

plication to them. In the words of William James, we would experience a "buzzing, blooming confusion." Hence, some additional proof is needed that these appearances actually do conform to the pure concepts. Now, when the problem is posed in this way it has no solution, for what Kant aims to prove is precisely that appearances *cannot* be given to us unless they conform to the pure concepts. The categories are conditions of the possibility of consciousness itself, Kant later argues. There can be no appearances "given in intuition independently of functions of the understanding."

Rather than dwell on the inconsistency of the Deduction, we may simply view this passage as an introduction which assumes a theory whose essentials Kant eventually intends to disprove. In effect, he is saying: "If you start from the *Dissertation*, you come first upon the problem of knowledge of noumena. The natural solution is to restrict all knowledge to phenomena, but this will not suffice, for as Hume has shown, there are difficulties even with *a priori* knowledge of appearances. We may formulate this new problem by saying that the pure concepts, unlike space and time, are not conditions of something appearing, and hence need a special justification. However, by the time we have finished, it will turn out that in fact the pure concepts *are* conditions of something appearing, and have a cognitive status like that of space and time. When this point is reached, we will be able to see that intuitions and concepts are actually joint elements in cognition, each one indispensable for knowledge."

The Inadequacy of Associationism. Paragraph 8. Kant briefly points out that associationistic explanations of the concept of causation, and other pure concepts, are doomed to failure. They can never account for the *necessity* which we think in a pure concept.

Analysis of § 14

The purpose of § 14 is to suggest briefly the line which will be taken by the Deduction. The key phrase, "*a priori* conditions of the possibility of experience," is introduced and explained, and by this step the entire argument is carried forward to a new stage. In the previous § 13, Kant had asked how pure concepts could be valid of objects if they were not, like space and time, conditions of their being known by the mind. Here, it is suggested for the first time that the pure concepts are just such conditions. Kemp Smith has quite justly remarked that this marks the transition to the first truly critical position.[10]

Superficially, the argument of the section is simple: either objects determine their representations, or representations determine their objects; in the former case, knowledge is *a posteriori*, in the latter case it is *a priori*. Thus, the only way to explain the *a priori* validity of the pure concepts is to claim that they determine their objects. Or, to put it differently, the pure concepts are "*a priori* conditions of the possibility of experience." Space and time determine the way in which objects *appear*, and the categories determine the way in which objects are *thought*. Together, the forms of sensibility and conception constitute the conditions of a possible experience.

This is a fair enough summary of the argument, but it does not begin to suggest the importance of the section. In the first paragraph especially, we have a rare opportunity to observe Kant making a fundamental philosophical move — what has elsewhere in this commentary been characterized as the epistemological turn. I shall return to this again and again, for it is a key to virtually every section of the *Critique*.

In the *Dissertation*, Kant adopts a philosophical standpoint which is common to Descartes, Leibniz, and other figures in western thought. He presupposes a world of independent entities (things-in-themselves)[11] and a knowing subject. His problem, then, is to bring the two together, to explain how the subject knows the objects, how much it knows, and what the status is of that knowledge. It must be stressed that Kant's point of view is, as it were, that of the external observer who can see both the object and the subject. For this reason he never in the *Dissertation*

---

[10] Kemp Smith, p. 222.

[11] It is not correct, strictly speaking, to equate things-in-themselves with noumena, as we shall see in the analysis of the chapter on Phenomena and Noumena. "Things-in-themselves" is a metaphysical term, and signifies the absence of conditions or restrictions on the being of the entities. "Noumena," on the other hand, is an epistemological term, meaning "knowable only through intelligence" (cf. *Dissertation*, § 3). The difference may seem slight, and it is certainly treated as such by Kant, but in fact an appreciation of its implications illuminates many passages in the *Critique*.

doubts either the existence or the knowability of things-in-them-selves. Now such a picture makes ontology logically prior to epistemology: *what is* is decided independently of *what we can know to be.* The *Critique of Pure Reason* records Kant's effort to reverse this order of dependence. By and large, he was success-ful, though to the very end he continued to slip into statements about the existence of unknowable entities. What distinguishes the passage which we are now examining is the picture it gives of Kant in the very act of first working out a doctrine of *epistemo-logical priority.* Let us go through the first paragraph of § 14 and examine the argument in some detail. For convenience, the para-graph can be divided into four segments.

(1) There are only two possible ways in which synthetic representations and their objects can establish connection, obtain necessary relation to one another, and, as it were, meet one another.

This sentence clearly expresses the notion of objects and a sub-ject waiting to be brought into contact. Kant speaks here, as al-ways, of representations rather than of the conscious subject who possesses them. This is a perfectly legitimate mode of speech, for according to the *Critique* the self is known only through its activi-ties and the contents of its consciousness. Referring to the self gains nothing, therefore, and runs the risk of falling into the error of the Paralogisms. This remark may help to clarify some of the puzzling passages in which Kant identifies a faculty with its ac-tivity, or an activity with its product. For example, in A 119 he says, "The unity of apperception in relation to the synthesis of imagination is the understanding." We would more naturally expect him to say, "The unity of apperception in relation to the synthesis of imagination *is produced by* the understanding."

(2) Either the object alone must make the representation possible, or the representation alone must make the object possible.

The sentence is unclear because of the ambiguity of the phrase "make possible" (*möglich macht*). This might be interpreted as a synonym for "cause to exist," as when an object's interaction with the sense-organs produces a sensible representation, or per-ception. Such in fact is the implication of the subsequent sen-tences. However, a different meaning is suggested by the word "alone." Why does Kant say that either the object *alone* makes the representation possible, or the representation *alone* makes the object possible? At the risk of carrying interpretation to excess, I venture to see in this phrasing a hint of the shift to an epistemological point of view. It is with regard to the question of justification or confirmation that this either/or makes sense. Either the representation must wait upon the object, in which case the knowledge based upon it is *a posteriori*, or the representation precedes and determines the object, in which case the knowledge is *a priori*. The causal dependence gives way to logical or evidential dependence as the problem of *a priori* knowledge comes to the fore. It is not yet clear, however, how we are to interpret the statement that an *a priori* representation "makes possible" its object. The next sentences give Kant's answer.

(3) In the former case, this relation is only empirical, and the representation is never possible *a priori*. This is true of appearances, as regards that in them which belongs to sensation. In the latter case, representation in itself does not produce its object in so far as *existence* is concerned, for we are not here speaking of its causality by means of the will. None the less the representation is *a priori* determinant of the object, if it be the case that only through the representation is it possible to *know* anything *as an object*.

Here the implications of the word "alone" are made explicit. The *a priori* representation does not produce the object, as is the case when we form an idea of an action and then perform it (this is the meaning of the reference to causality of will). Rather, says Kant, the representation determines the object in the sense that *only through it is the object knowable*. It would be easy to miss the truly earth-shaking significance of this move. In these few sentences, Kant carries out his Copernican revolution, and in the image of a later revolutionary, stands philosophy on its head. Previously, the object was assumed to exist, the problem being to explain how it could be known.[12] Knowledge therefore was conditional upon an independently existing realm of being. Now, however, Kant proposes to reverse this order, making the realm of existing objects dependent upon the subjective conditions of knowledge. The *a priori* representations determine what can and cannot be known as an object, and hence what can and cannot be

[12] It is common to read that Descartes first substituted questions of knowing for questions of being. For my reasons for attributing this revolution rather to Kant, see the discussion of the "epistemological turn" in the Concluding Remarks below.

considered to exist. The realms of being and knowledge are co-
terminous, and even more significantly, the latter defines the
former. What can I know? becomes the first and fundamental
question of all philosophy. By taking with absolute seriousness the
egocentric predicament from which Descartes so quickly extricated
himself, Kant achieves a thorough reorientation in philosophy.

(4) Now there are two conditions under which alone the knowledge of
an object is possible, first, *intuition*, through which it is given, though only
as appearance; secondly, *concept*, through which an object is thought
corresponding to this intuition. It is evident from the above that the first
condition, namely, that under which alone objects can be intuited, does
actually lie *a priori* in the mind as the formal ground of the objects. All
appearances necessarily agree with this formal condition of sensibility,
since only through it can they appear, that is, be empirically intuited and
given. The question now arises whether *a priori* concepts do not also serve
as antecedent conditions under which alone anything can be, if not intuited,
yet thought as object in general. In that case all empirical knowledge of
objects would necessarily conform to such concepts, because only as thus
presupposing them is anything possible as *object of experience*. Now all
experience does indeed contain, in addition to the intuition of the senses
through which something is given, a *concept* of an object as being thereby
given, that is to say, as appearing. Concepts of objects in general thus
underlie all empirical knowledge as its *a priori* conditions. The objective
validity of the categories as *a priori* concepts rests, therefore, on the fact
that, so far as the form of thought is concerned, through them alone does
experience become possible. They relate of necessity and *a priori* to objects
of experience, for the reason that only by means of them can any object
whatsoever of experience be thought.

In this long passage, Kant expands upon the preceding sentences,
repeating his thoughts several times in an effort to make them clear.
A few comments may be helpful, though more extended discussion will be reserved for the *Deduction* proper. It should be recalled here that the term "experience," when strictly used, is
synonymous with "empirical knowledge" [see for example, B 147].
A mere play of unorganized perceptions would not be experience
(*Erfahrung* in the terminology of the *Critique*). Hence when
Kant says, in the next paragraph of § 14, that the categories are
a priori conditions of the possibility of experience, this means that
they are conditions of *knowledge*.[13]

---

[13] However, Kant sometimes strays from this usage, to the confusion of the
reader. See below, p. 159, for a discussion of this problem.

Kant has not at this stage decided precisely how the pure concepts are conditions of a possible experience. He says rather weakly that "all experience . . . contain[s] . . . a *concept* of an object as being . . . given," but there is no indication of the nature of this concept, nor of its relation to the given perceptions. The decisive shift in Kant's view on this question comes when he introduces the factor of unity of consciousness. It first appears in the Deduction in A, and is then made the focal point of the argument in the rewritten Deduction in B.

Summary of Section 1

As the analysis of Section 1 required an exceedingly close attention to particular sentences in the text, the general train of thought may have temporarily disappeared from view. Before going on to the Deduction itself, therefore, it will be helpful to summarize the argument of §§ 13 and 14:

§ 13

a. Before making use of a concept which purports to yield *a priori* knowledge, we must explain how it obtains relation to its objects, and must demonstrate that its employment is legitimate [Par. 1–4].

b. There are two difficulties concerning the pure concepts of understanding, which claim *a priori* validity:

(1) These concepts supposedly apply to independent reality, and it is not clear how subjectively produced representations can be related to things-in-themselves [Par. 5];
(2) Furthermore, even with respect to mere appearances, it is difficult to see how concepts can be *a priori* valid, for such validity involves a necessity and universality which the appearances do not exhibit [Par. 6–7].

c. Our problem, therefore, is how representations can relate *a priori* to their objects.

§ 14

a. This problem admits of two possible answers: either the objects determine the representations, or the representations determine the objects. The former relation, however, does not give *a priori* knowledge. Hence, the latter must be the case.

b. We have already seen that this is so for the forms of sensibility, space and time. It remains only to demonstrate that the pure concepts of understanding determine, or make possible, their objects. What this means, we shall see, is that conformity to the pure concepts is the condition of being an object of knowledge.

c. But as knowledge of objects is *experience*, we can say instead that *the pure concepts are conditions of the possibility of experience*. This we shall now prove.

SECTION 2. THE SUBJECTIVE DEDUCTION

Introduction

Section 2 is entitled "The *A Priori* Grounds of the Possibility of Experience." According to Kant, it "seeks to investigate the pure understanding itself, its possibility and the cognitive faculties upon which it rests; and so deals with it in its subjective aspect" [A xvi–xvii].

Although this latter exposition is of great importance for my chief purpose, it does not form an essential part of it. For the chief question is always simply this: — what and how much can the understanding and reason know apart from all experience? not: — how is the faculty of thought itself possible? [A xvii]

Kant asserts that this investigation of the faculty of knowledge is in the nature of a search for causes (i.e., a psychological rather than philosophical inquiry), and "to that extent is somewhat hypothetical in character." Then, with an inconstancy which reveals his very great indecision on this point, he adds in a parenthesis, "though, as I shall show elsewhere, it is not really so." The problem is one which has caused a great deal of discussion among commentators on the *Critique*, both philosophical and scholarly.

On the one side are those who claim, in conformity with Kant's own statements, that the *Critique* demonstrates the need for an absolute separation of psychology and philosophy. In the place of genetic accounts of the (empirical) origin of concepts or descriptions of mental faculties,[14] Kant introduces a new kind of investi-

---

[14] What Kant calls with reference to Locke a "physiology of the human understanding" [A ix]. Compare A 86–87.

gation of the *a priori* conditions and limits of knowledge, called Transcendental Philosophy. This discipline is not dependent upon dubious hypotheses concerning the workings of the mind, and therefore can stand in the Objective Deduction without the assistance of the materials of the Subjective Deduction.

On the other side are those who point out that the Subjective Deduction, whatever its status may be *vis-a-vis* psychology and philosophy, is an absolutely indispensable part of the Analytic as a whole. It contains material, found nowhere else in the *Critique*, which we must have in order to understand the very terms in which Kant phrases his argument. This is most clear with regard to the central term of the Analytic: synthesis. The Subjective Deduction does not merely give us a physiological account of the origins of synthesis; it tells us what the word "synthesis" means. Until we know that, we know nothing about the *Critique*.

Though this all may seem like a sectarian quibble among disciplines, it actually involves a very significant philosophical point. Kant is struggling in the Deduction with the apparently contradictory notion of *synthetic unity*. On the face of it, there can be no such thing as the unity of a manifold (literally, the oneness of a manyness). Yet consciousness exhibits just this property, for all the varied and everchanging contents of consciousness are united as *my* thoughts. How to explain this fact without lapsing into spatial metaphors of containment ("in the mind") is in a sense the central problem of the Deduction. Now Kant could say that this unity is just a fact, even if we do not understand how it is possible, and that he can draw inferences from it (in the Objective Deduction) without depending on any hypothetical explanation which he may suggest (in the Subjective Deduction). But such a course would be wholly superficial. A serious philosophical argument cannot be based on a metaphorical premise. Therefore the Objective Deduction must be preceded by an analysis of synthetic unity *which will explain what it is by telling how it is produced*. Here we see the indissoluble tie between the two sides of the Deduction. Kant thinks — to anticipate a bit — that a manifold acquires unity by being subjected to a certain operation, which in general can be called "reproduction according to a rule." In the case of the unity of the manifold of contents of consciousness, this process of reproduction according to a rule is called *synthesis*. Now

the unity of consciousness is not some object which can be separated from the process which creates it. It is a characteristic which
the contents of consciousness have *by virtue of having been synthesized*. Hence it is quite misguided to assert that we can describe
the *unity* without committing ourselves to any definite theory
about the *synthesis*.[15]

The text of Section 2 consists of an introductory passage of several paragraphs followed by four sub-headings. For purposes of
analysis and reference, I shall number the paragraphs of these five
parts independently. Thus, the introductory passage (including the
"preliminary remark") has six paragraphs, subsection 1 has three,
subsection 2 has 3, subsection 3 has twelve, and subsection 4 has
seven. The reader will find it much easier to follow the discussion
if he marks off in his text the paragraph numbers as well as the
division of the argument.

The first four paragraphs of the introduction recapitulate the
material of § 14 of Section 1, just preceding. The notion of *a priori*
conditions of the possibility of experience is presented, and the
categories are asserted to be the means alone by which "an object
can be thought." These four paragraphs constitute one layer or
stage (stage II) of the Subjective Deduction.

Kant then presents an account of the "subjective sources" of
a priori knowledge, which he claims are three in number. These
are announced in paragraphs 5–6, and then dealt with one at a time
in subsections 1–3. The analysis ends with paragraph 2 of subsection 3, and this constitutes another (stage III) of the stages of
the Subjective Deduction.[16]

In paragraph 3 of subsection 3, a new problem is introduced:
the meaning of the notion of an "object of representations." In the
remainder of subsection 3, we are given the theory of the Transcendental Object $= x$. This constitutes yet another stage of the
Deduction — in terms of logical progression, it is the first stage.

Finally, in subsection 4, Kant recasts the argument which he has

---

[15] It should be pointed out that from time to time Kant makes precisely this
mistake. In the Metaphysical Deduction, it will be recalled, he tried to distinguish
the unity of the rule of synthesis from the synthesis itself, assigning the former
to understanding and the latter to imagination. I suggested in my analysis of that
passage that the distinction was illegitimate. The above may help to explain why.

[16] Strictly speaking, this account of the mechanism of synthesis *is* the Subjective
Deduction proper.

already developed in order to show that it is an answer to Hume's associationist scepticism. This is the last stage of the Subjective Deduction.

The four parts of the Deduction represent stages in the development of the argument, from a position slightly more advanced than the doctrine of the *Dissertation* through successive revisions to the final argument of the *Critique*. The first stage is the doctrine of the Transcendental Object $= x$. The second, third, and fourth stages proceed in order in the Section. The following table should make the structure of the Section clear.[17]

Organization of Section 2 of the Deduction in A

Pages in A	Sections and paragraphs in A	Stage of the argument
A 95– 97	Introduction, Paragraphs 1–4	II
A 97–104	Introduction, Paragraphs 5–6; [1]; [2]; [3] Paragraphs 1–2	III
A 104–110	[3] Paragraphs 3–12	I
A 110–114	[4]	IV

Let me make it clear that I am not claiming any chronological priority of composition for the stages which I have listed as "earlier." The order is purely logical, as exhibiting a natural progression of argument. The original patchwork theory was historical, and an attempt was actually made to establish a relative dating of Sections, paragraphs, and even sentences. However, it should not be surprising if my divisions along logical lines agree with the chronological divisions of Kemp Smith and Vaihinger. Their principal tool was internal textual analysis, and they simply assumed that more primitive versions of an argument must date from an earlier time. While this is in general a reasonable supposition, I see no reason for engaging in fruitless controversies over the

[17] This breakdown is a simplification and revision of the official patchwork theory. According to Kemp Smith, who includes all three sections of the Deduction in A in his analysis, the stages which I have called II and IV are merely earlier and later substages of II. The Subjective Deduction, here labeled stage III, is called stage IV by him. I accept from his account the explication of stage I and the recognition that it is the first form of the Deduction argument. Thus, although I have slightly shifted about the order of exposition, I adopt *in toto* Kemp Smith's and Vaihinger's identification of the dividing points in the text of Section 2. Their acuteness in this matter seems to me a very strong evidence of their genuine understanding of Kant's argument. Without the guidance of Kemp Smith's commentary I should never have hit upon the interpretation offered here.

biographical believability of the patchwork hypothesis. By resting my analysis on textual analysis alone, I hope to convince the reader of its correctness as reconstruction even if as history it is dubious.

The commentary on Section 2 which follows is quite long and, even in the simpler patchwork theory, rather involved. I have therefore sought for some method of exposition which would allow the reader to follow the analysis in a single line without having to skip back and forth in the text. The order I have selected is by no means completely satisfactory, but it should be possible for an attentive reader to grasp the essentials of this chapter in one consecutive reading.

I begin with a systematic presentation of the theory which I claim to find in the Deduction. I develop it, step by step, through its first three stages, showing at each point what problems or inadequacies lead Kant on to the next stage, and ending the discussion of each stage with a provisional statement of the argument thus far. In this way the reader can watch the theory grow, from a rather brief and incomplete proof-sketch in stage I to the full doctrine of *a priori* synthesis in stage III.[18] Then, with the completed analysis as a guide, I trace a path through section 2, following the order of stages of the argument. My purpose there is both to explain the text in terms of the analysis and to justify the analysis by reference to the text.

This is, strictly speaking, the reverse of the proper order for a commentary. I should first analyze the text and only then present my findings in systematic form. But if I were to proceed in that way, the reader would be forced to hold his breath through many pages of detailed textual exegesis before discovering their purpose.

After dealing systematically and textually with stages I–III, I turn to stage IV, in which Kant gives his answer to Hume. There, by an analysis of Hume's original attack on causality, I exhibit a weakness in the argument of the Deduction, and try by this means to explain why Kant went on to develop a new and more complicated version of the argument in Section 3. The order of discussion is thus: (1) exposition of stages I–III of the argument; (2) textual exegesis of stages I–III; (3) exposition and textual exegesis of stage IV; (4) analysis of stage IV and the Deduction argument.

[18] Stage IV, which is merely a reworking of stage III, will be dealt with later.

The Argument of the Deduction in A: Stages I–III

The Premises of the Argument

In each of the versions of the argument of the Deduction the premise is the same. The starting point is the *cogito*, "I think," of Descartes. Or rather it is a revised form of the *cogito* which expresses what Kant believes to be the most general fact about any consciousness: its unity. A second and subsidiary premise concerning the contents of consciousness is implied by Kant's statements at various points. This enthymeme, which proves to be the key to the early stages of the Deduction proof, is the assertion that the representations contained in consciousness can be viewed in two ways, either as objects of awareness *simpliciter* or as *representations* of something other than themselves. Let us examine these premises in order.

The Unity of Consciousness. "It must be possible for the 'I think' to accompany all my representations; for otherwise something would be represented in me which could not be thought at all, and that is equivalent to saying that the representation would be impossible, or at least would be nothing to me." [B 131-2] In this way, Kant introduces in the revised version of the Deduction the idea of the unity of consciousness. Following Descartes, though with very different results, he adopts the "I think" as the absolutely first principle of all philosophical speculation. But Kant does not merely assert "I think." Rather he states that the "I think" can be attached to each of my mental contents. Thoughts are not like stones in a heap, or rabbits in a hat. They do not simply lie in the mind as an aggregate of unconnected contents. They are all bound up together as the thoughts of *one mind*. They are all *my thoughts*, and only mine.[19]

The force of this statement, however, is not on the face of it obvious. "All my mental contents are my mental contents" is merely a tautology, and "an 'I think' attaches to all my mental contents" does not seem much better. What is the characteristic to which Kant is trying to call our attention? Light may be thrown

---

[19] The unity of consciousness is a fact of logic, not a datum of introspective psychology. Kant only makes this clear later in the Analytic. Cf. below, pp. 186–187, and compare pp. 175–177. The doctrine of the Second Edition with regard to this point marks an advance over that of the First Edition.

on the problem if we make use of a trick first suggested by Brentano.[20] Imagine, then, that we have written a six-word sentence on two different pieces of paper. We tear up the first piece so that each scrap contains just one word. (Suppose, for example, that the sentence is "The unicorn is a mythical beast.") The other piece we leave intact. Then we line up six people on one side of the room, each with a scrap of the first piece, and opposite them we stand a seventh person, to whom we give the whole sentence written on the untorn paper. Each member of the group of six reads the word which he has been given. Jones reads "The," Brown reads "unicorn," and so on. Smith, the seventh man, reads "The unicorn is a mythical beast." Now, every word of the sentence is contained in the consciousness of some member or other of the group of six.[21] Similarly, every word of the sentence is contained in Smith's consciousness. But the two cases are absolutely different, for while in the former it is true that the separate parts of the sentence are contained in *some* consciousness, they are not contained in the *same* consciousness, and hence there is no *unity of consciousness* of them, as there is in the case of Smith. William James puts the point in the following way:

Take a sentence of a dozen words, and take twelve men and tell to each one word. Then stand the men in a row or jam them in a bunch, and let each think of his word as intently as he will; nowhere will there be a consciousness of the whole sentence.[22]

The fact is that one consciousness of twelve words is not the same as twelve consciousnesses of one word each. Following Kant's terminology, we may characterize the difference by saying that the one consciousness of all twelve words binds them together, or conceives them as a unity. These descriptions are metaphorical, but whether or not they can be reduced to literal terms (as, in fact, will later be done), the state of affairs to which they point seems undeniable.[23]

[20] William James took it from Brentano, and Kemp Smith in turn quotes it from James. Cf. Kemp Smith, *op. cit.*, p. 459 note.

[21] If we can be permitted for the sake of the demonstration to ignore the difference between words and concepts.

[22] William James, *Principles of Psychology*, volume I, p. 160.

[23] It goes without saying that when I adopt the voice of direct argument in this manner, I am representing what I believe to be Kant's views. Many parts of the Deduction seem to me to be valid, and the above is one such example, but it is not the role of a commentator to decide about the truth of the text he is analyzing.

We can get a further insight into the unity of consciousness by showing that it is not merely a matter of association of ideas, as Hume had argued. This point is of great importance in understanding how Kant's position differs from Hume's. As we shall see, the relationship which Kant asserts to hold between the unity of consciousness and the association of the contents of consciousness is one of entailment rather than equivalence. Kant claims that if a manifold of representations are bound up in one consciousness, then it follows that they are related to one another by association. But he denies the converse: perceptions or concepts may stand in associative relations *without being part of the same consciousness.*

To say that two ideas are associated is to say that when one of them is thought, the other is, or tends to be, thought also.[24] Thus, the idea of bread brings with it the idea of butter and pepper reminds us of salt. Somewhat more to the point, the image of the face of a friend calls to mind ideas of his stature and dress, his personal characteristics, and his past actions. Now it might be supposed that associations of this sort are what constitute the "unity of consciousness." Hume develops this view with characteristic deftness in the section of the *Treatise* entitled "Of personal identity."[25] The following lengthy extracts will put the whole theory before us:

> But setting aside some metaphysicians of this kind, I may venture to affirm of the rest of mankind, that they are nothing but a bundle or collection of different perceptions, which succeed each other with an inconceivable rapidity, and are in a perpetual flux and movement. . . . The mind is a kind of theatre, where several perceptions successively make their appearance; pass, re-pass, glide away, and mingle in an infinite variety of postures and situations. There is properly no *simplicity* in it at one time, nor *identity* in different; whatever natural propension we may have to imagine that simplicity and identity. The comparison of the theatre must not mislead us. They are the successive perceptions only, that constitute the mind. . . .
>
> What then gives us so great a propension to ascribe an identity to these successive perceptions, and to suppose ourselves possest of an invariable and uninterrupted existence thro' the whole course of our lives?
>
> [*Treatise*, pp. 252–53]

[24] Note that it won't do to add that they are thought *by the same mind,* for it is precisely this notion of one mind or one consciousness, which is supposed to be definable in terms of association.

[25] Hume does not raise directly the question of the unity, or as he would put it, the *identity* of consciousness, but rather that of the unity of personality or self. The two questions, however, would come to the same thing on both his view and Kant's.

After examining the matter, Hume asserts that:

> the true idea of the human mind, is to consider it as a system of different perceptions or different existences, which are link'd together by the relation of cause and effect, and mutually produce, destroy, influence, and modify each other. Our impressions give rise to their correspondent ideas; and these ideas in their turn produce other impressions. One thought chaces another, and draws after it a third, by which it is expell'd in its turn. In this respect, I cannot compare the soul more properly to any thing than to a republic or commonwealth, in which the several members are united by the reciprocal ties of government and subordination, and give rise to other persons, who propagate the same republic in the incessant changes of its parts. And as the same individual republic may not only change its members, but also its laws and constitutions; in like manner the same person may vary his character and disposition, as well as his impressions and ideas, without losing his identity. [*Treatise*, p. 261]

Thus, turning Plato's analogy around, Hume portrays the soul as a republic writ small. Is the image an appropriate one? Is a system of causal connections relating perceptions to one another all that we mean when we speak of the unity of the self? The answer is *no*, as can best be seen by considering cases in which the laws of association are operative, while yet we would refuse to say that the ideas are bound up in one consciousness.[26] Let us imagine two men, A and B, who exhibit the following curious relationship: every time A smells bacon frying, B, wherever he may be, finds himself thinking of eggs. If A sees a fire, B imagines heat. In short, the contents of B's mind are, as a matter of discoverable fact, causally associated with those of A's.

Such a situation would certainly raise questions about the nature of the causal relation between the minds of the two men. We might even be led to postulate some sort of psychic influence. But the one thing which we would *not* be led to suppose is that A and B were *one mind* in two bodies. Against such a suggestion is the fact that A does not think of eggs when he smells bacon, and that B does not find himself thinking of bacon when the idea of eggs pops into his mind. In short, the associated ideas are not all in the same mind. To say this, however, is just to assert the existence of a self

---

[26] The variation in language from philosopher to philosopher makes it difficult to discuss these questions without a continual flow of terminological explanations. Thus Hume's most general word for any content of consciousness is "perception," while Locke's is "idea" and Kant's is "representation." I shall use these interchangeably, letting the context indicate the precise meaning.

which is something other than a mere aggregate of associated thoughts and perceptions.

Kant struggled with the problem of consciousness throughout the period when he was writing and revising the first *Critique*. The analysis of the unity of consciousness, though it played an essential role in the Deduction, was never carried far enough to resolve its difficulties and obscurities. Even the preliminary account given above is largely an inference from statements which Kant did not fully explain. Nevertheless, Kant's realization of the complexity of consciousness marks a major advance on the rationalist theories of Descartes and Leibniz or the empiricist doctrine of Hume. Where they concentrated their attention on the objects of awareness, he sought the nature of awareness itself. Out of his analysis of the structure of consciousness there developed the revolutionary argument of the Deduction.[27] In the end, Kant failed to find a satisfactory theory of the self which could reconcile the transcendental ego, the empirical ego, the moral self, the noumenal self, and all the faculties of reason, will, judgment, imagination, understanding, feeling, and sensibility which he attributed to them.

The Double Nature of Representations. In the terminology of the *Critique*, the generic name for all mental contents is "representation" (*vorstellung*).[28] Categories, empirical concepts, ideas, pure intuitions, and perceptions are all referred to in the *Critique* as *representations*. There is some doubt as to the proper classification of feelings (*Gefühle*), such as pleasure and pain; as Kant is not concerned with them and considers them irrelevant to cognition, he leaves the matter open.

Representations, viewed in one light, are merely the contents of our consciousness, the immediate objects of awareness. But at the same time they perform the function of referring beyond themselves to the objects which they purport to represent. Needless to say, this referential function exists whether or not there really is some object to be represented. It is precisely because the concept of a unicorn purports to represent that we can call it fictitious. As Kant puts it in the Deduction, "All representations have, as repre-

---

[27] Cf. Kemp Smith, pp. xxxix–xlv.
[28] Cf. A 320 = B 376–77. The other definitions given there do not conform to Kant's customary usage. Compare with Hume's use of "perception" [*Treatise*, opening sentence] and Locke's use of "idea" [*Essay*, Book I, chapter 1, § 8].

sentations, their object, and can themselves in turn become objects of other representations." [29]

A. S. Pringle-Pattison, commenting on Locke's use of the analogous general term "idea," gives the following lucid account of the distinction between the two functions of mental contents:

Endless controversy has gathered round this definition ["idea" = "whatsoever is the object of the understanding when a man thinks"] and round Locke's actual use of the term 'idea.' It is important to remember, in the first place, the distinction signalized by Descartes between an idea as a mental state, a psychical occurrence, and the same idea as functioning in knowledge and conveying a certain meaning. The former he called the *esse formale seu proprium* of an idea, and in this respect all ideas stand upon the same footing. . . . The treatment of ideas so regarded belongs to psychology. But ideas not only exist as facts in the mental history of this or that individual; they have also, in the modern phrase, a 'content' or meaning; they signify something other than themselves. We regard them, in Descartes's words, 'as images, of which one represents one thing and another a different thing', and this is the important aspect of ideas for us. He calls it their *esse obiectivum seu vicarium*. So regarded, ideas are the subject-matter of epistemology or theory of knowledge, and it is in this light that Locke appears to contemplate them in the definition.[30]

Kant's concern, as we shall see, is not with one aspect of representations rather than the other, but precisely with the fact that there are these two aspects.

Perhaps it would be well to add here that the distinction between perception as an object of consciousness and perception as consciousness of an object is valid even if one adopts a phenomenalist analysis of objects as constructs of perceptions. A visual perception of a table is not, on any reasonable phenomenalist theory, a piece of the table, like a leg or drawer. As Kant makes brilliantly clear in the Second Analogy, an object viewed as a perceptual construct is a collection of judgments, not a jigsaw puzzle of little bits of immaterial matter. An understanding of this fact would have saved

---

[29] A 108. The sentence comes from Stage I of the Deduction. Note the reference to representations becoming the "objects of other representations." The point is that in order to treat representations as mental contents, we must make judgments about them by means of other representations (which are thereby employed *as representations*). Thus, I may say of my perception of a house that it is a vivid perception, a fleeting perception, a perception similar to one previous, a perception which I had last Tuesday, etc. Representations treated as contents of consciousness are events, and so have causes, effects, etc.

[30] Locke, *Essay*, p. 15, note by editor.

us from some of the sillier sorts of sense-data phenomenalism with which this century has been afflicted.

Stage I of the Argument: The Transcendental Object = x

At this point, I begin the stage-by-stage development of the argument of the Analytic. The final version, in the form of a proof of the causal maxim, will not appear until page 278, after an analysis of the Second Analogy. The four preliminary versions are all inadequate or incomplete in greater or less degree. Thus the first form of the argument, given a few pages further on, is little more than a skeleton of a proof. Each succeeding restatement embodies some clarification, addition, or advance in insight which Kant has put forward in order to overcome the failings of the preceding version. The second version substitutes the categories for the overly abstract concept of the object = x. The third version incorporates the analysis of "synthesis," thereby making a tremendous advance over the first and second versions. The fourth version revises the argument to bring out its relevance to Hume, and the fifth and final version completes the Analytic by successfully explaining the nature of "necessary connection." All this, unfortunately, demands a good deal of patience on the part of the reader. I must ask that he hold in reserve his objections or questions until the whole plan is laid before him. At times, in order to avoid endless repetition, I have been forced to state Kant's doctrines with a confident air, as if their meaning were quite transparent, when in fact I am preparing to show that they are in need of clarification. To this extent, I may seem to suffer from the fault of repeating Kant instead of explaining him. But by the end of the book, I think I have dealt with the major difficulties of Kant's argument. My claim is not to show that it is a valid argument, but only to show that it is a clear, coherent, unmetaphorical argument, and one which is worthy of serious consideration. Let us now turn to the first and crudest form of the Deduction.[31]

The task which Kant sets himself in the *Critique* is to prove rigorously that we have genuine empirical knowledge, assuming as his only premise the fact of the unity of consciousness. In other

---

[31] I might add, as a further justification for the somewhat unusual mode of exposition, that each "stage" of the argument corresponds exactly to a separate portion of the text. It is in this sense that the deduction is a "patchwork."

words, he wants to deduce the possibility of knowledge (and its actuality as well) from the unity of consciousness.[32] As I indicated in the Introduction, this is equivalent to showing that *the possibility of empirical knowledge is a necessary condition of consciousness*. In later stages, Kant makes this more specific by proving that *the A PRIORI validity of the categories is a necessary condition of consciousness*. At this point, however, he is not ready to introduce the categories and demonstrate their function in *a priori* knowledge.

The problem of the first stage, then, is to discover a chain of argument which will link the unity of consciousness with the possibility of knowledge. Kant can proceed in two ways, either by deducing consequences progressively from the unity of consciousness, or by ascending regressively to this premise from the possibility of knowledge. In fact he does both, meeting in the middle with the proposition that the concept of the Transcendental Object $= x$ must have universal applicability to the contents of consciousness. This proposition, he claims, can be deduced from the mere unity of consciousness, and in turn implies the possibility of knowledge. Hence it serves to establish the connection between the two and thereby complete the proof.[33]

Let us begin "from below" with the conclusion which we wish to reach: the existence of knowledge. What is the defining mark of knowledge that sets it off from mere subjective fancy? The answer, as Hume recognized in his analysis of causal judgments, is *necessity*. Knowledge is the assertion of a necessary connection between the subject and the predicate of a judgment. When I state, for example, that all bodies are heavy, I am not merely reporting

[32] In order to avoid excessively clumsy expressions, I have stated this in a shorthand manner. Strictly, one deduces propositions from other propositions, not facts from facts. Thus, Kant is seeking to show that the proposition "I am conscious and my consciousness has a unity" implies the proposition "It must be possible for me to acquire genuine empirical knowledge." More strictly still, the latter should perhaps state: "It must be possible for me to formulate, and assert with justification, valid propositions concerning the experienced world."

[33] I hope it is clear how this procedure differs from the method of "retreat and advance" which Kemp Smith describes (cf. above, Introduction, Chapter 3). The proof which Kant offers is perfectly straightforward and deductive, but in expounding it he employs a partially regressive style. In a similar manner, one might state a geometrical proof of, say, eight steps by first *ascending* from step eight to step five, and then *descending* from step one to step five. In the present instance, the universal applicability of the concept of the Transcendental Object is *proved from* the original premise of the unity of consciousness. It therefore becomes (like step five) a mere step in the final proof. See the statement of the proof at the end of this section.

the fact that on past occasions I have found the property of weight to be conjoined with the properties of spatial extension and impenetrability. I am asserting that there is an objective connection among these properties, such that I *must* connect them in my judgment. Now it is sometimes the case that a merely logical connection exists between the subject and predicate of a judgment, as when I say that all bodies are extended. Here the necessity derives from the meanings of the subject and predicate terms alone, for "body" is defined as "that which fills space." But "all bodies are heavy" is not such an analytic judgment. Hence there must be some other kind of necessity of connection between "body" and "weight." Kant calls such a connection a *synthetic unity* and the problem thus becomes that of synthetic judgments *a priori*.[34]

What is it that enables us to connect with necessity two concepts which have no analytical unity? (At this point, remember, Kant is not arguing, but merely expounding regressively.) Consider for example the various perceptions I have of the desk in front of me. What binds these representations to one another and distinguishes them from any arbitrary selection of representations which I might make? What is the difference between asserting that this extended body is metallic, and saying (merely as a figment of my fancy) that it is made of stone? Kant, be it noted, is searching for the general characteristic which distinguishes any cognitively valid judgment from an arbitrary juxtaposition of representations. He is not concerned with the rules or actual evidence by which I decide that this particular desk is indeed metal rather than stone.

Kant agrees completely with Hume's insistence that there is nothing in the representations themselves linking them together. The sight of the top of the desk does not compel me to conclude that it feels hard; its shape does not entail its weight. (If such con-

[34] Cf. A 6 ff. Note that the terms "*a priori*" and "*a posteriori*" do not refer to types of judgments but rather to *ways of knowing* a judgment. This point is frequently misunderstood by readers of the *Critique*. The two classes which between them include all judgments are *analytic judgments* and *synthetic judgments*. It is obvious, Kant thinks, that we can know all analytic judgments *a priori*, which is to say we can assert them as necessarily and universally true. His problem is to show that we can also know certain synthetic judgments *a priori*, and indeed that this possibility is a consequence of the mere fact of consciousness. The German for "synthetic *a priori* judgments" is "synthetische Urteile a priori," which indicates this distinction in meaning by placing the "a priori" after the noun. Kant never writes "synthetische *a priori* Urteile." Grammatically, "analytic" and "synthetic" are adjectives which modify the noun "judgment," while "*a priori*" and "*a posteriori*" are adverbs which modify the verb "know" and its cognates.

nections existed, the propositions asserting them would be analytic.) Speaking in the most general way, what binds these diverse representations together is simply the idea that they are all representations of the *same object*. The shape and solidity of the desk do not go together by virtue of some direct identity or similarity between them; they are the shape and solidity of *the* desk, and hence we can join them in the judgment, "the rectangular desk is solid." This is what we mean when we say that the judgment is true, and not just an idle fancy. As Kant says:

> The object is viewed as that which prevents our modes of knowledge from being haphazard or arbitrary, and which determines them *a priori* in some definite fashion. For in so far as they are to relate to an object, they must necessarily agree with one another, that is, must possess that unity which constitutes the concept of an object. [A 104-5]

If we reflect on this notion of an *object of representations*, we realize that it signifies something independent of our knowledge, standing over against the mind and serving as the objective anchor of our judgments. In Kant's language, it is a "ground of unity of representations," which means a ground of synthetic unity. But, Kant argues, "it is easily seen that this object must be thought only as something in general $= x$, since outside our knowledge we have nothing which we could set over against this knowledge as corresponding to it" [A 104]. In fact, since we can never go beyond our representations, the source of their unity must be sought in the *concept* of an object $= x$, and not in the object itself.

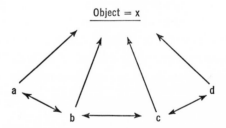

Object = x

Thus, the organizing and uniting principle of our representations in a mode of knowledge is the concept of an object $= x$. The diagram indicates the way in which relation to an object creates a connection among diverse representations.

This regressive exposition has established a relation between the applicability to representations of the concept of an object $= x$, and the possibility of valid modes of knowledge. It has shown, Kant believes, that *if* the concept of the Transcendental Object $= x$ is applicable to all the contents of consciousness, *then* they will all be capable of being joined in valid empirical judgments. As Kant says in the last paragraph of Stage I of the Deduction:

> The pure concept of this transcendental object, which in reality through-
> out all our knowledge is always one and the same, is what can alone con-
> fer upon all our empirical concepts in general relation to an object, that
> is, objective reality. This concept cannot contain any determinate intuition,
> and therefore refers only to that unity which must be met with in any
> manifold of knowledge which stands in relation to an object. [A 109]

We have discovered the second half of the proof by an analytic or regressive investigation. Now we shall attempt to complete it by a progressive argument, descending from the unity of consciousness to the universal applicability of the concept of an object $= x$. The discussion of the unity of consciousness earlier in this chapter served to demonstrate that it is more than a network of associative relationships, as Hume thought. But we have not yet explained what is meant by the term "unity of consciousness." Unity would seem to imply impossibility of separation, and yet Hume showed that any two distinguishable mental contents are capable of being separated. It does not help us much to use images like "in the mind" or "bound up in one consciousness," for they are all physical metaphors and obviously illegitimate as literal descriptions of the mind. Representations are not in the head, nor are they tied together like stalks of wheat in a sheaf.

Hume makes the point very acutely in his discussion of the concept of identity, or what Kant would call synthetic unity.

> One single object conveys the idea of unity, not that of identity. On the
> other hand, a multiplicity of objects can never convey this idea . . . The
> mind always pronounces the one not to be the other, and considers them
> as forming two, three, or any determinate number of objects. . . .
> Since then both number and unity are incompatible with the relation of
> identity, it must lie in something that is neither of them. But to tell the
> truth, at first sight this seems utterly impossible. Betwixt unity and number
> there can be no medium; no more than betwixt existence and non-existence.
> After one object is suppos'd to exist, we must either suppose another also
> to exist; in which case we have the idea of number: Or we must suppose
> it not to exist; in which case the first object remains at unity.
>
> [*Treatise*, p. 200]

It would seem that if we consider representations to be merely objects in consciousness, we will never find an explanation for this paradoxical synthetic unity, which in Hume's words falls "betwixt unity and number." But suppose we employ the subsidiary premise of our argument, and recall that the contents of consciousness have a double nature: they are representations as well as objects of consciousness. Now we see that there is a way in which the contents of consciousness can establish necessary relations with one another. This is possible only if they are referred, *qua* representations, to an object which serves as the ground of their unity. Furthermore, since all the contents of consciousness are bound up in a single unity, they must all be referred as representations to a *single ground of unity*, which can be called the Transcendental Object $= x$.

Thus, the unity of consciousness is possible only if the concept of the Transcendental Object $= x$ is applicable to all the contents of consciousness. And as the first part of our analysis showed, the concept of the Transcendental Object $= x$ is applicable to all the contents of consciousness only if they are capable of being united in valid modes of knowledge.[35] Combining the two, we get: "If I am conscious and my consciousness has a unity, then it must be possible for me to acquire valid empirical knowledge." Which is what was to be proved.

The formal proof can be stated as follows:

FIRST VERSION OF THE DEDUCTION

To Prove: I possess valid synthetic judgments *a priori*.

Proof

1. All the contents of my consciousness are bound up in a unity. [Premise]
2. The contents of my consciousness have the double nature of representations. [Premise]
3. The only way to unify a diversity of mental contents is by referring them *qua* representations to an object as ground of their unity. [Premises 1 and 2 and analyses of unity of consciousness and concept of an object, above]
4. If all the contents of my consciousness are bound up in a unity, then they must all be referred *qua* representations to a *single* object $= x$ as the ground of their unity [3, and analysis of object $= x$, above];

or, alternatively

[35] "P only if Q" is another way of saying "If P then Q."

5. If all the contents of my consciousness are bound up in a unity, then the concept of an object $= x$ applies to all the contents of my consciousness. [Analysis of concept of transcendental object $= x$, and 4]

6. Representations have objective reality conferred upon them, and thereby yield knowledge, by having applied to them the pure concept of an object in general $= x$ which they are thought as representing.

[Analysis of knowledge, above]

or, alternatively

7. If the concept of an object $= x$ applies to all the contents of my consciousness, then they yield knowledge in the form of judgments asserting a necessary connection among representations. [6, by conversion]

8. By 5, 7, 1, and the rules of logic, we get:

The contents of my consciousness yield knowledge in the form of judgments asserting a necessary connection among representations.

["If P then Q, and If Q then R, and P" implies "R"]

which is to say:

I possess valid synthetic judgments *a priori*. Q.E.D.

Stage II of the Argument: The Pure Concepts of Understanding

The first version of the argument, although it can be put in the guise of a formal proof, is quite obviously no more than a proof-sketch. It is condensed, opaque in certain key questions, and metaphorical where it should be literal. In succeeding stages of the Deduction Kant eliminates these flaws, one at a time, until finally the proof is completed in the Second Analogy.

The first difficulty which comes to view is the vagueness of Kant's statements about the relation between empirical concepts and the concept of the object $= x$. This latter is said to refer "only to the unity" of a manifold of representations. It also is described as "conferring relation to an object" on empirical concepts. But we are not told at all how this is done. Kant clearly must work out a more detailed and adequate account of the notion of objectivity, and connect it with an expanded theory of the concept of an object $= x$.

Furthermore, it is not at all evident how we can have *a priori* knowledge, if our concepts must either be empirical or else the vacuous concept of the transcendental object. From the former we can derive at best synthetic judgments *a posteriori*, and the latter by Kant's own insistence yields no knowledge whatsoever. Again the problem is to explain how an *a priori* but empty concept can shed an aura of necessity on content-ful but *a posteriori* empirical concepts.

More seriously still, Kant appears to be caught in the assertion that something can be the cause of itself. He claims that the unity of consciousness, and thereby consciousness itself, is possible only through the application to the given manifold of the pure concept of an object $= x$. But this pure concept, as it has no content itself, must work by means of empirical concepts, such as "body." Now empirical concepts are formed, according to Kant, by abstracting certain common characters from experience and putting them together into a class notion.[36] This can only be done after I am conscious, presumably. So it would appear that empirical concepts are ingredients in the very mental activity (unification of consciousness) whereby they first become possible. They both precede and depend upon consciousness.

The difficulty again stems from the inadequacy of the concept of an object $= x$. What Kant needs at this point is a theory of pure concepts which teaches that they (1) originate in the mind itself rather than in experience, (2) serve conjointly as the means for the synthesis or unification of the manifold of consciousness, and (3) constitute, as it were, a spelling out of the concept of an object of knowledge. Such a theory would explain the possibility of *a priori* knowledge, for the pure concepts, like space and time, would be innate "conditions of the possibility of experience." It would also avoid the circularity of the stage I argument, for the pure concepts would precede consciousness and make it possible. They would not be abstracted from experience *a posteriori*. The pure concepts would also take the place of the overly abstract concept of an object $= x$, and hence would make it easier for Kant to explain precisely how objective reference is conferred on a manifold.

What Kant needs at this point is of course *the categories*. They serve all the purposes listed above, and in stage II of the Deduction Kant substitutes them for the concept of the transcendental object. Thereafter in the Deduction the object $= x$ is dropped from the

---

[36] This is done through the logical employment of understanding. Cf. *Logic*, I, 1, § 3. "The empirical concept arises out of the senses through the comparison of objects of experience and contains through the understanding merely the form of universality."

argument and is not mentioned again.[37] The revised proof is as follows:

SECOND VERSION OF THE DEDUCTION

To Prove: I possess valid synthetic judgments *a priori.*

Proof

1. All the contents of my consciousness are bound up in a unity. [Premise]
2. The contents of my consciousness have the double nature of representations. [Premise]
3. The only way to unify a diversity of mental contents is by referring them *qua* representations to an object as ground of their unity. [Premises 1 and 2 and analyses of unity of consciousness and concept of an object, above]
4. If all the contents of my consciousness are bound up in a unity, then the concept of an object = x applies *a priori* to them.
   [See steps 4–5 of First Version of Deduction]
5. The categories, or pure (i.e., *a priori*) concepts of understanding, are modes of the concept of an object = x. They spell out what is contained in it, and thereby serve as rules for the unification of consciousness. [Metaphysical Deduction and comments above]
6. If all the contents of my consciousness are bound up in a unity, then the categories are *a priori* applicable to them.
   [4 and 5, by substitution]
7. Representations have objective reality conferred upon them, and thereby yield knowledge, by being connected to one another with necessity by means of the concept of an object in general = x.
   [See step 6, First Version]

   or, alternatively

8. If the concept of an object = x is employed to synthesize all the contents of my consciousness, then they yield knowledge in the form of judgments asserting a necessary connection among representations.
   [7]
9. If the categories are *a priori* applicable to the contents of my consciousness (i.e., are employed to synthesize the manifold of consciousness), then the contents of my consciousness yield knowledge in the form of judgments asserting a necessary connection among representations.
   [5, 8, by substitution]
10. By 1, 6, 9, and the rules of logic:
    The contents of my consciousness yield knowledge in the form of judgments asserting a necessary connection among representatives, which is to say:

    I possess valid synthetic judgments *a priori.* Q.E.D.

---

[37] It is this fact which is used by Kemp Smith in dating A 104-110 as the first layer of the Deduction.

Stage III of the Argument: The Analysis of Synthetic Unity

The substitution of the categories for the undefined concept of an object $= x$ is an improvement in the argument of the Deduction, but it obviously leaves a good deal to be explained. No real reason has been offered for supposing that the categories are modes of objective reference. Indeed, if we set to one side the Metaphysical Deduction, we are still completely in the dark as to the identity and existence of any pure concepts of understanding. This failing in the argument is not made good anywhere in the Deduction proper. Not until the Analytic of Principles does Kant give us a genuine proof of the validity of the individual categories. We must therefore not expect more than a general reference to some pure concept or other in any of the versions of the Deduction.

More serious still is Kant's failure thus far to present a convincing analysis of the pivotal notion of *synthetic unity*. As Hume argued in the passages quoted earlier, it is an apparent contradiction to ascribe a unity (or "identity") to a diversity of impermanent mental contents. What then does it mean to say that the contents of consciousness have a synthetic unity?

Kant's first attempt at meeting this demand is his account of the role played in cognition by the concept of an object. The results of this analysis find expression in the first and second versions of the proof. But it is obvious that the matter has not been satisfactorily dealt with. The concept of an object does not literally draw representations to itself like pointed arrows; nor is an object in any literal sense a ground or base. Kant has not even told us yet *what* a pure concept is and *how* it functions.

In this next stage, Kant carries his theory a great distance forward by providing just such an analysis of synthetic unity. He does so by way of a description of the activity of synthesis. In the Metaphysical Deduction, Kant had said of synthesis that it was "a blind but indispensable function of the soul, without which we should have no knowledge whatsoever, but of which we are scarcely ever conscious" [B 103]. Nevertheless, in the Subjective Deduction [A 97–104 = stage III] he analyzes in detail the several aspects of the synthesizing activity of imagination. The result is to give us our first real insight into the nature of synthetic unity.

The discussion which follows is the real heart of this book.

What I have attempted to do is to develop a complete theory of the mental activity of synthesis, basing my arguments on the suggestions in the Subjective Deduction. Out of the theory will come answers to such questions as, What is synthetic unity?, How can necessary connections be established among discrete elements of experience?; and a step will be taken toward answering Kant's recurrent question, What is an object (of knowledge)? Because the *Critique* only provides clues, but not a completely elaborated theory of synthesis, I have been forced to employ a certain amount of philosophical argument which can at best be attributed to Kant by inference. Many passages support my interpretation, and they have been cited in the textual exegesis which follows this section, but I must nevertheless admit that at times I exceed the customary limits of "reading into" a text. My defense — and indeed the principal claim of this entire commentary — is that only by such a technique can I succeed in making good sense and a reasonable argument out of the Deduction. I shall begin the analysis of the activity of synthesis with an examination of rules and rule-directed activities.

Rules and Synthetic Unity. The clue to a complete understanding of synthetic unity is provided by a passage in Section 2 of the first-edition Deduction. Kant states:

All knowledge demands a concept, though that concept may, indeed, be quite imperfect or obscure. *But a concept is always, as regards its form, something universal which serves as a rule.* The concept of body, for instance, as the unity of the manifold which is thought through it, serves as a rule in our knowledge of outer appearances. But it can be a rule for intuitions only in so far as it represents in any given appearances the necessary reproduction of their manifold and thereby the synthetic unity in our consciousness of them. [A 106, emphasis added]

The significant words for our purpose are contained in the second sentence of the paragraph: "a concept is always, as regards its form, something universal which serves as a rule." Throughout the Analytic Kant speaks of rules of synthesis, by which our intuition is generated or a manifold reproduced.

(1) The Nature of Rule-Directed Activities. As a first step toward interpreting the statement that concepts have the form of rules, let us consider some of the significant characteristics of the functioning of rules in general. An activity, of whatever sort, may

be either haphazard or else performed according to a plan. In the latter case we can formulate a set of prescriptions in conformity with which the activity is done. If we compare a potter with a child slapping clay, for example, we see that they differ not only in the products of their acts, but also in that we can state a rule which the potter follows. Roughly speaking, it might run something like this: (1) Place a large handful of clay on the wheel; (2) smooth it while slowly turning the wheel; (3) make a depression in the center of the clay with the thumbs, etc., etc. For the child no such rule would exist, though we might perfectly well give a blow-by-blow *description* of his mud-patting.

In like manner we can distinguish an aimless wanderer from a purposeful pedestrian by the latter's adherence to a walking plan or set of directions: "Go down Massachusetts Avenue, turn left on Trowbridge, etc." Here again, we can describe the itinerary of the wanderer, but cannot state a rule which he is following.

There are three characteristics of rule-grounded activities which are important for our purposes. In the first place, an activity performed according to a rule can legitimately be said to proceed correctly or incorrectly. It makes no sense to say that the child is properly or improperly slapping mud, for there is no rule or standard of mud-patting against which the action can be judged. But if the potter sprinkles sand on the turning clay, or probes it too soon with his thumb, or molds it asymmetrically, we can say that he is not making the bowl *correctly*. That is, he is not following the rules of bowl-making. Similarly, the rambler's twists and turns are all neither right and wrong, but simply right and left. Should the pedestrian turn off on Plympton Street, however, we say "He has taken the wrong turn. He has not followed the directions."

Secondly, in the case of at least some rule-directed activities, the order of the steps of the activity is not haphazard, but is determined by the rule: *first* the clay is placed on the wheel, *then* it is shaped, *then* it is baked. To paint the clay first would be to disobey the rules of pottery-making. This is not the case, notice, merely because of physical necessity, as one might say that the pedestrian cannot turn on Trowbridge before he has got there. Even in the case of interchangeable stages of a rule-directed activity, the first may occur first because the rule prescribes it so. A good example of this is a musical composition, which is distinguished from any number of other possible compositions solely by the order in which its component notes are to be played.

The third significant characteristic of a regulated action is its coherence. All the parts or stages of the activity belong together by virtue of the rule, and are set off from other activities which may be accidentally associated with it, for example by occurring at the same time. The sequence, furthermore, has a clearly defined beginning and end. Suppose, to dwell a bit longer on our simple example, that one is asked to describe the playing child. Lacking any notion of a plan or rule which the child is following, we are forced to make a random catalogue, guided perhaps by nothing more than temporal sequence: first he slaps the mud, then scratches his ear, then wiggles his toes, and finally lets out a cry. But in describing the potter's movements, a knowledgeable spectator will group together in one narrative chain all the stages in the making of a bowl, omitting whatever incidental actions may occur in the same span of time. The potter scratches his ear while making the bowl, but not as part of the bowl-making process. Thus, out of a kaleidoscope of events, certain ones are selected as forming a *single* activity by virtue of their concordance with a single rule. In like manner, a description of the pedestrian will include all the turnings of his walk, but will exclude his facial gestures, whistling, and breathing, which are not parts of the activity dictated by his sheet of directions.[38]

These three characteristics of rule-directed activities, and in particular the third of them, provide a solution to the problem of synthetic unity. The paradox of a multiplicity which has unity without losing its diversity — the problem which the ancients called the one and the many — is resolved by the notion of a rule-directed activity. Its stages are several and separable, but they proceed according to a rule which serves to set them off and unify

[38] Mrs. Ingrid Stadler has pointed out to me that one can distinguish between rules, strictly so called, and plans, techniques, standards, etc. Thus, the pedestrian in my example might better be described as following directions or following a plan than as acting according to a rule. Correspondingly, the potter is employing a technique or, in the Greek sense, practicing an art. Although this point is valid, I do not think it works against my analysis of rule-directed activities, for in the three respects which I have singled out for attention, all of these species of purposeful activities are alike. It would be a mistake, let me add, to make too much of the legalistic overtones of "rule" in Kant's statements. That metaphor leads us away from a literal explanation of "synthetic unity" and "necessary connection."

them. Thus is found, in Hume's words, "a medium betwixt unity and number" [*Treatise*, p. 201].[39]

A final point of great importance must be mentioned concerning the distinction between haphazard and rule-governed activities. Contrary to what might appear to be the implication of the examples cited above, there is in principle no activity which by the nature of its component stages either *must be*, or *cannot be*, rule-directed. The child might possibly do at random just the things laid down in the pottery manual, and the rambler might perfectly well wander along the path of the pedestrian. Equally, one might follow a rule which prescribed mud-slapping, ear-scratching and toe-wiggling, or apparently aimless wandering. This is not to suggest that an observer would be unable to distinguish rule-directed from non-rule-directed activities. In the case of the present examples, he could do so simply by asking the potter or walker. The point is that any sequence of steps could be built into a rule, or occur by sheer chance.[40]

(*2*) *Two types of rule-directed activities.* A distinction can now be drawn between two different types of rule-directed activities. The first sort are activities concerned with the working up of a product, as in the case of the potter and the bowl, or with the carrying out of a planned sequence of actions, as in the case of the pedestrian on his walk. These we may call first-order rule-directed activities. The second sort of rule-directed activity consists in the formulation of a rule in accordance with which a working-up or a carrying-out is done.

Not all such rule-determinings are themselves rule-directed. Some of these second-order activities may themselves be performed haphazardly. A child, for example, may select at random a set of

---

[39] There is yet some explaining to do, strictly speaking, for the notion of a rule-directed activity will at best explain the unity of a series of mental acts, not the unity of a manifold of mental contents. This extension can be completed only after we have analyzed the nature of synthesis itself. Then it will be seen that the contents of consciousness are unified by virtue of their being all reproducible in imagination according to a rule. In other words, their unity consists in the nature of their generation.

[40] The reader should by now have some glimmering of where this is all leading. The distinction between subjective association and objective causal connection, for example, will turn out to be a matter of rule-directedness. The first characteristic of rule-governed activities — that they are susceptible to criticism as correct or incorrect — will then be called upon to explain the distinctively normative feature of knowledge as opposed to mere apprehension.

rules and make them into a game. Then, having convinced some friends to join him, he can play his game — i.e., he can perform the activities enjoined by his rules. This play will be governed by the rules, but the activity of *choosing* the rules will have been unregulated. Some cases of rule-determining activities, however, are themselves governed by rules. For example, suppose that a toy manufacturer were to tell his office boy to create a new game. "Make up a game," he says, "which will require four players, use a deck of cards, take no more than an hour, and be playable only with a special set put out by our firm." This second-order rule-directed activity of game-making contrasts with the unregulated game-making of the child, analogously to the ways in which pottery making (a first-order process) contrasts with casual mud-slapping.

First, it would make no sense to criticize the child for making up a bad game, for he has no standard by which to judge. The office boy, on the other hand, can quite well be said to have performed his task well or ill, according as he has or has not followed his employer's stipulations. Second, the office boy can explain why the steps of the game appear in their assigned order (because they must accommodate four players, or must consume less than an hour, for example). But the child has no particular reason for putting the hop before the skip, rather than the other way round.[41] Finally, the office boy has a preconceived notion of the extent and number of the steps in the rule (or game) which he is creating, while the child merely adds on steps till he grows weary, having no criterion by which to determine the unity and completeness of the game.

Lest the reader think that I have wandered far from the subject of this commentary, led on by idle desire to explore the varieties of rule-directed activities, I will simply remark here that the distinction between first and second order rules proves to be the key to the distinction between empirical and pure concepts.

The Nature of Synthesis. Thus far I have discussed certain of the aspects of rule-directed activities in order to throw light on the

[41] This is not to suggest that children always compose their games haphazardly. Actually we can discern a good many rules of thumb governing the selection of forms of play. With a little directed questioning of the sort that Socrates used with the slave boy in the *Meno*, a child might be made to express quite a few criteria of a "good game."

problem of synthetic unity. We have seen that an activity performed according to a rule has a coherence and completeness which is precisely the unity of a diversity. It remains to consider directly that activity which Kant attributes to the mind, and whose guiding rule is contained in the concept of an object, namely *synthesis*. The doctrine of the Analytic would be considerably clarified by the foregoing, even if we continued to rely on the figurative descriptions of synthesis which Kant gives in the Metaphysical Deduction. With the suggestions provided by the analysis of rules, we are in a better position to understand how the mind can give unity to a manifold of perceptions by going through it, taking it up, and connecting it according to a concept which serves as a rule. Nevertheless, the theory must necessarily remain partially obscure until we can state in detail the nature of this going through and taking up, this grasping, this synthesis.

The inadequacies of such locutions as "holding together" and "connecting" are obvious, and need little comment. Perceptions do not move past the mind like parts on a conveyor belt, waiting to be picked off and fitted into a finished product. There is no workshop where a busy ego can put together the bits and snatches of sensory experience, hooking a color to a hardness, and balancing the two atop a shape. The whole picture of construction or arranging conjured up by Kant's phraseology is unsatisfactory if pressed even a little. A further difficulty, in its way more serious still, is introduced by the factor of the passage of time, for the manifold which is run through stretches out in time.[42]

Now a perception which is past lies beyond the reach even of this sort of displacement. Could we make sense of the idea of re-

---

[42] We touch here on some of the most complicated points in the interpretation of the *Critique*. According to certain versions of Kant's theory, the synthesizing process actually generates the temporal order, and hence cannot itself be spoken of as in time. This implication, for example, is essential to the resolution of the Antinomy of freedom and determinism in the Dialectic. On the other hand, the description actually given of synthesis makes it a process *in time*. It might be argued, of course, that since our language permits us to speak coherently only of the phenomenal, any attempt to describe non-temporal activities is doomed to failure. However, this condemns the word "synthesis," as well as the process which it names, to complete obscurity. Since the argument of the *Critique* cannot finally be understood until its key terms are clear, it seems preferable to emphasize the passages in which Kant offers us some explanation of the nature of synthesis, even if his theory is thereby left open to attack. The problem of the generation of the time-order is discussed below.

arranging a presented visual field, we would still be unable to explain how the mind takes a color from last week, and groups it with a shape from yesterday and another perspectival view of just a moment ago. If Kant is to be understood as employing anything other than complex and untranslatable figures of speech, some way must be found to restate his theory which avoids these difficulties.

A first possibility, which Kant uses frequently in the *Critique*, is to substitute "thinks together" for "holds together" and "thinks as a unity" for "grasps as a unity." As I had occasion to note in the Metaphysical Deduction, this move is naturally suggested by the two senses of the word "begreifen," but such a solution, unfortunately, leaves the problem unchanged. If there is an unreduced figurative content in "holds together," then the substitution of "thinks" merely squeezes it all into the second word. What we need here is a completely new description of synthesis which, so far as possible, remains completely literal.

The key to an understanding of synthesis lies in the mental activity which Kant calls *reproduction in imagination*. It is an observable fact about men that they are able to recall past experiences, reproducing in the present copies or memories of perceptions from some earlier time. How this is done is a mystery which Kant does not attempt to resolve, and we do not seem to be any clearer on this point today. Even if some causal explanation could be put forward involving the physiology of the brain, it is hard to see how it would make the fact of memory any less opaque.

As noted above, Kant's ambiguity permits several interpretations on this point. If synthesis is considered productive of time itself, then a very neat solution exists to the problem of memory. Instead of becoming entangled in the ever more constricting bonds of a solipsism of the present moment, Kant can claim that the mind is present to different moments of time precisely because it creates them. Nevertheless, a heavy price is paid for this convenient line of argument, for it deprives us of our sole insight into the nature of synthesis, namely reproduction in memory. Kant cannot have it both ways at once: either he must analyze synthesis independently, and then use it to explain the functioning of memory, or he must begin with memory as a familiar mental capacity and explain synthesis in terms of it. It was undoubtedly this dilemma which led

Kant to speak so equivocally of the Subjective Deduction in the Preface to the first edition.[43]

Kant develops the notion of reproduction in imagination in Section 2 of the first-edition Deduction, A 97–104. The following exposition and analysis will make no attempt to deal with the text in detail. That will be done in the latter part of this chapter, along with the commentary on the other parts of the Deduction.

The starting point of the synthesizing process is the given manifold of intuition, resulting from an affection of sensibility — in other words, a diversity of perceptions.[44] This manifold of intuition, whatever its origin may be, must conform to the conditions of inner sense, and hence must have the form of time. In other words, sensibility presents a succession of representations. But this manifold cannot yet be *conceived* as a succession of representations, for to apply to it even so general a concept requires that it be thought as *a* manifold, and hence that it be unified. In short, the manifold must be synthesized before concepts can be applied to it.[45]

Now, if I kept forgetting the last representation of the manifold every time I came to a new one in the temporal order, I would not be thinking them together in one consciousness. There would be merely a succession of unitary and disjoint apprehensions, not a unity. If I look at a tree, then forget it and look at another, then forget it also and look at a third, and so on, I can not in any meaningful sense be said to have seen the forest. What I must do, therefore, as I proceed from one moment to the next, is to reproduce the representation which has just been apprehended, carrying it along in memory while I apprehend the next. In looking at a forest, I must say to myself, "There is a birch; and there is an elm, plus the birch which I remember, etc." [46] The result of this repeated recollecting — or synthesis of reproduction in imagination, as Kant calls it — is the apprehension in one consciousness

[43] "The latter [i.e., the Subjective Deduction] is, as it were, the search for the cause of a given effect, and to that extent is somewhat hypothetical in character (though, as I shall show elsewhere, it is not really so) . . ." [A xvii].

[44] Leaving to one side the possibility of a pure manifold; we shall have to consider later on what we are to make of Kant's theory of pure intuition.

[45] More accurately, synthesis is the application of concepts to the manifold. Kant tends to obscure this identity by distinguishing between imagination and understanding, or between reproduction and recognition.

[46] Needless to say, this is a rather flatfooted description. But then, the mind works with such rapidity and deftness that any attempt to spell out its activities must seem ponderous by comparison.

of a variety of representations which were originally disjoint. By carrying them forward, the mind has made it possible to think them as a unity.

But this is not yet enough. I must apprehend the succession by reproducing it, but I must also be aware that what I have just reproduced is identical with what I apprehended a moment ago. To put it crudely, I have to know what I'm doing. Merely reproducing the earlier contents will not suffice [A 103]. When I count a row of twelve stones, I look at the first one and say "one." Then I look at the second, think of the first, and say "two." In saying "two" I am aware that I previously said "one" and I can recall that act, knowing as I recall it that it was the *precursor* of this "two," not merely prior to it. The process is repeated up to "twelve," at which time I am aware of myself as having performed a series of *connected* acts. If I merely found myself saying "twelve" after a while, or if I could recall previous utterances of "one," etc., but didn't recognize them as the earlier stages of a single activity whose culmination was the "twelve," then I could not know that I had just counted twelve objects. In general, when I apprehend a succession of representations by reproducing them in imagination, I must become conscious of two things: first, that the present representations exactly resemble those which they reproduce, and second, that the representations before my mind belong to one set or group, and hence are unified. The process whereby I become conscious of these two facts is called by Kant "the Synthesis of Recognition in a Concept" [A 103].

How does the mind perform this last synthesis? What is it to be aware of a group of representations (thoughts and perceptions) "as a unity"? What is the difference between calling an idea or image to mind at random and reproducing or recognizing it? The answer lies in the analysis of *rules*. The mind's activity in reproducing the successive intuitions of a manifold is not random, but regulated. It proceeds in accordance with a rule which determines the mind to act thus and in no other way. When I count the twelve stones, I do not recall any past representations which please my fancy. I am bound by the rules of counting to label the first stone "one." I must then recall that "one" while labelling the second, and I must recall it as "one," not as "three" or "fifteen." I must continue on, obeying the rules, until I have reached "twelve." I then recall the previous eleven steps, and I am aware at that point that those recollected steps were performed *in accordance with the rule*. This is what we meant when we said that the steps had to be remembered as a series of *connected* acts. They are connected by being successive stages of a single rule-directed activity. The whole process, which enables me to know that there are twelve stones, is governed by a rule — in this case, the rule of counting. To conceive of "twelve" is actually to be conscious of the rule by which the mind has reproduced the succession of representations. As Kant says, "a concept is always, as regards its form, something universal which serves as a rule" [A 106]. To be exact, it is the rule for the reproduction in imagination of a manifold of intuition.

Kant is not always careful to distinguish a concept from the act of conception, but we may say with some confidence that he thinks a concept to be a rule, and conception to be the consciousness of the rule. As we have seen, a rule-directed activity has a unity which consists in its various stages conforming to the same rule. The synthetic unity of a manifold, therefore, is the characteristic possessed by a collection of mental contents by virtue of their having been reproduced by the imagination in accordance with a single rule. The consciousness of that synthetic unity is the conception of the rule by which it has been produced.

Thus far, the explanation of synthesis as a rule-directed reproduction in imagination has proceeded as if the previous analysis of rules applied literally and without distortion to it. This is not the case, however, for in at least two extremely important ways the mental activity of synthesis differs from such rule-governed activities as the potter's bowl making and pedestrian's walking described above. First of all, Kant does not think that the mind has any choice in the sorts of rules which it will apply to representations. The categories, which we shall see are the rules by which the mind forms its empirical concepts, are beyond a certain point inexplicable.[47] To be sure, they can be deduced from the general characteristics of time-consciousness, but we can neither understand why inner sense has the form of time, nor choose to synthesize the presented manifold in another way. All this contrasts

[47] Cf. B 145–146, where Kant makes this point quite forcefully.

with the potter and the pedestrian, who can choose to follow many different rules, or none at all for that matter.[48]

A second difference between synthesis and the rule-directed activities which we have examined is that the operation of the mind is pre-conscious as well as unavoidable. The pedestrian, we may suppose, is aware of the rules he is following: he has them on a piece of paper, can recall them if necessary, can repeat them when asked. But Kant does not suppose that even the most self-aware among us is always conscious of the rules by which perceptions are reproduced, or the general types to which these rules conform. We may at times become conscious of these rules; indeed, Kant defines a concept as the awareness of the unity of the rule by which the perceptions are reproduced. Nevertheless, since the activity of reproduction is what *produces* unity of consciousness and thereby makes concepts possible, awareness of the rules of synthesis must always be subsequent to the synthesizing itself.

We see reflected here a conflict which runs all through the *Critique* and which Kant never successfully resolved. On the one hand, his rationalist orientation and concern with the conditions of knowledge incline him toward an emphasis on concepts, judgments, reasoning, and the other conscious processes of cognition. On the other hand, his discovery of the problem of consciousness, and his distinction between appearance and reality, force him to assign the generative processes of the mind to a pre-conscious transcendental limbo. Kant obscures this ambiguity to a certain extent by attributing the non-conscious functions to faculties of the mind whose operations are customarily considered conscious, such as imagination. He also attempts to resolve the conflict by distinguishing synthesis itself from the bringing of synthesis to concepts [A 79]. This won't do, however, for the concept is simply the rule according to which the synthesis is performed, and hence must precede, not follow, it.

[48] This sort of problem frequently arises when a philosopher takes a concept which is originally applicable to a limited, optional activity, and extends it to a non-optional situation. Socrates' extension of 'virtue' from the virtue of sheep-herding or shipbuilding to the virtue of being a man is one example; the modern attempt to view moral reasoning as a kind of game is another. These conceptual graftings are productive, but one must be careful to avoid drawing conclusions whose legitimacy is essentially dependent on a *limited* use of the concept in question.

The Argument of Stage III. We are now in a position to re-state the argument of the Deduction, including in it the clarification of "synthetic unity" and the account of synthesis. Notice that the categories are still introduced arbitrarily, although their function is now much better understood.

THIRD VERSION OF THE DEDUCTION

To Prove: I possess valid synthetic judgments *a priori.*
Proof

1. All the contents of my consciousness are bound up in a unity. [Premise]
2. The only way to introduce synthetic unity into a manifold of contents of consciousness is by reproducing it in imagination according to a rule. [Analysis of synthetic unity, above]
3. The categories, taken as a whole, constitute the most general *a priori* rule of synthesis. [Analysis of categories, above]
4. If all the contents of my consciousness are bound up in a unity, then they have been synthesized according to the categories [2, 3]
5. Contents of consciousness have objective reality conferred on them, and thereby yield knowledge, by being brought into necessary connection with one another *qua* representations, for necessity of connection is the defining mark of objectivity. [Analysis of objectivity, above]
6. But synthesis according to rules confers a necessity of connection on a manifold. [Analysis of synthesis, above]
7. If all the contents of my consciousness are synthesized according to the categories (*rules* of synthesis), then they yield knowledge in the form of judgments asserting a necessary connection among representations.
   [3, 5, 6]
8. By 1, 4, 7 and the rules of logic:
   The contents of my consciousness yield knowledge in the form of judgments asserting a necessary connection among representations, which is to say:
   I possess valid synthetic judgments *a priori.* Q.E.D.

If this version of the argument is compared with the first and second versions,[49] it will be seen that the subsidiary premise concerning the double nature of representations has been omitted. Somehow, the analysis of synthesis has at the same time provided a means of incorporating that assumption into the proof. This fact is actually one of the most interesting consequences of the theory of synthesis just outlined, and reflects the great advance which the third version marks over its predecessors.

In explaining the notion that mental contents function as repre-

[49] Cf. pp. 116–117, 119 above.

sentations, it was tacitly assumed that the object which they represent is a separate entity. The problem therefore arose of describing the relation between the object and its representation. Kant at first followed Descartes and others in adopting a general form of the copy theory of representation. The concept or perception was considered, either literally or metaphorically, to be a copy of its object. So Kant explained the synthetic unity of an assortment of mental contents by asserting that they must all, in their role as representations, represent one and the same object — their connection in the mind mirroring the connection of states or properties in the object. This is the meaning of the diagram on page 114, above.

However, this is for Kant the beginning of his philosophical inquiry, not the end. The explanation as it stands is obviously unsatisfactory for several reasons. It is, firstly, a highly figurative account of mental operations. The relation of representing, indicated in the diagram by the arrow, is still unanalyzed. Secondly, and from Kant's viewpoint very much more importantly, the theory of representation as stated makes *a priori* knowledge of the phenomenal world seem impossible. If the object is separate from its representations, then we are again faced with the problem of *a priori* knowledge of the independently real. Instead of examining directly the relation of representing, Kant turns his attention to the nature of the object, and to the characteristic of synthetic unity which the manifold of representations seems to possess. In the course of his investigation, he comes indirectly upon a new answer to the question, What is it for a mental content to represent an object?

The first step in the solution of this problem is the recognition that it is the *concept* of the object, and not the object itself, that is the focus or ground of the unity of the representations. Somehow their relation, as mental contents, to the concept of the object confers upon them a necessary unity. Through the analysis of concepts as rules, and of synthetic unity as rule-conferred, it becomes clear that the unity of the manifold of representations is the unity of a variety which has been reproduced according to a rule.

Now we can see what has become of the relation of representing. *To say that mental content R represents object O is to say that R is one of a variety (= manifold) of mental contents which has been, or can be, reproduced in imagination according to the rule which is the concept of O.*

Some of the above may not be entirely clear at this stage. Only in the Second Analogy does Kant directly attack the problem of the relation between a phenomenal object and its representations. His solution there, although stated with almost cryptic terseness, is precisely that which I have outlined here. The following sentence, from A 197, contains the heart of his new theory:

If we enquire what new character *relation to an object* confers upon our representations, what dignity they thereby acquire, we find that it results only in subjecting the representations to a rule, and so in necessitating us to connect them in some one specific manner . . .

This is the most advanced stage of development reached by the argument of the Deduction. Its lacunae and shortcomings, including one very serious flaw which I shall discuss presently, are not remedied by Kant until the Second Analogy of the Analytic of Principles.

The fourth stage of the argument, which appears in subsection 4 of Section 2 and again in the Objective Deduction of Section 3, is really no more than a restatement of the third version. Its purpose is to show more clearly how that argument refutes the sceptical doubts of Hume. I shall deal with it after completing the detailed textual exegesis of stages I-III.

The Text of Stages I-III of the Deduction: A 95–110

Stage I—The Transcendental Object = x [A 104–110]

The discussion of the Transcendental Object = x, which immediately follows the Subjective Deduction, is one of the most compactly written passages in all of Kant's works. Its ten paragraphs could profitably be examined word by word, a style of commentary which would unfortunately swell this book out of all reasonable proportions. With the exception of the doctrine of the transcendental unity of apperception, which shall be treated more fully in the discussion of the Second Edition Deduction, all the leading ideas and arguments have been touched upon in the last chapter. Hence, it will be possible to limit detailed analysis to a few especially difficult passages, the reader being assigned the task of explaining the text in terms of the interpretation presented above.

General Discussion of the Passage. The passage appears in the text directly after the Subjective Deduction, which occupies most of the first half of Section 2 of the Deduction. It begins an entirely new train of thought, and Kant makes the transition from the preceding paragraph simply by asserting that "at this point we must make clear to ourselves what we mean by the expression 'an object of representations'." It is possible to see why Kant placed the passage here, though the reason is not terribly good. The Subjective Deduction consists of a description of three syntheses, or stages in the process of synthesis. The third and last is the Synthesis of Recognition in a Concept — after the manifold has been gathered together by a Synthesis of Reproduction in Imagination, the *unity* of that synthesis must be brought to consciousness in a concept.[50] This gives Kant his lead-in to the passage we are discussing, for it is strictly the *concept* of an object of representations that he explores. Nevertheless, the presuppositions of the Subjective Deduction are, on several crucial points, contradictory to those of the doctrine of the object $= x$.

Kemp Smith has dated this passage as the earliest in the entire first edition Deduction, and claims for himself the discovery "that the doctrine of the transcendental object is . . . a pre-Critical or semi-Critical survival." [51] In partial support of this view, he points out that all mention of the transcendental object is dropped from the portions of the second edition which Kant revised. The principal argument for Kemp Smith's conclusion is the assertion that in most of the references to the doctrine, including the present one, the transcendental object is identical with the thing-in-itself. Since Kant very early gave up the idea that we can have knowledge of things-in-themselves, any passage which identifies the object-of-knowledge with a thing-in-itself must be a "pre-Critical or semi-Critical survival."

It is not clear from Kemp Smith's remarks how he thinks this offending remnant found its way into the inner recesses of the

[50] Cf. the discussion of synthesis, above, and the commentary, below, on the passage.
[51] Kemp Smith, p. 204.

Critical edifice. That the passage requires explaining, we may grant. But with Paton, we must refuse to believe that Kant snatched a sheet of paper from his desk and sandwiched it into the Deduction of the Pure Concepts of Understanding without noticing that it contained "thoroughly un-Critical teaching," a fact which "was very early realized by Kant himself."

The phrase "transcendental object" appears more than thirty times in the *Critique*, either as *transzendentale Objekt* or as *transzendentale Gegenstand*. In the Aesthetic it is used once, at A 46, and clearly means "thing-in-itself." In the Analytic proper, outside of the present passage, it is used only once at A 191 in the Second Analogy, and again it seems clearly to refer to an unconditioned reality, or thing-in-itself. The remaining occurrences are in the chapter on Phenomena and Noumena, the Amphiboly, and the Dialectic (A 250, A 251, A 253, A 277, A 288, A 358, A 366, A 372, A 379, A 390, A 393–4, A 478, A 494, A 495, A 538, A 539–41, A 545, A 557, A 565, A 613, A 679, and A 698). Here, too, the meaning is always thing-in-itself, or independent reality. The question, then, is whether Kant saw in the concept of the transcendental object some elements of the mature Critical doctrine, which he could make use of in the Deduction as an aid to expounding his very complicated theory.

I think in fact that this is exactly what happened. Kant began the development of the Deduction argument by recognizing that intelligence, as well as sensibility, could yield knowledge only of things as they appear. His first problem then was to re-analyze the concept of objectivity in order to explain how our awareness of appearance could be knowledge. As I explained in the systematic exposition of the early stages of the argument, a crucial step in the solution of this problem was Kant's claim that "object" must be replaced by "object of knowledge," and that in turn by "concept of an object of knowledge." The concept of an object in general $= x$ is the pure form of objectivity. It is provided by the mind, which imposes it on the given manifold of perceptions, thereby rendering them "objective," which is to say giving them relation to an object of knowledge. Now at this stage it still has not been explained what an empirical object is, and therefore it is undetermined whether the "transcendental object $= x$" is a thing-in-itself or not. In later stages of the argument, Kant grapples with the problem of distinguishing between object and representation within the realm of appearances. As we shall see presently, the fourth stage of the argument is devoted to precisely that distinction. It fails, however, and hence Kant must return to the problem for a last time in the Analogies, where it is finally solved and the argument of the Analytic brought to completion.

In the second and succeeding stages, the categories are substituted for the object $= x$. Nevertheless, this concept of an object in general has a legitimate place in the development of the theory of the Analytic. What is of value in it is absorbed into the doctrine of the categories and the theory of *a priori* synthesis. Hence, I think Kemp Smith is wrong to assimilate this first stage of the Deduction proper to the transitional exposition of § 13.

Detailed Analysis. The entire passage consists of ten paragraphs — the third through the twelfth of subsection 3. In order to clarify the analysis, I will divide them into five segments: (1) paragraphs 3–4; (2) paragraphs 5–6; (3) paragraphs 7–9; (4) paragraph 10; and (5) paragraphs 11–12. Paragraph 10 contains the deduction proper, the rest of the passage being explanation and commentary.

(*1*) *Statement of the problem — Paragraphs 3–4.* The defining characteristics of knowledge are objectivity and necessity. Knowledge is precisely a combination of representations which is non-arbitrary; it is what we must think, not what we wish to think. In this way the most obscure and indistinct knowledge is distinguished from the most vivid and affecting fiction. The customary way of explaining these characteristics of knowledge is by reference to an independent object, to which the representations must be made to conform. If the properties of weight and impenetrability are combined in iron, then I must combine the representations of those properties in my concept of iron. Truth is the conformity of thought to object.

In the *Dissertation* the sensuous representations, or appearances, have as their objects the things-in-themselves. To be sure, the physical and mathematical propositions formulated about the appearances do not apply to things-in-themselves *qua* things-in-themselves. Nevertheless, the appearances are appearances of things-in-themselves, and are not in any sense *objects*.[52]

When Kant gave up the position that we can have knowledge of things-in-themselves, because of the inadequacies of his theory of pure concepts, he was forced to reconsider his rather undeveloped account of knowledge of appearances. If the objects of my sensuous representations are nothing to me, then in what sense can those representations be said to give me knowledge? How can I know of their conformity to an object which is necessarily hidden from me? (Needless to say, the *Dissertation* theory is open to criticism even if noumena *are* presumed to be knowable, for Kant nowhere explains the connection between the metaphysical knowledge *via* pure concepts and the physico-mathematical knowledge *via* sensuous concepts. It would appear, however, that Kant was led to reconsider the entire theory only after the doctrine of pure concepts had been questioned. This order of reasoning is reflected in paragraph 3, where Kant sets up the problem.)

At this point, there are two alternative lines of reasoning which Kant may follow. He may decide that there is no sense at all to the notion of an object of representations, and hence that we do not have any knowledge, strictly so called. There is nothing left, then, but to explore for their psychological interest the subjective mechanisms by which we generate our beliefs in objects and their causal connections.[53] Or, he may decide to reinterpret the phrase, "object of representations," thereby preserving the characteristics of objectivity and necessity by explaining them in a different way. As the opening paragraph of the passage makes clear, Kant chose the latter alternative.

The first step is to reconsider the function of the object in

---

[52] This point is obscured from modern readers of the *Critique* by Kant's later use of "phenomena" or "appearances" to refer to *empirical* objects. In the present passage, however, Kant has not yet developed a coherent theory of empirical objects. The entire subject, as we shall see below, is one which Kant never settled to his satisfaction. Throughout the writing and re-writing of the *Critique* he wavered between the view that there are only unknowable noumena and subjective appearances of them, and the more complex view that there are noumena, empirical objects which are appearances of noumena, and subjective representations which are in some sense representations of the empirical objects. The connections between this problem and the arguments of the Objective Deduction, the Refutation of Idealism, and the Analogies produce much of the confusion which makes the Analytic so difficult to understand.

[53] This, of course, is the line which he thought Hume had taken.

cognition.[54] We saw before that the object coerces the mind, forcing it to combine representations in conformity with the connections in the object. Now, cognition is not a matter of mental picture-building, in which internal images are fitted into a replica of an object. It is the formulation of judgments, whereby a connection is asserted between the representations named by the subject and predicate terms. In the judgment, "All bodies are heavy," it is asserted that the concept of weight is necessarily connected with the concept of body (extension plus impenetrability).[55] The function of the object, then, is to serve as the ground of the necessary unity of the representations in a judgment. In other words, objectivity and necessity, the marks of knowledge, are relations of representations *to one another, not to an independent object.*

(2) *Transformation of the problem — Paragraphs 5–6.* Thus far Kant's argument runs along familiar lines. In moving from a correspondence theory of truth to a coherence theory, he emulates Berkeley and Hume. In paragraph 5 [A 105], however, his thought becomes difficult and important. He introduces in rapid succession most of the key notions of the Deduction. It will be necessary, therefore, to examine the argument sentence by sentence.

(*a*) But it is clear that, since we have to deal only with the manifold of our representations, and since that *x* (the object) which corresponds to them is nothing to us — being, as it is, something that has to be distinct from all our representations — the unity which the object makes necessary can be nothing else than the formal unity of consciousness in the synthesis of the manifold of representations.

Kant is arguing here in what he calls the regressive, or analytic, manner. He assumes that we have knowledge and hence that our

---

[54] There is an unfortunate ambiguity in the word "cognition," which may mean either the act of knowing or that which is known. This is compounded by the lack of any English equivalent for "eine Erkenntnis," literally "a knowledge." Kemp Smith uses "a mode of knowledge," and some modern epistemologists have coined the term, "knowledge-claim." In the light of Kant's own theory, the most accurate equivalent would be "a judgment," for all judgments are *prima facie* knowledge-claims, and all knowledge claims take the form of judgments. Such a usage, however, would obscure the reasoning by which Kant arrives at this important conclusion. Hence, when the words "cognition" and "knowledge" are used, the reader will be asked to determine from the context whether it is *knowing* or the *proposition known* which is intended.

[55] The connection, however, is not analytic. Hence, as Kant says many times, there must be some "third thing" which connects the subject and the predicate.

representations have an object, and then asks what that can mean. The ultimate purpose of the Deduction, of course, is to prove this assumption from some premise even more certain, but at this point he is merely trying to clarify and relate the concepts with which he is dealing. The argument of the sentence turns on the double nature of representations, which we have already explored. A manifold of representations of an object has a unity, for as Kant says in the preceding paragraph, "they must necessarily agree with one another (*untereinander übereinstimmen*)." But this unity cannot be, as we might at first suppose, the unity *in the object* of the states represented by the manifold of perceptions, for the object is hidden from us, and hence we could never have any knowledge at all. On the assumption that we do have knowledge, therefore, we must seek the unity elsewhere. If we cannot discover the unity on the side of the object, then perhaps we can discover it on the side of the subject. Perhaps, that is, the manifold has a unity simply *qua* mental contents. Or, as Kant puts it, the unity of the manifold of representations of an object is "nothing else than the formal unity of consciousness in the synthesis of the manifold of representations." The full significance of the word "formal" will be explained below. Kant is trying to suggest that the concept of an object of representations ($= x$) contributes the basic *form* of synthetic unity, and not any particular details about which properties are to be combined with which.

(*b*) It is only when we have thus produced synthetic unity in the manifold of intuition that we are in a position to say that we know the object. [*Alsdann sagen wir: wir erkennen den Gegenstand, wenn wir in dem Mannigfaltigen der Anschauung synthetische Einheit bewirkt haben.* Kemp Smith's translation is a bit loose.]

This sentence carries the argument one step further. If the unity in knowledge is a subjective unity of a manifold of perceptions, then it must be a unity which the mind itself has produced. Kant does not here defend the assertion that the unity of consciousness must be produced rather than given. Ultimately such a defense would involve the notion of conception or intelligence as active, and the analysis of synthesis as a rule-directed activity. This latter is rather hastily introduced in the next sentence.

(*c*) But this unity is impossible if the intuition cannot be generated in accordance with a rule by means of such a function of synthesis as makes the reproduction of the manifold *a priori* necessary, and renders possible a concept in which it is united.

In this one sentence, Kant throws into the argument the whole complex theory of synthesis which is expounded in the Subjective Deduction and elsewhere.[56] The general sense should be clear from the preliminary exposition of the Deduction but several points demand particular attention. The principal unclarity of the sentence is the distinction between an intuition being *generated* and *reproduced*. The proper interpretation of these two words actually involves the most far-reaching problems of Kant's philosophy. Although this is not the place to explore the issue at length, a few remarks may indicate what is at stake. Kant sometimes distinguishes between two different kinds of synthesis. *Transcendental synthesis* is performed on a manifold of pure intuition by *productive* imagination, and its outcome is the objective phenomenal world; *empirical synthesis* is performed on a manifold of empirical intuition (perceptions) by *reproductive* imagination, and its outcome is our knowledge of the phenomenal world. According to this view, which is found in the Objective Deduction of the first edition (Section 3), the syntheses are performed by different faculties of the mind and are numerically distinct. At other times, Kant makes no distinction between transcendental and empirical acts of the mind, while in the Subjective Deduction, he describes both syntheses as *reproductive*.[57] The cause of this indecision is Kant's desire to do justice to the scientific world of real empirical objects, while yet preserving his belief that those objects are products of the activity of the mind. In the sentence which we are discussing, if "generated" (*hervorgebracht*) be read as a synonym for "reproduced," then the passage can be taken either as expressing the Subjective Deduction position or else as taking no stand at all on the relation of the two types of synthesis. If it be taken to mean "produced," however, the passage must be referred to the position of the Objective Deduction. It is just this sort of ambiguity on Kant's part which makes possible such a wealth of conflicting interpretations of the Deduction.

[56] The presence of this theory of synthesis in the context of the doctrine of the transcendental object shows the impossibility of any simple dating procedure for passages of the Deduction.
[57] Cf. the discussion of Section 3, pp. 164 ff.

(*d*) Thus we think a triangle as an object, in that we are conscious of the combination of three straight lines according to a rule by which such an intuition can always be represented. This *unity of rule* determines all the manifold, and limits it to conditions which make unity of apperception possible. The concept of this unity is the representation of the object $= x$, which I think through the predicates, above mentioned, of a triangle.

The example with which Kant concludes the paragraph reveals, albeit rather cryptically, the major point of the entire passage. This is that the concept of the object $= x$ operates in conjunction with particular empirical concepts. The concept of a triangle or a body (see next paragraph) is a rule for the reproduction of perceptions, while the concept of an object of representations is merely the concept of the unity of such a rule. It is this something extra, this *unity of rule*, which gives objectivity to a manifold of representations, and thereby makes possible what we call knowledge of objects. A similar point, it will be recalled, was alluded to in the original definition of synthesis, in the Metaphysical Deduction.[58] It is explained more clearly in paragraph 12 of the present passage.

Paragraph 6 merely repeats, with a new example, the argument which has been sketched in paragraph 5. It also contains the statement which was used in the analysis of synthesis given above, namely: "a concept is always, as regards its form, something universal which serves as a rule." Kemp Smith's translation of the last sentence of the paragraph might seem to imply that the representations of impenetrability and shape follow from the representation of extension, which of course Kant would deny. The German, however, makes it clear that they are merely taken with the representation of extension, all of them following from the concept of body.

(*3*) *Transcendental apperception — paragraphs 7–9.* Kant now draws a breath and starts on a new element in his argument, viz. transcendental apperception. This extremely difficult subject will be dealt with in more detail when we come to the second-edition version of the Deduction. With respect to the present passage, the reader is referred to Kemp Smith's generally excellent treatment of it in his *Commentary*, pp. 207–212.[59]

---

[58] Cf. § 10, "The Pure Concepts of the Understanding, or Categories," paragraph 5 = A 79 = B 104.

[59] With one exception, however. Kemp Smith asserts, p. 207, that Kant was

Despite its obscurity and undeveloped character, the doctrine of transcendental apperception cannot be ignored as merely a remnant of Kant's rationalist days. It is actually a first attempt to deal with a problem with which Kant struggled until the end of his life, and which remains the most serious weakness of his system: the nature of the self. For Kant, the problem of the self is posed in a very special way. He accepts the Cartesian starting-point — the introspectively discoverable fact of thought; but he rejects the Cartesian conclusion that the self revealed through thought is better known than the material objects of which it thinks. Kant wishes to prove that our knowledge of objects is both real knowledge — the very best we can have — and knowledge only of appearances. In order to prove the first, he must deny that the self is any better known than objects, for otherwise the status of scientific knowledge is diminished, and a rational metaphysics of the self takes its place. But in order to prove the second, he must develop an elaborate theory of the activities of the self, based on an analysis of consciousness. In short, he must write an entire book about the self, while insisting at every turn that we can have no knowledge of it.

Such a dilemma in itself would be sufficient to cause Kant great difficulty but the problem is by no means limited to these epistemological and metaphysical considerations. Kant also has in his mind an elaborate ethical theory which is based upon a conception of this same self. Having limited knowledge to make place for faith, Kant must now find words to speak about the very realm of noumenal reality which his theory asserts to be beyond our reach.

In this passage Kant distinguishes between the changing contents of consciousness and the logical conditions of the unity which those contents possess. Descartes had professed to discover the source of that unity — the self itself — by a simple introspection. But Hume reported that when he looked for this self, all he ever found was "some particular perception or other, of heat or cold, light or shade, love or hatred, pain or pleasure" [*Treatise*, p. 252]. The problem, again in Hume's words, is that

unaware of Hume's theory of the empirical self. Actually, the *locus classicus* for Hume's view, in which he describes the self as a "heap or collection of different perceptions," was known to Kant through the 1772 translation of Beattie's *Essay on Truth*. Cf. my "Kant's Debt to Hume via Beattie," *Journal of the History of Ideas*, January-March, 1960.

"self or person is not any one impression, but that to which our several impressions and ideas are suppos'd to have a reference." [60] This single something, to which all mental contents are referred, is the transcendental unity of apperception.

The reader who has struggled with paragraphs 7–9 may at this point feel rather puzzled. Transcendental apperception is described as a "pure original unchangeable consciousness." Presumably then it is *someone's* consciousness. This conclusion does not rest on an unexamined supposition that consciousness is always the state of some simple substance (Descartes' mistake). It rests on Kant's own description of apperception as not merely unified, but itself a *source* of unity. Apperception is active, it does something. As Kant says in the first sentence of paragraph 10, it "forms out of [*macht aus*] all possible appearances . . . a connection." Later in the Deduction, when the theory has reached a somewhat revised stage, the unity of apperception is identified with the understanding — that is, a faculty or function of the mind [A 119]. All of this suggests that there is some being whose consciousness is thus unified, and who performs the act of making a connection among appearances. And yet it is precisely this inference which Kant denies over and over. In the Paralogisms and elsewhere he insists that we can have no knowledge of any transcendent self. Only the empirical self is knowable, and as an empirical entity its existence is dependent upon precisely the same conditions as are material objects.

At first sight, it may appear that Kant is guilty of what have lately become known as category mistakes. He says that consciousness *does* something, that a unity *is* the understanding, whereas we would expect him to say that a conscious *being* does something, and that the understanding *has* or *produces* a unity. Actually, as was suggested above, the reason for Kant's strange choice of words is his desire to mark precisely the boundary which divides the knowable from the unknowable. All that is known and knowable

[60] *Treatise*, p. 251. The reader may discern an uncommon fondness on my part for quoting Hume. The reason, beyond a liking for the elegant and compendious manner of his expression, is my conviction that Hume has been much slighted as a creative thinker, and that he has a great deal to contribute to a positive theory of knowledge. There is much in the *Treatise* which could, with suitable terminological adjustments, be fitted comfortably into the *Critique*. Though this is outside the subject of this commentary, the occasional references to Hume may stir the reader's interest further in that direction. (Cf. my "Hume's Theory of Mental Activity," *Philosophical Review*, July 1960.)

lies within the limits of consciousness. Hence the generating conditions of consciousness are unknowable, for they necessarily lie outside consciousness. Any description of those conditions must therefore refer only to their effects, which are discoverable by reflection on, or analysis of, consciousness. Transcendental activities such as synthesis must be equated with the experiential structures which they produce. Hence the unity of apperception *is* the understanding in the sense that it is all we can know about the understanding. We might say that for Kant, consciousness is like the light flowing from a flashlight. It shines everywhere save on its source, which is always hidden precisely because it is the source (a simile, needless to say, which will not bear much pressure).

Having said all this, we must remember that Kant rarely adheres to it. He has an extremely detailed theory of the nature and operations of the faculties of the mind, and does not hesitate to call upon it for support, as in the Metaphysical Deduction. What is more, Kant tells us nothing about the connection between sensibility, understanding, imagination, and the other transcendental faculties, and the observable phenomena of perception, memory and reasoning. To a considerable degree, one's final judgment on the Critical Philosophy will rest on whether one thinks a coherent theory of the self in all its facets can be drawn from the pages of the three *Critiques*.

(4) *The Deduction — paragraph 10.* Having gathered together in paragraphs 3–9 the various materials for this argument, Kant here sketches the proof that the concept of an object finds application in experience. Because of its extreme condensation, the paragraph is open to several interpretations, and this has allowed some commentators to claim that it is consistent with Kant's later views, while others, like Kemp Smith, have asserted the contrary. The central idea, which indeed is retained throughout the *Critique*, is that the subjective unity of consciousness and the objective unity of knowledge are merely two sides of the same synthetic unity of representations. This, of course, is based on the double nature of the representations, which has already been discussed. In this paragraph, however, Kant seems to claim that the concept of an object in general $= x$ is a projection or externalization of the self's immediate awareness of its own unity of act, a

unity from which the unity of knowledge flows. As thus interpreted, the doctrine is open to the criticism that it seems to make knowledge of objects dependent upon self-awareness. In later developments of this theory, Kant draws a distinction between the generative conditions of consciousness and the unities — subjective and objective — which flow from them. It then becomes possible for him to describe unity of consciousness and knowledge of objects as interdependent.[61]

The deduction contained in this paragraph is, strictly speaking, only a deduction of the concept of an object $= x$. The categories are not mentioned at all, a fact which greatly detracts from the argument. The argument may be represented by the formal proof given as Stage I in the preliminary analysis above.[62] The concept of an object $= x$ must be applicable to experience, because only by relating representations to one another by means of it can a synthetic unity of consciousness be produced.

(5) *Additional comments — paragraphs 11–12.* Kant concludes the passage with a reasonably clear statement of the implications of the preceding paragraphs. The relation between particular concepts and the concept of the object $= x$ is made unambiguously clear:

> The pure concept of this transcendental object, which in reality throughout all our knowledge is always one and the same, is what can alone confer upon all our empirical concepts in general relation to an object, that is, objective reality. This concept cannot contain any determinate intuition, and therefore refers only to that unity which must be met with in any manifold of knowledge which stands in relation to an object.

The concept is "one and the same" because it is the reflection of transcendental apperception which is "numerically identical . . . pure original unchangeable." It contains no determinate intuition because, if it did, it would be capable of giving us knowledge of the object $= x$, which as a thing-in-itself is unknowable. Hence the concept is merely the abstract form of unity of representations. As the defining characteristic of knowledge (i.e., relation to an object), it is one and the same throughout all the instances of knowledge. Notice the use of the phrase "pure concept" to apply to the concept of the transcendental object. As this term is elsewhere re-

[61] See, for example, the second-edition Refutation of Idealism, B 274–279.
[62] Cf. pp. 116–117.

served for the categories (as in the title of the Deduction chapter), its use here is one more evidence that Kant did not have the categories in mind when he wrote this passage.

Stage II — The Categories as Conditions of the Possibility of Experience. A 95–97.

In this brief passage of four paragraphs, Kant introduces the central idea that the categories are conditions of any possible experience (= consciousness). The passage is, in its teaching and language, an extension of § 14 of Section 1, which directly precedes it in the text. For this reason, Kemp Smith classifies the two together as belonging to his stage II of the Deduction. Because of Kant's decision to retain §§ 13 and 14 in the second edition, however, it seemed better to treat them separately as an introduction to the entire Deduction.

The contrast between this version of the argument and that of the transcendental object is brought out quite clearly by the first paragraph. "An *a priori* concept which did not relate to experience," says Kant, "would be only the logical form of a concept, not the concept itself through which something is thought." But this is a perfect description of the concept of an object $= x$, which "cannot contain any determinate intuition" [A 109]. The problem is that in order for knowledge to be possible, there must be an object *in experience* to be known. To say that we can only think an object through a concept for which no intuition is possible, is the same as to say that no knowledge is possible. Hence the pure concepts through which an object is thought must be such as to find application in experience. In other words, they are the categories, not the concept of an object $= x$. At this point, it is not explained what sort of thing can be both an object of knowledge and a mere appearance. Nevertheless, Kant firmly asserts the principle that in whatever sense we interpret "object," the object of knowledge must be revealed in experience.

The only paragraph which offers any difficulty is the third, in which Kant says some curious things about the "elements of all modes of *a priori* knowledge" and the nature of fictions and impossible concepts. The following commentary by Paton seems reasonable, though as he himself indicates, Kant's meaning is open to question:

Kant makes one new point. Although the categories must have this relation to experience if they are to be thoughts of an object, and even if they
are to arise in thought, nevertheless, once I possess the categories, I can invent concepts of objects which are either impossible in themselves or incapable of being given in any experience.

For example, I can invent the concept of spirit or soul, that is, the concept
of an immaterial substance possessed of reason; I do so, however, by leaving
out something which is a necessary condition of possible experience. Kant
does not tell us what is left out. I take it to be 'the permanent' which is
given in intuition. This we can find only in outer intuition, and so only in
material substances; and it is necessary, if the category of substance is to
have validity.[63]

The latter part of paragraph 4 is obviously a hasty transition
to the Subjective Deduction, which is inserted at this point. It is
not clear from what has gone before that an account of the "subjective sources" of the possibility of experience is required for the
argument.

Stage III — The Subjective Deduction. A 97–104.

The heart of Section 2 of the Deduction is Kant's detailed analysis of "the subjective sources which form the *a priori* foundation
of the possibility of experience" [A 97]. The passage actually
represents an extension beyond the doctrine of the Objective Deduction in Section 3, and according to Vaihinger was composed
during the last stages of the preparation of the *Critique*, in 1780.
Nevertheless, for simplicity of organization and commentary, it
will be dealt with here, before we go to Section 3.

The Subjective Deduction consists of two introductory paragraphs (paragraphs 5–6 of Section 2) and three subsections, ending with paragraph 2 of the third subsection. The purpose of the
passage is to spell out the several components of the process of
synthesis. Despite its points of conflict with the rest of the argument, this account is Kant's only attempt to tell us precisely what
"synthesis" means, and it is therefore deserving of our closest attention.

Preliminary Discussion. Synthesis, Kant has said, is a function of the soul "of which we are scarcely ever conscious." How,
then, are we to explore its workings? Since it is supposedly the

[63] Paton, I, 351–352.

activity which generates consciousness itself, introspection can at best reveal its products or effects. And yet, Kant cannot merely leave unexamined the key concept of his theory. Somehow he must find within experience some clues to the nature of synthesis.

His solution is to study the activities of the empirical self — the ordinary mind which imagines, reasons, remembers, and perceives — and then to ascribe a set of parallel operations to the transcendental faculties of the mind. This involves him in postulating two distinct manifolds, to which the two synthesizing processes are applied. The complications of such a view are tremendous, accounting for much that is puzzling and confusing in the Deduction. An attempt will be made to sort things out in the commentary on Section 3. For the present, let us ignore this aspect of the Subjective Deduction and confine ourselves to Kant's analysis of the stages of the synthesis.

The first step in cognition is the affection of our sensibility, which produces a manifold of intuition. This is the material of knowledge, without which our concepts are empty and void of reference. Sensibility in us is always passive, receptive. But knowledge is the assertion of judgments, which combine these sensible representations in some definite manner or other. Such judgments always assert a unity — knowledge, indeed, is precisely the discovery of the one in the many. Now the diversity of perceptions presented to the mind can only acquire a unity if the mind actively puts them together. In short, for the given manifold of intuition to become knowledge, it must be *synthesized*.

It might be noted in passing that Kant here sets himself against the widespread identification of knowing with seeing. It is common among some empiricists to speak as if the paradigm of knowledge were the case of viewing an object under optimal conditions of background, light, etc. Once the object is in place, all you do is open your eyes and look. Perception is then conceived as an internal picture-show, so that, on analogy with seeing an object, we can at least be certain of our sense-data, if nothing else. For Kant the principal mistake of this theory would be the description of knowing as passive. Since all consciousness is awareness of meanings by the use of concepts, it follows that the more passive and receptive the mind is, the less is it conscious. The highest degree of awareness comes in the act of self-reflection, when the contents of consciousness are most completely brought under concepts and made the objects of judgments.

Kant asserts that the synthesizing process has three stages, which in typical fashion he assigns to three different faculties of the mind. There must first be apprehension of the representations in intuition; then reproduction of them in imagination; and finally, recognition of the reproduced representations in a concept. Each of these syntheses, furthermore, with the possible exception of the last, takes place at both the transcendental and the empirical levels. The three subsections of the Subjective Deduction describe in order these three pairs of transcendental and empirical syntheses.

The key to the analysis, as stated in paragraph 1 of the first subsection, is that all intuitions, if they are to become part of our consciousness, must be subjected to a temporal ordering. The following quotation from the Aesthetic summarizes Kant's view:

Time is the formal *a priori* condition of all appearances whatsoever . . . since all representations, whether they have for their objects outer things or not, belong, in themselves, as determinations of the mind, to our inner state; and since this inner state stands under the formal condition of inner intuition, and so belongs to time, time is an *a priori* condition of all appearance whatsoever. [A 34]

Save for the passage which we are now discussing, Kant makes almost no reference in the Deduction to the temporal form of consciousness. The Analytic of Principles, on the other hand, is concerned with little else. As we shall see, it is by drawing out to the fullest the implications of time-consciousness that Kant eventually succeeds in completing the argument of the Deduction. For the present, however, he carries the analysis only far enough to explain more precisely the nature of synthesis.

The central ideas of the theory of three-fold synthesis have already been explained above, and the reader is urged to review that account before going into the textual analysis.[64]

Analysis of the Text: (1) The Synthesis of Apprehension in Intuition. As described in this passage, the synthesis of apprehension in intuition precedes the synthesis of reproduction in imagination. It is the process whereby a given manifold of intuition, having a temporal ordering, is first held together as *a manifold*. A total

---

[64] See stage III of the Argument, pp. 120 ff.

chaos has no cognizable form whatever. As soon as we call it "chaos" we impart to it the bare form of a something. In other words, we prepare to think about it, focus attention on it, draw a line around it. This first and most fundamental act is the synthesis of apprehension, so called because by means of it we first apprehend the manifold of intuition.

Kant places this synthesis first because of his conviction that cognition must proceed from sense to imagination to understanding. As we shall see in the chapter on Schematism, Kant treats imagination as the faculty which mediates between intuition and conception, bringing together these two absolutely different elements of cognition. In the Objective Deduction, this becomes the view that imagination, as the faculty of synthesis, mediates between sensibility, the faculty of intuition, and understanding, the faculty of concepts. Here the single synthesis of imagination is expanded into three syntheses. Kant still preserves the pattern, however, and so it is that the synthesis of apprehension must come first.

Actually, a careful reading of the text reveals that the synthesis of reproduction is a condition of the synthesis of apprehension, for the way in which the manifold is "run through, and held together" [A 99] *is precisely by reproducing it*. Hence the synthesis of reproduction should have been placed first in the three-fold synthesis. Because of this complication, no mention was made of the synthesis of apprehension in the preliminary exposition, above.

This little confusion, and a variety of other ambiguities, hesitations, contradictions, and obscurities in the Analytic, all stem from Kant's failure to decide once and for all how much of the structure of experience is ascribable to intuition and how much to synthesis. In the Aesthetic it all seemed quite simple: the spatio-temporal form of appearances is due to the passive conditions of sensibility, and the connections of those appearances are due to the active conditions of understanding. In the Analytic, however, Kant becomes increasingly aware of the links between the forms of sensibility — especially time — and the forms of understanding. Ultimately, the categories are seen to be nothing more nor less than *modes* of *time-consciousness*. The closer analysis of the unity of consciousness also reveals the degree to which even bare perception depends upon the synthetic activities of imagination. By the time

we have reached the Analogies, the neat dichotomy between in-
tuition-Aesthetic and understanding-Analytic has broken down.
The result is an immeasurable improvement of the Critical Philosophy, but at the same time a hopeless confusion of the role of
intuition in cognition. It is not surprising, therefore, to discover
that most of the revisions in the second edition deal with the problem of inner sense.[65]

There is only one sentence in the Synthesis of Apprehension
subsection which calls for special comment. In the second paragraph, Kant says:

> Every intuition contains in itself a manifold which can be represented as
> a manifold only in so far as the mind distinguishes the time in the sequence
> of one impression upon another; for each representation, *in so far as it is
> contained in a single moment*, can never be anything but absolute unity.

Kant appears to think that at any one moment in time I can only
perceive one simple sensation and no more. Such a view, however,
would not only be wrong, but also totally out of harmony with
the rest of the *Critique*. Paton offers the following explanation:

> [Kant's] view is more plausible, if we take it as expressing a limit reached
> by analysis. . . . [I]f we were to abstract from the time-element in our
> consciousness, and ignore the continuous successive synthesis by which we
> hold together what is given at different times in different places, we should
> be left with something which has no parts outside one another, or before
> and after one another.[66]

This interpretation is equally unintelligible, or so it seems to me.
I suggest that when Kant asserts that "each representation, *in so
far as it is contained in a single moment*, can never be anything
but absolute unity," he undoubtedly means that we could never

---

[65] The problem which Kant faces is a perennial one in philosophy. If one distinguishes a formal and a material element in cognition, and if one identifies the
formal with the conceptual, then it will always appear paradoxical to say anything
about the material element. Whatever one says will be expressed by means of
concepts, and hence will fall on the side of the formal. Eventually, the material
becomes ineffable and indeterminate. The next step, which is frequently taken by
the disciples of such a philosophy, is to drop out the material element altogether,
since it plays no assignable role. Thus Kant's theory tends to degenerate into an
idealism, *à la* Hegel or Fichte, in which the mind generates its own world without
the aid of a given manifold of intuition. An historical parallel to Kant's theory
can be found in Aristotle's doctrine of form and matter. The distinction is pressed
until Aristotle arrives at prime matter, which has no specifiable characteristics.
How such an un-thing as prime matter can serve to individuate substances is one
of the mysteries of ancient philosophy.

[66] Paton, I, 358.

know a representation as diverse in a single moment. In order to know a diversity of representations, even if they are given as simultaneous, the mind must run over them *one after another.* If I am presented with a variegated visual field, for example, I keep recalling it in memory as I say to myself: "There is a green patch and a red circle and a blue patch and a black dot." Such a process takes time, even though it is the analysis of a perception which was presented at one instant.

(2) *The Synthesis of Reproduction in Imagination.* In this sub-section, the longest by far of the three, Kant repeats the arguments concerning the affinity of the manifold, fleshing them out by appeal to the temporal character of association.[67] A suggestion of a distinction between association and objective affinity is to be found in the notion of a transcendental synthesis of a manifold of pure intuitions. This however is not developed, and I shall not consider it here.

Paragraph 1 contains several of Kant's all-too-infrequent examples. The point which they are designed to prove is obscure, however, for here as elsewhere Kant shifts rapidly from the regressive to the progressive modes of exposition. Consider the example of the cinnabar (which, incidentally, is an ore of mercury). Kant says: "If cinnabar were sometimes red, sometimes black, sometimes light, sometimes heavy, . . . my empirical imagination would never find opportunity when representing red colour to bring to mind heavy cinnabar." Hence, he concludes, "we must assume a pure transcendental synthesis of imagination as conditioning the very possibility of all experience." Kant here starts from the assumption that we do have knowledge of phenomena like cinnabar, and infers the existence of a transcendental synthesis as a condition of such knowledge. He is therefore reasoning regressively, assuming what he hopes to prove. In the very next sentences (the second half of paragraph 2), he turns around and argues progressively. Briefly, his reasoning is as follows: if I did not reproduce the representations as I ran over the manifold, I could not even apprehend them as a whole; reproduction in imagination, so far from being merely an accidental and *a posteri-*

---

[67] For a discussion of affinity and the problem of an objective ground for association, see the analysis of stage IV of the Deduction, below. The subject makes its appearance in A 112–113.

ori function of the empirical self, is thus actually one of the transcendental conditions of the possibility of consciousness in general; so we can always be certain that our representations will exhibit associations which permit the formation of rules of reproduction. This proof, as I have shown below, is inadequate.

(3) *The Synthesis of Recognition in a Concept.* The argument of this passage has already been explained in the preliminary exposition of the Deduction. It should be noticed that Kant does *not* distinguish transcendental and empirical syntheses of recognition, as he does for the other two syntheses. The reason, as I remarked in connection with the Metaphysical Deduction, is that Kant identifies concepts and consciousness. He is hesitant, therefore, to ascribe a synthesis of recognition in a concept to the transcendental realm, which is presumably outside the limits of consciousness. Ideally, what Kant needs to complete his analysis is a pure *a priori* consciousness, which stands to empirical consciousness as the transcendental syntheses of apprehension and reproduction stand to their empirical counterparts. Such a consciousness is provided by the doctrine of transcendental apperception, and this is undoubtedly one of the reasons why Kant decided to insert at this point the theory of the transcendental object $= x$.

Stage IV of the Deduction: Kant's Answer to Hume. A 110–114.

Thus far the development of the Deduction argument has been determined entirely by what we may call the Herz considerations — that is to say, the difficulties and inadequacies of the *Dissertation* doctrine which Kant set forth in the 1772 letter to Marcus Herz. As we have seen, however, these form only one of the problems which Kant struggled to solve during the '70's. The second great problem was that posed by Hume's critique of *a priori* knowledge in general, and particularly by his devastating analysis of causal inference. In this passage, Kant finally introduces this long-deferred topic and takes the first steps towards a solution. As if in recognition of his debt to Hume, Kant confines the discussion to causation, even though later on he systematically broadens it to encompass all twelve categories. As the text is reasonably clear, I shall combine the general discussion with such close analysis as is necessary.

Hume's attack on causal inference was designed to prove that both particular causal judgments and the causal maxim itself lack any rational justification. His argument, as we have seen, depends on two principles: that what is distinguishable is separable, and that what is conceivable is possible. From the first principle it follows that since the impression of an object is distinguishable from the idea of its supposed cause, the two can be separated, and one imagined without the other. The second principle then allows us to infer that the object can at least possibly occur without its "cause," and hence that the two are not *necessarily* connected. So too, the concepts of event and cause are distinguishable, hence separable. But then the contrary of the proposition, "Every event has a cause," is conceivable, and so possible. Hence, the proposition itself is not a necessary one.[68] Having proved to his satisfaction that causal inferences are logically indemonstrable, Hume goes on to ask where they come from. In Kant's language, he undertakes to answer *quid facti*, having disposed of the question *quid juris*. His answer is the theory of association, according to which a constant conjunction of like objects creates a mental habit, and also generates an internal impression of necessary connection. The following paraphrase from Beattie's *Essay on Truth*, which Kant undoubtedly read, gives the skeleton of the theory quite adequately:

When we think we perceive our mind acting on matter, or one piece of matter acting upon another, we do in fact perceive only two objects or events contiguous and successive, the second of which is always found in experience to follow the first; but that we never perceive, either by external sense, or by consciousness, that power, energy, or efficacy, which connects the one event with the other. By observing that the two events do always accompany each other, the imagination acquires a habit of going readily from the first to the second, and from the second to the first; and hence we are led to conceive a kind of necessary connection between them. But in fact there is neither necessity nor power in the objects we consider, but only in the mind that considers them; and even in the mind, this power

[68] There are tremendously significant differences between these two lines of argument, though Hume himself treats them as similar. To say that fire is distinguishable from heat and "event" from "cause," is to use the word "distinguish" in two rather dissimilar senses. The first leans heavily on a notion of imagination, while the second seems to involve definition and logical consistency. This confusion on Hume's part is compounded by the fact that his theory of association *only* explains particular causal inferences. He never gives in the *Treatise* an associative or other explanation of the belief in the causal maxim.

or necessity is nothing but a determination of the fancy, acquired by habit, to pass from the idea of an object to that of its usual attendant.[69]

Kant accepts Hume's criticisms of the rationalists. In his language this amounts to saying that the causal maxim is synthetic, not analytic. He is also prepared to accept, or at least he has no desire to quarrel with, Hume's account of the psychological mechanisms of association. What he wants to prove is that the causal maxim is a necessary truth despite the fact that it is not a mere truth of logic; in short, that it is a synthetic judgment *a priori*. The materials for this proof are the arguments already developed in the earlier stages of the Deduction.

In the first three paragraphs of the passage, Kant recapitulates the theory of *a priori* conditions of experience thus far developed. While doing so, he slightly alters several points in order to prepare the way for the discussion of Hume's criticisms. The most important matter concerns the question whether perceptions could possibly enter consciousness without conforming to the categories. In § 13, it will be recalled, Kant appeared to state that it would be possible. He said there that "appearances might very well be so constituted that the understanding should not find them to be in accordance with the conditions of its unity" [A 90]. Using the same example which occurs in the present passage, he went on to say that under such circumstances, the concept of cause and effect might find no application, and hence be "empty, null, and meaningless." Nevertheless, he added, making his meaning unambiguously clear, "appearances would present objects to our intuition."

Now, the very heart of the entire Deduction is the claim that perceptions must conform to the categories, and thus give knowledge of objects, in order even to be admitted to the unity of consciousness. In Kant's view, sense-datum languages and the uninterpreted given, those foundation-stones of contemporary phenomenalism, are sheer impossibilities. As I indicated in the preliminary exposition of the Deduction, Kant claims to prove that the validity of the categories is a necessary condition of consciousness itself.

It is clear, therefore, that Kant must give up the position taken in § 13. He does so in a very finely graded series of steps stretch-

---

[69] Quoted in my "Kant's Debt to Hume via Beattie," p. 119.

ing throughout the second and third sections of the Deduction in A. The almost wistful tenacity with which Kant clings to the notion of an unsynthesized manifold, despite its obvious incompatibility with his central argument, suggests some deep philosophical problem which has not been resolved. In fact, as I shall demonstrate in my discussion of the problem of inner sense, that problem does exist, and Kant seems never to have successfully dealt with it.

The question of the possibility of an unsynthesized manifold is so important that it might be well to break the flow of the commentary here and deal with it systematically. I shall assemble a series of passages in which we can observe Kant slowly changing his mind. The end result, reached in Section 3 of the Deduction, is that no perception could ever enter consciousness save under the condition of having been synthesized according to the categories. We can distinguish five separate steps in the transition.

(1) In § 13, as we have seen, it is flatly stated that an unsynthesized manifold is possible:

Objects may, therefore, appear to us without their being under the necessity of being related to the functions of understanding; and understanding need not, therefore, contain their *a priori* conditions. . . . For appearances can certainly be given in intuition independently of functions of the understanding. . . . Appearances might very well be so constituted that the understanding should not find them to be in accordance with the conditions of its unity. Everything might be in such confusion that, for instance, in the series of appearances nothing presented itself which might yield a rule of synthesis and so answer to the concept of cause and effect. This concept would then be altogether empty, null, and meaningless. But since intuition stands in no need whatsoever of the functions of thought, appearances would none the less present objects to our intuition. [A 89-91]

(2) In § 14, the first seeds of doubt are sown. Kant has just finished saying that "understanding need not contain" the *a priori* conditions of objects of experience. Now, however, he says that in fact understanding does contain such conditions, in the form of the categories:

[The categories] relate of necessity and *a priori* to objects of experience, for the reason that only by means of them can any object whatsoever of experience be thought. The transcendental deduction of all *a priori* concepts has thus a principle according to which the whole enquiry must be directed, namely, that they must be recognized as *a priori* conditions of the possibility of experience, whether of the intuition which is to be met with in it or of the thought. Concepts which yield the objective ground of the possibility of experience are for this very reason necessary. [A 93–94]

(3) A decisive step is taken away from the initial position in subsection 4 of Section 2, "Preliminary explanation of the possibility of the categories," which I have called the fourth stage of the Deduction. In paragraph 2, Kant asserts:

Unity of synthesis according to empirical concepts would be altogether accidental, if these latter were not based on a transcendental ground of unity. Otherwise it would be possible for appearances to crowd in upon the soul, and yet to be such as would never allow of experience. Since connection in accordance with universal and necessary laws would be lacking, all relation of knowledge to objects would fall away. The appearances might, indeed, constitute intuition without thought [*gedankenlose Anschauung*, literally "thought-less intuition"], but not knowledge; and consequently would be for us as good as nothing. [A 111]

We still cannot be certain whether Kant thinks that we would be conscious of this thought-less intuition. With the tantalizing phrase, "as good as nothing," he pulls back from the flat statement that the perceptions would not enter consciousness.

(4) Two paragraphs later, Kant returns to the subject, and again leaves the impression that we cannot be conscious of unsynthesized perceptions, without however actually saying so.

Without such unity [of the synthesis according to the categories] . . . [no] unity of consciousness would be met with in the manifold of perceptions. These perceptions would not then belong to any experience, consequently would be without an object, merely a blind play of representations, less even than a dream. [A 112]

(5) In the Objective Deduction in A, some ten pages after the last passage just quoted, Kant finally states in absolutely unambiguous language that we cannot be conscious of an unsynthesized manifold.[70] Speaking of the distinction between subjective association and objective connection or affinity, Kant writes:

Now if this unity of association had not also an objective ground which makes it impossible that appearances should be apprehended by the imagination otherwise than under the condition of a possible synthetic unity of this apprehension, it would be entirely accidental that appearances should fit into a connected whole of human knowledge. For even though we should

[70] See below, pp. 179–180, for an analysis of the passage.

have the power of associating perceptions, it would remain entirely undetermined and accidental whether they would themselves be associable;
and should they not be associable, there might exist a multitude of perceptions, and indeed an entire sensibility, in which much empirical consciousness would arise in my mind, but in a state of separation, and without
belonging to a consciousness of myself. This, however, is impossible. *For it
is only because I ascribe all perceptions to one consciousness (original apperception) that I can say of all perceptions that I am conscious of them.*

[A 121-122. Emphasis added.]

In keeping with the principle of interpretation which I have
adopted, I shall not attempt to judge whether this progression reveals a parallel alteration in Kant's thoughts or a chronology of
composition. It is significant, however, that the completely un-
ambivalent statement comes in a passage in which Kant is presenting the argument of the Deduction, for that argument will not
work unless the categories are viewed as necessary conditions of
any consciousness whatsoever.

In § 4, the confusion is compounded by Kant's cavalier use of
his own special terms. In the second sentence of paragraph 2, for
example, "experience" clearly means "empirical knowledge," as
on Kant's definition [B 147] it should. But in the beginning of
the first sentence of paragraph 3, it is used as a synonym for "consciousness." Since this latter sense is required for the argument,
Kant may very well have intended it here. The confusion is especially unfortunate, for the Deduction turns on the argument that
empirical knowledge is a necessary condition of consciousness itself (i.e., that we can deduce the possibility of empirical knowledge *from* the mere fact of consciousness). If Kant is going to use
"experience" sometimes to mean empirical knowledge and sometimes to mean consciousness, his argument will take the form of
the tautology that "experience is a necessary condition of experience." There are quite a few passages in the *Critique* which have
an apparent air of triviality for just this reason.

Paragraph 4 introduces the example of causation. The concept
of a cause is said to be "nothing but a synthesis (of that which
follows in the time-series, with other appearances) *according to
concepts.*" The full-scale discussion of causation in the Analogies
makes it clear that Kant agrees with the so-called regularity theory
of causation. In so far as appearances are concerned, regular suc-

cession is the only relation common to all instances of causal influence.[71]

Finally, in paragraph 5, Kant prepares to answer Hume, without however mentioning him by name. The progression of thought is somewhat confusing, for Kant appears to use the very arguments which Hume had discovered and employed in his critique of the rationalists. Thus, Kant points out that "experience does indeed show that one appearance customarily follows upon another, but not that this sequence is necessary." Compare this with the following statement in the *Enquiry Concerning Human Understanding*, from which Kant drew his knowledge of Hume's philosophy: "When we look about us towards external objects . . . we are never able . . . to discover any power or necessary connexion; any quality, which binds the effect to the cause, and renders the one an infallible consequence of the other. We only find, that one does actually, in fact, follow the other [*Enquiry*, p. 63]. The two statements make the same point.

Kant goes on to assert that the empirical rule of association — the constant conjunction of cause and effect — must itself rest on some objective ground. In effect Kant says to Hume: You are right to claim that necessity is not given in the succession of appearances, but you are wrong to conclude that therefore the only necessity is the subjective, accidental feeling of necessity produced by the habit of association. That very association is only possible because it is grounded in an objective affinity. The perceptions of flame and heat are associated in experience because the states which they represent are united *in the object*. This is why we *must* conjoin them in our judgments. What remains, then, is to explain *how* it can be that appearances "stand and *must* stand under unchanging laws."

The most natural reaction to this paragraph is to turn against Kant his complaint about Beattie and others, that "they were ever taking for granted that which [Hume] doubted, and demonstrating with zeal . . . that which he never thought of doubting." [72] First Kant insists that necessity is not given in experience — which Hume never doubted — and then he takes for granted

---

[71] It is a bit more complicated than this. See the discussion of the Second Analogy, below.

[72] *Prolegomena* (tr. Beck), p. 6.

that there is more to causal necessity than a habit of association —
which Hume most vigorously denied. The trouble, here as elsewhere in the *Critique*, is that Kant mixes up the regressive and
progressive methods of exposition. He is not going to show *how*
appearances stand under unchanging laws; he is going to show
that they do and must. And this really will be an answer to Hume,
who only professes to account for our belief, while denying that
it can be given a proof.

The proof is stated in the sixth paragraph. It follows directly
from the arguments of paragraphs 1–4. Appearances, in order to be
anything for us, must enter into consciousness, and hence be bound
up in a synthetic unity with all other appearances. This can come
about only if appearances submit themselves to the *a priori* conditions of synthetic unity, namely, the categories. Now Kant concludes:

> The representation of a universal condition according to which a certain
> manifold can be posited in uniform fashion is called a *rule*, and, when it
> *must* be so posited, a *law*. Thus all appearances stand in thoroughgoing
> connection according to necessary laws, and therefore in a transcendental
> affinity, of which the empirical is a mere consequence.

The formal proof of the affinity of the manifold is merely a
revision of the argument of stage III. It can be stated in the following manner:

FOURTH VERSION OF THE DEDUCTION

To Prove: All appearances stand in thoroughgoing connection according
to necessary laws.

Proof

1. All the contents of my consciousness are bound up in a unity. [Premise]
2. The only way to introduce synthetic unity into a manifold of contents
   of consciousness is by reproducing it in imagination according to a rule.
   [Cf. Third Version of the Deduction]
3. The categories, taken as a whole, constitute the most general *a priori*
   rules of synthesis. [Cf. Third Version of the Deduction]
4. If all the contents of my consciousness are bound up in a unity, then
   they have been synthesized according to the categories. [2, 3]
5. But, by 1, 4, and *modus ponens:*
   The manifold of contents of my consciousness must have been synthesized according to the categories,
   which is to say,

6. The manifold of contents of my consciousness must have been posited in uniform fashion according to a rule. [5 and 3]

7. But the representation of a universal condition according to which a certain manifold *must* be posited in uniform fashion is a *law*. [A 113]

8. Therefore, by 6 and 7,

All appearances (contents of consciousness) stand in thoroughgoing connection according to necessary laws. Q.E.D.

Thus Kant refutes Hume.

Analysis of Stage IV: Has Kant Answered Hume?

The argument of stage IV looks very much like an answer to Hume. If we assume for the moment that its several steps are valid, then Hume must apparently confess that his sceptical doubts have been removed for even he cannot deny the premise of the proof, that he is conscious. However, if we examine the proof more closely, and then go back to the arguments of the *Enquiry* and the *Treatise*, we discover that the matter is a bit more complicated than it seems.

Hume actually casts doubt upon several distinct philosophical propositions which require separate justification. To be sure, these propositions all refer to causal inference, and they are related to one another quite closely, but it is still necessary to avoid confusing them. One of the propositions concerns the supposed necessity of connection between cause and effect. Hume pointed out that when we examine pairs of events or objects which are said to be causally connected, we find nothing more in the objective situation than a constant conjunction of resembling pairs. To these repeated relations of contiguity and succession he gave the name *association*. But obviously association by itself does not exhaust the notion of causal connection, for frequently we refuse to assert that repeatedly conjoined events are so related.[73] Hence we must locate the "necessity of connexion" elsewhere — in a subjective habit of mind induced by the constant conjunction, says Hume.

But even if we give up the attempt to discover some *objective* distinction between mere association and necessary connection, we might still be able to rely upon past associations as a clue to future

[73] To cite a famous example, the noon whistle at a factory does not cause the departure of the 12:01 train from a nearby station, even though they may be so conjoined daily for years.

ones, and thereby certify our causal inferences.[74] To do so we must appeal to some form of the principle of the uniformity of nature, but as Hume quite quickly showed, this principle falls victim to the same criticisms which have refuted the claims for necessity of connection. In part 2 of Section IV of the *Enquiry* he writes:

These two propositions are far from being the same, *I have found that such an object has always been attended with such an effect,* and *I foresee, that other objects, which are, in appearance, similar, will be attended with similar effects.* I shall allow, if you please, that the one proposition may justly be inferred from the other: I know, in fact, that it always is inferred. But if you insist that the inference is made by a chain of reasoning, I desire you to produce that reasoning. [*Enquiry*, p. 34]

Thus Hume can be viewed as issuing two challenges to the defenders of causal inference. Taking them in reverse order, inasmuch as the second is a weaker challenge than the first, they are: (1) to prove that the observable associations of events are invariable and universal, and hence constitute a sound basis for inferring the future from the past; and (2) to explain the difference between mere association and necessary connection, and to prove that every event has a necessary connection with some other which is its cause.

I think it is fair to say that Kant has met the first challenge with the argument of the Deduction as it is stated in the fourth version. All the representations of consciousness are there demonstrated to stand in thoroughgoing, or universal, connection according to rules, which is to say that they are bound together by universal associations.

Kant also believes that he has met the second challenge, which he describes in the Deduction as the problem of the *affinity of the manifold*. The conclusion of the proof is that "all appearances stand in thoroughgoing connection according to necessary laws." But in a curious way, Kant has actually proved too much by his argument. Every representation, it now turns out, is bound up in necessary connection with other representations, and this seems to be the only sort of connection possible. In short, Kant appears to

[74] It may not yet be entirely clear that these two propositions are distinct. Rather than go into the matter more deeply here, I will leave this important point to be clarified below, in the analysis of the Second Analogy. Hume himself seems not to have appreciated the distinction, probably because of his deliberate confusion of objects and perceptions. Cf. *Treatise*, p. 202.

have eliminated altogether the category of subjective association, just as Hume had attempted to eliminate the category of necessary (objective) connection.

This will not do, however. What Kant needs to be able to explain is the *distinction* between mere association and necessary connection. He must show that such a distinction exists within the bounds of experience, and that some subjective associations are backed up by, or "grounded in," objective connections. He does not want to prove that all subjective associations are so grounded, of course, for in fact some repeated associations of perceptions are merely accidental and do not reveal causal connections. Kant's problem, it should be noted, is to explain the difference between grounded and ungrounded association, *not* to give rules for telling which associations in particular are which.

Suggestions of a possible line of development have already appeared in the distinction between transcendental and empirical syntheses, which is first broached in the Subjective Deduction, and then is echoed in the penultimate paragraph of Section 2.[75] The full working out of this new addition to theory is reserved for Section 3, the Objective Deduction. In the Second Analogy, however, we shall find Kant giving up the doctrine of transcendental synthesis, and proposing instead a new and more satisfactory distinction between association and objective connection.

SECTION 3 — THE OBJECTIVE DEDUCTION

Preliminary Exposition

We saw in analyzing stage IV of the Deduction (Section 2, subsection 4) that Kant had failed to explain the notion of objective affinity. He sought to distinguish his view from Hume's by asserting that the subjective associations of perception are backed up by an objective connection in the (empirical) object. But his argument succeeded only in establishing that all representations are bound up in necessary connections. This conclusion, while a considerable advance over Hume, falls short of Kant's goal.[76] He still

---

[75] "Thus all appearances stand in thoroughgoing connection according to necessary laws, *and therefore in a transcendental affinity, of which the empirical is a mere consequence.*" [A 113–114. Emphasis added.]

[76] It might be pointed out that Hume comes extraordinarily close to a view like Kant's in several passages of the *Treatise.* After accounting for our beliefs in

needs some way of distinguishing subjective from objective con-⟩
nection.

This problem is actually only one facet of a much larger issue
with which Kant comes to grips in the Analytic, namely, the
nature and status of the phenomenal world of science. Kant's
original aim, when he worked out the compromise theory of the
Dissertation, was to reconcile the claims of metaphysics and natural
science. He did so by degrading the objects of science to the status
of appearances, while assigning metaphysics to the domain of reality. Appearances, or phenomena, were said to be conditioned by
the forms of sensibility (space and time), and were thus representations. Their precise status was obscured by Kant's assertion
that they were caused by noumena, and hence in some sense "had
objects," even if they gave no knowledge of objects. The following passage from the *Dissertation* captures perfectly Kant's
ambiguity:

> But although phenomena are, properly, appearances (*species*), not ideas
> (*ideae*), of things, and express no internal and absolute quality of the objects,
> the knowledge of them is none the less quite genuine knowledge. For, in
> the first place, so far as they are sensual concepts or apprehensions, they
> bear witness, as being caused, to the presence of an object — which is op-
> posed to idealism. On the other hand, to take judgments about what is
> known by sense, the truth of a judgment consists in the agreement of its
> predicate with the given subject. But the concept of the subject, so far as
> it is a phenomenon, can be given only by its relation to the sensitive faculty
> of knowledge; and it is by the same faculty that sensitively observable
> predicates are also given. Hence it is clear that the representations of sub-
> ject and of predicate arise according to common laws, and so allow of a
> perfectly true knowledge.[77]

When Kant came to the conclusion that the noumenal world was
absolutely unknowable, the world of phenomena was, as it were,
promoted. Kant's task now became the construction of a the-

---

causal inference and in the existence of bodies by appeal to an assortment of
mental propensities, Hume writes: "In order to justify myself, I must distinguish
in the imagination betwixt the principles which are permanent, irresistable, and
universal; such as the customary transition from causes to effects, and from effects
to causes: And the principles, which are changeable, weak, and irregular; such as
those I have just now taken notice of. The former are the foundation of all our
thoughts and actions, so that upon their removal human nature must immediately
perish and go to ruin" [*Treatise*, p. 225]. These universal principles are, it turns
out, propensities to reproduce perceptions in imagination. Their function is re-
markably like that of the categories.
[77] *Dissertation*, § 11.

oretical underpinning for physical science. To do this it was necessary to demonstrate the possibility of empirical knowledge, and to ascertain the status of the objects of knowledge. In the process, needless to say, he did not want to explain science *away*. This was the fault he found with Hume and Berkeley. Each, in analyzing the nature of empirical knowledge, seemed to arrive at the conclusion that empirical knowledge was impossible.

Now an essential characteristic of science and of empirical knowledge in general is *objectivity*. Again and again Kant drives this home as he rejects Hume's "merely subjective necessity" [B 5] or says that Berkeley "degraded bodies to mere illusion" [B 71] through failing to ascribe "objective reality" [B 70] to space and time. But the term "objective" has two very different meanings which Kant himself never clearly distinguished. In the first sense, "objective" may be taken to mean "having to do with objects." The world is conceived as a collection of independent material things, literally outside the mind of an observer or knower. In contrast with objects are mental contents, inside the mind of the knowing subject and therefore subjective. The fundamental distinction is drawn between object and subject. Science deals with objects, not with mental contents. Its general propositions describe the relations and characteristics of material objects and are therefore "objective."

In the second sense, "objective" denotes not the status of material objects but the characteristics of our knowledge. A body of propositions is said to be objective if it asserts truths which are necessary and universal. Knowledge, unlike mere fancy and conjecture, conforms to an independent standard; it is of an object whose nature we do not determine arbitrarily. Hence we can speak of our knowledge-claims as possessing truth or falsehood, whereas imaginative fantasies can only be labeled interesting, suggestive, or distasteful. On such a view of objectivity, no presupposition is made concerning the nature of the anchor to which knowledge is fixed. Although a copy-theory might suggest itself most naturally as an account of the relation between representations and their objects, other analyses can equally well preserve the defining characteristics, necessity and universality. In the earlier stages of the development of the *Critique*, Kant was concerned principally with the second sense of objectivity, i.e., necessity and universality. For this reason he allowed himself to make statements which have a very strong subjectivist tone. The following examples, selected from the Aesthetic and the Dialectic, explain why the first reviewers of the *Critique* saw in it a version of Berkeley's idealism:

Matter [is not] a thing in itself, but merely a species of representations in us.
[A 360]

But this space and this time, and with them all appearances, are not in themselves *things;* they are nothing but representations, and cannot exist outside our mind. [A 492]

Appearances . . . cannot exist in themselves, but only in us. [A 42]

Neither bodies nor motions are anything outside us; both alike are mere representations in us; and it is not, therefore, the motion of matter that produces representations in us; the motion itself is representation only, as also is the matter which makes itself known in this way. [A 387]

Nevertheless, the similarity to idealism is only apparent. Material objects are not reduced to mere internal perceptions. Rather, both external objects and the self are considered as products of the same mental activity. The internal time-order of consciousness is a product of synthesis no less than the causal and substantial order of physical objects. It is this fact, demonstrated by the Transcendental Deduction, that provides Kant with his Refutation of Idealism. Contrary to the idealistic contention that the existence of the self is immediately evident and undeniable, while the existence of objects is problematic or even illusory, Kant argues that "both are in the same position" [A 38 = B 55]. As he says in the Paralogisms:

in the connection of experience matter, as substance in the appearance, is really given to outer sense, just as the thinking "I," also as substance in the appearance, is given to inner sense. [A 379]

As we have seen, this theory does not explain the nature of objective affinity. In order to distinguish subjective association from objective connection, it seemed necessary for Kant to reinstate the material object as an entity independent of our perceptions. We can account for the complications and innovations introduced in the Objective Deduction by reference to this problem alone, and for the purpose of explaining the Analytic, it might be sufficient to go no further. However, there is a second problem which looms larger and larger in Kant's later work, in response to which he drew out the implications of the Objective Deduction position. As this line of thought is one of the major trends in the *Critique*, it is worth while pausing for a bit to examine it.

The problem to which I refer is that of explaining the physiological facts of perception in terms of the theory that objects are merely logical constructs. Kant believed quite firmly that perceptions are the effects of an interaction between physical objects and the sense organs.[78] Erich Adickes, in his study of Kant's theory of "double affection," has gathered together some of the many passages in which reference is made to the physiology of perception.[79] In the *Critique* he cites

Colors are not properties of the bodies of the intuition of which they are attached, but only modifications of the sense of sight, which is affected in a certain manner by light. [A 28]

as well as passages in B 124, A 115, A 96, B 145, B 208, B 209, B 260, and B 520. With reference to B 208–09, Adickes writes:

In both cases [the first and second edition Anticipations of Perception] bodies around us in space are not complexes of sensations, but objects which stand over independently against sensations; they are not put together out of sensations, but rather are causes of sensations.[80]

As Adickes repeatedly insists,[81] we must keep in mind that empirical objects are the empirical causes of perception. It is not the Transcendental Object or the thing-in-itself which causes the manifold of intuition in inner sense, but rocks and trees and books, interacting with eyes, ears, and noses. It is easy to see why Kant thought this view inconsistent with his earlier theory of mental activity, according to which perceptions are the components of physical objects. What distinguishes a random collection of perceptions from an object is the existence of a rule for the reproduction of the object-perceptions. But if a complex of perceptions is to be understood as the *cause* of the selfsame perceptions, we are led to the apparently impossible conclusion that something is both cause and effect of itself. For example, my visual perception of a table would be part of the table, for a table is simply a manifold of empirical intuition (perceptions) ordered by a rule in certain ways.

[78] For a more detailed discussion of Kant's views, see the analysis of the Anticipations of Perception, below.

[79] Cf. Adickes, *Kants Lehre von der Doppelten Affektion Unseres Ich*, pp. 6–8.

[80] Adickes, pp. 7–8.

[81] *Ibid.*, p. 18.

However, as the perception is the effect of the action of the table upon my eyes, it would be an effect of itself.

These anomalies, added to the problem of affinity and Kant's always powerful attachment to a realistic interpretation of natural science, induced him to alter his theory. He sought a way of preserving the distinction between unconditioned reality and conditioned experience, while further allowing a distinction, within the realm of experience, between perceptions and objects. In his own terms, he wished to distinguish the transcendentally real (things-in-themselves), the empirically real (objects), and the empirically ideal (perceptions). The means to this end was the theory which Adickes calls *double affection*. It appears explicitly and unambiguously only in the working papers which Kant left at his death, now published by Adickes as Kant's *Opus Postumum*. In what follows, I have relied heavily upon the discussions of Adickes, Kemp Smith, and Weldon.[82]

Kant proposes to identify empirical objects with appearances, and to classify perceptions as representations of appearances (or, as Kant says in the *Opus Postumum*, "appearances of appearances"). But this raises again the problem which the whole *Critique* is designed to solve, for the empirical objects, relative to their perceptual representations, are independent entities. Hence it is impossible to explain how a synthesis of perceptions can yield *knowledge, unless the objects themselves are also products of a mental synthesis.* This is in fact the line which Kant's argument takes. The empirical objects must be subject to all those conditions of sensi-

---

[82] A considerable portion of Kemp Smith's *Commentary* is devoted to distinguishing the earlier and later versions of Kant's theory, which he labels respectively the Subjectivist and Phenomenalist doctrines. He identifies the Phenomenalist theory with the true Critical teaching, relegating much of the *Critique* to the status of pre-Critical remnants on the grounds of its Subjectivist leanings. The difference between the two, very crudely, is that Subjectivism allows for the existence only of things-in-themselves and appearances (= representations), while Phenomenalism maintains the three-fold classification of noumena, empirical objects, and perceptions described above. Although I have drawn on Kemp Smith's analysis, I have not chosen to follow him in this interpretation. The reasons for this are three: First, the terminology of Subjectivism and Phenomenalism is confusing — the latter word today would be more likely to convey the sense of the former; Second, I do not think that the two theories distinguished by Kemp Smith are the only alternatives open to Kant, and in the analysis of the Analogies I will try to show that Kant himself suggested a third; Finally, I do not agree with Kemp Smith in his evaluation of the different versions — the form of "Subjectivism" at which Kant arrives in the Analogies is, in my opinion, the most defensible line of thought in the *Critique*.

bility and conception which in the earlier theory limit perceptions. Objects must be the products of a working up of a manifold of intuition according to the categorial rules of synthesis. Perceptions are then the empirical effects of objects upon bodily sense-organs. Considered as mental entities, perceptions conform to various rules of association which are merely contingent and barren of objective (cognitive) significance. Considered as representations of objects, on the other hand, perceptions are capable of yielding objectively valid cognition. They do so because of the necessary conformity of the objects to the categories.

Thus there are *two* affections, transcendental and empirical, producing *two* manifolds and requiring *two* syntheses. Following Weldon's account,[83] we can describe the situation in the following manner: First the independent things-in-themselves affect the transcendental self; as a result of this affection, and in conformity with its inherent forms of intuition and conception, the transcendental self synthesizes the world of empirical objects, *among which is the empirical self;* in this spatio-temporal world certain physical objects interact with the body of the empirical self and thereby affect the self sensibly; the product is a manifold of sensuous intuition (perception), on which the empirical self works, making judgments concerning the world of objects by interpreting its perceptions as *representations*. Transcendental affection — transcendental synthesis — empirical affection — empirical synthesis (judgment); these are the four stages in the order of their logical dependence.

The judgments of the empirical self are objective because they assert the existence of experiential structures which the transcendental self has synthesized into the world of objects. Whereas previously the acts of judgment and synthesis were fused, here they are at least logically distinguishable. The synthetic acts of the transcendental self are out of time (and in fact produce time). They therefore cannot properly be spoken of as preceding any given act of the empirical self. It may perhaps be better to speak only of one synthetic act, whose product is the entire empirical world, infinite in space and time [cf. A 540–541].

This theory provides solutions for the problems outlined above. The objects of natural science are accorded an independent status

[83] Weldon, pp. 252–256.

within the world of experience. Their role as determinants, rather than determinations, of the empirical mind is safeguarded. At the same time, our *a priori* knowledge of them is accounted for by their dependence on transcendental activities of the mind. The physiology of perception is also explained in a common-sense manner — material objects interact with the senses to produce a manifold of empirical intuition. Finally, the problem of objective affinity, with which we began, is resolved by the distinction between transcendental and empirical faculties. The associations of empirical imagination are grounded in the objective connections of transcendental imagination. As Kant indicates by his names for these faculties, we *re*produce in association what we have already *pro*duced by a transcendental synthesis. In this way, the laws of nature are seen to be the products of the mind itself. Paraphrasing Burke, we might say that for Kant, Nature is man's Art.

Nowhere in the *Critique* is the mechanism of double affection spelled out in the above manner. The distinction between empirical reality and empirical ideality is found in B 44. The doubling of transcendental and empirical faculties occurs, in one form or another, in the Subjective Deduction, the Objective Deduction in A, and various other passages. The recognition of empirical affection (i.e., the physiological causes of perception) is implied in several places, as Adickes shows. Nevertheless, the *Critique* as a whole presents a sort of dynamic equilibrium between this and the earlier theory. Kant repeatedly slips from one to the other, now identifying phenomena and representations, now distinguishing them.

The reason for this indecisiveness, undoubtedly, was Kant's inability to answer the very serious criticism which can be directed against the theory of transcendental synthesis. In the first place, we are told nothing about the origin and nature of the pure manifold on which the transcendental synthesis is performed. As we have seen, Kant holds that the self is capable of affection by some independent entity, the result being a manifold of sensuous intuition conforming to certain inherent forms of the self (space and time). So long as Kant identifies this manifold with perceptions, he is firmly in touch with the facts of our experience, but when he separates the manifold produced in the interaction of the transcendental self and the thing-in-itself from the empirical manifold of perception arising from physiological causes, he seems to drift into the region of speculative metaphysics. There is no argument, save analogy, to show that the operations of the transcendental self proceed similarly to those of the empirical self. What meaning can we give to the affection of an unknowable self by an unknowable object?

This problem resolves itself naturally into two: what is the pure manifold, and what is the pure synthesis? The first will be discussed below in connection with the Schematism chapter; it is one of the most vexing issues in the study of the *Critique*. The second is directly relevant to the Objective Deduction, however, for transcendental synthesis is supposedly the source of the possibility of *a priori* knowledge. As I understand Kant, he holds that subjective associations are grounded in objective connections which productive imagination has produced by an *a priori* synthesis of the pure manifold. Now, if this is to explain anything at all, we must assume that the forms of synthesis employed by the transcendental and empirical imaginations are identical. Otherwise, there is no reason why a subjective association of the representations of cinnabar and redness should bear any relation to an objective connection of qualities in an empirical object.[84] Thus Kant's position implies a parallelism of transcendental and empirical synthesis. This is precisely what lies behind the Subjective Deduction; momentarily Kant recognized where his argument had led, and matched the empirical syntheses of apprehension and reproduction with transcendental counterparts. Later on, he retreated from this view, for which he could find no real justification, and contented himself with a general doubling of the faculties of sense, imagination, and understanding.[85]

At this point Kant's theory is in danger of collapsing into the preliminary version of the Objective Deduction. According to the theory of transcendental synthesis, empirical intuition (i.e., perception) is the mind's window on the world of empirical objects.

[84] We cannot quite say, "to an objective connection of redness and cinnabar," since Kant considers colors to be empirically subjective. It would be more accurate, in his view, to speak of the configuration of matter whose interaction with the eye produced the *sensation* (not perception) of color; in modern terms, the wavelength of electro-magnetic radiation.
[85] There are special reasons why Kant cannot maintain that transcendental imagination is reproductive rather than productive. To explain them would involve the whole subject of inner sense, and hence I have ignored them here. See below.

But if these objects are independent of the empirical mind (though both may be grounded in the transcendental mind), then what meaning can we give to the claim that they are known by the empirical mind? The answer forced on Kant is a sort of pre-established harmony of faculties. The unseen transcendental synthesis organizes objects in a way which is paralleled by the association of perceptions. What possible justification can be given for this claim? It will not do to evoke the necessary conditions of unity of consciousness, for there is no connection, according to this theory, between *transcendental* synthesis and *empirical* unity of consciousness.[86] All Kant can prove is that there could be no unity of empirical consciousness without association. This tells him nothing about objective affinity, and so the doubling of faculties and syntheses fails to solve at least one of the problems for which it was designed.

This failure is actually quite instructive. Faced with the necessity of establishing the independence of the phenomenal world, Kant lapses into the very way of conceiving objects which he wishes to destroy. He postulates a distinct transcendental manifold and synthesis so that he can preserve the common-sense view of the relation of empirical mind to empirical object. Even though both these latter may be the products of a mental process of generation, they are numerically distinct from one another. But such a theory can only lead to the repetition of all the arguments which originally doomed the *Dissertation* doctrine. If Kant must presuppose that the transcendental synthesis is guided by the same rules which determine empirical association, then he might as well assume that "subjective conditions of thought can have objective validity," and have done with it. What he needs is an interpretation of the concept of objectivity which permits him to distinguish subjective from objective connection within the realm of perception and empirical consciousness. I shall try to show that he comes very close to just such an interpretation in the Analogies. Though I believe that Kant reached his philosophical apex there, it will not help to say, in the manner of Kemp Smith, that the Analogies represent the only truly Critical position. The evidence of the

---

[86] The reader can see here the motive for Kant's distinction between empirical and transcendental consciousness (apperception). The latter, however, whatever it may be, is known only by its effects, which appear in empirical consciousness.

Opus Postumum makes it quite clear that Kant chose to follow other, and as I have suggested, less profitable lines of thought.

Textual Analysis of Section 3

The Objective Deduction is set forth in Section 3, "The Relation of the Understanding to Objects in general, and the Possibility of knowing them *a priori*." It consists in all of nineteen paragraphs, including the "Summary Representation of the Correctness of this Deduction" at the end. For convenience we can divide the section into four parts: (1) paragraphs 1–6, in which the theory of transcendental and empirical faculties is stated; (2) paragraphs 7–9, a review of the empirical synthesis of the Subjective Deduction; (3) paragraphs 10–11, the Deduction proper; and (4) paragraphs 12–19, in which some implications of the foregoing are made explicit, and several matters are discussed in greater detail.

Paragraphs 1–6

The opening paragraphs of the section set forth the distinction between transcendental and empirical faculties, and indicate the significance of this distinction for the Deduction argument. After spelling out the theory with all possible clarity in the preliminary exposition, I must now retreat somewhat into the hesitancy of "on the one hand, on the other hand," for the language of the passage is ambiguous, particularly with respect to the numerical distinctness of the pure manifold. Sometimes the two sets of faculties seem to be completely separate, as when Kant says that "only the *productive* synthesis of the imagination can take place *a priori;* the reproductive rests upon empirical conditions" [A 118]. At other times, however, the distinction is rather a logical one, with one mental activity being assigned several cognitive roles. Thus, in the important footnote to A 117, the last sentence apparently means that pure apperception is not a distinct consciousness, but merely a logical possibility of asserting a certain proposition (namely, that the "I" can be attached to all other representations in consciousness). It is the lamentable imprecision of Kant's exposition in these crucial sections which allows him to preserve so many alternative lines of thought without being forced to choose among them. It would be too lengthy an enterprise to go through the paragraphs sentence by sentence, indicating where Kant leaned this way, and where that. I shall restrict myself to comments on some of the more important points.

Paragraph 1. In describing the three subjective sources of empirical knowledge, Kant makes an effort to bring his list into line with the three-fold synthesis of the Subjective Deduction. The result is simply to confuse the reader, for the two triads do not quite jibe. Kant relates imagination to the earlier synthesis of reproduction by adding a parenthetical "and reproduction." Similarly, apperception is paired with the synthesis of recognition in a concept. The trouble comes with sense, for in the Subjective Deduction Kant postulated *both* a sensible manifold (with its mysterious *synopsis*) *and* a synthesis of apprehension in intuition. Quite obviously Kant has given up this last, rather dubious, synthesis for the simpler view that sense presents a manifold to imagination.[87]

Paragraph 2. The trio of faculties, intuition, imagination, and apperception, make their entrance. The important part of the paragraph is the opening clause together with the first parenthesis: "But all perceptions are grounded *a priori* in pure intuition (if they are regarded as representation, in time, as the form of inner intuition). . . ." The use of "grounded in" [*zum Grunde liegen*] makes it impossible to tell exactly what the relation is between perception and pure intuition. The parenthesis, however, strongly suggests that Kant is here using "intuition" in the strict sense to refer to the *a priori form* of perception. The meaning, then, would be that (spatial) perceptions, as contents of consciousness, necessarily appear in time, which is the form of inner sense and hence of all consciousness whatsoever.

Paragraph 3 and footnote a. In this paragraph and long note, Kant enunciates the principle which stands at the head of his system. In the reconstruction of the argument given above, it is the premise from which all else is deduced. As stated by Kant, it reads: "All the variety of *empirical consciousness* must be com-

[87] The synthesis of apprehension in intuition is not a mere confusion, however. It indicates Kant's awareness of the synthetic element in even the bare apprehension of spatio-temporal relations. In the Axioms of Intuition, Kant revises the doctrine of the Aesthetic in such a way as to throw doubt on the whole account of mathematics which it contains. This and other passages reveal Kant's growing dissatisfaction with the theory of sensibility on which he based the *Critique*. Although dating from the *Dissertation*, it remained substantially unchanged until the late portions of the first edition and the revisions of the second edition.

bined in one unified self-consciousness." [88] The ambiguity of Kant's position is here exhibited to perfection. He begins the footnote by asserting that all representations must be capable of appearing in empirical consciousness, for otherwise they would be nothing to us (i.e., for representations, to be is to be apperceived). Thus far there is no need of supposing a numerically distinct transcendental consciousness. The next sentence, however, states that "all empirical consciousness has a necessary relation to a transcendental consciousness which precedes all special experience, namely, the consciousness of myself as original apperception." This suggests that there are two distinct consciousnesses. But the last sentences of the footnote entirely contradict this implication. Kant says:

> But it must not be forgotten that the bare representation 'I' in relation to all other representations (the collective unity of which it makes possible) is transcendental consciousness. Whether this representation is clear (empirical consciousness) or obscure, or even whether it ever actually occurs, does not here concern us. But the possibility of the logical form of all knowledge is necessarily conditioned by relation to this apperception *as a faculty*.

Instead of a "pure original unchangeable consciousness," as Kant describes transcendental apperception in Section 2 [A 107], we have the logical possibility, *which may not even be actualized*, of attaching the bare representation "I" to all the contents of consciousness.

Although the vacillation of Kant's thought is extremely confusing, occurring as it does even within the confines of a single sentence, its source is not difficult to discern. Throughout the Deduction, Kant employs in conjunction two quite different sorts of arguments, viz., logical and psychological. The first category includes analyses of the meanings of certain concepts such as "object" and "cause," and inferences concerning the epistemological relationships among the elements of cognition. The second category consists of descriptions of the mental activities which Kant asserts to be the generative conditions of experience. Now Kant would like to think that only the logical arguments are necessary

---

[88] Kemp Smith follows Vorländer in substituting *einzigen* for *einigen*, thus making the statement read "combined in one single self-consciousness." I see no reason for altering the text, since both versions make sense and express Kant's thought.

for his purposes. As I indicated above, he conceives the weakness of Locke and Hume to be their concentration on psychological factors alone. Thus in the Preface to the first edition he deprecates the psychological Subjective Deduction, basing his claims solely on the logical Objective Deduction. Nevertheless, the most cursory examination of the *Critique* reveals its absolute dependence on its theory of mental activity. Kant may not need a description of association, *à la* Hume, but he very much needs his account of transcendental synthesis. The Deduction proves, if it proves anything, that a necessary condition of knowledge (a logical question) is the *a priori* synthesis of a manfold of intuition by imagination (a psychological question). So far is Kant from demonstrating the separability of logic and psychology, as has long been fashionable to assert, that he actually demonstrates their complete inseparability.

Kant's failure to recognize this fact and his continued adherence to the view expressed in the Preface explains the ambiguity of the passage we are discussing. Since it appears in the Objective Deduction, Kant obviously struggles to turn the psychology into logic. So transcendental consciousness becomes the *possibility* of attaching one representation to others, and this possibility is then the logical form of knowledge.

Paragraph 4. This is the first mention of productive imagination, the transcendental faculty which accounts for the objective affinity of appearances. Kant never explains the use of this term. Presumably, he means to suggest that the productive synthesis actually makes the connections of the manifold which empirical imagination then merely reproduces. What this means, however, I confess I do not know. The interpretation of synthesis which I have presented is based on the idea of rule-directed reproduction in memory — the calling to mind of past representations. Productive imagination cannot be explained as some sort of regular remembering, and Kant gives us no other clues as to the mental function which is involved.

Paragraphs 5–6. The categories now make their entrance into the Deduction, though Kant says little or nothing about them. The categories are the *a priori* modes of knowledge contained in the understanding. But the understanding is nothing but "the unity of apperception in relation to the synthesis of imagination." Hence the categories, or pure concepts, are the functions of unity of the synthesis which pure imagination imposes on the manifold. Apperception brings that synthesis to concepts, or, more precisely, recognizes the unity of the synthesis in concepts. The categories are precisely those concepts. As stated in the Metaphysical Deduction, they are the functions of unity in synthesis.

All this comes perilously close to sounding like double-talk. It will not be possible to explain it completely until we have examined the detailed discussion of the categories in the Analytic of Principles. The following restatement may provide some clue as to what Kant means: The mind is presented with a manifold of intuition, on which it performs an operation. This operation, of "running through and holding together," is not done haphazardly but according to a rule, and it therefore has the unity — the synthetic unity — which belongs to rule-directed activities. The unity of the activity of the mind can be described briefly by saying that an 'I' can be attached to every mental content. Now this *unity of apperception*, although absolutely simple in itself, is not produced by a simple rule. In fact the rule by which the manifold is unified is rather complex, with twelve modes or facets. These various aspects of the rule for synthesis can be called functions of synthesis; to express the fact that they are the facets of the rule which gives unity to the synthesizing process, we may call them functions of unity in synthesis. Taken together, they constitute the rule which produces the unity of consciousness, and as the existence of such a rule is a logical condition of all possible consciousness, these functions of unity in synthesis may be identified with the transcendental unity of apperception. In short, the categories (functions of unity in synthesis) *are* the unity of apperception. But they are also the contents, or repertory of acts, of the understanding. Therefore, "the unity of apperception in relation to the synthesis of imagination *is* the understanding" [A 119].

Paragraphs 7–9

Starting from below, as he puts it, Kant now rehearses quickly the teaching of the Subjective Deduction, the three paragraphs corresponding to the first three subsections of Section 2. In this case, however, the progression of the argument is altered somewhat to prepare the way for the Deduction in the next paragraphs. Empirical apprehension, reproduction, and recognition (not here mentioned by name) are introduced in order, with no reference to the corresponding transcendental faculties. This allows Kant to use the problem of objective affinity as the bridge between the empirical and the transcendental. On the whole, these paragraphs and the immediately succeeding ones are admirably clear. The contrast between the coherence of Section 3 and the confusion of Section 2 adds weight to the patchwork analysis which has been given of the latter. Here and in the second-edition Deduction Kant shows that he is quite capable of presenting his argument in connected form.

Paragraphs 10–12

Kant springs the trap, as it were, with the argument from objective affinity. If subjective association did not have an objective ground, "it would be entirely accidental that appearances should fit into a connected whole of human knowledge." Perceptions might enter into consciousness, yet lack all connection with one another or relation to my self-consciousness.[89]

This passage is clearly written with Hume in mind. There is a rather remarkable passage in the *Enquiry Concerning Human Understanding* which is the perfect statement of the view Kant is rebutting. After describing the subjective, associative mechanisms of custom from which we derive our causal beliefs, Hume writes:

Here, then, is a kind of pre-established harmony between the course of nature and the succession of our ideas; and though the powers and forces, by which the former is governed, be wholly unknown to us; yet our thoughts and conceptions have still, we find, gone on in the same train with the other works of nature. Custom is that principle, by which this correspondence has been effected; so necessary to the subsistence of our species, and the regulation of our conduct, in every circumstance and occurrence of human life. Had not the presence of an object, instantly excited the idea of those objects, commonly conjoined with it, all our knowledge must have been limited to the narrow sphere of our memory and senses; and we should never have been able to adjust means to ends, or employ our natural powers, either to the producing of good, or avoiding of evil. Those, who delight in the discovery and contemplation of *final causes*, have here ample subject to employ their wonder and admiration. [*Enquiry*, pp. 54–55]

[89] Needless to say, the "or" in this sentence might as well be changed to "and hence." The lack of connection to one another and lack of relation to my self-consciousness are two sides of the same coin. To relate them all to one self-consciousness is to associate them together — that is precisely the point of Kant's argument.

Much as Kant delighted in final causes, this bald assertion of a pre-established harmony must have appeared to him the very abdication of philosophy. His answer is to prove that we are not at the mercy of an inexplicable and unpredictable correspondence between the accidental associations of perceptions and the objective connections of nature. For we could not even become conscious of our perceptions unless they were bound up in one consciousness, and hence associated according to a rule. "All appearances, without exception, must so enter the mind or be apprehended, that they conform to the unity of apperception." If they do not so conform, they are nothing to me. Hence, the associability of perceptions is not a miracle to be wondered at, but a demonstrably necessary condition of their appearance in consciousness.

In discussing stage IV of the Deduction (Section 2, subsection 4), I pointed out a weakness in Kant's argument. He sought to prove that objective connection, *as well as* subjective association, could be found in the world of experience; but his argument actually proved that objective connection, *instead of* subjective association, tied all representations to one another. The theory of productive imagination and the transcendental faculties is designed to provide the needed explanation of objective affinity. As the argument of paragraph 10 makes clear, however, Kant is still faced by the same problem: how to distinguish, within experience, between mere association and objective connection. A satisfactory solution only appears in the Second Analogy.

Paragraphs 13–19

The Deduction proper ends with the argument of paragraphs 10–12. Kant appends seven more paragraphs in which several matters are gone into at greater length.

Paragraphs 13–14. The emphasis placed upon the separation of sensibility and understanding and their union through the mediation of imagination, is repeated in the Schematism, to which I shall proceed presently. I agree with Kemp Smith that Kant obscures his real argument by this insistence, though the reasons for doing so are quite strong. The example of the triangle in paragraph 13 reveals Kant's continuing uncertainty about the precise roles of apprehension, reproduction (or production), and recognition. He seems to suggest that apprehension gets us as far as what today would be called sense-experience, while imagination and apperception generate knowledge. The last sentence of paragraph 14 takes it all back, however, by repeating the claim that the full three-fold process is necessary before we can even be conscious of appearances. It is useless to attempt a schematic or orderly representation of Kant's thought about these questions, as he never successfully resolved them for himself.

Paragraphs 15–19. Kant concludes the Deduction with a bold statement of the extraordinary and paradoxical conclusion of his argument: man himself legislates to nature! The mind imposes on the material world those laws which it then discovers there. The understanding is "the lawgiver of nature." That Kant was quite sensible of the singularity of this view is demonstrated by his reserving it for the last paragraphs of the Deduction. Only after the entire position has been set forth does he dare to assert such a corollary.

Kant immediately takes up the crucial problem of the relation of the highest rules, or laws, to particular empirical laws. He cannot mean that the mind determines every detailed causal relation of material objects. To assert this would imply that by pure reason alone we could discover the truths of empirical science; there would be no need for experiment or observation. This, of course, is precisely what Kant wished to deny, and he is forced therefore to explain more precisely the nature of the "highest laws" (which can be found in the Analytic of Principles). His first answer to this question is not terribly helpful. Empirical laws, he says, "are only special determinations of the pure laws of understanding," and hence in some sense depend upon those pure laws. This tells us nothing about how the law of the parallelogram of forces is related to the causal maxim, however. The entire subject will be discussed at length in a later chapter. For the moment, let me just note that for Kant, experience determines that *fire* causes *heat*, while the mind determines that fire *causes* heat. As modern phenomenalists would say, there is an irreducible given element in experience which guides the mind's interpretations.

Finally, I call the reader's attention to paragraph 16, where confirmation may be found for my interpretation of synthesis in terms of rules. The unity of apperception, says Kant, "acts as the rule" for unifying the manifold, and "the faculty of these rules is the understanding." Laws are simply objective rules, the highest of which (i.e., those based on the categories) "issue *a priori* from the understanding itself."

THE DEDUCTION OF THE PURE CONCEPTS OF UNDERSTANDING IN THE SECOND EDITION

(In the second-edition version of the Deduction, Kant attempted to remedy some of the inadequacies of the first-edition argument. As that argument is only completed in the Analogies, below, the reader may wish to go directly on to Book Two of the Analytic and return to this chapter later.)

The Transcendental Deduction is the only section of the Analytic which Kant completely rewrote for the second edition of the *Critique*. His decision to do so is evidence of his realization that the first edition version was unsatisfactory, at least in exposition. The new Deduction is slightly longer than the passage which it replaces. Instead of two sections representing the subjective and objective sides of the argument, we are offered a single coherent discussion, divided for convenience into thirteen brief subsections (§§ 15–27 in the second edition numbering). Section 1 of the Deduction in A (§§ 13–14) has been retained, despite its reflection of *Dissertation* and early Critical doctrines.

In point of clarity and coherence, the new version is unquestionably superior to the old. However, its philosophical interest lies mainly in its clarification of arguments already stated in the first edition. Much of importance has been omitted, and with one very significant exception, there are no new theoretical developments. It is for this reason, as I explained, that I have devoted so much space to the first edition. The exception is the discussion of inner sense which appears in §§ 24–25. This very difficult passage, together with a passage added to the Aesthetic and a footnote to the

Preface in B, contains the theory of inner sense which Kant advanced to meet some of the difficulties of the first edition.

What I shall do, therefore, is to begin with some comments upon points of interest or difficulty in §§ 15–23 and 26–27. Then I shall return to §§ 24–25 and, with the help of T. D. Weldon's brilliant treatment of these sections, attempt to clarify them somewhat. I must warn the reader that this topic is still in large measure opaque to me, so that I cannot hold out the promise of a definitive explication.

§§ 15–23 and 26–27

The progression of argument in the Deduction in B is quite straightforward. Kant begins with the manifold of sensibility, handed, as it were, to the Analytic by the Aesthetic. He propounds in general terms the problem of connection of a manifold, which requires that a *synthetic unity* be produced (§ 15). Then he states the official starting premise of the Deduction, which is the fact of the transcendental unity of apperception (§ 16). Now he introduces, one by one, the several elements of the proof. First the concept of the object of knowledge is analyzed, and its relation to the unity of apperception indicated (§ 17). Then the unity of consciousness is carefully distinguished from the unity of apperception (§ 18). After this, the Metaphysical Deduction is briefly recapitulated, with functions of judgment (§ 19) and then the categories (§ 20) being defined. Kant now pauses for extended discussions of the nature and limits of the categories (§§ 21–23) and of the distinction between inner sense and apperception (§§ 24–25). Finally, the Deduction is formally stated (§ 26, first part), and Kant concludes with some general remarks about science (§ 26, second part) and a summary (§ 27).

§ 15 — The Possibility of Combination in General

Knowledge begins with the affection of the self, producing a manifold of sensible representations. The form of that manifold may well lie within us, as the Aesthetic has shown, but the combination through which we obtain knowledge can never be *given* with the manifold. Rather it must be introduced into the manifold by an act of the mind which can be called "synthesis." For "we cannot represent to ourselves anything as combined in an object which we have not ourselves previously combined" [B 130].

The critical arguments of Hume had revealed the impossibility of connection being given with perceptions. That several representations had come before the mind in contiguous spaces or at the same time might be perceived (although strictly speaking, even such relations as these were for Kant the products of synthesis), but that they stood in some connection to one another could never be given. As I have indicated above, it is because all perceptions are spatio-temporal that such connection cannot be given. The parts of space and time are all external to one another, so that no intrinsic connection of them is possible. As Hume would put it, they are distinguishable, and hence separable, from one another. It is the passivity of human intuition which produces this spreading out of the object, and which thereby necessitates the combination of the manifold according to subjective forms of cognition.

Kant adds an extremely significant observation which considerably improves upon the teaching of the Metaphysical Deduction. Combination, he says, is representation of synthetic unity of the manifold, and *synthetic unity is a property of analytic as well as synthetic judgments*. The discussion of analytic and synthetic judgments in the Introduction conveyed the impression that only the latter raised any problem for philosophy, and even then merely when known *a priori*.[1] Kant himself represents his problem as, How are synthetic judgments *a priori* possible? But in any act of judgment there is a combination of distinct representations, and the possibility of that combination in one consciousness must be explained. For example, when I judge that All unmarried men are men, I form the concepts "unmarried man" and "man," and then assert a connection between them. To be sure, the connection may in this case rest upon nothing more than the laws of logic, but it must still be possible for me to unite the separate consciousness of the two concepts in one consciousness [B 131, note a]. Hence all thinking, and indeed all consciousness, stands in need of an explanation in respect to its most general characteristic: synthetic unity.

[1] Cf. Section IV, A 6–10.

§ *16. The Original Synthetic Unity of Apperception*

Kant gives expression to this universal property of all consciousness in the proposition which marks the formal starting point of the Deduction:

It must be possible for the 'I think' to accompany all my representations; for otherwise something would be represented in me which could not be thought at all, and that is equivalent to saying that the representation would be impossible. . . . All the manifold of intuition has, therefore, a necessary relation to the 'I think' in the same subject in which this manifold is found.
[B 131–132]

Here the *cogito* of Descartes is restated in a form which Kant believes truly expresses the correct implications of the method of doubt. The principle of the unity of apperception is at once the most general and the best-known proposition available to human beings.

It will be recalled that in the first edition Objective Deduction, Kant was undecided whether the unity of apperception is a logical or a psychological fact.[2] He now decides that it is a logical fact — that is to say, the principle of the unity of apperception asserts merely that I must be able to attach the 'I think' to all my representations; whether I actually do so is beside the point. As Kant puts it:

the manifold representations, which are given in an intuition, would not be one and all *my* representations, if they did not all belong to one self-consciousness. As *my* representations (even if I am not conscious of them as such) they must conform to the condition under which alone they *can* stand together in one universal self-consciousness . . . [B 132]

At this point Kant makes a most extraordinary statement, which he then repeats in the next sub-section. The principle of the unity of apperception "is itself . . . an identical, and therefore analytic, proposition" [B 135]. It merely says that all my representations are my representations [B 138]. But how can a tautology serve as the highest principle of transcendental philosophy, from which all else is claimed to follow? The answer is that the principle is a tautology because it *defines* the nature of an understanding whose fundamental act is the synthesis of a given manifold [cf. B 145]. The synthetic proposition which is added to this in order to yield

[2] Cf. above, pp. 175–177.

a genuine advance in knowledge is simply the assertion that human understanding *is* such an understanding [cf. B 139].[3]

§ 17. The Principle of the Synthetic Unity is the Supreme Principle of all Employment of the Understanding

This section carries forward the conclusions of the preceding one by introducing the concept of the object of knowledge. Kant's exposition here is admirably clear and precise, and expresses unambiguously the epistemological turn on which the Critical doctrine depends. Knowledge is the "determinate relation of given representations to an object." But an object is merely a "that which"; it is "that in the concept of which the manifold of a given intuition is *united*." Hence the connection which we locate *in the object* is nothing more nor less than the unity which the understanding imposes upon the *consciousness* of the representations. So to think the representations together in one consciousness is precisely to confer upon them relation to an object. The *subjective* condition of unity of consciousness is at one and the same time the *objective* condition "under which every intuition must stand in order *to become an object for me*" [B 138]. Here Kant is restating the analysis of A 104–106, without however any reference to the object in general = *x*.

§ 18. The Objective Unity of Self-Consciousness

Until now, no clear distinction has been drawn between the merely empirical unity of my consciousness as a phenomenal object, and the necessary unity of consciousness (apperception) in the act of synthesis which the understanding performs. The former concerns the associations which serve to specify and define my particular empirical character. It must not be confused with the latter, which is the condition alike of empirical objects *and* the unity of empirical consciousness.[4]

§§ 19–20. Recapitulation of the Metaphysical Deduction

Having established the principle of the unity of apperception as his *pou sto*, Kant introduces the categories by way of a doctrine

---

[3] See also A 117 note a, where Kant states that the proposition asserting the unity of *empirical* consciousness is synthetic, not analytic.
[4] See below, the discussion of inner sense and apperception.

of judgment. As judgment is the assertion of a unity of representations by means of the copula 'is,' the functions of unity expounded in the Table of Judgments will yield the modes of combination in general (§ 19). When applied to a manifold of sensible intuition, they give the modes of synthesis, or Table of Categories (§ 20). This way of leading into the categories *after* a discussion of the unity of apperception is much superior to the original discussion in the Metaphysical Deduction. Here the revolutionary implications of Kant's theory have been spelled out, so that we can see, for example, the connection between analytic and synthetic unity. It is still the case, however, that the Tables of Judgments and Categories are *ad hoc* at this point in the argument. Rather, Kant should modify his exposition slightly so that he claims here merely the *existence* of such tables, and not yet their possession. In practice, he does just this, for the second edition Deduction makes no more detailed reference to particular categories than did the first edition.

The reader should note Kant's criticism of the doctrine that all judgment consists of a subject term and a predicate term. As it has become a commonplace to say that Kant thought all judgments were of the subject-predicate form, that he was unaware of the existence of relations, and that his entire enterprise is therefore vitiated by an inadequate logic, it may be worthwhile to point out that nothing could be further from the truth. The same unity of consciousness is demanded by the proposition "Squares have more sides than triangles but fewer sides than octagons" as by the proposition "All men are mortal."

§§ *21–23. The Nature and Limits of the Categories*

Having defined the role of the categories in *a priori* synthesis, Kant takes the opportunity in the next three sections to clear up certain ambiguities in his theory. What he says here has an authoritative ring, for it appears in the context of the argument which he himself considered the core of his philosophy. Nevertheless, he does not always adhere to his own statements, so that it would be dangerous to claim that any particular utterance is what he really believed about some subject.

The first point of interest is the very forceful and explicit denial that the categories have any validity for an intuitive understanding (§ 21). The following passage is perfectly unambiguous:

[The categories] are merely rules for an understanding whose whole power consists in thought, consists, that is, in the act whereby it brings the synthesis of a manifold, given to it from elsewhere in intuition, to the unity of apperception . . . [B 145]

In my commentary on the Schematism, I will discuss the question whether the categories have a problematic extension beyond the limits of our sensibility.[5] I will argue that Kant had little interest in other forms of sensible intuition, and hence was principally concerned to decide whether the categories are potentially applicable to things in themselves or only to a spatio-temporal manifold. The present section may appear to contradict that assertion, and so I will try to explain why I do not think it does.

The theory which Kant is expounding in the Deduction makes synthesis out to be the act of combining a manifold in one consciousness. As thus described, the process seems quite indifferent to the nature of the manifold, so long only as it is a manifold of sensibility. Hence, Kant can say with perfect consistency that there is no explaining "why space and time are the only forms of our possible intuition" [B 146]. But when it comes to describing precisely what synthesis is, and showing how it confers unity on a multiplicity, Kant presents us with an account (in the Subjective Deduction) which makes essential and indispensable use of the temporality of consciousness. If I am correct in believing that we cannot understand the *Critique* at all without that explication of the concept of synthesis, then Kant must forego his reference to other forms of sensible intuition, and recognize that he is postulating a much more intimate relation between the forms of sensibility and the acts of understanding than he has hitherto allowed.

In § 22, the term "knowledge" is taken in a very strict sense, with the consequence that pure mathematics becomes merely potential knowledge. Its actualization in the form of applied mathematics depends upon the presentation of objects in space. The implication of this passage [B 146–147] would seem to be that pure space is *not* an individual given *a priori*, for if it were, then presumably pure mathematics would have its own separate ob-

[5] Cf. below, 214–218.

ject. There is no doubt that this view is superior to that of the Aesthetic, and that it is more consistent with the rest of the Analytic. Why Kant did not stick to it throughout the *Critique* is something of a mystery.[6]

§ 26. Transcendental Deduction . . . of the Pure Concepts

The first three paragraphs of this section complete the Deduction. The argument relies upon the Metaphysical Deduction in the first paragraph, and by its reference to the synthesis of apprehension in the second paragraph suggests the doctrine of the Subjective Deduction. I confess myself unable to understand the first part of paragraph three, but the concluding sentences seem clear enough. The bare act by which perceptions are apprehended under the forms of space and time (synthesis of apprehension) must, as a combination of a manifold in one consciousness, conform to the categories, for they are the rules for any such synthesis. Since

experience is knowledge by means of connected perceptions, the categories are conditions of the possibility of experience, and are therefore valid *a priori* for all objects of experience. [B 161]

It is instructive to compare this last formulation of the solution of the Deduction with the first expression of the problem, as it appears in § 13. The latter, it will be recalled, reflected a very early stage in the development beyond the *Dissertation*. Kant stated the task of the Deduction in these terms:

That objects of sensible intuition must conform to the formal conditions of sensibility which lie *a priori* in the mind is evident, because otherwise they would not be objects for us. But that they must likewise conform to the conditions which the understanding requires for the synthetic unity of thought, is a conclusion the grounds of which are by no means so obvious. *Appearances might very well be so constituted that the understanding should not find them to be in accordance with the conditions of its unity.*
[A 90. Emphasis added.]

The problem was that perceptions apparently might enter consciousness without submitting to the categories. The solution, as is clear in § 26, is that the conditions which perception must meet in order merely to enter consciousness are at one and the same time the conditions of their subsumption under the categories.[7]

---

[6] Cf. for example, B 160 with note a, just a few pages further on in the Deduction.
[7] Cf. above, pp. 93–94.

In the second part of § 26, Kant deals briefly with the relation of the categories to natural science. The passage stands to the rest of the Deduction as A 125–128 stands to the first edition Objective Deduction. Here, as there, Kant states that the understanding dictates laws to nature, and here too he asserts that particular laws cannot "be *derived* from the categories, although they are one and all subject to them" [B 165]. What this means is left quite undetermined, and as I will indicate in my general discussion of Kant's philosophy of science, the critical writings nowhere contain a definitive clarification of the issue.

§ 27. Outcome of this Deduction

Kant concludes the Deduction with a general summary and some architectonic flourishes. The footnote to B 166 lapses back into the view that the categories have perfectly universal problematic applicability. The context of this utterance, namely practical reason, indicates once again that it is Kant's ethical and religious doctrines which draw him back from the conclusions of B 145 and B 149.[8]

§§ 24–25. Kant's Theory of Inner Sense

The one portion of the Deduction in B which presents serious problems of interpretation is the inserted discussion of inner sense, which is contained in the second half of § 24 and in § 25. The passage should be read with General Observation II in the Aesthetic [B 66–69], which was added by Kant in the second edition. The two, taken together with the new Refutation of Idealism, constitute Kant's answer to the charges of idealism which were directed against the first edition of the *Critique* by its earliest readers. The theory of inner sense also serves to clarify and fill out some of the obscure aspects of the doctrine of the Analytic. In what follows, I have relied very heavily on the excellent discussion by Weldon.[9] The interpretation which he offers cannot be substantiated merely by appeals to the text. It is a reconstruction, based on a plausible hypothesis, of the theory which Kant must have had in

---

[8] At this point, Kant ceases the numbering of subsections which he has added to the second edition Analytic of Concepts. One of my students, somewhat dazzled by the architectonic, pointed out that there are twenty-seven such subsections, which is not only the cube of three, but also precisely the number of distinct types of categorical propositions. I remarked that I doubted it had any significance, but one never knows!

[9] *Op. cit.*, pp. 257–270.

mind when he wrote the cryptic passages of B 66–69 and § 24. As with all good commentary, its justification is that it allows us to explain why Kant wrote precisely the words he did, even though they seem strange or incomprehensible on first reading.

According to the rationalist tradition from which Kant wished to dissociate himself, the self is apprehended by consciousness through the act of introspection. It is this self-consciousness which revealed to Descartes his thinking self. The self thus known is the real, or in Kant's terms the noumenal, self — literally a *noumenal* self because it is an object of intelligence. The body, and also the feelings of pleasure, pain, etc., may be perceived by the senses, but the soul is known to itself through an act of conscious awareness. This special character of self-knowledge places the natural world at an epistemological disadvantage and makes necessary a special proof of the possibility of knowledge of material objects. Such a proof must be unsatisfactory, however, for since the standards of genuine knowledge are read off from the paradigmatic knowledge of the self (clarity and distinctness), and since the self is the only object which can be directly and immediately apprehended, material objects will inevitably be degraded to a less secure status. In Descartes' case this failure is made particularly vivid by his reliance upon the goodness of God, which in the circumstances is a virtual admission of defeat.

Kant accepted Descartes' orientation, placing the fact of consciousness at the head of his system. At the same time, however, he wished to certify our scientific knowledge of material objects. For this purpose (and in order to achieve certain results in Ethical theory), he must deny any privileged access to the real self. This involves elaborating a theory of the nature of consciousness in its relation to empirical knowledge, as well as a theory of the phenomenal self, or self as appearance. In the context of the *Critique*, this latter means that Kant must explain how the self is given to itself as an object of knowledge. Since an object can, according to the Aesthetic, be given only through the affection of sensibility, and since the empirical self is not a material thing, it follows that Kant must present a doctrine of an *inner sense* whereby the self appears to itself as phenomenon.[10] Hence Kant begins his discussion in § 24 by saying:

[10] Cf. Kemp Smith, pp. 295–296.

This is a suitable place for explaining the paradox which must have been obvious to everyone in our exposition of the form of inner sense (§ 6): namely, that this sense represents to consciousness even our own selves only as we appear to ourselves, not as we are in ourselves. For we intuit ourselves only as we are inwardly *affected*, and this would seem to be contradictory, since we should then have to be in a passive relation [of active affection] to ourselves. [B 152–153]

As soon as we try to imagine what kind of account of inner sense can be given in the framework of the *Critique*, we encounter an apparently insurmountable problem. Weldon states it with great clarity as follows:

the five special [bodily] senses, as again [Kant] states explicitly in the *Anthropology*, constitute between them the outer sense, and from this the inner sense has somehow to be distinguished. The difficulty which at once presents itself is that the immediate data of consciousness are already exhausted and therefore there is in fact nothing left for inner sense to do. We might at first suppose that, in so far as it is clearly regarded as being cognizant of my own states, it could have as its content the non-cognitive states of the self. . . . But this interpretation is quite un-Kantian and cuts clean across both the division of faculties and the doctrine that sense *qua* cognitive is representative. . . .[11]

The difficulty, quite simply, is that the manifold of sensibility is composed of perceptions having a spatial form, and they are one and all representations of material objects, belonging to *outer* sense. The fact that the original manifold is spatial rather than spatio-temporal can very easily be missed by even the attentive reader. Kant does say, after all, that "Time is the formal *a priori* condition of all appearances whatsoever. . . . But since all representations, whether they have for their objects outer things or not, belong, in themselves, as determinations of the mind, to our inner state . . . [time] is the immediate condition of inner appearances (of our souls), and thereby the mediate condition of outer appearances" [B 50]. Nevertheless, in the paragraph just preceding this in the Aesthetic, he asserts that "[Time] cannot be a determination of outer appearances; it has to do neither with shape nor position, but with the relation of representations in our inner state" [B 49–50]. In the long footnote to the Preface in B, he says, "[W]e derive the whole material of knowledge, even for our inner sense," from "things outside us" [B xxxix note].

[11] *Op. cit.*, p. 259.

The significance of this is twofold: first, Kant must somewhere discover a manifold of inner intuition which can serve as the representation of the self, rather than of outer objects; and secondly, he must explain how, by the affection of inner sense, a temporal form is imposed upon the spatial manifold of outer intuition.[12] Kant never spells out such a theory, although he makes a number of cryptic and suggestive remarks in §§ 24–25, B xxxix n, and B 67–68. Weldon therefore postulates that "he is . . . taking for granted a contemporary theory without troubling to make explicit what exactly that theory is. . . . [I]t happens that there is evidence in his correspondence to show us whose theory it was most likely to be."[13] Weldon identifies it as that of the psychologist Tetens, whose *Philosophische Versuche über die menschliche Natur und ihre Entwicklung* was published in 1777.[14] The following lengthy extract from Weldon's account gives the elements of Tetens' views.

The essence of this view was as follows. . . . [The] function [of inner sense] is to provide immediate awareness of awareness, and its existence is obvious to introspection. . . . [A]wareness and awareness of awareness are never in fact simultaneous. It is never true to say "I know that I am thinking" but only "I know that I have thought," and this is ultimately his ground for maintaining the representative character of inner sense [i.e., it represents past, and hence absent, events of awareness]. . . . [T]he mind in the act of thinking modifies its ideas (by abstraction, concentration, etc.). This modification is accompanied by a corresponding modification of the *ideae materiales* in the cortex, and to this physical modification corresponds the event in consciousness which I describe as awareness of awareness and which constitutes the content of my inner sense. To put the matter in a sentence, what I am aware of by means of inner sense is my own past acts of awareness. . . .

The upshot of all this is a psychological theory of perception which is both odd in itself and difficult to harmonize with Kant's theory of knowledge. Nevertheless it does seem to be consistent with what he says both in the *Aesthetic* and the *Analytic*. The view is simply that the content of im-

---

[12] There is a further problem, which Weldon says is central to the question of inner sense, namely, how the self manages to project an objective temporal order into outer appearances, distinct from the subjective temporal order of their apprehension in consciousness. As I believe that Kant has treated this problem successfully in the Second Analogy, I have not introduced it into the present chapter. Weldon's general discussion of the problem of subjective and objective succession is one of the finest parts of his *Commentary*. Cf. Weldon, pp. 263–265. See also below, pp. 262–269.

[13] Weldon, pp. 260–261.

[14] Kemp Smith also refers to Tetens. Cf. his *Commentary*, p. 148 and p. 294.

mediate awareness is (a) non-cognitive states with which we are here not concerned; (b) intuitions which are representations of objects (including my own body); (c) intuitions which are representations of myself as perceiving. These are literally scattered about among my perceptions of things and are entirely separate both from one another and from those perceptions.[15]

There are several points of ambiguity in Weldon's account which reveal the difficulties of the doctrine which Kant is apparently espousing. First of all, Kant frequently asserts that all the representations of outer sense have, *qua* contents of the mind, a temporal order which is the order of their apprehension. This subjective time order serves as the starting point for the synthetic re-working of the manifold into phenomena. In the Analogies, Kant's focus is so completely on the problem of subjective and objective time order that he neglects even to mention the fact that the manifold is constituted solely of perceptions of outer sense. Now, it is not clear from the last paragraph of Weldon's exposition, quoted above, whether the given manifold does or does not have the form of time. If only the intuitions of inner sense are temporal in form, then the third category, (c), of contents of consciousness, namely the awarenesses of awarenesses, will be the only elements of the manifold of consciousness to exhibit relations of succession and simultaneity. The outer perceptions will have a spatial ordering, but not a temporal ordering. In the language of mathematicians, the manifold on such an interpretation possesses the properties of a partially ordered set.

Although this matter seems very much a technical quibble, it actually cuts to the heart of Kant's theory of synthesis. In order for the argument of the Analogies to stand up, the manifold must be presumed to have a temporal ordering upon its entrance into consciousness. Synthesis is then the re-ordering of the manifold in a new, rule-governed, and hence objective, time order. But as time is the form of inner sense, through which the self comes to know itself, Kant must somehow make the argument consistent with the conditions of such self-knowledge. He must find a place for an affection of the self by itself, and explain how *that* affection first produces a manifold in the form of time.

Lest the reader lose patience with these complications, and con-

<hr/>

[15] Weldon, pp. 261–262.

clude that they merely show the absurdity of Kant's theory, let me add as an aside that the problem is quite real and independent of any particular epistemology, so long as it attempts to do justice to the facts of empirical knowledge. Consciousness is the vehicle by which we apprehend the world of material objects. Hence, from a subjective point of view, the limits of the mind are the limits of the knowable world. All other sentient beings are merely particular forms of the subjective contents of my consciousness. Thus far the facts suggest a radical solipsism. At the same time, however, the contents of my consciousness, together with certain dispositions and propensities and capacities, constitute a single empirical self among many in an intersubjective world of conscious human beings. Furthermore the same consciousness which reveals the world to me, also, through self-consciousness, apparently reveals my own self to me as well. Now one may not find Kant's account of this situation convincing, but it seems to me impossible to deny that it exists, and that some rather complicated analysis of it is called for from any serious epistemological theory. So far as I can discover, it is pretty much ignored by contemporary phenomenalists and sense-data theorists. Nor does the continuing debate about the possibility of knowing other minds really deal with the problem. The issue is not closed by the assertion that we can know other minds; quite to the contrary, it is precisely our ability to do so which raises so many complications. Solipsism, after all, is a very simple doctrine to maintain consistently. Its failing is that it is too simple to account for the fact that, through consciousness, we apprehend an objective world of persons and things. For those who mourn the passing of the grand systematic questions in philosophy, but are unable to keep faith with the secular religions of 19th century metaphysics, this familar double aspect of ordinary consciousness may serve as a good starting point for investigation. I suspect that the working out of its implications would involve all of the issues of epistemology and metaphysics which today are treated in isolation.

Returning to the problem which faced Kant, one natural explanation would seem to be that the outer and inner senses are simultaneously affected, producing a manifold which is spatial, *qua* representative, and spatio-temporal *qua* content of consciousness. Although the end result of Kant's theory is quite similar to this, it will not do as it stands. The problem is that inner sense, like outer sense, must be representative. Now if the content of inner sense is the spatial manifold *simpliciter*, then it will represent outer objects and not the empirical self. Since the spatial manifold is the content of subjective consciousness, that manifold must itself become the object of a new manifold of representations. Then it will be the case that the spatial perceptions viewed as representations will represent outer objects, while the same perceptions viewed as objects will be represented by a manifold in inner sense. This is what Kant means in the Subjective Deduction by the assertion that "All representations have, as representations, their object, and can themselves in turn become objects of other representations" [A 108].

In order to discover precisely what Kant's theory is, let us turn to the text, where in a few brief passages he gives us all the clues which we have to work with. The first and clearest passage is General Observation II to the Aesthetic, B 67–69. Kant states there that "the representations of the *outer senses* [i.e., the five bodily senses] constitute the proper material with which we occupy our mind" [B 67]. Thus the given manifold is spatial and representative of outer objects. Now, he continues, "the time in which we set these representations . . . underlies them as the formal condition of the mode in which we posit [*setzen*] them in the mind." And he goes on, "Since this form does not represent anything save in so far as something is posited in the mind, it can be nothing but the mode in which the mind is affected through its own activity (namely, through this positing of its representation), and so is affected by itself" [B 67–68].

This is a difficult passage to understand, and the principal obscurity surrounds the word "positing." What precisely is the activity of positing, or setting, representations in the mind? And in what sense does that activity confer upon the representations the form of time? Kemp Smith offers the following explanation:

[Kant] would seem to mean that the mind in the process of "setting" representations of outer sense *in space* affects itself, and is therefore constrained to arrange the given representations likewise in time. No new content, additional to that of outer sense, is thereby generated, but what previously as object of outer sense existed merely in space is now also subjected to conditions of time. The representations of outer sense are all by their very nature likewise representations of inner sense. To outer sense is due both their content and their spatial form; to inner sense they owe only the additional form of time; their content remains unaffected in the process of being taken over by a second sense.[16]

Although at first reading this interpretation appears plausible, a closer examination reveals several ways in which it contradicts Kant's teaching, and fails to explain the text. According to Kemp Smith, the act of positing (or, as he more accurately translates in his *Commentary*, of *setting*) is an act whereby the given manifold is set *in space*. Presumably this means a synthesis of the manifold which imposes upon it the form of space. Such a synthesis, however, is clearly contrary to the doctrine of the Aesthetic, where the spatial form of the manifold is attributed to a passive affection of the mind, not to an active synthesis performed by the mind. To be sure, Kant states in the Axioms of Intuition that a synthesis underlies the empirical consciousness of spatial relations [B 202]. But it is not clear how Kant can make that assertion consistent with his doctrine of sensibility, which is the subject of the present passage.

More serious however is Kemp Smith's statement that "the representations of outer sense are all by their very nature likewise representations of inner sense. To outer sense is due both their content and their spatial form; to inner sense they owe only the additional form of time." This is clearly impossible on Kant's view, for several reasons. If the representations are representations of outer sense, then as I explained above, they will represent outer objects only. This is clear from Kemp Smith's comment that their content is due to outer sense. How can a perception whose content is a shade of color or a degree of impenetrability (hardness) be said to *represent* the empirical self? To be sure, such a perception may be a part of the empirical self, and consequently a representation *of it* will be a representation *of* the self. But it itself can only be a representation of an outer (material) object.

Kemp Smith appears to have confused two related but separate questions. The first, to which his interpretation provides an answer, is How does the manifold of spatial intuition acquire its temporal form? The second, which he cannot answer, is How can the self represent itself to itself in inner sense? Weldon's account is clearly on the right track. It treats the spatial manifold as composed of

[16] Kemp Smith, p. 294. Emphasis added.

acts of awareness of outer things. These awarenesses then become the objects, in turn, of reflective acts of awareness of awareness. Because the self is affected by its own activity, its acts of awareness (of outer things) become set in the form of time. In short, while the awarenesses of outer things have the form of space, the awarenesses of those awarenesses are strung out in temporal order. So it is that time is "the immediate condition of inner appearances (of our souls), and thereby the mediate condition of outer appearances" [A 34].

The last portion of General Observation II finally throws a little light on all this. "In man," Kant says, "[the] consciousness [of self] demands inner perception of the manifold which is antecedently given in the subject. . . ." That is now quite clear —we come to know ourselves by an inner perception of the spatial manifold which constitutes the content of consciousness. He continues: "If the faculty of coming to consciousness of oneself is to seek out (to apprehend) that which lies in the mind, it must affect the mind, and only in this way can it give rise to an intuition of itself." Now we see what the "positing" is which affects the self: it is the seeking out, or apprehending, of that which lies in the mind. In other words, reverting to Weldon's account, the mind is initially presented with a spatial manifold. In order to bring this manifold to consciousness, the mind must seek it out, which is to say focus attention upon it. This act affects the mind, for in this case the object on which the self is focussing is the content of its own consciousness. The result of the affection is to set the self-awareness of the spatial manifold in a temporal order. That order is the *subjective* order of the empirical consciousness of outer objects, for it is the order in which the perceptions of outer objects appear in the mind, rather than the order in which the outer objects themselves stand to one another.[17]

There remains one point which is not yet clear: the precise nature of the mental activity which Kant called positing, or setting, and which in the explanation above I have described as a focussing of attention. In § 24, we are given this final piece of information by Kant. The second paragraph states:

What determines [i.e., affects] inner sense is the understanding and its original power of combining the manifold of intuition, that is, of bringing

[17] Cf. the Second Analogy.

it under an apperception. . . . The understanding, that is to say, in respect
of the manifold [of outer intuition] which may be given to it in accordance
with the form of sensible intuition, is able to determine sensibility inwardly.
[B 153]

It is the synthesizing of the spatial manifold which affects inner
sense, so that when the synthesized manifold is brought to consciousness, it is apprehended in a temporal succession.

It is now possible to explain precisely how Kant's Refutation
of Idealism works, and why he was so confident that his position
was distinct from that of Berkeley. According to the theory just
set forth, the self becomes conscious of itself and gains knowledge
of itself by seeking out and bringing to self-consciousness its own
contents. Now these contents are spatial perceptions, and the act
of bringing them to consciousness is simply the act of synthesizing
them. But by synthesizing the manifold of spatial perceptions we
gain knowledge of material objects outside us (this has been
shown in the Deduction). Hence, it is only *through* knowledge
of outer things that the self can know itself. So Kant says, in the
note on the Refutation added to the Preface in B:

I am just as certainly conscious that there are things outside me, which are
in relation to my sense, as I am conscious that I myself exist as determined
in time. [B xli note]

With the help of Weldon's account of Tetens' psychological
theory, it has proved possible to make sense of some very difficult
and obscure passages in the Deduction and the Aesthetic. It remains to ask how this complex doctrine of inner sense fits into the
interpretation of the Analytic which has been set forth in this
Commentary.

In my discussion of the final version of the argument of the
Analytic, as it is completed in the Second Analogy, I point out
that the most serious flaw in the proof is the postulation of a
pre-conscious subjective temporal order.[18] The analysis of synthesis which I have developed in connection with the first-edition
Deduction presupposes that the manifold of intuition, *as given*,
possesses the form of time. The mind then reproduces it in imagination, thereby reorganizing it in an objective order which has a
synthetic, or rule-governed, necessity. But it here appears that

[18] Cf. pp. 279–280, below.

Kant only attributes a spatial order to the given manifold. Its temporal order — *even its subjective temporal order* — is described as the product of the synthesis by which the objective world-order is produced.

This is not merely evidence of my faulty interpretation, however, for the argument of the Analogies clearly depends on the one temporal order being given, and the other being produced by synthesis. So it seems that at the root of Kant's theory in the Analytic there is an unresolved contradiction.

One solution suggests itself, although I confess that I do not think it does the job. In the Subjective Deduction, Kant distinguishes between the Synthesis of Apprehension in Intuition and the Syntheses of Reproduction and Recognition [A 98 ff]. Later on, he alters this classification slightly and attributes the synthesis of apprehension to the faculty of imagination. Thus he says in the Second Analogy:

The apprehension of the manifold of appearance is always successive. . . . The appearances, in so far as they are objects of consciousness simply in virtue of being representations, are not in any way distinct from their apprehension, *that is, from their reception in the synthesis of imagination;* and we must therefore agree that the manifold of appearances is always *generated* [*erzeugt*] in the mind successively.[19]

From these passages it would seem that the subjective time order is due to a synthesis of imagination, which generates the order of subjective apprehension, while the objective time order is due to a second and supervening synthesis of understanding, whose material is the manifold as ordered by the first synthesis.

So we come back, once again, to Kant's attempt to split off the activity of imagination from the activity of understanding.[20] The former is responsible for our consciousness of, and indeed for the generation of, the subjective time order of the manifold of spatial perceptions. The latter produces the objective time order of phenomena. There are several reasons why this way out of the dilemmas of inner sense seems to me not successful. First of all, it gives too much to the creativity of the self. In the Analogies, Kant portrays the self as beginning with a given subjective time order out of which it constructs the natural world. On the present

[19] B 234–235. For "synthesis of imagination," see A 94, omitted in B.
[20] Cf. pp. 68–77 above.

view, even the subjective order itself is attributed to the self. Here as elsewhere Kant tends to slip toward the idealist doctrine that the self spins the world, *in toto*, out of itself. More serious philosophically, however, is the fact that by attributing the initial time order to a synthesis of imagination, Kant cuts himself off from the kind of explanation of "synthesis" which I presented above. I can only repeat my conviction that until he can give a coherent non-metaphorical account of the activity of synthesis, in terms of which he can explain its curious capacity for bestowing synthetic unity on a manifold, Kant has no theory at all. Hence it is better to try to adjust the doctrine of inner sense to the theory of synthesis than the other way around.

KANT begins the second book of the Analytic with a flourish of the architectonic. General logic, following the structure of the intellect, deals with the three faculties of understanding (*Verstand*), judgment (*Urteilskraft*) and reason (*Vernunft*), whose corresponding objects are concepts, judgments, and inferences. As it abstracts from all content, general logic takes no notice of the possible objects of knowledge, and its conclusions are therefore unlimited in their application. Whatever it discovers from the analysis of concepts, judgments, and inferences is valid for all thought and all being. Needless to say, the truths of general logic are all analytic propositions.

Transcendental logic sets itself a more ambitious goal, and is correspondingly more limited in the scope of its conclusions. It retains a certain content, namely that of pure *a priori* modes of knowledge, and its conclusions, which are synthetic or ampliative in nature, are valid only for the objects of experience. This restriction carries with it the seeds of a possible error, for if the propositions of transcendental logic are treated as if they belonged to general logic — if, that is, a universal validity is ascribed to them — then the result will better be called a logic of illusion, or Dialectic, than a logic of truth, or Analytic. Just this error has been committed by past philosophers, Kant claims. It is the source of the rational theology and cosmology which has till now been put forward as *a priori* metaphysical knowledge.

For purposes of systematic neatness, and because of the logical structure of certain of the dialectical errors which he aims to expose, Kant blames all of the fallacies of transcendent metaphysics on the third of the three faculties of knowledge, namely reason. Consequently, when he divides transcendental logic into Analytic and Dialectic, he assigns concepts and judgments to the former, and inferences to the latter. So we get the Analytic of Concepts, the Analytic of Principles, and the Dialectical Inferences of Pure Reason. Unfortunately, things are not quite so simple; or perhaps we should say fortunately, for the complications carry us closer to the truth, not farther from it.

In the first place, Kant denies his own distinction between the faculties of understanding and judgment by entitling the second chapter of the Analytic of Principles the "System of all Principles of Pure Understanding," rather than "System of all Principles of Judgment." This terminological inconsistency may seem unimportant, but in fact it reflects one of the most significant conclusions of the Deduction. The point is that the distinction between concepts and judgments is illegitimate in Transcendental Philosophy, however adequate it may be for school logic. The categories, or pure concepts, are *a priori* rules, which is to say laws. The principles are not *applications* of the categories, despite Kant's own insistence to the contrary; they *are* the categories. This will become clearer as we proceed through the rest of the Analytic.

Secondly, it is misleading of Kant to attribute all dialectical illusion to reason alone. His reasons for doing so derive from the broader scheme of the Critical Philosophy. Dialectical illusion, strictly so called, is the confusion of appearance with independent reality. Reason, as the faculty both of logic and of ethical judgment, has a legitimate realm of transcendent employment. It is natural, therefore, to attribute the contradictions of transcendent metaphysics to reason's illegitimate extension of the categories and principles beyond the realm of appearance, to things-in-themselves. As an account of mental faculties, this may have its virtues, but as a scheme for a logic it is inadequate. Inferences have a perfectly legitimate employment within the confines of experience, and ought therefore to be treated as part of the Analytic. Kant recognizes this fact in his doctrine of the regulative employment of reason (cf. Appendix to the Dialectic), which assigns an essential and constructive scientific role to reason. Conversely, dialectical illusion may result from other elements of logic than inferences. This, too, Kant acknowledges by including a Book on the Concepts of Pure Reason in the Dialectic.

TRANSCENDENTAL JUDGMENT
IN GENERAL

This section is of little help to the reader who is trying to find out what the Analytic of Principles is about. The doctrine of judgment expounded here has no essential connection with the problem of the application of the pure concepts, even supposing for the moment that there is a problem which can be thus defined.

Judgment is said to be the "faculty of subsuming under rules; that is, of distinguishing whether something does or does not stand under a given rule" [A 132]. Kant has in mind the ability to decide, for example, whether a given act is murder or manslaughter, or again, whether a bit of matter conforms to the concept of salt or sugar. The point is that even if you know the criminal law or the rules of chemistry perfectly, you must still decide which law or rule is applicable to the case at hand.

Now Kant claims that transcendental logic can actually give rules for judgment, even though general logic cannot. The source of these rules, as we might expect, is the set of conditions which are placed on transcendental logic by its limitation to the objects of experience. "Transcendental philosophy has the peculiarity that besides the rule (or rather the universal condition of rules), which is given in the pure concept of understanding, it can also specify *a priori* the instance to which the rule is to be applied" [B 174]. It is obvious, I think, that Kant is here confusing the giving of rules of thumb for the application of concepts ("mother wit") with the laying down of the conditions under which alone those concepts can have legitimate employment. It is this latter task which the Schematism is intended to perform.

CHAPTER I

THE SCHEMATISM OF THE PURE CONCEPTS OF UNDERSTANDING

The Schematism is occasioned by a variety of architectonic considerations which obscure and misrepresent Kant's real teaching. The first aim of a commentary, therefore, should be to show how this is so, and why it has happened. At the same time, Kant includes in the chapter some extremely important material on the nature of the categories and their relation to empirical concepts. Furthermore, the doctrine of the Schematism, even though perhaps inconsistent with the conclusions of the Deduction, reflects certain broad principles which Kant continued to hold throughout the *Critique*, particularly in the Dialectic. In what follows, I shall try to say something about all three of these subjects.[1]

The Argument of the Schematism

According to Kant, a Schematism is needed because of the special characteristics of the pure concepts. A concept is by nature universal.[2] It can be applied to an object because of a partial identity between it and the representation of the object. Thus, the concept 'man' applies to Socrates because it and the concept 'Socrates' both contain the characteristics 'rational' and 'animal.' The same homogeneity, as Kant puts it [A 137], exists between the concept 'cinnabar' and a perception of a piece of the stuff. In this latter case, the concept can apply to an intuition because it (the concept) contains sensible predicates (redness, weight) which have previously been abstracted from experience. In the

[1] Cf. Kemp Smith, pp. 334–342.
[2] Cf. Kant's *Logic;* § 1, Anmerk. 2: "It is a mere tautology to speak of universal or common concepts, a mistake based on an incorrect division of concepts into universal, particular and individual. Not the concepts themselves, but only their use can be so divided."

case of 'Socrates' and 'man,' both concepts contain sensible predicates derived from experience.

But the pure concepts are by definition devoid of all sensible content [cf. B 3]. There cannot be any partial identity between them and the sensible appearances to which they are to be applied. Some account must be given, therefore, of the manner in which the categories apply to appearances. Kant proposes to bridge the gulf between category and appearance with a "third thing," which bears a partial identity to each at the same time. It must be both intellectual like the category and sensible like the appearance. Time meets both these conditions:

[A] transcendental determination of time is so far homogeneous with the category, which constitutes its unity, in that it is universal and rests upon an *a priori* rule. But, on the other hand, it is so far homogeneous with appearance, in that time is contained in every empirical representation of the manifold. Thus an application of the category to appearances becomes possible by means of the transcendental determination of time, which, as the schema of the concepts of understanding, mediates the subsumption of the appearances under the category. [B 177–78]

Each category must be provided with a "transcendental determination of time," by means of which it can be brought into contact with appearances. This Kant proceeds to do in the second half of the chapter.

The artificiality of both the problem and the solution is evident upon reflection. To take the second first, the solution is a sheer *non sequitur*. If A is identical with B in respect R, and B is identical with C in respect R', then what sense does it make to say that B "mediates between" A and C? Either appearances can be subsumed under the categories without the aid of the schemata, or else they cannot be subsumed at all. Bachelors and spinsters are both unmarried; spinsters and mothers are both women; but it does not follow that bachelors are mothers. As Kemp Smith points out, Kant undoubtedly has a quite different sort of subsumption in mind here, namely that whereby the minor term of a syllogism is brought under the major term. In a syllogism in Barbara, for example, the major term A is related to a middle B, by the fact that All A are B. Similarly, the middle and minor bear the relation All B are C. A is then subsumed under C in the conclusion, All A are C. But here a partial identity does exist between A and C.

The middle term serves to demonstrate this identity, not to make up for the lack of it.

The problem itself is the result of Kant's failure to take notice of his own conclusions. Whatever the nature of ordinary class concepts may be, the Deduction proves that pure concepts are rules for synthesis. They direct the process of working up a manifold of intuition into a unified and organized empirical knowledge. Now, the relation between a rule for organizing something and the something to be organized is nothing like the relation which Kant claims to exist between a class concept and one of its instances.[3] It makes no sense to ask whether a rule is homogeneous with that which it regulates.

Despite this confusion, the argument of the Schematism comes to an exceedingly important conclusion: the categories are *a priori* valid of experience in general only in so far as they are related to the various modes of *time-consciousness*. This proposition ought not to come as a complete surprise to one who has followed the argument of the Deduction with care. The categories are there described as the rules for the synthetic unity which is imposed on the contents of consciousness by the activity of transcendental imagination. As time is the form of inner sense, it follows that whatever appears in consciousness must be part of a temporal order of representations. Hence, we might expect that the categories, in their application to the manifold, would express the structure of time-consciousness in general. The Subjective Deduction, as we saw, made use of the temporal ordering of consciousness in its explication of the synthesizing process, but Kant only draws out the full significance of time in the Analytic of Principles.

In commenting upon the Metaphysical Deduction, I had occasion to note the *ad hoc* character of the tables of Judgments and Categories. There seemed no justification for some of the items in the Table of Judgments other than to prepare the way for the categories, and even the latter appeared in several instances to serve the interests of systematic neatness more than the demands of logic. This sense of arbitrariness is increased by the doctrine of Schematism. How is it that there are just the right number

---

[3] Strictly speaking, categories and class concepts might be very much alike if it turned out that even the latter were rules. As we shall see, Kant seems to think this is the case, but if so, then the whole problem should never have arisen.

of transcendental determinations of time? Could the understanding contain a category which failed to find its mode of time? Would a transcendental determination of time, as it were, coerce the understanding into producing a corresponding category? The whole business smacks of that pre-established harmony which Kant elsewhere rejects as the very denial of philosophical explanation.

To a certain extent, we are here seeing just one more example of the distortions of the architectonic. Kant has a great deal to say about two of the categories, causality and substance. He can make a pretty fair case for community, and he sees a way of getting his dynamical theory of matter into the system under the heading of Quality. So he searches about for plausible 'determinations of time' to cover the other categories, and comes up finally with the system of schemata. Because he makes so much of the synthetic character of experience, Kant must lay the burden of his argument on the categories of *relation*. The whole Deduction argument makes sense only if one thinks of the categories as ways of relating perceptions (or pure intuitions). Thus it is not surprising that the Analogies of Experience occupy as many pages as the Axioms, Anticipations, and Postulates taken together, or that the really important contribution of the Analytic of Principles is to be found in the Second Analogy, of causation.

Looked at in this way, even the connection between the categories of relation and their schemata appears fortuitous. Since the understanding and the forms of sensibility are initially distinct and independent, it is merely a happy accident that causality and substance can find so interesting a temporal interpretation. Suppose, however, that we turn Kant's entire argument upside down. Instead of beginning with the Table of Categories and hunting for time-determinations, what happens if we begin with time as the form of inner sense, and try to derive a Table of Categories by analysis of time-consciousness? The answer, as we shall see in the Analogies, is that we arrive at precisely the desired categories of relation! With this simple revision, the entire Analytic suddenly falls into a perfectly logical form. Omit the Metaphysical Deduction and how does Kant's argument run? First, a proof that the mere fact of the unity of consciousness implies the applicability to experience of certain *a priori* forms of synthesis (the Deduction); then, the addition to the argument of the fact that consciousness has a temporal form (the Schematism); lastly, the deduction of the particular forms of synthesis by an examination of the structure of time-consciousness (the Analogies). Starting with the unity of consciousness, we arrive finally at the validity of the causal maxim. This reorganization of the Analytic diminishes somewhat the plausibility of the system of categories — those which cannot be drawn out of time-consciousness must simply be abandoned — but it adds immeasurably to the power of the argument. Kant can be seen actually to deduce the causal maxim from the nature of subjective consciousness.

The appearance of a pre-established harmony between the categories and the modes of time consciousness also points up a rather important shift which takes place in Kant's conception of the relation of sensibility to understanding. In the *Dissertation*, they are viewed as perfectly distinct and separate mental faculties. The forms of sensibility are said to determine the character of phenomena and the pure concepts of understanding to yield knowledge of noumena. With the move to a Critical theory, understanding is limited to phenomena, and thus the two faculties become co-equal but independent sources of forms (conditions) of experience. This view is clearly expressed in Section 1 of the Deduction in A. Kant there asserts that appearances could meet the conditions of sensibility, and thus enter consciousness, without necessarily also meeting the conditions of understanding and thereby yielding knowledge.

But such a doctrine is inadequate to meet the sceptical doubts of Hume and so Kant finally comes to see that sensibility and understanding are inseparably linked. The categories, so far from being independent forms of thought which must find their temporal interpretation in schemata, become modes of time-determination. More strictly, they become rules for the synthesis of a temporal manifold. As such, they are shown to be universal and necessary conditions of all time-consciousness.

Categories, Schemata, and Empirical Concepts

Paragraphs 6 and 7 contain an analysis of schemata, and some exceedingly important remarks on the nature of empirical concepts. Kant begins by distinguishing a schema from an image.[4]

[4] The use of examples from mathematics makes it appear that Kant is talking

No image can ever adequately express what is contained in a concept, for the image is particular in a way that a concept is not. If I conjure up the picture of a man, he will be some particular height or other, with a determinate color of hair, etc. The concept, on the other hand, abstracts from these qualities, thus making it possible to think many individuals at once through their common characteristics. This is just the problem with which the empiricists had struggled in their attempts to derive all our ideas from perceptions. Although Kant adopts the terminology of the rationalists, and structures his *Critique* with their classifications of logic, his solution to the puzzle of the generality of concepts turns out to be more akin to that of Hume.

The solution is the *schema*. When I imagine a dog or a triangle or a man, I generate an image according to a rule. In the case of the triangle, the rule tells me to draw a plane figure having three straight sides which meet at three vertices. The rule is attached to the concept of a triangle, and it remains the same no matter what sort of triangle I draw. Now, there are an unending variety of images which can be generated in accordance with this rule, no one of them any more of a triangle than any other. A given image is subsumable under a concept when it has been generated by means of the schema of the concept. Kant defines the schema, therefore, as a "representation of a universal procedure of imagination in providing an image for a concept" [B 179].

Sometimes, of course, we do not actually produce an image for a concept, as when we think of very large numbers. It suffices to call to mind the rule by which we could provide an image if we so desired. Again, in reasoning about mathematical objects, we base our arguments on the schema rather than the image. It is not what can be read off from *this* equilateral triangle (such as that it is five inches on a side), but what follows from the rule for constructing equilateral triangles, that is sought in a geometrical proof.[5] Kant makes these points in an effort to prove that the

about the schemata of pure concepts, for mathematics refers to objects in pure intuition. Actually, however, what he says applies to empirical concepts primarily, for only they have *images* in the strict sense. See below.

[5] This point is quite important for Kant's theory of mathematics. Kant holds that geometry is synthetic, not a succession of tautologies, and he seems to base this on the view that the constructions of figures in each proof are essential and cannot be expressed by definitions. It follows from this that the schemata, rather than either the actual figures *or the concepts,* are the critical elements of mathematics.

schema, and not the image, is what truly represents the concept, but his argument really seems to prove that the schema is the concept. He comes very close to recognizing this in paragraph 7, when he states that the empirical concept "always stands in immediate relation to the schema of imagination." In the next sentence, the two are virtually identified: "The concept 'dog' signifies a rule according to which my imagination can delineate the figure of a four-footed animal. . . ." The concept is not merely associated with a rule of imagination, it signifies such a rule, or, as Kant asserts in the Deduction, a concept is "something universal which serves as a rule" [A 106].

Thus far, the discussion of schemata has concerned only empirical concepts and perhaps the pure sensible concepts of mathematics. But what of the pure concepts of understanding? Their schemata, Kant asserts, "can never be brought into any image whatsoever" [A 142], the reason for this being that the schema of a pure concept "is simply the pure synthesis, determined by a rule of that unity, in accordance with concepts, to which the category gives expression" [A 142]. This explanation, as it stands, is hopelessly murky. The real reason why categories cannot be brought to images is that they are not ordinary first-level rules at all. Rather they are *types* of rules. They bear the same relation to empirical schemata that empirical schemata bear to images.[6] To understand this, let us revert to the example of the potter which was used in explaining the nature of rule-directed activities.

The potter, it will be recalled, is engaged in an activity whose successive stages are determined by a rule. Suppose that a visitor to the pottery asks the general question, How does one make earthenware? The potter may answer somewhat as follows: First place a certain amount of clay on the wheel; then turn the wheel at the proper speed, shaping the clay in the desired manner; etc., etc. Now not even the quickest pupil could possibly learn from this description how to make earthenware, for the potter is not giving the rules for bowl-making, plate-making, or vase-making. He is really giving a rule-type with whose use the pupil can construct pottery-making rules. This rule about rules, or second-

---

[6] I have dispensed with the distinction between categories and their schemata for the purpose of exposition. The rather complex problem of the difference between the two is discussed below.

order rule, if formulated as a rule, might read: First lay it down how much clay shall be placed on the wheel; then prescribe the speed at which the wheel shall be turned; then specify the shaping movements of the hands; and so forth.

The point of this digression is that categories are *second-order rules*. They lay down the general conditions to which first-order empirical concepts must conform. Kant hints at this notion in B 174, when he speaks of "the rule (or rather the universal condition of rules), which is given in the pure concept of understanding." The parenthetical emendation makes all the difference. A universal condition of rules can only be a rule for rules, in Kant's philosophy. Once the relation of categories to empirical concepts is made explicit, we see why it is impossible to give an image for a category. The rules for generating pottery-making rules are exemplified by pottery rules, not by pottery. In like manner the categories are exemplified by empirical concepts. Thus the images of the category of causation are simply the particular empirical concepts of causal connection which we call causal laws, and the images of the category of substance are the various empirical concepts of objects. To use Kant's example, the category of substance stands to the concept "dog" as it in turn stands to the image of a particular dog.

This analysis of the structure of the categories can command support from the text, and it allows us to make a good deal more sense of the later teaching of the Analogies, but it is by no means certain that Kant would have accepted it completely. He might well have preferred either of two other methods of distinguishing categories from empirical concepts, which must at least be mentioned. The first consists simply of repeating that *pure* concepts are those which contain nothing from sensation [B 34]. Although this does set off the categories from empirical concepts, it tells us nothing more about the relation between them.

An alternative to degrees of purity as a distinguishing mark is provided by the theory of transcendental synthesis which Kant adumbrated in the Objective Deduction. According to that doctrine, at least as spelled out in the *Opus Postumum*, the categories are rules for synthesizing a manifold of pure intuition, while empirical concepts are rules for synthesizing a manifold of empirical intuition. Both are therefore what I have been calling first-order rules. But this interpretation runs afoul of all the problems connected with pure intuition, and besides is practically useless in helping us to understand the Analytic of Principles.

The Broader Implications of the Schematism

Kant could have simplified the Analytic considerably by identifying the categories with their schemata, instead of maintaining the distinction between them. There are very powerful considerations which weigh against such an identification, chiefly relating to the doctrines to be expounded in the Dialectic and the later *Critiques*. Though these subjects lie outside the scope of this commentary, some mention must be made of them if we are to understand the forces shaping the Analytic.

In the *Dissertation*, Kant held that the pure concepts have absolutely universal application, while the forms of sensibility (space and time) are valid only for the realm of appearances. The application of the categories to appearances, therefore, constituted a limitation of them by sensibility. Kant expressed this in the *Dissertation* by the statement that propositions with sensible subjects and intellectual predicates are legitimate, while the converse sort are not.[7] Even after giving up the doctrine that the categories apply to things-in-themselves, he continued to represent them as at least possibly universal in scope.

There are at least three different views of the scope of the categories in the *Critique*, no one of which ever seems to have won out over the others in Kant's mind. The first, just mentioned, is that the application of the categories to independent reality is problematic, but in no sense internally inconsistent. This teaching can be found in the chapter on Phenomena and Noumena, the following extract from which is typical:

If I remove from empirical knowledge all thought (through categories), no knowledge of any object remains. For through mere intuition nothing at all is thought, and the fact that this affection of sensibility is in me does not amount to a relation of such representation to any object. But if, on the other hand, I leave aside all intuition, the form of thought still remains — that is, the mode of determining an object for the manifold of a possible intuition. The categories accordingly extend further than sensible intuition,

[7] See summary of *Dissertation*, pp. 20–21 above.

since they think objects in general, without regard to the special mode (the sensibility) in which they may be given.[8]

The importance of this first view is that it preserves the meaningfulness of assertions about independent reality which are couched in terms of the categories. It thus remains open to us to believe what we cannot know.[9] The (causal) freedom of the will, the immutability of the (substantial) soul, and the existence of God, can all be made articles of faith, since they are at least not inconsistent.[10]

The second view, a significant revision of the first, is that the categories have at least problematic application to all forms of *sensible* intuition: "the pure concepts of understanding . . . extend to objects of intuition in general, be the intuition like or unlike ours, if only it be sensible and not intellectual" [B 148]. When thus extended, of course, they yield no knowledge. It is still true to say that sensibility limits understanding, but it is now the peculiar characteristics of human sensibility, rather than the characteristics of sensibility in general, which are the limiting conditions. Since the categories are rules for the synthesis of a manifold of intuition, and since only sensible intuition requires to be unified by synthesis [B 138–39], it would not make the least sense to attempt to apply the categories to things-in-themselves. A rule for synthesizing a manifold can have even problematic application only to a manifold.

The third view constitutes a still further constriction of the categories. It teaches that the categories are modes of time-consciousness, and so extend only so far as a sensibility like ours. Once the move has been made from the first to the second position, it seems to me inevitable that this last step should be taken, for any attempt to explain exactly how the categories function will necessarily involve the characteristics of rule-directed reproduction *in time*. When abstracted from that condition, the categories become

[8] B 309. In the last sentence Kemp Smith adopts Erdmann's reading of the parenthesis as *die Sinnlichkeit* = the sensibility, in place of *der Sinnlichkeit* = of sensibility. The difference is actually quite relevant to the present discussion, for if we read "of sensibility," then the passage implies that the categories have a problematic extension only to other possible forms of sensible intuition. The continuation of the passage lends weight to Erdmann's emendation.

[9] "I have therefore found it necessary to deny *knowledge*, in order to make room for *faith*." [B xxx]

[10] See the Antinomies of Pure Reason. It takes a bit of stretching to get God out of the category of community.

meaningless, mere titles of concepts, as Kant says at one point [A 696].

Although the second of these conceptions of the categories has a good deal of theoretical interest, it plays almost no role in Kant's thought. The few passages in which he speaks of other forms of sensible intuition give the impression of having been added merely to tie down a loose end in the theory. The first and third alternatives, on the other hand, are both intimately involved in the Critical system, and they pose a genuine and very difficult choice for Kant. Originally, the *Critique* was conceived as a middle way between the extremes of rationalism and empiricism, or in Kant's language, Dogmatism and Scepticism. Kant's solution was to develop a critical method which considers whether a question can be decided before attempting to answer it [A 388–89]. Thus, in the Dialectic Kant argues only for the undecidability of all propositions concerning things-in-themselves, not for their falsehood. Now, a presupposition of this position is the doctrine that pure concepts have a problematic applicability to independent reality, since if the rationalistic dogmas concerning God, freedom, etc., could be shown to be strictly *meaningless* or *contradictory*, the critical balance would be tilted in favor of empiricism. In the Dialectic, therefore, Kant is committed to the first theory of the categories mentioned above.

While working out the details of the Analytic, however, Kant found himself driven farther and farther from the *Dissertation* doctrine of pure concepts, and closer to a picture of them as rules for the synthesis of a manifold of intuition. This development, if carried over into other parts of the Critical Philosophy, would have necessitated a fundamental reconstruction of Kant's ethical and theological views.

The various difficulties of interpretation which adhere to Kant's doctrine of categories come together in the question whether we can distinguish the pure categories from the schematized categories. Paton has gone into this matter at very great length.[11] He maintains, with copious quotations from all parts of the *Critique*, that we can actually discover pure categories, schematized categories, and transcendental schemata, as well as the functions of judgment. To prove this he reconstructs the quartet for each of the cate-

[11] Cf. Paton, II, 17–78.

gories which is given a schema. For example, the logical function of hypothetical judgment (If p then q) yields the pure category which Paton describes as "the concept of the synthesis of ground and consequent." The schematized category corresponding to this is "the concept of the synthesis of ground and consequent where the consequent succeeds the ground in time," better known as the category of cause and effect. The transcendental schema, finally, is *necessary succession*.[12] Paton offers similar definitions for quantity, quality, modality, and the other two categories of relation.

In contrast to Paton's view we may cite Kemp Smith, who holds that the distinction between categories and schemata is completely artificial. Speaking with his customary assurance as to the deeper significance of Kant's thought, Kemp Smith writes:

> The true Critical teaching is that category and intuition, that is to say, form and content, mutually condition one another, and that the so-called schema is simply a name for the latter as apprehended in terms of the former.[13]
> What Kant usually means when he speaks of the categories *are* the schemata.[14]

In deciding between these two extreme interpretations, it seems to me that we must split the prize, for each has a distinct virtue. Paton's theory would surely have won Kant's approval, had he ever been confronted by it. The parallel tables, the neat pigeon-holes, the excess of terminology, all would please Kant's taste for architectonic. At the same time — and this is the fatal weakness of Paton's entire commentary — the elaboration of the details of the system leaves us as puzzled about its *meaning* as we were to begin with. Kemp Smith, on the other hand, tells us something which makes philosophic sense, however much it may require us to ignore certain of Kant's repeated utterances as "pre-critical." Just as it is hard to see the distinction between a rule for synthesis and the unity of the rule,[15] so there appears to be little difference between a category and a schema, let alone between a schematized category and its schema.

If a commentator makes the claim that Kant did not mean what he said, then he ought to explain what led Kant to write the passage

[12] *Ibid.*, pp. 53–54.
[13] Kemp Smith, pp. 335–36.
[14] *Ibid.*, p. 340. Compare Paton, vol. ii, p. 69. Cf. also Kemp Smith, p. 195.
[15] See the discussion of the Metaphysical Deduction, above.

at all. Kemp Smith attributes the misleading doctrine of Schematism to architectonic considerations, but this is not a sufficient explanation. The importance of its contents alone shows that Kant was not simply filling up an empty slot in the system. I have tried to account for the Schematism by pointing to its historical precedents in the *Dissertation*, and by referring to Kant's ethical and theological interest in distinguishing pure from applied categories. Coupled with the influence of the architectonic, these factors undoubtedly explain the presence of the Schematism in the *Critique*.

The Problem of Pure Intuition

The theory of the Schematism is based on Kant's doctrine of pure intuition, and it may therefore be appropriate to make some general comments here on that vexing subject. No aspect of the *Critique* is more difficult to interpret, or more often repeated as an integral part of the Critical teaching. I cannot undertake to clarify the notion of pure intuition, as I do not at all understand it, but it may help to indicate the reasons for Kant's adherence to it. For an excellent discussion of the entire question, the reader is urged to consult Kemp Smith.[16]

The term "pure intuition" first appears in the *Dissertation*,[17] where it clearly denotes the pure form of, or purely formal aspect of, sensibility. Space and time are there described as "law[s] of the mind, according to which it combines in a fixed manner the sensa produced in it by the presence of the object." [18] We acquire our concepts of space and time by a self-reflective attention to "the action of the mind in co-ordinating its sensa." [19] The implication of this seems to be that space and time are *a priori* only in the sense of lying ready in the mind as potentialities. As Kant says, they are thus far *acquired* rather rather than *connate*.

In the *Critique* Kant introduces a new and baffling notion of pure intuition: not a pure form of intuition, but an actual, separate, given manifold of pure intuition. At first this might be supposed to mean merely that the mind can abstract the forms of sensible intuition from the content [sensation], thereby leaving a "pure mani-

---

[16] Kemp Smith, pp. 88–98.
[17] § 14 and elsewhere.
[18] § 15.
[19] *Ibid.*

fold." The initial definition of pure intuition in the Aesthetic encourages such a view:

If I take away from the representation of a body that which the understanding thinks in regard to it . . . and likewise what belongs to sensation, impenetrability, hardness, colour, etc., something still remains over from this empirical intuition, namely, extension and figure. These belong to pure intuition, which, even without any actual object of the senses or of sensation, exists in the mind *a priori* as a mere form of sensibility. [B 35]

Countless other passages, however, demonstrate that Kant has a very much more difficult notion of pure intuition than this. In the Deduction in B, for example, he states that

space and time are represented *a priori* not merely as *forms* of sensible intuition, but as themselves *intuitions* which contain a manifold . . . [B 160]

In the Metaphysical Exposition of space in the Aesthetic, space is described as "an infinite *given* magnitude" [B 39] which is furthermore "an *a priori* intuition, not a concept" [B 40]. I have already indicated, in discussing the Objective Deduction in A, that Kant's theory of transcendental synthesis required just such a separate pure manifold of intuition.[20]

What are we to make of this doctrine? That it is essential to many of Kant's theories, and not an idle speculation or temporary aberration, is I think unquestionable. But when we attempt to give some concrete meaning to it, we come up against Kant's unclarity on a subject central to the *Critique*: the distinction between the formal and material elements in cognition. Kant invariably associates the formal element with that which is contributed by the mind, and hence can be known *a priori*, while the material element is identified with the given object of knowledge which in its particularity can only be known *a posteriori*.[21] Transcendental phi-

---

[20] This point of interpretation has been very hotly debated by Kant commentators. Such passages as B 160 seem to me conclusive, but no doubt many students of the *Critique* will disagree. Vaihinger is quite definite in his treatment of the problem (*Commentar*, ii, pp. 102-111). Thus, on page 104 he says: "Diese Form (der Anschauung) ist also nicht bloss etwas künstlich erst aus der Erscheinung Abstrahirtes, was nur an der Erscheinung stattfände . . . sondern sie ist etwas für sich allein, unabhängig von der Materie und vor aller Erscheinung in uns Existirendes. Und zwar existirt in uns vor allen Erscheinungen nicht nur etwa bloss die potentielle Form . . . sondern es liegt in uns schon von vorneherein eine fertige, actuelle Anschauung. . . ." Vaihinger cites A 52, A 373, B 305, and also *Dissertation* § 12: "Raum und Zeit, die *objecta* der *Mathesis pura, sunt omnis intuitus non solum principia formalia, sed ipsa intuitus originarii.*"

[21] See, for example, the Preface to the *Groundwork of the Metaphysics of Morals*.

losophy therefore concerns itself with the form of experience — its content is left to the unpredictable given.

In the *Critique*, intuition is frequently identified with the content, or material element, of cognition, and concepts with the formal element. Thus, in the famous passage from the Introduction to the Transcendental Logic, Kant says:

> Without sensibility no object would be given to us, without understanding no object would be thought. Thoughts without content [n.b.] are empty, intuitions without concepts are blind. [B 75]

At the same time, however, the distinction between form and matter can be carried into the manifold of intuition itself, where the pure form — be it space or time — is distinguished from the matter, namely sensation [cf. B 34]. As formal elements in cognition, space and time are mind-dependent and knowable *a priori* — whence the doctrine of the Aesthetic. Indeed, even sensation can be analyzed into a form (its degree of intensity, or qualitative magnitude) and a content or matter (its particular quality).[22] Thus it appears that the manifold of intuition, which is matter for concepts, is itself a combination of matter and form, at several different levels.

Whenever the form-matter distinction is employed by a philosopher, the question arises whether either can exist without the other. The logical answer should be *no*, but there are usually pressing reasons why the philosopher wishes to say *yes*. And it is always *form without matter* that he is interested in. The best examples are Aristotle's prime mover and active intellect, both of which are blatant contradictions of the whole form-matter, actuality-potentiality system of distinctions which he has developed. Kant finds himself in just such a quandary. He insists that in cognition concepts and intuitions are as form to matter — or alternatively, that in perception pure intuition and sensation are as form to matter. Therefore, he ought to conclude that concepts without intuitions, or intuition with sensation, are mere potentialities lying ready in the mind to be actualized in experience. In fact, he often says just that. But at the same time he very much wants to say that concepts without intuitions are at least meaningful, and that intuition with-

---

[22] See the discussion of the Anticipations of Perception, pp. 232–238.

out sensation can exist as an actual manifold of pure (i.e., content-less) sensibility.[23]

I have several times indicated Kant's motives for insisting that concepts without intuitions are not quite totally blind. There are equally weighty reasons for his claim that pure intuition can exist without sensational content. The first of these is the function of pure intuition in the justification of *a priori* mathematics. Kant apparently believed that mathematics was *a priori* in a psychological as well as a logical sense. That is, he seems to have held that the truths of geometry could be known literally before (in time) experience of objects in space. For this to be possible, space would have to be a complete intuition, or given individual, which "exist[s] in the mind [and] precedes the objects themselves" [B 41]. The objects of geometry are constructed in this pure space; the applicability to empirical objects of the theorems of geometry is guaranteed by the (apparently fortuitous) fact that space is the pure form of empirical intuition as well as a pure *a priori* intuition.

Having said all this, I must now take back much of it, for Kant several times denies the status of knowledge to pure geometry, precisely on the grounds that it has no object.[24] Furthermore, the ambiguity of his language always permits the commentator to read the pure manifold — as an independent entity — out of existence. For a demonstration of the slipperiness of the subject compare Kemp Smith and Paton on the precise sense of "a priori." [25]

[23] The double view of perception, as not only matter for concepts but also a combination of pure intuition and sensation, helps to explain Kant's vacillations on the possibility of unsynthesized perceptions entering consciousness. In so far as they are merely matter for cognition, perceptions cannot be apprehended until a conceptual form has been impressed upon them. But viewed as sensations which have already acquired a spatio-temporal ordering, perceptions seem quite adequate candidates for contents of consciousness. This confusion dates back to the *Dissertation*, where space and time are considered products of mental activity rather than passivity. The relativity of all such form-matter, active-passive distinctions allows Kant to maintain many incompatible doctrines in an uneasy suspension.

[24] "Mathematical concepts are not, therefore, by themselves knowledge, except on the supposition that there are things which allow of being presented to us only in accordance with the form of that pure sensible intuition. Now *things in space and time* are given only in so far as they are perceptions. . . . Consequently, the pure concepts of understanding, even when they are applied to *a priori* intuitions, as in mathematics, yield knowledge only in so far as these intuitions . . . can be applied to empirical intuitions" [B 147]. Notice that although Kant is here denying that pure mathematics is knowledge, he is not retracting his claim that there is a pure *a priori* separate spatial manifold of intuition.

[25] Kemp Smith, pp. 91–92, and Paton, vol. I, pp. 136–143.

The second and more important function of pure intuition is as the material for the transcendental synthesis. According to the theory of double affection, it will be recalled, the transcendental ego exercises its productive imagination upon a pure *a priori* manifold of sensuous intuition, from which it constructs the world of nature. In this world, among other things, is the empirical self, which is then affected by physical objects according to the laws of the physiology of perception. The result is a quite distinct manifold of perceptions (empirical intuition) on which reproductive imagination operates. The consequence is a set of subjective habits of association (reproduction) which mirror the objective connections already established by transcendental synthesis.[26] In order for this rather elaborate theory to have any plausibility at all, there must be a pure manifold independent of, and not merely abstracted from, the manifold of perceptions.

It is not difficult to show that the postulation of such a manifold contradicts other equally important parts of the Critical system. For example, Kant repeatedly asserts that empty space cannot be an object for us [A 214, A 487]. If not, then how can it be the stuff of (phenomenal) objects? Furthermore, as the real in space is matter, corresponding to sensation in perception [A 20], productive imagination could not possibly make a material world out of a manifold of content-less intuition.

Such considerations as the above explain why Kant persisted in a complicated and implausible theory which conflicts with so much of the rest of his philosophy. His perseverance was made easier by the thoroughgoing ambiguity of the key term, "pure intuition." It is always open to Kant to speak of pure intuition when he means pure *form* of intuition. As the word "manifold" (*mannigfaltige*) means "variety" or "diversity," the phrase "manifold of pure spatial intuition" can be interpreted as "variety of spatial relations, considered independently of that which they relate." Such an interpretation makes a great deal of sense, but it cannot be made to serve either the theory of transcendental synthesis or Kant's psychologistic version of the apriority of mathematics.

In the version of the argument of the Analytic which I have defended as Kant's best line of thought, the problem of pure intuition does not arise. Time and space are *a priori* forms of empirical in-

[26] See the analysis of Section 3 of the Deduction in A.

tuition and nothing more. The schemata, or schematized categories, are pure determinations of time only in the sense that they are second-order rule-types for the reproduction of a manifold, having nothing in them concerning the particular perceptual content of that manifold, but relating solely to its temporal ordering.

CHAPTER II

SYSTEM OF ALL PRINCIPLES OF PURE UNDERSTANDING

After setting forth the pure concepts of understanding (Analytic of Concepts) and having considered the manner in which the faculty of judgment may employ these concepts to form synthetic propositions (the Schematism), Kant states that it is now time to exhibit the system of principles which results from such employment. I have already suggested that this is a misleading representation of the aim of the Analytic of Principles. Actually, as we shall see, the Analytic of Principles is the deduction of the particular categories.[1]

The second paragraph of the introductory section [B 188] contains a rather startling assertion which requires some comment. The principles (*Grundsätze*), Kant says, are our highest and most universal modes of knowledge, and might therefore be supposed to stand beyond all possible proof.[2] Nevertheless, he continues:

This characteristic does not remove them beyond the sphere of proof. This proof cannot, indeed, be carried out in any objective fashion, since such principles lie at the foundation of all *knowledge* of objects. This does not, however, prevent our attempting a proof, from the subjective sources of

---

[1] Cf. Kemp Smith, pp. 343–44.

[2] The proof of a proposition usually consists of a syllogism of which it is the conclusion. In order to construct such a syllogism one needs premises, which then can be considered "higher" than the propositions to be proved. Kant is not merely referring to the purely logical point that in a deductive system some proposition or other must be the premise, and hence not deducible from higher propositions *in the system*. In accordance with traditional metaphysics, Kant is maintaining that certain propositions are *in their nature* better known than all others, so that no syllogistic proof with less well-known premises would increase their certainty. Cf. Aristotle, *An. Post.*, 71^b 25 — 72^b 4. One wonders how Kant pictures to himself a principle (*Grundsatz*) which was not *grounded* on any *higher* judgment. The confusion of higher and lower with necessary and sufficient conditions has already been discussed above. The last word in mixed metaphors is Kant's "supersensible substrate of nature," in *Critique of Teleological Judgement*, p. 67.

the possibility of knowledge of an object in general. Such proof is, indeed, indispensable, if the propositions are not to incur the suspicion of being merely surreptitious assertions. [A 149]

Kant surely cannot have meant what this passage seems to assert. The principles, for example the causal maxim, must be given a perfectly rigorous proof if the aims of the *Critique* are to be achieved. How could we be able to prove objectively that the applicability of the category of causation to objects of experience is an *a priori* condition of the possibility of experience, and yet only be able to offer a subjective proof of the causal maxim? Once more Kant is led by considerations of system into a misrepresentation of his views. The causal maxim is shown in the Second Analogy to be a logical consequence of the unity of consciousness.

What Kant has in mind here, undoubtedly, is the importance of the Subjective Deduction in the proof of the Principles. Since the proof turns on the characteristics of time-consciousness and the nature of synthesis, it draws primarily on section 2 of the Deduction rather than section 3. Nevertheless, it is an objective proof in whatever sense the Objective Deduction itself is objective.

SECTION I. THE HIGHEST PRINCIPLE OF ALL ANALYTIC JUDGMENTS

This section is required by the Architectonic. As he is expounding a transcendental logic, parallel to general logic, Kant must treat of analytic as well as of synthetic judgments. He therefore takes the opportunity to repudiate an earlier position and to clarify considerably the nature of the law of contradiction. As ordinarily stated, the law involves the concept of time. Aristotle, for example, gives the following version:

The same attribute cannot at the same time belong and not belong to the same subject and in the same respect.[3]

The conditions "at the same time . . . to the same subject and in the same respect" were added to rule out dialectical paradoxes directed against the principle, such as that a man who slakes his thirst is both thirsty (before) and not thirsty (afterward), or that a cube painted red and black on different sides is both red and not red. In the *Dissertation* Kant accepted this formulation and came

[3] *Metaphysics,* 1005[b] 18–22.

to the rather unusual, but quite consistent, conclusion that therefore the law of contradiction applied only to appearances:

So far is it from being possible that anyone should ever deduce and explain the concept of time by the help of reason, that the very principle of contradiction presupposes it, involving it as a condition. For A and not-A are not incompatible unless they are judged of the same thing *together* (i.e., in the same time); but when they are judged of a thing successively (i.e., at different times), they may both belong to it.[4]

Although this argument is, strictly speaking, correct, it proves only that the law of contradiction has been misstated, not that it applies only to phenomena. In the present section Kant offers a revised version, namely that "No predicate contradictory of a thing can belong to it."

Thus formulated, it denies the validity of any judgment of the form S is P, when the subject-term S contains the predicate 'not P.' For example, "An unlearned man is learned," with S = unlearned man and P = learned.

SECTION 2. THE HIGHEST PRINCIPLE OF ALL SYNTHETIC JUDGMENTS

With a great flourish and fanfare, Kant presents the highest principle of all synthetic judgments: "every object stands under the necessary conditions of synthetic unity of the manifold of intuition in a possible experience" [A 158]. This, of course, is not a new deduction from previous results; it is merely a statement of the conclusion of the Deduction. So far as the progress of the argument is concerned, the section is completely redundant. The form in which Kant recapitulates his argument, however, is interesting as an example of the extreme empiricist tendencies which find expression in scattered portions of the *Critique*.

In A 156, for instance, Kant asserts that the concepts of space and time would be "without objective validity, senseless and meaningless," if they did not have a necessary application to objects of experience. In other words, pure mathematics is meaningful only because it finds application to objects in applied mathematics. In A 157 Kant goes so far as to say that pure mathematics would be "nothing but a playing with a mere figment of the brain, were it not that space has to be regarded as a condition of the appear-

---

[4] *Dissertation*, § 14. Cf. also § 28.

ances which constitute the material for outer experience." In the second-edition Deduction the more moderate statement is made that pure mathematics is *knowledge* only in so far as it can be applied to objects of experience.[5]

The last sentence of the section is an example of the obscurity which is caused by Kant's ambiguous use of terms. Unless the sentence is to be construed virtually as a tautology, the first instance of the word "experience" must be interpreted as meaning "empirical consciousness," while the second instance must mean "empirical knowledge." Thus understood, the whole is merely a repetition of the Deduction principle.

SECTION 3. SYSTEMATIC REPRESENTATION OF ALL THE SYNTHETIC PRINCIPLES OF PURE UNDERSTANDING

The system of principles follows the Table of Categories. As already indicated in the Schematism, there are separate principles only for the categories of relation and modality. The distinction between the mathematical and dynamical principles is quite important, but Kant's account of it is misleading. The Axioms of Intuition and Anticipations of Perception tell us the general characteristics of perceptions, *considered simply as contents of consciousness*. Whatever their significance or proper interpretation, they will have extensive and intensive magnitude. The Analogies of Experience and the Postulates of Empirical Thought tell us what sorts of connections will be discoverable among perceptions, *considered as representations of objects*. The distinction between the mathematical and dynamical principles, therefore, can be viewed as deriving from the double nature of representations. Kant expresses his meaning better in B 222–23, where he renames the two groups "constitutive" and "regulative" principles.

It should be noticed that Kant made parallel revisions, in the second edition, in the Axioms, Anticipations, Analogies, and in each of the three individual Analogies. In each case he substituted a new statement of the principle and a paragraph headed "Proof." [6]

---

[5] Cf. B 147. For the terms "pure" and "applied," see B 206. Kant, of course, was ignorant of the notion of formal systems versus interpreted systems. The developments in logic during the past century have made it much clearer in what senses pure mathematics is and is not knowledge.

[6] Cf. B 202–203, B 207–208, B 218–19, B 224–25, B 232–34, B 256–58.

The reason for these substitutions is not stated, but I would suggest as an hypothesis that it is connected with the distinction between mathematical and dynamical categories just mentioned. In A 160 = B 199, Kant explains that the mathematical principles concern "the mere *intuition* of an appearance in general," while the dynamical categories concern "its *existence*." The first-edition statements of the principles seem to play up this ground of distinction, while the second-edition restatements play it down. For example, the principle of the Axioms in A is: "All appearances are, in their intuition, extensive magnitudes." In B this is changed simply to "All intuitions are extensive magnitudes." Again, the principle of the Analogies in A states: "All appearances are, as regards their existence, subject *a priori* to etc." In B appears the more straightforward: "Experience is possible only through the representation of a necessary connection of perceptions." The revisions of the individual Analogies confirm this hypothesis. The only doubtful case is the principle of the Anticipations where, for reasons which shall be discussed later, Kant was forced even in the first edition to emphasize the involvement of the appearance as well as the "mere intuition" of it. Nevertheless, even here the change in the second edition has the effect of de-emphasizing sensation in favor of the object. Having altered the form of the principle, Kant is then forced in each case to add a paragraph containing a new proof. For the most part, of course, the proof simply rehearses the arguments already contained in the first edition. I think it can be assumed, then, that Kant phrased the principles in the first edition so as to follow the distinction between mathematical and dynamical categories, and then decided that this requirement unduly distorted their meaning.

Axioms of Intuition

This section occupies a very peculiar place in the Critical system. According to the division of the Critique which Kant establishes in the Introduction, it should not really exist at all, for mathematics is supposed to be dealt with in the Aesthetic. What is more, the proof of the principle is a flat contradiction of one of the proofs employed in the Aesthetic. The exposition reveals one of the deepest flaws in Kant's philosophy, namely the inadequate and inconsistent account which it gives of the role of intuition in knowledge. With all this, the section succeeds in making some valuable contributions to the philosophy of mathematics.

The principle of the Axioms is: "All intuitions are extensive magnitudes." An extensive magnitude is one "the representation of [whose] parts makes possible, and therefore necessarily precedes, the representation of the whole" [A 162]. What this means is that in representing an extensive magnitude, we represent successively each of its parts, adding them one at a time. Consequently, thinking (representing) the whole is dependent upon first having thought of the parts. It is this fact, it will be recalled, which Kant takes as the source of the problem of the *Dissertation*. There, however, he distinguishes a sensitive from an intellectual representation of a whole, and attributes the character of extensive magnitude only to the former. The qualification "extensive" is required to distinguish it from intensive magnitude, which is treated in the Anticipations. The proof in A is quite simple: It is impossible to call up an image of a line save by drawing it in imagination — producing it, as the geometry texts say. The same is true of a span of time, which we represent by going through it successively. But all our intuition is either spatial or temporal, and so, given the definition of an extensive magnitude, it follows that "All intuitions are extensive magnitudes." The proof in B grounds this argument in the more general conclusions of the Deduction. An intuition can be apprehended in consciousness only if its manifold is synthesized, which is to say, only if the representation of the parts precedes and makes possible the representation of the whole.

This proof should come as something of a shock to the reader who has mastered the Aesthetic, for it is the direct contradictory of an argument offered there to prove that space and time are intuitions rather than concepts. The third argument of the Metaphysical Exposition of Space reads in part:

Space is not a discursive or, as we say, general concept of relations of things in general, but a pure intuition. For, in the first place, we can represent to ourselves only one space; and if we speak of diverse spaces, we mean thereby only parts of one and the same unique space. Secondly, these parts cannot precede the one all-embracing space, as being, as it were, constituents out of which it can be composed; on the contrary, they can be thought only as *in* it. Space is essentially one; the manifold in it, and therefore the general concept of spaces, depends solely on [the introduction of] limitations. [A 24–25]

In terms of the teaching of the *Critique* itself, we can assert unequivocally that Kant is wrong here, and right in the Axioms of Intuition. If the Deduction argument is granted, then the apprehension of a unified space necessarily presupposes a synthesis. It can be pleaded in defense of the Aesthetic that it purposely omits all reference to the contribution of understanding in order the better to study sensibility [A 22]. This argument is valid *only* if we maintain that sensibility and understanding are separate and independent faculties, neither of which conditions the other, though of course both together condition knowledge. Kant started by holding this position, but the Deduction forced him to place synthesis at the origin of all consciousness, whether of pure intuition or of empirical objects.

In A 164–65 we find another of Kant's all too brief discussions of mathematics. Since it is easy to suppose that Kant identified arithmetic with time and geometry with space, it is worth while stating that this is not at all the case. Mechanics is the science associated with time, while arithmetic requires both forms of intuition.[7] Kant recognizes that arithmetical propositions like "7 + 5 = 12" differ from axioms of geometry, but he is not entirely clear why they do. Had he known of the possibility of axiomatizing arithmetic, he would have realized that there are in formal arithmetic precise analogues of Euclid's axioms.[8]

Kant recognizes that inclusion of the Axioms of Intuition requires some explanation. The demonstration of the validity of mathematics has presumably already taken place in the Aesthetic. What, then, does this new principle tell us? Kant's answer is extremely important, for it reveals the true significance of the whole system of principles. The Axioms, he says, are "those principles upon which the possibility and a priori objective validity of mathematics are grounded. These latter must be regarded as the foundation of all mathematical principles" [B 199]. Near the end of the *Critique*, in the section known as the Discipline of Pure Reason, the role of the Axioms is made unambiguously clear:

[7] Cf. Kemp Smith's excellent discussion of the problem, *Commentary*, pp. 128–134. Kemp Smith points out that this common misinterpretation of Kant derives from an ambiguous passage in the *Prolegomena* and from an early, widely-read exposition of the Critical Philosophy by one of Kant's disciples.

[8] Kant actually mentions one such axiom, that equals added to equals yields equals. He asserts that this proposition is analytic, but in a formal reduction of arithmetic to logic it would appear as a theorem of the system.

In the Analytic I have indeed introduced some axioms of intuition into the table of the principles of pure understanding; but the principle (*Grundsatz*) there applied is not itself an axiom, but serves only to specify the principle (*Prinzipium*) of the possibility of axioms in general, and is itself no more than a principle (*Grundsatz*) derived from concepts. For the possibility of mathematics must itself be demonstrated in transcendental philosophy.

[B 761]

In other words, the principle stands to the axioms of a particular mathematical system as a meta-systematic assertion of their possibility, not as a higher axiom from which they can be deduced.

An examination of the passages in which Kant demonstrates the validity of mathematics — the Aesthetic, the Axioms, etc. — reveals that he never attempts anything like a detailed proof of Euclid's axioms. He uses simple geometrical and arithmetical examples, but these are always discussed in such a way as to be aids to exposition rather than steps in the argument. In fact, all that Kant ever seeks to prove is that there is an *a priori* mathematics of three-dimensional space (confining ourselves for the moment to geometry). Having before him the model of Euclidean geometry, which for millenia had served as the ideal of deductive certainty, and lacking any knowledge of the possibility of alternative geometries, Kant simply made a natural transition from the proposition, There is a valid mathematics of space, to the further conclusion, Euclidean geometry is valid. If he wished reassurance for this inference, he had only to turn to the second great system of knowledge, Newtonian physics, where the geometry of Euclid played a central role.

It has on many occasions been argued that the discovery of non-Euclidean geometries, and their application to the universe in relativistic physics, flatly disproved Kant's arguments in the *Critique*. Actually, however, this is not at all true. What Kant claims to prove is that there must be *some* mathematics of space, in as much as space is a three-dimensional extensive magnitude. Whatever the merits of his argument, it is quite consistent with the existence of other geometries than Euclid's.[9]

[9] These comments are quite superficial, and do not touch upon any of the deeper issues involved in the new physics and mathematics. The terms of the problem have been so much altered by researches into the nature of formal systems, by the reduction of mathematics to logic, and by the recognition of the interdependence of physical and mathematical systems, that we can give no simple answer to the question whether Kant's philosophy of mathematics has been refuted.

Anticipations of Perception

To the reader who is unfamiliar with Kant's other writings, this section must appear utterly baffling. Kant makes strange references to the "real in appearance," and goes on at great length about continuity, the void, and other cosmological topics. All this, furthermore, in a section supposedly devoted to our *a priori* knowledge, or "Anticipations." The explanation lies in Kant's physical theories, which he sought in this section to introduce into the Critical Philosophy. Most of the unclarity of the section can be removed by a brief detour into several related subjects. We shall have to review the dynamical theory of matter, as contained in his *Metaphysical First Principles of Natural Science*, and Kant's view of perception, which is expounded in the Aesthetic and the present section.

The Dynamical Theory of Matter

Kant held a dynamical theory of matter, in contrast both to the theory of the atomists and to the Cartesian theory, the latter identifying matter simply with extension. According to Kant's theory, the real in the phenomenal world is matter, defined variously as "the movable, in so far as it fills a space," or "the movable, in so far as it is something having a moving force," or simply as "the movable in space." [10] To fill space, Kant explains, is to resist the entrance into that space of another movable. A body, which is to say a quantity of matter filling a space, may be displaced from its space, but never "penetrated." In short, the resistance offered by matter is what we ordinarily call *impenetrability*. Matter fills space by virtue of a special moving force (*bewegende Kraft*), which is the fundamental characteristic of all phenomenal being.

One body can move another in only two directions, Kant asserts: either toward it, or away from it. There are thus two moving forces, an attractive force, ordinarily called *gravity*, and a repelling force, the above-mentioned *impenetrability*. Matter is thus a sort of field of force, occupying a space into which it resists the movement of other bodies, and also reaching out to attract all the bodies

[10] *Prolegomena, and Metaphysical Foundations of Natural Science*, trans. and ed. by E. B. Bax, pp. 169, 214, 150.

in other spaces. The attractive force works at a distance, the repellent force does not.

Contrary to the atomists, Kant holds that matter fills a space homogeneously with varying degrees of intensity — the force can be stronger or weaker, in short. Solidity and mass are thus not determined by the quantity of matter — by the number of atoms and amount of void between them — but by the intensity of the matter filling the space. A quantity of matter is always compressible into a smaller space, given a sufficient compressing force. The smaller the space, the greater the density, hence the greater the resistance to further compression. Conversely, matter will expand until the diminution of its density brings its repellent force into equilibrium with the repellent forces which surround it. The limits of these processes of expansion and contraction are the filling of an infinite space, with zero density, and the compression into an infinitesimal space, with infinite density. Both limits are of course impossible to attain.

Kant does not believe in the existence of a void, but he contents himself in the *Metaphysical Foundations* with a proof that the void is undemonstrable. The argument is that we can at least conceive of a space filled through and through with matter of such low density that its force falls below the minimum required to affect our sense organs or instruments of measurement. This being the case, when we encounter a volume of space which presents no appearance to us, we can never know whether it is a void or merely an excessively rarefied matter. Kant uses this argument in the Anticipations, as we shall see.

Kant's Analysis of Empirical Intuition

Perception is defined by Kant as *empirical intuition*. It can be analyzed into two elements: the form of perception is space and time; the content is sensation. When Kant speaks of pure intuition, he means intuition in which abstraction has been made from all sensation — in other words, purely formal intuition (or, perhaps, the pure form of intuition. Kant usually confuses the two). Kant agrees with the view that sensations are subjective, depending on the constitution of the organ of sense. In the Aesthetic, for example, he writes:

The taste of a wine does not belong to the objective determinations of the wine, not even if by the wine as an object we mean the wine as appearance, but to the special constitution of sense in the subject that tastes it. Colours are not properties of the bodies to the intuition of which they are attached, but only modifications of the sense of sight, which is affected in a certain manner by light. [A 28]

It is thus the intuition of the object, not the sensation caused by its interaction with the sense organ, which gives us knowledge of phenomena. Empirical objects have neither colours nor tastes nor smells nor sounds, but only such properties as cause those sensations in the perceiver. This point must be kept firmly in mind when we come to discuss the doctrine of the Analogies. Even there, where he comes closest to the theory of material objects which today is called phenomenalism, Kant speaks of constructs of intuitions, not sensations.

But sensation is capable of an internal analysis, for we may distinguish two aspects or dimensions of a sensation of color or heat. There is first the quality (redness, say), and second the degree of its intensity. These are related as matter and form. Now Kant follows Aristotle in holding that it is form, never matter, which yields knowledge. There would appear, therefore, to be a possibility that even the subjective content of perception might have cognitive significance, in its degree of intensity if not in its quality.

It should begin to be obvious what Kant has in mind. According to his physical theory, a body or substance is simply a quantity of matter filling some determinate volume of space. The sole characteristic of the matter is the intensity of its force, as measured by its gravitational pull and its resistance to other matter. Consequently, a phenomenal substance, or empirical object, is defined completely by (1) its spatial configuration and motion, and (2) the degree of intensity of the moving forces of its matter. In short, it is defined by its *extensive* and *intensive* magnitude. Now perception is our sole source of knowledge of the empirical world — this principle Kant accepts from the empiricists. Therefore perception must contain dimensions, as it were, which are adequate to the representation of the objective characteristics of substances — otherwise these latter would in some measure be unknown to us. But knowledge is conveyed always by objective form, never by subjective matter. Therefore, the extensive and intensive magnitudes of substances must find their representation in the extensive and intensive magnitude of perception. The spatio-temporal form of perception gives us information concerning the extension and motion of bodies, while the intensity of the sensation tells us of the degree of the moving forces.

The Argument of the Anticipations

Keeping the foregoing in mind, the reader should be able to make sense of most of the Anticipations, though even when understood it is not especially convincing. The phrase, "sensation, and the *real* which corresponds to it in the object" [A 166 — the statement of the principle in A] is now clear. The real in the object is matter, the stuff of phenomena. The long discussions of continuity and void are designed to support the dynamical theory, or at least to give it an equal footing with the atomic theory by showing that the latter can never be proved [cf. A 174].

There are a great many objections to the teaching of the Anticipations, and it may be worthwhile to discuss a few of them, as they throw light on the rest of the Critical System. In the first place, Kant is required by the Deduction to attribute all *a priori* knowledge to a transcendental synthesis. Here, as elsewhere, we must explain the possibility of such knowledge by an *a priori* rule for synthesis of the manifold. But there is no obvious sense in which the apprehension of a specific degree of intensity in a sensation can be attributed to a synthesis. As Kant himself says, it is an instantaneous process [B 209–210], and therefore cannot involve a successive synthesis. Hence Kant is forced, in one of the most artificial arguments of the *Critique*, to claim that any given degree of intensity in a sensation is capable of being generated by a gradual increase from absolute negation or absence = o, up to the required intensity. He even goes so far as to state that we can "determine *a priori*, that is, can construct, the degree of sensations of sunlight by combining some 200,000 illuminations of the moon" [B 221].

Even if this were true, and it is manifestly implausible, it still would not suffice to harmonize the Anticipations with the general doctrine of synthesis, for Kant asserts that a synthesis of this sort would be possible, not that it has actually taken place. If there has not been an instantaneous synthesis, bringing the intensity of a sensation up to its perceived level, then how can we know *a priori* that it *would* have a determinate degree — knowledge on which can be based a theory of matter? And worse still, if such a synthesis actually occurs — if we put together 200,000 moon-illuminations to form sunlight — then the representation of the former precedes and makes possible the representation of the latter. By Kant's definition, then [B 203], sunlight would have *extensive* magnitude. Quite clearly, the theory will not work. Kant has violated his own precept in attempting to lay an *a priori* foundation for a particular theory of matter.

The Anticipations also raise the complex problem of the relationship between perceptions and appearances. As I stated in commenting on the first edition Objective Deduction, Kant vacillates between two positions, which for convenience we can call subjectivism and the theory of double affection. According to the first, phenomenal objects are merely representations in the mind, resulting from a synthesis of the manifold of intuition. Although Kant never quite puts it in this way, we may say that for subjectivism an object is simply a way of interpreting a manifold of perceptions. The sensational content is excluded from the interpretation, or better, is interpreted as subjective and cognitively valueless. The second theory, of double affection, distinguishes between perceptions and phenomena within the world of appearance. Perceptions are the (empirical) effects of an interaction between phenomena and the sense-organs. As such, they are representations of the phenomena, which in turn are appearances of the unknowable realm of independent reality.

Most of the time Kant manages to confuse these two positions by ambiguous references to pure intuition, transcendental synthesis, and so forth. When he speaks of *a priori* synthesis, for example, it is almost never clear whether he means an independent synthesis of an independent manifold of pure intuition, or simply a synthesis of an empirical manifold according to *a priori* principles.

The Axioms and the Anticipations are obviously fertile grounds for these confusions. Kant characterizes them in the preface to the system of principles as being concerned with "the mere *intuition* of an appearance in general" [B 199]. If he has in mind the subjectivist theory, then this would mean that the Axioms and Anticipations deal with the *a priori* knowable character of empirical intuitions considered merely *qua* perceptions, rather than with those connections of perceptions through which objects are constructed. But if the double-affection theory is uppermost in his mind, then Kant will presumably mean that the two sections tell us what we can know *a priori* about perceptions *rather than the phenomena of which they are the empirical representations.*

In the Axioms, Kant manages to avoid any clear commitment to either alternative by using the device which served him so well in the Aesthetic. This is the confusion of pure intuition with pure form of intuition. On the subjectivist theory, pure intuition must mean pure form of intuition, for there is only one manifold, and that is empirical. On the theory of double affection, however, the pure manifold is perfectly distinct. The connection between pure and empirical intuition, as already indicated in the discussion of pure and applied mathematics, is made possible by the fact that space is both a pure intuition (the object of pure mathematics) and a pure form of intuition. It follows, therefore, that on either the subjectivist or double-affection theory, a principle valid for pure intuition will also be valid for empirical intuition. Hence we need not worry in the Axioms about the precise status of appearances. Whether they are constructs of pure intuition or modes of interpreting an empirical manifold, it will be true that "all appearances are, in their intuition, extensive magnitudes" [A 162].

The problem can be avoided in the Axioms because it is always possible to abstract from the sensational content of a perceptual manifold, leaving then just the spatio-temporal relations as a manifold of pure intuition. But we cannot abstract from the quality of a sensation without also abstracting from its degree of intensity as well. Kant is compelled, therefore, to treat matter as something independent which *corresponds* to the degree of the sensation, rather than as a *construct* of intensities of sensation. This commits him in the Anticipations to the double-affection theory, for the perception is there a representation of what is itself only appearance. The statement of the principle, particularly in the first edition, is unambiguously clear: "In all appearances sensation, and the *real* which corresponds to it in the object (*realitas phaenomenon*), has an *intensive magnitude*, that is, a degree" [A 166].

But the principle, as thus stated, is not concerned with mere intuition. It asserts that both sensation *and the real which cor-*

responds to it are intensive magnitudes. In short, Kant's desire to establish the dynamical theory of matter leads him to claim more than he ought, on his own view, to be able to prove. Even if he can demonstrate as an *a priori* principle that all sensation has intensive magnitude, how will he make the transition to the principle that matter or substance also has intensive magnitude? In the paragraph added in B, Kant shows that sensation must have a degree, and he then concludes simply by asserting:

Corresponding to this intensity of sensation, an *intensive magnitude*, that is, a degree of influence on the sense, must be ascribed to all objects of perception, in so far as the perception contains sensation. [B 208]

The problem with which Kant is struggling is more than the product of his ambiguous doctrine of pure intuition or his outdated views on physical science. Even a very much more advanced theory of physics and perception must still explain how qualities which are admittedly "in the eye of the beholder" can nonetheless give information about objective structures and events. Kant is surely correct in denying that we learn about objects only from the spatial and temporal relations of our perceptions, rather than from the qualities of them as well.

Finally, it should be noted that the Anticipations, like the Axioms, fall outside the chain of argument from consciousness to causation. Kant cannot draw his dynamical theory of matter out of the deeper insights of the Deduction, nor indeed should he be able to do so according to his own doctrine. The most he can claim is to have shown that such a physical theory is consistent with his analysis of perception. Consequently, my contention that the Analytic forms a single coherent argument cannot be taken to apply to the Anticipations.

Analogies of Experience

With the Analogies of Experience we return once more to the mainstream of Kant's argument. The Axioms and Anticipations deal with important problems, and in the case of the Anticipations particularly, expound doctrines very near to Kant's heart. But in the development of the Analytic they represent offshoots, drawing on the conclusions already established but carrying the analysis no further. The Analogies pick up the argument where it was left in the Objective Deduction and carry it to its conclusion by the addition of the last essential factor: time-consciousness.

I have already indicated why the Analogies, of all the Principles, should play so important a role in the Analytic. The doctrine of synthesis bases itself on the proposition that experience is a connection of perceptions. The entire machinery of synthesis is introduced because Kant believes that the connections which we discover upon retrospective analysis could never be given, but must rather have been constructed. It is obvious that such a view will place a particular emphasis upon relations of perceptions, and hence, in Kant's system, on those rules for synthesis which come under the heading of relation in the Table of Categories.

The structure of Kant's position is not quite so simple as this brief explanation suggests. In the introduction to the Deduction, to be sure, it is asserted that perceptions can enter consciousness without exhibiting associative relations with one another [§ 14]. The problem then becomes one of showing that the categories — and Kant can only mean the categories of relation — apply necessarily to the perceptions. Very quickly, however, Kant changes to the view that consciousness itself presupposes a synthesis according to the categories. Here there is opportunity for a penetration of the categories into the internal structure of the perceptions themselves, and hence for the developments of the Axioms and Anticipations. Nevertheless, even after this deepening of the theory, Kant continues to place his emphasis upon substance, causality, and community. The demonstration of their principles remains the major goal of the Analytic.

Kant actually presents a separate principle for each of the three categories of relation, as well as a principle for the Analogies as a whole. Hence the section, which is quite long, breaks down into four parts.

The Principle of the Analogies

The general principle of the Analogies is stated in the first edition as: "All appearances are, as regards their existence, subject *a priori* to rules determining their relation to one another in one time" [A 176–77]. This formulation reflects both the distinction between mathematical and dynamical categories and the Schematism, with its modes of time-determination (*Zeitbestimmungen*).

For purposes of the argument, the second-edition version of the principle is equally significant, for it reveals the precise relation of the Analogies to the Deduction. As revised by Kant, it reads: "Experience is possible only through the representation of a necessary connection of perceptions" [B 218]. Strictly speaking, this is merely a restatement of the conclusion of the Deduction [cf. A 113–14, A 122]. Why then should Kant undertake to prove it again in the Analogies? The answer lies in the inclusion of the crucial phrase, "necessary connection."

It will be recalled that in the preliminary version of the Objective Deduction (Section 2, subsection 4) Kant introduced the problem of *objective affinity*. In order for the scepticism of Hume to be refuted, it was necessary to prove that the merely subjective associations of perceptions had an objective ground. In Kant's words, it was necessary "to make comprehensible to ourselves the thoroughgoing affinity of appearances, whereby they stand and *must* stand under unchanging laws" [A 113]. The first answer, given in the very next paragraph, consists of a proof that perceptions are necessarily associated with one another, since otherwise they could not even enter consciousness [A 113–14]. In my analysis of this argument, I pointed out that it lacked a way of distinguishing, within experience, between mere association and objective connection.

The doctrine of transcendental synthesis which appears in the Objective Deduction is, I suggested, an attempt to fill the gap in the theory. Ultimately, however, it fails to advance the argument beyond the stage reached in the preliminary exposition. Even if one accepts the extraordinarily complicated and implausible theory of double affection which lies implicit in the doctrine of transcendental and empirical syntheses, there is still no satisfactory explanation of the difference between objective and subjective connection. The proof in A 122, like that given earlier in A 113–114, merely demonstrates that there must be association of perceptions.

With this background in mind, the significance of the second-edition principle of the Analogies becomes clear. Kant intends to take another stab at explaining the nature of *necessary connection*. To do so he introduces an analysis of time-consciousness, and with the successful completion of the task, the Deduction is finally brought to a close.

If we exclude the two statements of the principle of the Analogies, the introductory section consists of six paragraphs in A and a single paragraph added in B [B 218 = A 176 to B 224 = A 181]. Following the arrangement adopted by Kemp Smith, I will call the added paragraph number 1, and the first-edition paragraphs numbers 2–7. The passage can then be divided into three parts: (1) paragraph 1, the proof in B; (2) paragraphs 2–3, the proof in A; and (3) paragraphs 4–7, a variety of comments by Kant on the Analogies in particular and the dynamical categories in general.

Paragraph 1 — The Proof in B. The proof which Kant gives of the revised principle is extremely compact and, in its final step, somewhat inadequate. I shall try therefore to set it forth in a more discursive form, while suggesting a revision which removes the weakness. Although its full import can only be grasped after the Second Analogy has been analyzed, we shall still be able to see here the clue to Kant's solution of the problem of necessary connection.

As translated by Kemp Smith, the paragraph consists of eight sentences, corresponding to five in the German. The proof contained therein proceeds in six steps. The following table shows the relationship of the English and German texts to the proof.

English sentences	German sentences	Steps in Proof
1	1	1
2,3	2	2
4,5	3	3
6	4 (first half)	4
7	4 (second half)	5
8	5	6

Steps one, two, and three review the conclusions reached by the Deduction. Steps four and five introduce the fact that the manifold of perceptions has a temporal form, and draw from this certain inferences. Step six, finally, applies these results to the argument of step two, and concludes with the proposition to be proved, viz., the principle of the Analogies. The proof is as follows:

To Prove: Experience is possible only through the representation of a necessary connection of perceptions.

Step 1:   Experience is an empirical knowledge, that is, a knowledge which determines an object through perceptions.

Kant sets up two equivalences, the first between "experience" and "empirical knowledge," the second between "empirical knowledge" and "knowledge which determines an object through perceptions." The latter phrase will here be dealt with in the succeeding steps. The principle to be proved is a conditional, "If experience, then representation of a necessary connection of perceptions," and by the first step Kant indicates that he interprets "experience" to mean "empirical knowledge" rather than "consciousness in general." The preliminary inference, from consciousness to empirical knowledge, has already been performed in the Deduction. To a certain degree the Analogies can be viewed as a second inference carrying the argument from empirical knowledge to necessary connection. Strictly speaking, however, the Deduction is inadequate even as a first step until the results of the Analogies have been used to strengthen it.

Step 2:   It is a synthesis of perceptions, not contained in perception but itself containing in one consciousness the synthetic unity of the manifold of perceptions. This synthetic unity constitutes the essential in any knowledge of *objects* of the senses, that is, in experience as distinguished from mere intuition or sensation of the senses.

Drawing on the Deduction, Kant carries a step further the analysis of the concept of experience. As a knowledge which determines an object through perception, it is a synthesis of perceptions. The knowledge contains in one consciousness, as Kant puts it, the synthetic unity of the various perceptions which represent the object. As we have seen, this means that the mind possesses a rule for connecting the perceptions, a rule which is the concept of the object.[11] The synthetic unity of the perceptions is the distinguishing mark of knowledge.

Step 3:   In experience, however, perceptions come together only in accidental order, so that no necessity determining their connection is or can be revealed in the perceptions themselves. For appre-

[11] To be precise, the concept contains the *unity* of the rule. This refinement, I have suggested, does not correspond to any real distinction in Kant's theory, but stems from his desire to isolate the activity of understanding from that of imagination. It is this aim which lies behind the separation of the category and the schema.

hension is only a placing together of the manifold of empirical intuition; and we can find in it no representation of any necessity which determines the appearances thus combined to have connected existence in space and time.

Now the problem is posed, and as in the discussion of objective affinity in the Deduction, Kant obviously writes with Hume in mind. It was Hume who proved so convincingly that necessity could not be given in perception. Heat may follow fire, Hume would say, but whichever way you turn the two perceptions about, you will never discover in them any indication that heat *must* follow fire. Subjective association, as apprehended in empirical consciousness, contains no necessity.

Step 4: But since experience is a knowledge of objects through perceptions, the relation in the existence of the manifold has to be represented in experience, not as it comes to be placed together in time [*wie es in der Zeit zusammengestellt wird*] but as it exists objectively in time.[12]

Packed into this brief sentence is the key to the problem of necessary connection. Knowledge is a connection of perceptions *qua* representations, not *qua* mental contents. When I form the judgment that cinnabar is heavy, I do not merely associate the representations of cinnabar and weight in my mind, as when I think sugar and salt or bread and butter; I assert that there is a connection *in the object* of that which is represented by the perceptions of red stuff and weight. Now the only sort of relation which all representations bear to one another is time-relation, for time is the form of all consciousness. Given the double nature of representations, there are two possible time-orders in which they can be arranged. The first is their time-order as mere contents of consciousness, their subjective time-order. It is to this which Kant refers by the phrase "as it [the manifold of perceptions] comes to be placed together in time." The second possible time-order of the contents of consciousness is their order *qua* representations, which is to say, the order in objective time of the states or events of which

[12] Kemp Smith translates *zusammenstellen* as "constructed." This gives an impression of active rearrangement which is just the opposite of that intended by Kant. If the subject of the clause were changed from the singular "manifold" to the plural "perceptions," an even more satisfactory rendering would be "as they [the perceptions] come to be juxtaposed." This almost entirely avoids the implication of activity.

they are representations. This order may be quite different from the first, for events or states of which we become aware successively may in the object be contemporaneous. Kant later gives the example of the sides of a house, which are perceived one after the other, but objectively co-exist. The phrase, "but as it [the manifold] exists objectively in time," quite obviously refers to this second order.

The sentence, when thus interpreted, asserts that in order to have knowledge through perceptions, it is necessary to connect the perceptions in their objective time-relations, which is to say, in an order not necessarily the same as that in which they are given. The first instance of "experience," incidentally, means "empirical knowledge," while the second means "consciousness."

We have finally come upon a distinction *within experience* between mere association and objective connection. It is the distinction between private and public time, as one sometimes finds it put. The full analysis and justification of this new addition to the theory is only presented in the Second Analogy. The argument which we are now explicating was added in the second edition, and tends to presuppose the later material.

Step 5:　Since time, however, cannot itself be perceived, the determination of the existence of objects in time can take place only through their relation in time in general, and therefore only through concepts that connect them *a priori*.

Time is not an object, or an objectively existing un-thing. It is not a hollow container, or a clothesline strung across eternity.[13] Therefore if we seek to set a representation in objective time, we cannot do so by attaching it to a pre-existing point of time. The only thing that can be done is to set it in its objective time-relations to other representations. In this way an objective time-order is constructed, and that *is* objective time.

This becomes much clearer if we recall the analysis of objectivity and synthetic unity given in the introduction to the Subjective Deduction. It was argued there that we connect mental contents by relating them, *qua* representations, to an independent object. Now we see that this amounts to reorganizing their relations to one another, so that their new relation is one of objective

[13] See the discussion of Kant's views on space and time in the Introduction to this work.

time order. Actually, as we shall see, this re-organizing process *creates* objective time.

At this point, the argument may appear circular. We begin by assuming that there is an objective time order, from which we can infer the existence of a reorganization, a synthesis, of the contents of consciousness. Then we turn around and say that the synthesizing process *produces* the objective time-order.[14] Later on we shall see that the argument is quite uni-directional. Kant proves the existence of an objective time-order and at the same time proves the causal maxim and the principle of community.

The above constitutes an explanation of the first part of the sentence, through the words "in time in general." Kant now makes a move which confuses the argument and momentarily loses the advantage won by this new analysis of objective connection. The words "in general" refer to the doctrine of the Schematism where, as we saw, Kant identifies general time-determinations with the categories. Without any real proof, Kant now asserts that the re-organization of representations in objective time relations must be done by the application of *a priori* concepts. This allows him to complete the proof in a rather facile fashion with:

Step 6: Since these always carry necessity with them, it follows that experience is only possible through a representation of necessary connection of perceptions.

The move from time relations in general to *a priori* concepts, and finally to necessary connection, is extremely superficial. It is not at all clear why *a priori* concepts must be used to hold together the manifold of perceptions in objective connection, nor is it clear what Kant means by the statement that *a priori* concepts "always carry necessity with them." It is as though Kant wearied of the argument after making the crucial point about the two time-orders, and simply brought it to an end with a mere sketch of remaining steps.

There are ways of relating objective time-order to necessary connection, as we shall see. The easiest way is simply to point out that necessity is what we mean by objectivity in this case. To say that an event A precedes an event B in objective time is to say that

---

[14] This, it will be recalled, is the claim of Weldon. Cf. his *Commentary*, 2nd ed., pp. 173-74, and pp. 54-56 above.

we must represent A as preceding B.[15] A more complicated way is to analyze necessary connection in terms of rule-directed synthesis. The necessity of the connection between two perceptions is seen to lie in the rule by which the perceptions are synthesized. But synthesis is a reorganization of the manifold according to a rule. It is in fact a reproduction in imagination according to a rule. Thus, we reproduce the manifold in a new order which is necessary because it proceeds according to a rule. That rule is nothing but the order of objective time relations. This will all be explained at greater length when we come to the Second Analogy.

Paragraphs 2–3 — The Proof in A. The first-edition statement of the principle, with its reference to the determination of the relations of appearances to one another in time, expresses more precisely the analysis of objective time which Kant presents. The proof follows quite straightforwardly from the Schematism. The categories of relation apply to appearances by means of their schemata, which are time-determinations. As there are three categories, there must be three relations of time to serve as schemata. Kant offers *duration, succession,* and *co-existence* as the correlates of substance, causality, and community.

Unfortunately for the clarity and soundness of Kant's argument, duration is in no sense a time-relation. We can say that A succeeds B or that A co-exists with B, but not that A endures B (at least not if A and B are perceptions). Kant is well aware of this, and a few pages later he states explicitly that "simultaneity and succession [are] the only relations in time" [B 226]. Given this inconsistency, it comes as no surprise that the First Analogy is extremely muddled, and its role in the Analogies as a whole rather anomalous.

Paragraph three repeats the argument of the Deduction in order to establish its connection with the Analogies in particular. Kant comes to the conclusion that the analogies are "rules of universal time-determination." The reader may find this confusing, for the schemata have already been described as rules of universal time determination.[16] What then is the difference between a schema and

---

[15] Here and always, "must" is quite compatible with freedom. We must represent it before B if we wish our judgments to be true. Needless to say, nothing forces us to utter true judgments.

[16] The schema is "a transcendental determination of time" [B 177], a "rule of synthesis of the imagination" [A 141].

a principle? The answer, I think, is that there is no difference between them at all. Indeed, the category, schema, and principle are all three of them the same rule for the synthesis of the manifold. The principles, and in particular the Analogies, are thus the deductions of the individual categories.

Paragraphs 4–7. After the two proofs, Kant makes a variety of comments on the Analogies as a whole. The distinction drawn between constitutive and regulative principles raises in a particularly acute form the problem originally posed by the Axioms of Intuition. The Analogies and Postulates, it is claimed, deal with the existence of appearances rather than with the appearances themselves. What Kant means is that they are relational, but since relation is one of the types of categories, he cannot also put the Postulates under that heading. The Axioms and Anticipations supposedly tell us something about the nature of the appearances themselves, namely that they are spatio-temporal and have degree. Leaving the Anticipations to one side, this is merely a repetition of the conclusion of the Aesthetic. Kant there emphasized the differences between concepts and intuitions in an attempt to prove, against Leibniz, that space and time are not merely sets of relations of appearances. The proofs included the claim that space and time are given as wholes, and hence cannot be discursive or relational. But in the Axioms this is all taken back, for Kant realizes that his own theory demands a synthesis as the condition of the representation of any whole in consciousness. Taking all these considerations together, it seems that the distinction between constitutive and regulative, or mathematical and dynamical, principles is not what Kant says it is. The spatio-temporality of perceptions is as much a fact about their relations as is their regular succession.

I suggested earlier that the constitutive principles might be viewed as dealing with perceptions *qua* mental contents, the regulative with perceptions *qua* representations. If the above remarks are just, this suggestion will not work. However, it will become clear in the analysis of the Second Analogy that Kant cannot successfully maintain the position of the Axioms. In order for his theory to hold together, he must posit a temporal ordering in inner sense *prior* to the synthesis of imagination. It should be apparent now why the subject of inner sense caused Kant so much trouble, and why in the Deduction he vacillates between a theory of synopsis *cum* synthesis and an alternative theory of synthesis alone. He needs a subjective time-order of inner sense which is not the product of a synthetic re-organization, but at the same time he cannot allow consciousness which is not based on a synthesis.

The cryptic remarks about mathematical analogies in the sixth paragraph deserve some comment. Kant distinguishes mathematical from philosophical analogies, and says of the former, "If two members of the proportion are given, the third is likewise given, that is, can be constructed." He goes on to speak of philosophical analogies in which although three terms are given, the fourth cannot be constructed. One simply obtains a relation between the third and fourth, analogous to that between the first and second. Kemp Smith, following Mellin, has in his translation changed the words "two" and "third" to "three" and "fourth," on the assumption that a mathematical proportion, like the philosophical, must have four terms. Actually, I think Kant meant just what he said. In the mathematical proportion "*a* is to *b* as *b* is to *c*" the second and third terms are identical. This ensures that the last term, *c*, will be homogeneous with the other terms (all numbers, for example), and therefore that it can be constructed. But in the proportion, "*a* is to *b* as *c* is to *d*," there is no guarantee that the fourth term will be anything like the second, and therefore we cannot *construct* it, but simply establish its relation to the third.[17] Because the terms are heterogeneous, *d* cannot be expressed in terms of *a*, *b*, and *c*.

The last paragraph of the section reiterates the distinction between schema and category and maintains that the latter "is restricted by no sensible condition" [B 224]. The bewildering variety of Kant's utterances on this subject go far to explain the appeal of the patchwork theory of the *Critique*. We need not attempt to date the several positions, however. Kant juggled them all in his mind, never content either to give one up or to commit himself to it completely.

The First Analogy

The First Analogy is a very difficult section, due both to the complexity of the problems with which it deals and to Kant's indecision as to exactly what he wished to say about substance.

[17] For the terms "homogeneous" and "heterogeneous," see A 162 note a.

The first of the principles of relation, it rests on the dubious time-determination of duration, which is not really a time relation at all. As we shall see, the ambiguities of Kant's arguments are in a sense contained in this initial confusion over the schema of substance.

The first and second edition versions of the principle and proof will be analyzed first. Following this, some of the general problems of the Analogy will be sorted out, and then the remaining paragraphs of the section will be commented upon briefly. I have drawn heavily from both Kemp Smith[18] and Paton[19] in my analysis of the First Analogy. Paton especially is helpful, thanks to his careful examination of the many philosophical issues which hinge on the concepts of substance and permanence.

The Principles and Proofs in A and B. (1) The two versions of the principle. The Analogy is supposed to deal with the concept of permanence, but there are at least two distinct senses in which we may speak of the permanent in nature. The first is the familiar Aristotelian notion of the substratum of change, an unchanging base in which attributes succeed one another: the same wood in tree and table, the same person as boy and man, the same marble as block and statue.

The second sense of the permanent is more strictly scientific, and derives from the concept of a closed system. In order for the equations of physics to apply to bodies, it is necessary to assume that the forces and masses of nature, however they may redistribute themselves, do not, as it were, leak out of the system. Similarly, nothing must be supposed to enter the system from outside. Like the concept of substratum, the idea of a closed system has both a relative and an absolute interpretation. For purposes of most calculations, we assume the solar system to be closed; that is to say, we posit a total absence of external forces operating on the planets and sun. Strictly speaking, however, the other stars do exert an influence on the solar system, and the theory in its complete expression must take this into account. Hence just as Aristotle postulates a substratum (prime matter) which is not itself a state of some more basic substratum, so Newtonian physics posits a closed-system universe which is not itself merely a semi-isolated

---

[18] *Op. cit.*, pp. 358–363.
[19] *Op. cit.*, vol. ii, pp. 184–220.

segment of a still larger system. In Kant's day, a customary expression of this presupposition was the principle of the conservation of matter.

These two concepts of permanence find expression in the two versions of the First Analogy. In the first edition, Kant formulates the principle thus: "All appearances contain the permanent (substance) as the object itself, and the transitory as its mere determination, that is, as a way in which the object exists" [A 182]. In the second edition, an entirely different principle is substituted for this, namely: "In all change of appearances substance is permanent; its quantum in nature is neither increased nor diminished" [B 224]. Kant thus moves from the concept of a substratum in the first edition to the conservation of matter in the second edition. As we shall see, neither version states with any exactitude a principle which can be proved in Kant's system.

Again following Kemp Smith's translation, I will analyze first the proof added in B.

(2) *The proof in B.*   The argument is extremely condensed and rests on unexpressed and undefended presuppositions. We may represent it in the following form:

Step 1:   Change and co-existence can only be represented as determinations of a permanent — that is, as succession or co-existence of states of something which does not change, and exists at all times.

Step 2:   Change (succession) and co-existence are modes of time [they are the *only two* time-relations, as Kant says in B 226]. As such, they must be represented as determinations of an unchanging and enduring time.

Step 3:   Thus time can serve as the permanent underlying change. But time itself cannot be perceived.

Step 4:   Consequently, there must be something which functions as the perceptible representation of time, i.e., a permanent substratum.

Step 5:   But, by a few definitional shifts, the permanent is *substance*. And as it has been proved to be unchanging, its *quantity* must be neither increased nor diminished. Q.E.D.

It can without hesitation be stated that this proof is a total confusion. There is no point in trying to reconstruct it, but a consideration of its faults is quite instructive.

The first step is a premise which is never explicitly stated in the proof. It expresses the Aristotelian view of substance, and the rest of the proof continues along this line, despite the quite different view embodied in the statement of the principle (i.e., the conservation of matter). This inconsistency is reflected in the last step, where Kant makes the transition from permanent substratum to constant quantity without the slighest justification.

The second step is quite dubious, both in itself and in its relation to the argument. Kemp Smith quotes Caird as saying:

> It may be objected that to say that "time itself does not change" is like saying that passing away does not itself pass away. So far the endurance of time and the permanence of the changing might even seem to mean only that the moments of time never cease to pass away, and the changing never ceases to change. A perpetual flux would therefore sufficiently "represent" all the permanence that is in time.[20]

Kemp Smith comments that the objection is not vital, since Kant need only claim for his argument that "Events are dated in a *single* time, not in an unchanging time." This remark is perfectly correct as regards the overall doctrine of the Analogy, but Caird is nonetheless justified in his criticism of Kant's argument. An examination of steps 1–3 reveals an equivocation on the phrase "determination of a permanent." In the first step, Kant employs the notion of the permanent as a backdrop for change, a stable standard against which alteration can be marked. In order to identify time with this substratum in step 2, Kant must describe time as *unchanging* in just the sense intended by step 1. Then he can move, in steps 3 and 4, to the perceptible representation of this substratum, namely substance. But if time is as easily called everchanging as unchanging, then the whole flimsy analogy is destroyed, and we are left with no connection between time and the permanent.

(3) *The proof in A.* The first-edition proof is contained in the second paragraph of the Analogy.[21] It is possible to distinguish four separate proofs in this single paragraph. The first argument:

> Our *apprehension* of the manifold of appearance is always successive, and is therefore always changing. Through it alone we can never determine whether this manifold, as object of experience, is coexistent or successive. For such determination we require an underlying ground which exists *at all times*, that is, something *abiding* and *permanent*, of which all change and co-

[20] Kemp Smith, *op. cit.*, p. 359.
[21] I.e., the second paragraph of the first edition. The first paragraph, consisting of three sentences, was omitted from the second edition and the proof in B substituted for it.

existence are only so many ways (modes of time) in which the permanent exists. And simultaneity and succession being the only relations in time, it follows that only in the permanent are relations of time possible. In other words, the permanent is the *substratum* of the empirical representation of time itself; in it alone is any determination of time possible.

The first two sentences state the fundamental problem of the Analogies, which is only fully explored in the Analogy of Cause and Effect. The problem, briefly, is to explain how we get objective time-relations of events out of a subjective time-order of perceptions; or, more strictly, it is to prove that we do, not simply to explain how we do it. But Kant adopts the analytic or regressive style of exposition throughout most of the Analogies. The exact logical status of the argument is actually rather complicated. Kant undertakes to prove, in the Analogies, that the principles of permanence, causality, and community follow from the premise that we have knowledge of objects. As he has presumably proved this latter in the Deduction, it is perfectly correct to take it now as the starting point for further conclusions. But in the Analogies Kant gives more content to the phrase "knowledge of objects" than his proofs in the Deduction warrant. In particular, he has not yet proved that the distinction between objective and subjective time-order is a necessary element in empirical knowledge. Hence it is illegitimate for him here to treat that distinction as already demonstrated and to base on it the proofs of his principles. To be sure, Kant might argue that the supposition of an objective time-order is one which everyone would willingly make, but to do so would greatly strengthen his premises, and correspondingly weaken his conclusions. In discussing the Deduction, I remarked that the two books of the Analytic only appear to be the earlier and later portions of an argument, and that in reality the conclusions of the Analogies necessitate a revision of the Deduction. One of the conclusions of this commentary is that when the teaching of the Analogies is fully understood, we can restate the Deduction argument in such a way that the distinction between objective and subjective time-order becomes a necessary consequence of the unity of consciousness. The principles of the Analogies, to the extent that Kant proves them from that distinction, thus require no premises which are not already laid down in the Deduction. The Analytic becomes truly one single argument, proving the proposition, "If there is a unity of consciousness, then all alterations take place in conformity with the law of the connection of cause and effect."

To return to the proof, Kant asserts that subjective consciousness reveals only a constantly changing succession of representations. As he says in A 107, "consciousness of self . . . is merely empirical, and always changing. No fixed and abiding self can present itself in this flux of inner appearances." But the states or events represented by the perceptions are sometimes successive, sometimes simultaneous. To use the famous example from the Second Analogy, as I walk around a building I see the sides of it one after another, but no one would suppose therefore that they exist in objective temporal succession. Since *all* subjective consciousness is successive, its temporal relations quite obviously cannot, by themselves, serve to distinguish mere subjective representation from representation of (objective) succession.[22] Therefore, Kant concludes, there must be an underlying, enduring, permanent substratum in which the distinction between objective succession and coexistence is grounded.

Thus stated, the argument is clearly unsatisfactory. Having introduced the new and revolutionary problem of objective and subjective time order, Kant does nothing here to link it to the notion of a permanent. It is not clear how a permanent would ground such a distinction, the word "ground" being Kant's vaguest term for any relation of dependence or even connection.

I might take occasion to comment here on a point which Kemp Smith makes much of, but which seems to me unimportant.[23] This is the fact that Kant sometimes claims that all apprehension is successive, and at other times describes both succession and simultaneity as modes of time. These, we are to suppose, are contradictory positions, representing divergent tendencies of Kant's

[22] I add the phrase, "by themselves," because the characteristics of subjective consciousness are all the guides we have in the objective reorganization of perceptions. The point is that some considerations other than position in subjective time order will have to be introduced. For example, if I see a flash of lightning and then hear the thunder, I assign the two to the same objective time on the basis of laws about the speed of sound and light and the causes of lightning and thunder. I do *not*, however, step outside of my own subjective consciousness and, as it were, peek around the edge of my perceptions at the objects themselves. As the police would say, it is all an inside job. This, of course, is precisely the problem which has harrassed philosophers from Descartes onward.

[23] Cf. Kemp Smith, pp. 358–59.

thought. Actually it seems simplest to recognize them as quite complementary aspects of a single position. What Kant almost certainly means is that subjective consciousness is only successive, but that appearances in objective time order can be either successive or co-existing. This is confirmed by the use of "apprehension" in the first sentence of the proof. Paton doubts that Kant thought the manifold to be merely successive and never simultaneous, his principal reason being that such a view is obviously false.[24] Nevertheless, as he quite justly asserts, the point is irrelevant to Kant's argument. All Kant need claim is that subjective succession (and simultaneity) differs from objective succession (and simultaneity), which is equally obviously true.

The second argument:

> Permanence, as the abiding correlate of all existence of appearances, of all change and of all concomitance [*Begleitung*], expresses time in general. For change does not affect time itself, but only appearances in time. (Co-existence is not a mode of time itself; for none of the parts of time coexist; they are all in succession to one another.) If we ascribe succession to time itself, we must think yet another time, in which the sequence would be possible.

This is a condensed version of the argument which was added in the second edition. Time itself does not change, but only appearances in time. If we supposed time itself to change, there would have to be an unchanging time in which it did. The permanent, in other words, is that which is unchanged through change. But since co-existence and change cannot be represented in pure time (the parts of time do not co-exist, and time does not change), there must be something in which they can be represented, namely the permanent.

The point about the parts of time not co-existing is a sheer confusion. The most charitable thing we can say is that Kant has not yet had a chance to explain co-existence. It is, for Kant, a concept involving causal interaction, and hence extremely difficult to treat at this point in the argument. As Kemp Smith has noted, the entire section suffers from a lack of any reference to space, in terms of which co-existence is a great deal more comprehensible. Not until the second edition revisions of the Refu-

[24] Paton, vol. ii, pp. 192–95.

tation of Idealism did Kant make a serious attempt to reinstate space in the argument of the Analytic.

The third argument:

Only through the permanent does existence in different parts of the time-series acquire a magnitude which can be entitled duration. For in bare succession existence is always vanishing and recommencing, and never has the least magnitude. Without this permanent there is therefore no time-relation.

This argument is new and quite suggestive. Kant seeks to account for our notion of an object as lasting through a period of time. It is a familiar paradox that we speak of a material object as remaining the same, even though all its parts are in constant motion. True or not, every schoolboy knows that the cells in the human body are entirely replaced over a seven-year period. What then makes this new body the same as the old one? More generally, since subjective consciousness reveals only successions of vanishing perceptions, how can we ever form the concept of that which endures? The essential feature of such an idea is unchanging permanence. Although Kant does not say so at this point, we can recall that the idea of change, as well as that of endurance, requires the permanent. Change, rather than mere succession, takes place against a background. Thus, the two notions of alteration and endurance are interdependent.

Aristotle explained this permanence through change by the concept of substance, or essential form. Through alteration the essence of the object endures while the accidents change. When a boy grows to manhood, for example, he remains both rational and animal. When substances themselves come to be or pass away, prime matter remains as the substratum of change. In contrast with the Aristotelian doctrine is that of the Atomists, who taught that change was merely a regrouping of imperishable particles. This is actually closer to Kant's position, for whom matter, though not as atoms, is the permanent. By emphasizing in the second edition the conservation of matter, Kant seems to adopt the Atomists' view that the stuff, rather than the form, of objects is the permanent in appearances. This, I shall try to show below, is contrary to the trend of the general argument in the Analytic.

The fourth argument is merely a repetition and summary of preceding arguments, and requires no comment.

Discussion of the Problems of the Analogy. By means of a close analysis of the first and second edition proofs, I have managed to raise most of the problems with which Kant deals in the First Analogy under the heading of permanence. Let me now try to relate them to one another systematically.

There are three distinct topics taken up in the First Analogy, and either related to one another or confused with one another. The first is the general concept of permanence through change. As we have seen, Kant emphasizes both the necessity of presupposing the permanent as a counterpart of change, and the inability of mere alteration to account for the idea of duration. The second, put forward as a solution to the first, is the category of substance and attribute. Ostensibly, of course, the whole Analogy is supposed to be nothing but an application of this category, or, if we interpret the Analytic as I have proposed, a deduction of it. Nevertheless, it is only in the first edition statement of the principle that the category of inherence and subsistence is emphasized. Finally, the third topic introduced into the Analogy is matter, which is also offered by Kant as the permanent. The second edition expresses this alternative by means of the law of the conservation of matter. Kant does not see substance and matter as alternative explanations of permanence; matter for him is substance, the real in appearances.

The permanent in general, substance, and matter are all three described in the Analogy as the perceptible representation of time. This suggestion is never made clear, and in so far as it depends on the statement that time is unchanging, can only be a confusion. It would have been much more reasonable to describe matter as the perceptible representation of space, for according to Kant's dynamical theory, matter is a moving force with spatial extension, and it is the force which causes perceptions. Kemp Smith quotes a marginal note to the First Analogy in Kant's own copy of the *Critique*, which shows quite clearly that he himself recognized the importance of space. Kant wrote:

Here the proof must be so developed as to apply only to substances as phenomena of outer sense [i.e., space], and must therefore be drawn from space, which with its determinations exists at all times.[25]

[25] Kemp Smith, p. 361.

What are we to make of the hodgepodge of concepts and arguments which Kant offers as his account of permanence? Is there any order in the Analogy, or is it just an unhappy confusion? The answer, I think, is that the elements of a coherent theory can be extracted from Kant's statements, but that to do so we must follow out suggestions which he never developed and suppress alternative lines of thought to which he clung. The clue is the contrast between two concepts of permanence which I developed in discussing the first and second edition versions of the principle. The permanent may be substance, the subject of predication, the substance in which attributes successively inhere. But it may also be the basis of a closed system of scientific explanation, the constant which allows laws to be formulated.

Now, the logic of Kant's own argument should have forced him to give up the traditional notion of substance and attributes, for the dynamical theory demands that substance be treated as force or energy. Change is then a variation of the intensity and distribution of energy. As Kemp Smith says, it is change *of*, not change *in*, substance.[26] The Second Analogy makes it clear that an object is to be identified with its states, so that the distinction between unchanging substratum and successive attributes breaks down. Kemp Smith very justly writes:

> We must, then, conclude that Kant offers no sufficient deduction or explanation of the category of substance and attribute, and as he does so nowhere else, we are driven to the further conclusion that he is unable to account for its use in experience, or at least to reconcile it in any adequate fashion with the principle of causality.[27]

When we turn to the second conception of permanence, that of matter, it seems at first that the situation is equally unsatisfactory. Matter should be defined in terms of space and force, rather than as the representation of time. No proof is given of the conservation of matter, and in fact on Kant's own principles, none should be possible *a priori*. The *Metaphysical Foundations of Natural Science* admittedly employs an *empirical* concept, motion, to explain the nature of matter, and hence the subject should not even be broached in the *Critique*.

[26] Kemp Smith, pp. 362–63. This criticism of the treatment of substance in the First Analogy is drawn from Kemp Smith's discussion.
[27] *Ibid.*

If we take the more general notion of a closed system, however, and combine it with the concept of substance which Kant should, on his own principles, have employed, we come out with an analysis of permanence which expresses quite well one of the central doctrines of the *Critique*. I do not put forward the following as an account of what Kant really meant, but as a suggestion of what he could have said.

Consider first the traditional notion of substance which Kant proposes to defend. What is substance? First and foremost, it is a complete, independent thing, typically a natural organism. Every such entity can be analyzed into its form and its matter, and contrary to what most modern students expect, substance is identified with form, not with matter. It is of the form that we predicate attributes, as when we say that man is mortal. Now, in this tradition form is conceived as static, the root notion being that of the shape of something. To be sure, form is the structure which makes possible an activity, but it is itself not an activity. In Kant's critical philosophy, on the other hand, form is conceived as a pattern or regularity in appearances. The categories are structures of experience in the sense of being laws to which appearances conform.

If Kant wished to preserve the concept of substance as the permanent, therefore, it would have been more consistent for him to identify it with a relatively lasting pattern of representations against which more fluid patterns appear as alterations. The permanent would then not be a stuff or matter; it would be a form or law. In these terms, how can we reinterpret the principle that there is a permanent, unchanging substance? Here it is absolute permanence, not relative permanence, which is at stake. Obviously this becomes the principle that all appearances fit together into one pattern, which cannot "change" *because there is no broader pattern against which one could compare it to discover its relative alteration*. In other words, the principle of permanence becomes the assertion that there is a single world-order of appearances, thoroughly interconnected according to laws. As we know, Kant in many places asserts that the existence of this order is conditioned by, and is itself a condition of, the unity of consciousness.

Curiously, this suggested revision also has much in common with the second edition revision of the principle, for clearly the principle of a universal world-order is, in the most general terms, the postulation of a closed system. Whether we posit conservation of matter or conservation of a mass-energy quantum or some other form of closure depends upon the evaluation of empirical data, and hence cannot be determined *a priori*. But the positing of a coherent world-order is the condition of any scientific explanation at all, and therefore is a legitimate principle of Transcendental Philosophy.

In the Introduction, I reviewed the controversy between Newton and Leibniz concerning the nature of space and time. Kant, it will be recalled, sought a middle way between Newton's doctrine of absolute space-time and Leibniz's analysis of them as relations of substances. Kant says that space and time cannot themselves be perceived, and he therefore describes them as containing a manifold of relations, which is to say, relations of appearances.[28] But against Leibniz, he denies that space and time are relations of things-in-themselves. The relational theory of time lies behind Kant's assertion that we can only place appearances in objective time by establishing their relations *to one another*. All the appearances having been thus ordered, it would make no sense to Kant to ask whether the whole series might commence ten minutes earlier.[29] This lack of any absolute ground is the mark of conditioned appearances rather than unconditioned reality, Kant believes. Now it seems to me that the concept of matter as the substratum of change is a throwback to the absolute universe, and that permanence as a total pattern of change is more in keeping with the doctrine which Kant develops in the Analytic. Let me repeat, however, that the above is speculation about a Kantian theory of permanence, not exposition of Kant's own views.

The Remaining Paragraphs: A 184–189. The seven paragraphs following the first-edition proof expound in a more discursive style the concepts and arguments employed in the two proofs. In

---

[28] Kant also says that we have a pure manifold of *a priori* intuition, but this is simply in flat contradiction with other parts of his philosophy. Since the doctrine of pure intuition is central to the *Critique*, it is impossible to dismiss it as Precritical, or a temporary aberration. On the other hand, the principles with which it conflicts are equally essential to the *Critique*. I have chosen here to emphasize these latter aspects of Kant's philosophy in order to develop a train of thought which seems suggestive.

[29] Though he never says so, a similar argument can presumably be made for space.

the second of these paragraphs, after giving an example of the scientific employment of the principle of permanence, Kant says, "The unity of experience would never be possible if we were willing to allow that new things, that is, new *substances*, could come into existence. For we should then lose that which alone can represent the unity of time, namely, the identity of the substratum" [A 186]. It seems fairly clear that if the unity of experience is guaranteed by the permanent, then this latter must be the *law* which unifies appearances and not any stuff of which they are made.

The two arguments given in A 188 also support my proposed revision of the Analogy. The first argument, which derives originally from Aristotle's *Physics*, seeks to prove the impossibility of absolute coming-to-be, or creation *ex nihilo*. However, what it actually succeeds in proving, if anything, is the necessity of some cause for that which begins to be. It therefore proves that the world-order can have no loose ends, no characteristics inexplicable in terms of itself; in short, that the world-order is a closed system.

The next paragraph is susceptible of a similar interpretation. If substances could come to be or cease to be, Kant argues, the unity of time would be destroyed (since time is nothing but the order of appearances). There would then be as many times as there were separate orders of appearances, an obvious impossibility. But this is not a proof of the existence of a permanent stuff. It is simply a new version, based on the temporal form of consciousness, of the Deduction proof of the thoroughgoing associability of perceptions. If a perception can not be included in the order of representations, then it will not be part of the unity of consciousness, and hence can not even appear in consciousness. Similarly, coming to be and passing away would (according to Kant) violate the laws which unite appearances, and so would destroy the unity of consciousness. Again, this argument supports the revision of the Analogy which I have suggested.

The Second Analogy

The Second Analogy is undoubtedly one of the most powerful pieces of philosophy ever written. In it Kant analyzes the nature and significance of the objective time order of events, demonstrates the *a priori* validity of the causal maxim, and states explicitly the doctrine that material objects are constructs of perceptions. The Analogy also brings to completion the argument of the Analytic, thereby laying the foundation for the entire Critical Philosophy.

The section, including the proof added in B, consists of twenty-eight paragraphs divided into two relatively independent parts. Paragraphs 1–16 contain a series of proofs and explanations of the principle of the Analogy, while the twelve remaining paragraphs discuss various problems connected with Kant's physical theory. Following the order adopted in the discussion of the First Analogy, I shall begin by analyzing the proofs in the first part of the section. Several problems will then be discussed, culminating in a revised and final statement of the argument of the Analytic. Finally, the material in the second half of the Analogy will be commented on briefly.

The Principles and Proofs in A and B. (*1*) *The Principle.* The two versions of the Principle are: in the first edition, "Everything that happens, that is, begins to be, presupposes something upon which it follows according to a rule"; and in the second edition, "All alterations take place in conformity with the law of the connection of cause and effect." There is no significant difference between these two statements. The first edition actually enunciates the law of causality, while the second edition merely refers to it. As indicated by the first of the paragraphs added in B, the second-edition principle attempts to relate this Analogy to the previous one by referring to alternations of a permanent rather than to events in general. The inadequacy of the First Analogy, however, deprives this move of any real value, and as the rest of the Second Analogy reveals, it is the first-edition statement of the causal maxim which best expresses the outcome of Kant's argument.

(*2*) *The proofs in A and B.* The twenty-eight paragraphs of the Analogy divide into two parts, sixteen and twelve paragraphs long. The first sixteen paragraphs [including the additions in B] contain the development and statement of the proof. The remaining paragraphs deal with a variety of related matters which Kant wishes to touch on.

All in all, we can divide the opening passage into five parts:

First, paragraph 3, which is to say the first paragraph of the first edition. This is probably the most important part of the Analogy, for in it Kant lays out the skeleton of the argument, and establishes its connections with the Deduction. *Second*, paragraphs 4–6, in which the formal proof of the first-edition principle is expounded. *Third*, paragraphs 7–12, in which Kant answers Hume's attack on the causal maxim, and restates the proof so that it is more clearly an extension of the Deduction. *Fourth*, paragraphs 13–15, containing a new proof based on the theory of inner sense. And *fifth*, paragraph 16, together with paragraphs 1–2 added in B. As Kemp Smith points out, these are two statements of the same proof, not essentially different from the proof of paragraphs 3–6. The purpose of these repetitions is to exhibit the relation of the Analogy to the various elements of the Analytic which have already been introduced. The theory is by this time so complex that Kant must go through the proof several times, now emphasizing one aspect of the Analytic, now another.

(a) *The meaning of "object" — paragraph 3.* Kant very significantly begins the Analogy by asking what we mean by "object," when the term is taken to signify *object of representations*. This question was first asked in the Deduction, it will be recalled, at the beginning of the passage on the Transcendental Object $= x$.[30] At that point, Kant could only explain "object of representations" as referring to some indeterminate thing $= x$, which served as the ground of the unity which was thought in the manifold of representations. In the later stages of the Deduction argument, Kant sought to reinstate the object of representations as a part of the phenomenal world. To do so he was forced to develop a complex and unsatisfactory theory of transcendental and empirical syntheses, the object of representations ($=$ perceptions) then becoming the product of the transcendental synthesis. Now, in the Second Analogy, Kant returns to the question which began the argument of the Deduction, and advances a final analysis of the concept of the phenomenal object. The manner of phrasing the question indicates Kant's awareness that he is here picking up the discussion which was inconclusively dropped at the end of the Objective Deduction.

The problem of the phenomenal object arises from an apparent

[30] A 104 ff.

contradiction in Kant's position. On the one hand, the phenomenal object is a mere appearance and therefore a mind-dependent entity. As the product of the synthetic activity of imagination, it cannot exist independently of the subject who knows it. On the other hand, a phenomenon is the object of representations which appear in consciousness, and hence in some sense must be distinguishable from those representations. As I have said, Kant's two provisional, and unsatisfactory, solutions were *first*, to make the object a mere unknowable *x*, and *second*, to make it the product of a parallel synthetic linking-up of a duplicate manifold. The object $= x$ does not adequately express the content of the concept of an object of representation, and the theory of double affection, despite its bold assumptions, fails to explain the nature of necessary connection. Hence Kant must offer a third explanation, which distinguishes between object and representation while positing only one manifold of intuition.

Thus far, the problem bears no special relationship to the Second Analogy, but Kant transforms it by introducing the factor of subjective and objective time order. Representations play a double role, as objects of consciousness (i.e., mental contents) and as the representations of empirical objects. As contents of consciousness they are apprehended in a temporal succession, for time is the form of inner sense. Now we might at first suppose that the succession of states in the object of these representations could only follow the order in which the representations themselves enter consciousness, for the object is merely an appearance, and hence nothing apart from the mind. But this supposition is obviously false, as the example of the house demonstrates. "The apprehension of the manifold in the appearance of a house which stands before me is successive [i.e., I perceive its sides one by one, or scan one side from top to bottom]. The question then arises, whether the manifold of the house is also in itself successive [i.e., whether the sides of the house exist objectively one after the other]. This, however, is what no one will grant" [A 190].

How are we to draw a distinction between representations and object which will make comprehensible a difference in their order of connection while yet preserving the status of the object as mere appearance? Kant captures the paradoxical nature of the question when he asks, "What, then, am I to understand by the question:

how the manifold may be connected in the appearance itself, which yet is nothing in itself?" [A 191]. The answer involves a rather subtle shift in meaning and interpretation of the key term, *object*.

The defining marks of knowledge are universality and necessity. Strictly speaking, however, these constitute an analysis of *objectivity* rather than of *object*. An object, as Kant explains in the Deduction, is merely that which grounds, or accounts for, or serves as the locus of, objectivity. Specifically, the object is that which coerces the mind's connection of representations in judgment; a proposition is true precisely if it connects in judgment what is connected in the object. Now, if the object cannot be a distinct entity from the representations of it, and if at the same time it must serve as the ground for their objective connection, then the object must be simply a *special way of organizing the representations*.

We already know that the concept of an object is a rule for synthesis of a manifold, which is to say a rule for organizing representations. The object thus becomes once more a *that which*. It is *"that* in the appearance which contains the condition" of the synthetic reworking of the manifold of perceptions. *Our problem, then, is not to find some entity on which we can pin the label "object," but rather to find some order of the manifold which is different from the order of subjective consciousness and has the requisite marks of objectivity.*

The solution lies in connecting subjective and objective time order with the double nature of representations. Subjective time order is the order of representations *qua* mental contents. When we synthesize these representations, we reproduce them in imagination according to a rule, and this reproduction produces an order of the manifold *qua* representations. As already indicated by the analysis of synthesis and rule-directed activities, the succession in this new order is a *necessary* succession. It is therefore an *objective* order. *Thus, the synthesis which produces the unity of consciousness is nothing more nor less than the establishment of an objective time order.* "Connection in the object" is interpreted to mean "connection of the contents of consciousness *qua* representations." "Appearance," Kant says, "in contradistinction to the representations of apprehension, can be represented as an object distinct from them only if it stands under a rule which distinguishes it from every other apprehension and necessitates some one particular mode of connection of the manifold" [A 191].

With the introduction of the factor of time-consciousness, and the distinction between objective and subjective time order, Kant has found the key to the solution of the unsolved problem of the Deduction. Here, within the realm of experience, is a way of distinguishing necessary connection from mere subjective association. Hume seems to have been unaware of the fact that there is a difference between the order in which we perceive events or objects and the objective order which we subsequently ascribe to them. His long and detailed discussion of the belief in material objects[31] considers only the problems of continued and independent existence. As I mentioned above, he deliberately refuses to speak in terms of the distinction between objects and our perceptions of them, and it is therefore impossible even for him to frame the proposition that the order of our perceptions of a house differs from the order of the parts which the perceptions represent.

The importance of Kant's discovery cannot be emphasized too strongly. The entire Critical Philosophy is, in a sense, an exhaustive study of the modes of necessity in judgment and experience. Kant sets himself against the tendency, common to both the rationalists and empiricists, to identify all necessity with the analytic necessity of logic. It was this overly simple view which led the rationalists to make the indefensible claim that all knowledge was expressible in analytic propositions (as Leibniz held), and it was the same view, turned against the rationalists, which prompted Hume to deny that we have any knowledge save that of relations of ideas (tautologies).

Kant agrees with Leibniz that physics and mathematics yield genuine necessary propositions, but he also agrees with Hume that such propositions are not analytic. Hence, the key to his investigation is the concept of synthetic necessity (or synthetic unity). The Critical enterprise hinges on his ability to give content to this notion, and to demonstrate that synthetic necessity is an indispensable ingredient of experience. The Deduction takes a great step in that direction by proving that the subjective associations described by the empiricists are a necessary and universal element in experience. But it is only the introduction of the

[31] Cf. *Treatise*, I, iv, 2, "Of scepticism with regard to the senses."

concept of objective time order that allows Kant to flesh out synthetic necessity and thereby "answer Hume."

This development has, of course, been foreshadowed in the Subjective Deduction, where Kant analyzes the stages of the synthesizing process. Nevertheless, the full significance of it only becomes apparent in the Second Analogy. Again, let me point to the importance of the fact that Kant here reintroduces the problem of the "object of representations." Throughout the Analytic, the direction of the analysis has been from "object" to "objectivity," and simultaneously from "object" to "concept of an object." The net result is to replace the traditional notion of substance, as the ground of objective connection, with a rule for the reproduction of a manifold in objective time relations. The analytic necessity of the judgment that attribute P belongs to the essence of substance S (which for Leibniz was the prototype of all true propositions) gives way to the synthetic necessity of the judgment that event E must be reproduced in imagination, and thus occurs in objective time order, after event C.

The treatment in paragraph 3, is regressive or expository in style. It remains for Kant to prove that the re-ordering of all my representations in objective time-relations is a necessary condition of the unity of consciousness.

(b) *The proof in A — paragraphs 4–6.* The order of representations in apprehension is always successive, whether they be representations of the side of a house or of the several positions of a moving boat. Therefore we cannot discover, by a mere examination of the contents of consciousness, any mark which distinguishes an objective sequence from a mere subjective succession. We cannot, that is, distinguish a *representation of succession* from a *succession of representations*.[32]

Let us approach the problem from a different angle in an attempt to discover a clue to the distinction. What, in general, distinguishes an actual event in the real world from a mere fancy of imagination? Putting to one side all considerations of "force and vivacity of perceptions," as Hume would say, the mark of the real is its unalterability, its demand that we adjust to it, rather than it to us. To say that A really preceded B is to deny that their order can be changed, now that it has occurred. The real is

[32] Cf. Weldon, pp. 264–265, whose discussion of this point is excellent.

precisely what we cannot tear up and rewrite. If the order cannot be altered, then it *must* be represented in that way and no other.[33] In other words, we must *always* so represent it. Thus, the objective reality of the temporal succession of A and B is expressed by a necessary and universal rule for their representation. This is just the desired distinguishing characteristic of a *representation of succession* — it is a necessary, or rule-grounded, succession of representation. But necessary succession according to a rule is causation, Kant holds in agreement with Hume. Hence the distinction between subjective and objective time order, which is involved in the concept of the objective in general, implies the uinversal validity of the causal maxim. To place an event B in the objective sequence ABC is to assert that it must follow A and precede C, which is simply another way of saying that it is an effect of A and the cause of C.

This, in brief, is the proof of the Analogy in paragraphs 4–6.

One very important matter remains unclear, due to a confusion in Kant's argument. The central point of the proof is contained in the following passage, which distinguishes between necessary and merely subjective succession:

I see a ship move down stream. My perception of its lower position follows upon the perception of its position higher up in the stream, and it is impossible that in the apprehension of this appearance the ship should first be perceived lower down in the stream and afterwards higher up. The order in which the perceptions succeed one another in apprehension is in this instance determined, and to this order apprehension is bound down. In the previous example of a house my perceptions could begin with the apprehension of the roof and end with the basement, or could begin from below and end above . . . [A 192]

In other words, Kant claims that succession of representations, if it is also a representation of (objective) succession, must necessarily have entered *subjective* consciousness in that order and no other. A succession of representations which is not a representation of succession, as for example the perception of the house, could have entered consciousness differently. Needless to say, Kant is not claiming that you can tell a necessary from a contingent succession in consciousness merely by looking at it. Quite to the contrary, necessity involves a synthesis according to *a pri-*

---

[33] Again, "must" carries a normative, not a deterministic, force.

ori concepts. The point is that necessary succession of representations is what Scholastics used to call the *real definition* of representation of succession.

Unfortunately, this position is simply false, as the least reflection will show. It is not true that we must perceive the boat at B after we have perceived it at A. We might hear its whistle at A after we see its smoke from B. Or, to be somewhat more fanciful, the light from A might be reflected back and forth between mirrors enough times to make it arrive after the light from B. By the same token, the accidents of my perceptual situation might make it objectively impossible for me to view the house in more than one order. In general, by manipulating the physical and physiological setting of a perceptual situation, a particular succession of representations p_1, p_2, p_3, . . ., p_n can be made compatible with any of the $n!$ alternative objective successions of the states represented by the perceptions. Kant is apparently led to the contrary position by an over-simplified identification of perception with sight, although even with regard to sight his conclusion is unwarranted.

Here, as elsewhere in the *Critique*, Kant goes beyond what his argument either requires or sanctions. Subjective succession is neither a sufficient nor a necessary condition of objective succession.[34] The real point of the argument, as Kant makes clear later in the Analogy, is not that we must *perceive* B after A, but that we must represent or *think* B after A. Objectivity is a characteristic of cognition, not of apprehension. It is therefore expressed in judgments which assert a connection of representations. However the representations enter consciousness, they must be thought in the order AB.

This statement can be looked at in either of two ways. If we adopt the standpoint of someone who already knows the objective time-order — that is to say, if we presuppose the objective time-order — then the statement is trivial. It simply asserts that when A precedes B objectively, we must think A as preceding B or else be in error. But if we adopt the standpoint of subjective consciousness alone, then the statement becomes a definition of the concept of objective succession. "A precedes B in objective time"

[34] If it were a necessary (but not sufficient) condition, then it would be possible to deduce certain facts about objective time order from the mere subjective order of perceptions alone. This, of course, would contradict Kant's entire theory of knowledge.

thus *means* "we must represent A as preceding B or else be in error, *no matter whether the perception of A precedes or follows the perception of B in subjective consciousness.*" There is no necessity in apprehension, but there is necessity in the synthetic reorganization of apprehension. We must *think* an objective time-order into our representations, by application of the categories. In particular, we think objective succession by means of the category of cause and effect.

(*c*) *The answer to Hume — paragraphs 7–12.* With paragraph seven, Kant begins a new line of thought. His purpose is to refute Hume's sceptical analysis of causal inference, and consequently the argument takes the form of a *reductio ad absurdum.* If we suppose with Hume that it is *not* necessary for every event to have a cause, then on the basis of the foregoing analysis we can deduce various contradictions. Kant is here following the pattern established in the Objective Deduction. On that occasion he first gave a direct proof of the validity of the categories (paragraphs 1–6 of Section 3), and then applied the conclusions against Hume, "starting from below," as he put it [A 119]. Also as in the Objective Deduction, Kant here ascends from the empirical to the *a priori*, and then draws a proof of the causal maxim out of the inadequacies of Hume's purely psychological analysis. Kemp Smith divides the present passage in two, treating paragraphs 10–12 as distinct from paragraphs 7–9, but in fact they form a connected argument parallel in structure to paragraphs 7–11 of the Objective Deduction.

Hume teaches that there is no rational justification for causal inference, and hence that we can give no more than a psychological account of the mechanisms which generate our belief in causal judgments. His theory, as it happens, is couched in language which deliberately obscures the distinction between the contents of consciousness, or impressions, and the objects which they represent. In the famous section in the *Treatise* "Of Scepticism with Regard to the Senses," Hume announces his decision to speak with the vulgar:

Now we have already observ'd, that however philosophers may distinguish betwixt the objects and perceptions of the senses; which they suppose co-existent and resembling; yet this is a distinction, which is not comprehended by the generality of mankind, who as they perceive only one being,

can never assent to the opinion of a double existence and representation.
. . . In order, therefore, to accommodate myself to their notions, I shall
at first suppose; that there is only a single existence, which I shall call indifferently *object* or *perception* . . . understanding by both of them what
any common man means by a hat, or shoe, or stone, or any other impression, convey'd to him by his senses." [*Treatise*, p. 202]

As a consequence of this identification of object and perception,
it becomes possible to frame the conclusion of Hume's analysis of
causation indifferently in either of two ways:

(1) Objects are observed to be repeatedly conjoined, and this
constant conjunction of like objects is all we mean by causation.
The observed conjunction induces in us a habit of thinking of the
one when the other is presented.

(2) Perceptions are observed to be repeatedly conjoined, and
this induces us to connect the two objects in our minds with that
vivacity or force which we call necessity. In short, from a repeated
subjective succession we develop a habit of association.[35]

Whether Kant was actively aware of these alternatives is difficult to ascertain. The double definition of cause appears in trun-
cated form in the *Enquiry*,[36] but the more striking analysis of
material objects finds almost no expression there. At any rate,
intentionally or not, Kant supplies refutations to Hume's conclusion in both its forms. The first formulation, which is dealt
with in paragraphs 7–8, may be summarized thus:

There is no necessity of connection between two events which
we denominate cause and effect; there is merely "an object,
followed by another, and where all the objects similar to the first
are followed by objects similar to the second." [37] Kant's answer

---

[35] At the conclusion of his analysis of causality, Hume offers two definitions of
cause. These are (1) "an object precedent and contiguous to another, and where
all the objects resembling the former are plac'd in a like relation of priority and
contiguity to those objects, that resemble the latter"; and (2) "an object precedent
and contiguous to another, and so united with it in the imagination, that the idea
of the one determines the mind to form the idea of the other, and the impression
of the one to form a more lively idea of the other" [*Treatise*, p. 172]. Hume's
apparent belief that these are interchangeable formulations can only be based on
an intentional equation of object and perception.

[36] *Enquiry*, pp. 76–77.

[37] *Enquiry*, p. 76. Hume speaks of objects, Kant of events. The difference is
significant, but cannot be explored here, as it leads into aspects of Hume's philosophy which are not relevant to the *Critique*. Suffice it to say that by the time
Kant has modified the substance-accident conception of the First Analogy, and
Hume has thought through the connections between causal beliefs and the belief
in body, their views are not very far apart. Hume gives the causal maxim as

is to argue that the very concept of an *event* involves necessary succession, and therefore causation. What, after all, is an event? It is not a mere succession of perceptions in consciousness; it is a happening (*etwas, was geschieht*), which is to say, the succession of one state upon another in objective time. But our previous analysis has shown that objective sequence involves necessity. Hence it is a flat contradiction that something in the field of appearance should begin to be, and yet not be preceded by something else which it necessarily follows.[38] Even to speak of a sequence of events is to presuppose a causal order of which they are a part, for the causal order *is* the objective temporal order.

Kant deals with the second, more psychological form of Hume's argument in paragraph 9. There he merely repeats the point that empirical association can never account for the necessity which is involved in causation. Hume, of course, would agree — that is just the source of his scepticism. But the proofs already given by Kant of the causal maxim constitute a sufficient refutation of Hume. If Hume, in identifying objects with perceptions, defines the habits of causal inference in terms of subjective association, then he is utterly unable even to explain the distinction between subjective and objective succession. Faced with the example of the house, Hume might account for our refusal to call the roof a cause of the foundation by pointing out that perceptions similar to them are not always conjoined in experience in a like order. But since he does not distinguish objective from subjective sequence, he can never explain why we assign the several parts of the house to the *same* time. In a sense, then, objective co-existence is even more puzzling than objective succession, for the latter at least finds its exemplar in subjective consciousness.

The foregoing is obviously less satisfactory than the refutation of the first formulation of Hume's argument. In the former case, Kant managed to show that Hume's own position presupposed the existence of necessary causal connections, but here he has simply shown that Hume cannot account for a distinction which is generally accepted. To destroy the sceptical position

---

"whatever begins to exist, must have a cause of existence," which is close enough to the first-edition version of the principle of causality.

[38] See A 188, in the First Analogy, where the impossibility of an empty time is proved. The argument given there also proves the impossibility of an uncaused event, though that is not what Kant is discussing.

completely, Kant must prove that the distinction between subjective and objective time order is valid. It is not enough merely to assume it and then prove its incompatibility with scepticism. This proof, which completes the argument of the Deduction, will be formulated after we have completed our examination of the proofs of the Analogy.

In paragraphs 10–12 Kant reiterates the argument of the *Analogy*, clarifying and expanding the points made in paragraphs 4–6. Paragraph 11 is an extremely clear statement of the new analysis of "object of representations" which was worked out in paragraph 3. Relation to an object, Kant asserts, cannot be explained by reference to an entity independent of my representations, for no matter how far I search in consciousness, I encounter nothing but representations. A correspondence theory, in other words, fails for lack of anything to correspond to. Consequently, writes Kant, "If we enquire what new character *relation to an object* confers upon our representations, what dignity they thereby acquire, we find that it results only in subjecting the representations to a rule, and so in necessitating us to connect them in some one specific manner" [A 197]. As Kant says in paragraph 3, "the object is *that* in the appearance which contains the condition of this necessary rule of apprehension" [A 191].

(*d*) *Paragraphs 13–15.* The proof contained in these paragraphs is extremely difficult, and seems to have been included by Kant in order to bring the Second Analogy into relation with the Objective Deduction theory of pure intuition and transcendental synthesis. That this double-affection theory is actually inconsistent with the teaching of the Analogy can be seen from Kant's retraction, in paragraph 15, of the assertion in paragraph 14 that we can cognize pure time.[39]

The proof is as follows: pure time has the formal property that any given part can only be reached by way of the parts which precede it. But since time cannot itself be perceived, we can only empirically cognize (*empirisch erkennen*) this order in the appearances which fill time. We must, in other words, "carry the time-order over into the appearances and their existence" [A 199]. This is done by establishing a necessary order among the appear-

[39] Cf. Kemp Smith, pp. 375–76.

ances themselves, which thus is succession according to a rule, or causation.

The difficulty with this argument is that it denies its own premise. If pure time contained a manifold which could be intuited *a priori*, then it would be possible to establish the time-position of appearances by relation to absolute time. If, on the other hand, time-position can only be established by a process of reciprocal interrelation of the contents of time, then what sense does it make to speak of a pre-existent time-order being "carried over" into appearances?

We are confronted here with yet another evidence of the internal inconsistency of Kant's theory of inner sense. It should be growing clearer why so many of the second edition revisions dealt with this problem. I treat the subject in more detail in my discussion of the second edition version of the Transcendental Deduction.

Kemp Smith's translation of *empirisch erkennen* as "empirically apprehend" in the last sentence of paragraph 13 is questionable. In his *Commentary*, page 375, *erkennen* is rendered as "recognize." Because of the special sense which Kant gives to "apprehension" in the phrase "synthesis of apprehension," it is probably better to reserve the term for the German equivalent, *Apprehension*. Similarly, "recognize" suggests "synthesis of recognition," and is therefore also an unhappy choice. In the present context the matter is more than a mere quibble, for Kant himself is uncertain about the status of subjective consciousness. The translation should, if possible, preserve this uncertainty, and not make it appear that Kant either affirms or denies the necessity of a synthesis for subjective awareness.

(*e*) *Paragraphs 16 and 1–2.* The concluding proof in the first edition (paragraph 16) and the new proof added in B (paragraphs 1–2) perfectly exemplify this ambiguity concerning apprehension and subjective time-order. Kant begins his argument in paragraph 16 with the statement that:

All empirical knowledge involves the synthesis of the manifold by the imagination. This synthesis is always successive, that is, the representations in it are always sequent upon one another. In the imagination this sequence is not in any way determined in its order . . . and the series of sequent representations can indifferently be taken either in backward or in forward order. [A 201]

If, however, I am to have knowledge of an event, something which actually happens, my cognition must be "an empirical judgment in which we think the sequence as determined. . . . Were it not so . . . I should have to regard the succession as a merely subjective play of my fancy" [A 201]. Consequently, the principle of necessary succession, or causal relation, is the "condition of the objective validity of our empirical judgments . . . that is to say, it is the condition of experience [= empirical knowledge]" [A 202].

The initial step of the proof seems to involve the postulation of two separate syntheses, one in imagination and the other in (or determined by) understanding. The first of these syntheses gives subjective consciousness, in which the sequence is indifferent, and hence can be viewed as a mere fancy. The second yields necessary succession and thereby objective time-order. It is a synthesis according to the categories, serving as the condition and source of empirical knowledge.

Kant has already offered us a distinction between the syntheses of imagination and understanding. It appears in the Subjective Deduction, where the labels "synthesis of apprehension" and "synthesis of recognition" are given to them.[40] In the Metaphysical and Objective Deductions also, the contributions of the two faculties are distinguished [B 104, A 115-16]. But the two syntheses are never described as two different organizations of the manifold. They are simply different aspects of the same running through and holding together. This is why I suggested that the distinction is largely artificial. In the present instance, Kant seems actually to hold that the order established by the synthesis of imagination is different from that imposed by the categories of understanding. Obviously such a position cannot be made consistent with the rest of the Analytic.

I have already indicated the nature of the quandary in which

[40] The synthesis of recognition is attributed by Kant to apperception. It is this, undoubtedly, which Wille had in mind when he suggested the substitution of "apperception" for "apprehension" in the fifth (English) sentence of paragraph 16. The change would certainly clarify the text, but it would also commit Kant more firmly to a view which he only half believes. The entire Analogy gives evidence of Kant's complete indecision on this point.

Kant finds himself. The central insight of the Second Analogy is the distinction between subjective and objective time order, with all the consequences which follow from it. To maintain this distinction Kant must claim that we are conscious of the subjective order. But the Deduction has already proved that all consciousness presupposes a synthesis. Therefore, if Kant wants to explain objective time order as itself a synthetic reworking of subjective succession, he must apparently postulate two syntheses rather than one.

Kant glosses over the problem in the proof added in B (paragraph 12), which is a variation of paragraph 16. He states that the imagination can connect two states, A and B, in either order. But instead of implying that we are *first* conscious of them in the order AB and *then* by the application of the categories judge whether their objective order is also AB, Kant simply states that the work of imagination is guided by a pure concept [B 234]. The relationship between imagination and understanding is the same here as in the Deduction—imagination synthesizes the manifold, and understanding imposes a necessary unity on that synthesis.[41]

We can now begin to see why Kant mistakenly supposes that subjective succession is a necessary, though not sufficient, condition of objective succession; why, for example, he says that "in the perception of an event there is always a rule that makes the order in which the perceptions (in the apprehension [*sic*] of this appearance) follow upon one another a *necessary* order" [A 193]. The reason is that he can thus avoid the most obvious case in which subjective and objective time-orders must be completely distinguished, namely the case in which A causes B, and yet B is perceived *before* A. The distinction between the successions AB and A′B′, when A is cause of B and A′ is not cause of B′, can be explained by saying that A *must* precede B in perception, whereas A′ might have followed B′. In other words, in the synthesis of the manifold of A, B, A′, and B′, the understanding compels imagination to place A before B, but leaves it undetermined whether A′ shall precede B′. But if B can be apprehended in subjective consciousness prior to A, then a reworking of the *already apprehended* manifold will be needed if we are to think A as a cause of B. This

[41] Just what that means, I confess I do not know. See the discussion of the Metaphysical Deduction above.

in turn seems to imply a preliminary synthesis of apprehension distinct from a synthesis of apperception (understanding), with all the difficulties mentioned above.

In a proof of the Third Analogy, added in B, Kant actually uses the phrase "synthesis of imagination in apprehension" [B 257]. The precise meaning is unclear, but Kant apparently identifies this synthesis with the *re*ordering of the manifold, rather than with the original order given in intuition. The relation of subjective consciousness to synthesis thus remains obscured.

The Completion of the Argument of the Deduction. With the materials provided by the analysis of subjective and objective time order, I am finally in a position to redeem my oft-repeated promise to exhibit the argument by which Kant proves the validity of the causal maxim. This will complete the answer to Hume, as well as the major task of the Analytic. Strictly speaking, Kant purports to demonstrate eight principles in all: the principle of the Axioms, that of the Anticipations, three Analogies, and three Postulates.[42] Actually, however, only the law of causality can be given a thoroughly rigorous demonstration. With the introduction of the form of outer sense (space), a parallel proof could be constructed of the law of community (Third Analogy), although the complications of this are immense. Also, revisions along the lines suggested above would yield a provable principle of permanence (First Analogy). The other principles, however, cannot be supported by anything stronger than the general arguments which Kant offers for them. These, while quite interesting in a variety of ways, are not formally deduced from the unity of consciousness.

Before proceeding to the final version of the argument of the Analytic, a last confusion must be cleared away. The official aim of the Second Analogy is to prove that the validity of the law of cause and effect is a necessary condition of experience in general. This is equivalent to the assertion that I can deduce the law of causality from the premise that I have experience. In this instance, experience is taken to mean empirical knowledge, so the conclusion of the Analogy becomes, "If I have empirical knowledge, then everything which happens presupposes something upon which it

---

[42] These last are not really objective principles of experience in the same sense, and Kant offers an "explanation" of them rather than a proof.

follows according to a rule." The Deduction has proved that the possession of empirical knowledge is a logical consequence of the mere fact of consciousness in general. The two conclusions together yield: "If I am conscious in general, then everything which happens presupposes something upon which it follows according to a rule." Expressed in the terms employed by Kant, the law of causality is a *necessary condition* of (the possibility of) consciousness in general. Since any philosopher, including Hume, must grant that he is conscious, it follows that the law of causality has been vindicated.

Stated in this way, the connection between the two parts of the Analytic is based on a fallacy: the term "experience = empirical knowledge" is employed equivocally. In the Second Analogy, the distinction between subjective and objective time order seems not to be deduced, but simply to be drawn out of the concept of empirical knowledge by analysis. In the Deduction, however, this component of the concept was never demonstrated to follow from the unity of consciousness. All that was proved was the existence of objective reference for our concepts, or, alternatively, the existence of synthetic judgments *a priori*. Consequently, it is open to a critic such as Hume to accept the conclusion of the Deduction and yet consistently to reject the argument of the Analogy. He need simply deny that some subjective successions are representations of objective co-existence.

The real state of affairs is somewhat different from what has just been described. The Analogies introduce into the Analytic a factor which should have been included from the very first, namely the temporality of consciousness. The Subjective Deduction actually does draw out some of the consequences of time-consciousness, but Kant's desire to preserve the distinction between schematized and pure categories prevents him from integrating those conclusions into the Objective Deduction. The artificial distinction between categories and principles also forces Kant to distort the structure of his argument. So in fact, to complete the Analytic we must go back to the argument of the Deduction and revise it for the last time. The reader is urged to review the discussion of Section 2 of the Deduction in A, and in particular the version of the proof which I called stage III.

The following is a proof of the law of cause and effect. It begins with the premise of the Deduction, that my consciousness has a unity, and adds to this the further premise that all my consciousness has the form of time. It concludes with the principle that every appearance presupposes something upon which it follows necessarily. In other words, the law of cause and effect is a necessary condition of consciousness in general.

FINAL VERSION OF THE ARGUMENT OF THE ANALYTIC

To Prove: There is an objective order of events, and everything in it which happens, that is, begins to be, presupposes something upon which it follows according to a rule.[43]

Proof:

1. All the contents of my consciousness are bound up in a unity. [Premise]
2. The only way to introduce synthetic unity into a manifold of contents of consciousness is by reproducing it in imagination according to a rule. [Cf. discussion of the Third Version of the Deduction.]
3. The defining mark of objectivity is necessity of connection.
   [Cf. Analysis of Deduction.]
4. Synthesis, i.e., reproduction in imagination according to a rule, confers necessity of connection on a manifold.
   [Analysis of Synthesis, Third Version of Deduction.]
5. If all the contents of my consciousness are bound up in a unity, then they have, *qua* representations, an objective order.
   [2, 3, 4, substitution and conversion.]
6. The contents of my consciousness have, *qua* representations, an objective order,

   which is to say,

   there is an objective order of events. [1, 5, *modus ponens.*]
7. The form of inner sense is time, and therefore all the representations of my consciousness, *considered simply qua mental contents,* must be arranged in a temporal order. [Additional premise]
8. But since these representations must be reproduced in imagination according to a rule before they can be admitted to the unity of consciousness [step 3], they must have a *rule-determined time-order* which is the order of their reproduction. [From 7]
9. Thus, any mental content, in order to be treated as a representation with

---

[43] Cf. A 189. I have added the first clause in order to forestall a possible criticism to which Kant leaves himself open. As he states the causal maxim, it is a hypothetical proposition asserting that *if* anything happens, *then* there is something upon which it follows, etc. But, Hume might reply, this merely proves that nothing "happens," in the restricted sense meant by Kant. Thus it is necessary also to prove that there is an objective order of happenings, or events, to which the causal maxim applies. For Hume's equivalent formulation of the maxim, see *Treatise,* p. 78.

objective reference, must be reproduced in a temporal sequence of representations according to a rule [3, 4, 8],

which is to say,

Everything which happens, that is, begins to be, presupposes something upon which it follows (temporally) according to a rule, *and*, there is an objective order of happenings (events) [6]. Q.E.D.

The weak links in the argument, from the standpoint of the *Critique*, are steps 8 and 9. Kant must somehow explain what it means to attribute a temporal order to perceptions *prior* to their reception into the unity of consciousness. In the very earliest stages of the Deduction, Kant held that perceptions could enter consciousness independently of their subsumption under the categories (§ 13). This, however, leaves open the possibility of a scepticism with regard to the possibility of empirical knowledge, for it teaches that the contents of consciousness (perceptions) are better known than the objects of consciousness. Because it was precisely this privileged position of the subjective which Kant wished to deny, he was led eventually to the doctrine that the objective validity of the categories is the condition of any consciousness whatsoever. The extraordinary complications introduced into the argument in order to prove this powerful claim account for much of the difficulty of the Analytic.

Kant's theory might appear untenable even if he could make the pre-conscious temporal order of perception plausible. It might be argued that perceptions can only have one order in consciousness, whether it is the subjective order carried over from the pre-conscious, or the objective order produced by a synthetic reorganization. The proof of the Analogy, however, demands two contrasting orders, both of them conscious. We must be able to say that we *become aware of* the sides of the house successively, not simply that the sides are preconsciously perceived in succession. Even if that last statement meant anything, it would not suffice for the proof.

This objection can be met by Kant, but it is important nonetheless, for it exposes one of the aspects of the Analytic which is most easily misunderstood. A house, in Kant's view, is not a little object constructed in imagination from a collection of sights and feels. Strictly speaking, it, like every other empirical object, is a set of *judgments*. The whole point of the Analytic is that we cannot have experience (= empirical *consciousness*) unless it has been brought into the form of experience (= empirical *knowledge*). The synthesis of the manifold of intuition is not a putting together of a three-dimensional jig-saw puzzle, which the mind can then by some miracle stare at from all sides simultaneously. Synthesis is cognition, the application of concepts and the formation of judgments. Kant makes this clear in paragraph 16 of the Second Analogy when he says: "If, then, my perception is to contain knowledge of an event, of something as actually happening, it must be an empirical judgment in which we think the sequence as determined." [A 201] We *apprehend* the subjective order of perceptions, but we *think*, or *judge*, the objective order. Necessity, which is the mark of objectivity, can only be an attribute of judgments. We could not even be aware of the subjective order of representations if we did not treat them as objects in turn, and formulate judgments about their relation to an empirical object, namely, the self.[44]

The two orders can exist in consciousness because perceptions have the double nature of contents of consciousness. As mental contents, they are apprehended in a subjective time-order. But as representations, they form the content of empirical judgments which assign them to an objective time-order. Needless to say, this does not resolve the anomaly, mentioned above, of a preconscious time-order.

The Remainder of the Analogy. The second half of the Second Analogy is devoted to a discussion of three problems related to causation, namely simultaneous causation (paragraphs 17–18), the dynamical concept of substance (paragraphs 19–22), and the continuity of change (paragraphs 23–28). The first two of these have a direct bearing on the interpretation of the Analogies, and therefore merit some consideration. The third should more properly have been confined to the *Metaphysical First Principles of Natural Science*.[45]

(*1*) *Simultaneous causation.* Kant suggests that his analysis of causation in terms of objective succession may seem to conflict with the fact that "the great majority of efficient natural causes are simultaneous with their effects, and the sequence in time of the

---

[44] Cf. the first part of paragraph 3, A 189–190.
[45] Cf. Kemp Smith, pp. 380–381, for a brief discussion and references.

latter is due only to the fact that the cause cannot achieve its complete effect in one moment." [A 203] But everything is quite all right, because the concept of succession refers only to the *order* of time, not to the *lapse* of time.

This distinction has a rather nice ring to it, but it is not immediately clear what it means. Either two states exist at the same objective time or at different times. If the former, then why say that one is prior to the other in the order of time? What additional information is conveyed by such a statement, save that one is cause of the other (which is what we are trying to define)?

Kant's examples, in this case, are quite helpful. As instances of simultaneous causation he cites a ball making an indentation on a cushion, and the sides of a glass producing a rise in the surface of a column of water by surface tension. The case of the ball and cushion is described in the following manner:

If I lay the ball on the cushion, a hollow follows upon the previous flat smooth shape; but if (for any reason) there previously exists a hollow in the cushion, a leaden ball does not follow upon it. [A 203]

The two are then said to be distinguished "through the time-relation of their dynamical connection," which is somewhat cryptic, but the distinction is clearly one of dependent and independent variables: the shape of the cushion is a function of the position of the ball. This makes it clearer what Kant has in mind, but it does not bring us any closer to an explanation of simultaneous causation in terms of the doctrine of the Analogy.

A solution might be worked out in terms of the nature of synthesis. Synthesis, we have seen, is reproduction in imagination according to a rule. In the case of the category of cause and effect, the rule is that the event judged to be cause must always be reproduced prior to the event judged to be effect.[46] Thus, even if A and B are simultaneous in objective time, the order in which they are reproduced is determined as AB.

This may be what Kant had in mind when he distinguished order from lapse of time. At any rate, it will not do. Objective time sequence is defined in terms of the necessary succession of appearances, and this is equated by Kant with causation. He still

[46] More precisely, the representation of the cause must be reproduced prior to the representation of the effect.

must explain how a cause and its effects can be simultaneous.[47]

The only way out, it seems to me, is for Kant to recognize that simultaneous causation is a case of reciprocity or community, and hence must be treated under the Third Analogy rather than the Second. After all, if the law of action and reaction is valid, then the cushion *does* stand as cause to the iron ball, though to be sure it is not the principal determinant of the ball's position. Needless to say, this is a postponement of the problem, not a solution of it. If causation demands sequence, reciprocal causation looks to be an absolute impossibility. What Kant eventually must do, as we shall see, is revise the concept of causation to bring it in line with the demands of the time-relation of co-existence.

(2) *The dynamical concept of substance.* The Second Analogy seems to teach a regularity theory of causation, and it is in that way that most modern readers interpret it. The principle of the Analogy in A, for example, speaks of succession according to a rule. The continuing dialogue with Hume actually supports such an interpretation, for Kant accepts much of Hume's analysis. In effect, he argues that the regularity described by Hume must be shown to be a necessary regularity, by means of a transcendental argument. Kant holds, in basic agreement with Hume, that we cannot understand the internal connection of cause and effect, but must rest content with what might be called a *de facto*, or hypothetical, necessity.[48]

It has often been claimed that the regularity theory of causation is inherently absurd, since if taken seriously it must lead us to conclude that day causes night, youth causes age, and the earlier positions of the boat cause the later positions. Actually, such a view can quite easily be maintained. What, after all, *causes* night? Night is a complex of states and relations of objects, regularly succeeded by other states and relations, in conformity with certain laws of motion. When we have stated the laws according to which night follows day, we have said everything there is to say. Only a billiard ball prejudice for push-and-pull causes stands in

---

[47] Note that since either the ball or the cushion can be perceived first, the one mark of causal connection on which Kant always relies is here missing.

[48] Cf. paragraph 22 of the Second Analogy. It is the necessity of a necessary condition of the possibility of experience, or as Kant might call it, a transcendental necessity.

the way of our accepting regularity, and Hume has effectively taken the thrust out of the billiard ball.

But Kant is not having any of this defense, for he *rejects* a regularity theory of causation, offering instead his dynamical theory of force. Kant, it will be remembered, defines substance (= matter) in terms of the two moving forces, attraction and repulsion. These are for him the operative causes of the physical universe. Thus he states, "Causality leads to the concept of action, this in turn to the concept of force, and thereby to the concept of substance" [A 204]. In paragraphs 19–20 Kant proposes action as the mark of substance and dynamical agency as the essence of causality.

This leads to a subtle revision of the regularity analysis of causation whereby the cause of an event becomes a preceding action of some substance, rather than a preceding event. "The rule, by which we determine something according to succession of time," writes Kant, "is, that the condition under which an event invariably and necessarily follows *is to be found in what precedes the event*" [A 200, emphasis added]. In the case of night and day, it is some prior action of substance — here, the earth or sun — which causes night to succeed day.

How is this conception of substance to be brought into harmony with the complex argument of the Analytic? How can dynamical agency be expressed in terms of synthesis of a manifold of perceptions? I do not know, and I am inclined to think that it cannot be done. The starting point of Kant's critical revolution was the conviction that, in Leibnizean language, our knowledge is limited to external relations as conditioned by space and time. The rational connections of noumena are obscured from us, and we must therefore restrict ourselves to the brute incomprehensibility of appearance. In seeking to retain the dynamical as opposed to the regularity theory of causation, Kant seems to be gripped by a nostalgic desire for real connection. The entire weight of the *Critique* is against the satisfaction of such a desire.

The Third Analogy

The Third Analogy should, by all rights, play a central role in the Analogies and thereby in the Analytic as a whole. It is based on the time-relation of co-existence, which according to the argument of the Second Analogy is the focus of the problem of objective succession. The Humean theory of association might conceivably satisfy the demands of necessary succession since some sort of succession at least can be found in subjective consciousness, but co-existence unequivocally requires a distinct time-order of appearances. Unhappily, Kant lets down after the exertion of analyzing objective succession and gives us a hasty account of co-existence which adds little or nothing to the remarks in the Second Analogy.

The statements of the principle in A and B are essentially the same, save for the significant reference in B to co-existence *in space*. This, as we shall see, is the heart of the problem of co-existence. Kemp Smith's translation of the first-edition principle seems to carry a particular reference to Newton's law of action and reaction through the phrase, "that is, in mutual interaction." Actually, however, Kemp Smith has rendered the same German word, *Wechselwirkung*, as "interaction" in A and "reciprocity" in B.[49]

The main proof in A is contained in paragraphs 1–3 of the first edition [A 211–213; paragraphs 2–4 if we include the proof added in B]. It is extremely obscure and, as it stands, unsatisfactory. It consists of three steps, represented by the three paragraphs:

Step 1: Things are co-existent if and only if the order of their perception is reversible, a matter of indifference (*gleichgültig*). In other words, if two things are objectively co-existent, it is possible in principle to perceive them in either order; and if it is possible for the order of perceptions to be reversed [whatever that means], then the objects which they represent must be co-existent. As thus stated, the first step appears to be an analysis of the meaning of "co-existent," and a statement of the sufficient conditions for its application to the objects of a manifold of perceptions.

[49] However, cf. *Metaphysische Anfangsgründe*, III, Lehrsatz 4, Beweis: "Aus der allgemeinen Metaphysik muss der Satz entlehnt werden, dass alle äussere Wirkung in der Welt *Wechselwirkung* sei. Hier soll, um in den Schranken der Mechanik zu bleiben, nur gezeigt werden, dass diese Wechselwirkung (*actio mutua*) zugleich *Gegenwirkung (reactio)* sei; allein ich kann, ohne der Vollständigkeit der Einsicht Abbruch zu thun, jenes metaphysische Gesetz der Gemeinschaft hier doch nicht ganz weglassen." ["The proposition, that all outer action in the world is *interaction*, must be borrowed from general metaphysics. Here, in order to remain within the limits of Mechanics, it will only be shown that this interaction (*actio mutua*) is at the same time *reaction (reactio)*. But I can not completely leave out that metaphysical law of community here without doing injury to the integrity of insight."]

Step 2: Kant argues by *reductio ad absurdum*. Assume the existence of several substances which do *not* mutually interact. Then "their coexistence would not be an object of a possible perception and . . . the existence of one could not lead by any path of empirical synthesis to the existence of another." Kant's meaning is revealed in the next sentence, which is couched in the form of a demonstration rather than explanation of the foregoing. A succession of perceptions of isolated substances would at best reveal to us their existence (i.e., that there were several substances) but could not serve to determine their objective time-relations (whether successive or co-existent). In support of this assertion, Kant admonishes us to "bear in mind that they (the non-interacting substances) would be separated by a completely empty space." We can gain some clue to the meaning of this rather cryptic statement from paragraph 5 of the Analogy [B 260–261].[50] There Kant is arguing, in the reverse direction, that a void could never be cognized since it is only by the reciprocal influence of matter in space that we can establish the several parts of space as co-existent and part of one experience. The relevance of this for the present passage seems to be this: if substances are completely isolated dynamically, having no reciprocal interaction, then the perceiving of one would bear no relation to the perceiving of another, and in passing from the first to the second, *it would be as if* one had traversed a void.

Step 3: Kant draws out the conclusion of the *reductio* given in the second paragraph. In order for two substances to be "empirically represented as *coexisting*," each must somehow determine the position of the other in time. But only by being cause of B can A determine its position in time, and likewise for A in relation to B. Hence there must be a dynamical community, or mutual interaction, of substances, if they are to be known as co-existing.

The third step of the proof is a good deal more comprehensible than the second, but it too is incomplete. Why must A and B determine each other in time in order for them to be empirically represented as co-existent? Surely that is just what needs to be proved, rather than assumed. And what does it mean to "empirically represent" two substances as co-existent? Reversible succes-

[50] The entire Analogy should be read in conjunction with §§ 2 and 16–22 of the *Dissertation*.

sion is presumably the clue to the Analogy, but it is not clear what role it plays in the proof.

Matters are considerably improved in the second-edition proof [B 257–58]. Here Kant bases his argument on the same premise which underlies the Second Analogy, namely that time itself cannot be perceived. As we cannot determine the objective succession of two appearances by assigning each independently to its position in objective time, we must construct objective time by means of the necessary relations of appearances to one another. In the case of objective co-existence the same principle is involved, though the argument is a little more complicated. Subjective apprehension only reveals reciprocal sequence of perceptions (first we look at the moon, then the sun, then back to the moon). For these perceptions to be the representations of co-existence, their objects must somehow establish objective time-relation to one another, namely the relation of co-existence. But since time cannot be perceived, this can only come about if each of the objects (A and B) determines the other's time position; which is to say, only if each is cause of the other, etc.

The argument of the Third Analogy has many weaknesses, and there is little to be gained from picking at the text haphazardly. Its inadequacies clearly stem from Kant's failure to think through the fundamental issues involved in substantial co-existence, rather than from momentary lapses to be made up by quotations from other parts of the *Critique*. A systematic discussion of the subject in its relation to the Analytic may therefore be more helpful.

Kant accepted Hume's analysis of causal connection as necessary succession. He claimed only to demonstrate the legitimacy of a nonpsychological necessity, by appeal to the unity of consciousness and the distinction between subjective and objective time order. What then would be a corresponding analysis of substantial interaction? Kant suggests another temporal relation, namely co-existence or simultaneity, but this is a distortion of the view which he himself espoused. For it is not *time* which is the order of reciprocally interacting substances, but *space*.[51] In the *Dissertation*

---

[51] Kant, it will be recalled, accepts as true the Leibnizean propositions, "Time is the order of non-contemporaneous things," and "space is the order of co-existing things" [Leibniz, *Selections*, p. 202]. His objection is to Leibniz's attempts to put these forward as *definitions* of space and time. Considered in that light, he says, they are circular. Actually, only the definition of time is circular. Space is defined

this is made much clearer, although of course substances are there considered to be things-in-themselves. Space is decribed as the "universal and necessary condition, sensitively apprehended, of the co-presence of all things." [52] Time is then characterized in parallel fashion as the sensitive representation of "all changes and successions."

The adjustment of the principle of the Third Analogy in B reflects Kant's awareness of the importance of space to the analysis of co-existence, but it would not have been easy to carry through the necessary revisions in the argument. Ultimately the Axioms, the Schematism, and even the Subjective Deduction would have been affected, and there is no evidence that Kant was either willing or able to overhaul the Analytic so thoroughly. Only in the new Refutation of Idealism, added in rebuttal of the critics who had called the *Critique* Berkeleyan, does Kant take steps to reintroduce space into the argument.

Kemp Smith has suggested a proof of the Third Analogy which "will show that just as the conception of causality is involved in, and makes possible, the awareness of time, so the conception of reciprocity is involved in, and makes possible, the awareness of space." [53] It is valuable both as an alternative line which Kant's thought might more consistently have followed, and as an indication of the deeper problems which such an alternative would have left unsolved. The proposed proof is as follows:

The parts of space have to be conceived as spatially interrelated. Space is not a collection of independent spaces; particular spaces exist only in and through the spaces which enclose them . . . The parts of space mutually condition one another. Each part exists only in and through its relations, direct or indirect, to all the others; the awareness of their coexistence involves the awareness of this reciprocal determination. But space cannot, any more than time, be known in and by itself; and what is true of space must therefore hold of the contents, in terms of the interrelations of which space can alone be experienced. How, then, can the reciprocal determination of substances in space be apprehended by a consciousness which is subject in all its experiences to the conditions of time? . . . [O]bjective coexistence is distinguished from objective sequence by reversibility of the perceptions

---

in terms of a temporal relation. Kant, of course, has other arguments against Leibniz's theory of space, such as that of the incongruous counterparts.

[52] *Dissertation*, § 22 scholium. See also § 16, where the mutual interaction of substances is said to be "called space, when viewed intuitively."

[53] Kemp Smith, *op. cit.*, p. 385.

through which it is apprehended. . . . There is also, as Kant observes in the second proof, [i.e., paragraph 5 of the Third Analogy] a further condition, namely, that the transition is in each case made through a *continuous* series of changing perceptions. . . . But even such reversibility of *continuous* series does not by itself establish coexistence. . . . An additional factor is therefore required, namely, the interpretation of the reversibility of our perceptions as being grounded in objects which, because spatially extended, and spatially continuous with one another, can yield continuous series of perceptions, and which, because of their thoroughgoing reciprocity, make possible the reversing of these series. To summarise the argument in a sentence: as the objectively coexistent, if it is to be known at all, can only be known through sequent representations, the condition of its apprehension is the possibility of interpreting reversible continuous series as due to the reciprocal interaction of spatially ordered substances.[54]

Kemp Smith's proposal is an attractive alternative to the original argument, but it suffers nonetheless from several flaws which seem to me fatal. In the first place, the premise of the proof is drawn from the Aesthetic doctrine that space, as an intuition, is prior to its parts. But as we have already seen, Kant directly contradicts this in the Axioms of Intuition, where he teaches that space can only be known through a synthesis of its parts. It is not really open to Kant to revert back to the Aesthetic on this point, even for the sake of a great increase in the power and coherence of the Analogies, for the argument of the Axioms is a direct consequence of the proposition on which the entire *Critique* is founded, viz., that all consciousness presupposes a synthesis. The problem, in other words, is not simply how to bring several discordant parts of the argument into harmony by a judicious revision, but how to connect space and outer sense with the entire theory of synthesis. The Subjective Deduction, Schematism, and Second Analogy weave time so intricately into the argument that it is difficult to see how space could be introduced into the Analytic.

This difficulty is reflected in the second fault of Kemp Smith's proof, which is that at best it only deduces substantial reciprocity from the fact that we have knowledge of objective co-existence, rather than deducing that fact in turn from the unity of consciousness.[55] In the Second Analogy, Kant begins by presupposing the

---

[54] *Ibid.*, pp. 385–86.

[55] Since I appear to have quoted Kemp Smith's suggested proof only to criticize it, I should state that it is much superior to the original, and has the great virtue of exposing the strengths and weaknesses of Kant's argument more fully. That

distinction between objective and subjective succession, but as I endeavored to show in my analysis of the text, he eventually carries the argument so deep that he provides the materials for a proof of that presupposition. Neither Kemp Smith nor Kant, however, suggests any way of grounding the Third Analogy in like manner, on the Deduction. The principal cause of this failure is the impossibility, already mentioned, of integrating the awareness of space into the Deduction treatment of synthesis. But in Kant's argument two other factors are responsible, both indicative of the unthought-out nature of the Third Analogy.

The first of these is Kant's inadequately analyzed concept of substance. The triads in the Table of Categories are supposedly so arranged that the third in each group is a synthesis of the first and second. Community or reciprocity, therefore, is presented as the mutual causality of substances. Now, the First Analogy offers a traditional conception of substance (in terms of subsistence and inherence) which the Second Analogy completely contradicts. In the Third Analogy, however, Kant reverts to the original notion of substance, and takes it for granted that he has proved its (or more properly, their) existence.[56] The aim of the Analogy, therefore, is to demonstrate that knowledge of these given substances presupposes their thoroughgoing reciprocity [cf. statement of the Analogy in B]. What Kant really needs is a new analysis of substance in line with the Second Analogy, and a proof that the existence of such substances is a necessary condition of the possibility of consciousness. Something very like the latter of these requirements is fulfilled by the second edition Refutation of Idealism, to which I shall come presently.

At the heart of Kant's difficulties with the argument of the Third Analogy is his failure to clarify the notion of reversible succession. In the Second Analogy we are given the example of the

---

he was, in the end, unable to do for Kant what Kant could not do himself, hardly constitutes a reflection on Kemp Smith.

[56] By identifying substance with matter, Kant allows himself to ignore the distinction between substance (= substratum of all change) and substances (= empirical objects). Individual substances become merely delineated volumes of matter. As such their demarcation is conventional rather than objective. This ambiguity frequently appears in physical theories which reduce the objects of ordinary experience to transient states of some permanent substratum. One can contrast here Aristotle and the Atomists, whose contradictory approaches to the subject are embodied by Kant in the first and second edition versions, respectively, of the principle of the First Analogy.

house whose component parts can be perceived in any order. In the proof added to the Third Analogy, the example is changed to the earth and moon. Kant says: "I can direct my perception first to the moon and then to the earth, or, conversely, first to the earth and then to the moon; and because the perceptions of these objects can follow each other reciprocally, I say that they are coexistent" [B 257]. Typically, the order of the perceptions in subjective consciousness is described as "indifferent" (*gleichgültig*). Now Kant is extremely confused about the meaning of "indifferent" here. If I look first at the earth, then at the moon, and again at the earth, there is nothing "reversible" about the series of perceptions. They form a series ABC, and even though A and C are similar, the series is not thereby different from the succession A', B', C' of perceptions of the positions of the boat. Similarly, if I scan a house from bottom to top and then top to bottom, the resultant perceptions are no more or less "reversible" than any other series. Once any perceptions have entered consciousness, their position in the order of *subjective* consciousness is once-for-all fixed, however we may reorganize them *qua* representations.[57]

The trouble is that reversibility, like necessity, is a modal concept, and hence cannot on Kant's own view be perceived. Kant is clear that necessity must be thought into perceptions, but he sometimes loses sight of the fact that the same is true for possibility. What is involved here is a kind of proposition which has received a great deal of attention in the last several decades, namely, the counterfactual conditional. To say that the order of perceptions of the earth and moon is reversible is to say that the moon *could have been* apprehended first, *even though it was not*.[58] Kant obviously has in mind the co-existence of ordinary empirical objects which last unchanged throughout a span of time. In the series EMM'E' of perceptions of the earth and moon, the object represented by E' is the same as that represented by E, and presumably not even

[57] This is simply another way of saying that the self is itself a phenomenal substance, whose contents of consciousness, as states of that substance, have a determinate position in objective time.

[58] Kant expresses this concept quite clearly in a footnote to the Postulates, B 290. "That a body should come to rest after having been in motion does not prove the contingency of the motion. . . . To prove the contingency of its motion, we should have to prove that *instead of* the motion at the preceding moment, it was possible for the body to have been *then* at rest, not that it is *afterwards* at rest . . ."

changed very much. But Kant does not have any right to presuppose the existence of such entities, since he has provided no
analysis of their concept, and has even defended a theory of substance which would exclude them as legitimate phenomena.

Kant is aware that reversibility is a matter of what could have
been, but he never quite succeeds in describing the fact. Oddly
enough, the closest he gets is in the Observation to the thesis of the
Fourth Antinomy, in the Dialectic. The subject is slightly different, but the idea is clearly stated:

In the strict meaning of the category, the contingent is so named because
its contradictory opposite is possible. . . . When anything is altered, the
opposite of its state is actual at another time, and is therefore possible.
This present state is not, however, the contradictory opposite of the preceding state. To obtain such a contradictory opposite we require to conceive, that in the same time in which the preceding state was, its opposite
could have [sic] existed in its place, and this can never be inferred from
[the fact of] the alteration. [A 459–460]

It is not easy to see how the notion of the counterfactual can be
worked into the argument of the Analytic. Necessity becomes succession according to a rule, and reversibility might then be interpreted as indifferent succession. In that way anything at time
T_1 would necessarily be represented as prior to anything at time
T_2, but no order of precedence would exist among all the things
at T_1, or at T_2. This, however, is precisely what Kant is trying to
disprove. His aim is to show that A and B can coexist at time T
only if they are in dynamical connection with one another. We
come once more, therefore, to the subject which Kant treated so
superficially in the Second Analogy: simultaneous causation.

Contrary to Kemp Smith, Kant quite clearly asserts that co-
existent substances stand in a relation of reciprocal, and therefore
simultaneous, causation.[59] He gives no explanation of how this is
possible, unfortunately, and there really does not seem to be any
way that he can. Causation is unequivocally identified with suc-

---

[59] Cf. A 212–213. Kemp Smith quotes the passage, *Commentary*, p. 388, but
chooses to ignore it. Considering the relation of the Third Analogy to the law
of action and reaction, the obvious reference to the mutual gravitational attraction
of co-existing bodies, and the combination of substance and causation to yield
community, it seems to me impossible to claim that Kant does not mean what he
says in A 212–213. That such a view is incompatible with the Second Analogy is
of course another matter. Kemp Smith is quite correct about that.

cession in the Second Analogy. It is here just as unequivocally identified with simultaneity.

The contradiction is not easily resolved, for Kant really is dealing with two distinct concepts of causation. The first is that of necessary succession, deriving from the analysis of Hume. It has been quite adequately treated in the Second Analogy. The second is the scientific concept of functional interdependence, expressed in such equations as the laws of motion. The law $F = ma$, for example, does not state that something, B, invariably follows something else, A. It asserts a relationship — presumably describable as causal — between the force on a body of given mass and the rate of the body's acceleration. The force and the acceleration (cause and effect) are strictly co-terminous. The acceleration begins as soon as the force is applied and ends as soon as it is removed.[60]

It is not clear how Kant can relate these two concepts to one another, but then, it is not clear how anyone would relate them to one another. If Kant wished to retain them both, for example in connection with time and space respectively, he would at least be forced to recognize a complexity in the notion of causation of which there is no indication in the *Critique*.

The foregoing discussion has been almost entirely a catalogue of the errors and inadequacies of Kant's argument and possible revisions of it. This suggests, what is in fact the case, that many of the weak strands in the system of the *Critique* come together in the problem of substantial co-existence. The plausibility of the Analytic, and thereby of the *Critique*, depends to a considerable degree on the possibility of solving the problem outlined above.

The Postulates of Empirical Thought in General

It is evident from the Table of Judgments that the problematic, assertoric, and apodictic moods are ways of asserting a judgment rather than aspects, or "functions of unity" of the judgment itself. This distinction between the fourth heading and the other three carries over into the Table of Categories, and reappears in the System of Principles. Kant acknowledges the peculiar status of the Postulates by offering only an Explanation of them, rather than the customary proof [cf. B 266]. Despite its incongruity with the rest of the System of Principles, however, the section contains

[60] Cf. Paton, II, 324 ff.

a very valuable account of the Critical interpretation of the central metaphysical terms, possibility, actuality, and necessity. As we would expect, Kant transforms them into epistemological concepts by relating them to the conditions of a possible experience.

In the first edition, Kant assigned his Refutation of Idealism to the Paralogisms, which deal in general with the dialectical attempts to prove that the self is the best known, or only known, entity. Because of the connection between the category of actuality and the problem of the existence of material objects — and perhaps also because the Refutation argument belongs essentially to the Analytic — Kant in the second edition inserted his new Refutation in the Postulates, just after the discussion of the Second Postulate. The argument has nothing especially in common with the teaching of the Postulates and I shall therefore treat it separately, taking the opportunity to connect it up with several related passages from other parts of the *Critique*.

The Postulates of Empirical Thought

Kant offers three postulates, thereby paralleling the Analogies rather than the Axioms and Anticipations. His discussion also is divided informally into three parts: (1) A 219–224, on possibility; (2) A 225–226, on actuality; and (3) A 226–234, on necessity, and a variety of related matters.

Kemp Smith is highly critical of the exposition of the Postulates on the grounds that Kant should have united the three postulates rather than separating them.[61] His argument is that according to Kant, the possible, actual, and necessary have precisely the same limits of application: whatever is actual is (causally) necessary, and whatever is not (or has not been, or will not be) actual must thereby be empirically impossible. Whether or not it is true that the three modalities are in Kant's view coextensive, it is certain that Kemp Smith has missed the point of Kant's separate discussion of them. For what Kant wishes to convey is that there is a *subjective* distinction among the three modal notions, whatever the objective identity. The function of the categories of modality is to express "the relation of the concept [of an object of knowledge] to the faculty of knowledge" [A 219]. In other words, modality is a characteristic of the knower rather than the known. Or, more

[61] Cf. Kemp Smith, pp. 391–403, esp. 392–394.

precisely, it is a characteristic of the relation between the knower and the known, viewed from the side of the knower. We see here again the anti-reductionist tendency of Kant's thought.

The First Postulate asserts that the possible is "that which agrees with the formal conditions of experience, that is, with the conditions of intuition and of concepts" [A 218]. This is a definition of *real* or *empirical* possibility, which has more stringent conditions, and hence a narrower field of application than logical possibility. In a footnote in the Preface to the second edition, Kant explains the distinction thus:

To *know* an object I must be able to prove its possibility, either from its actuality as attested by experience, or *a priori* by means of reason. But I can *think* whatever I please, provided only that I do not contradict myself, that is, provided my concept is a possible thought. This suffices for the possibility of the concept, even though I may not be able to answer for there being, in the sum of all possibilities, an object corresponding to it. But something more is required before I can ascribe to such a concept objective validity, that is, real possibility; the former possibility is merely logical.[62]

As an example of a concept which meets the conditions of logical possibility but not those of real possibility, Kant offers "two sided plane figure." He might also have cited the three concepts which appear so prominently in other discussions of unknowable possibles, namely God, freedom, and immortality.

It is difficult to assess this doctrine of the merely logically possible. Despite its crucial importance for the Dialectic and the rest of the Critical Philosophy, Kant never subjects it to the close scrutiny which such concepts as "object" or "necessity" receive. The doctrine derives from the *Dissertation*, where sensibility is viewed as the only limitation on empirical knowledge, and understanding is given a real employment in the realm of noumena. When the move is made to the position of the *Critique*, understanding as well as sensibility is treated as a limiting factor. Kant is then forced to discover a new home for those concepts which transcend the boundary of the knowable. His solution is to sharpen the line between understanding (*Verstand*) and reason (*Vernunft*), and to associate the transcendent concepts with the latter.

[62] B xxvi, note a. The last sentence of the note reads, "This something more need not, however, be sought in the theoretical sources of knowledge; it may lie in those that are practical."

It is on this basis that understanding is identified with the Analytic and reason with the Dialectic. These architectonic readjustments only touch the surface of the problem, however, for the implications of the Analytic run directly counter to any distinction between real and logical possibility. We have already seen the stages by which Kant moves from the *Dissertation* teaching that the pure concepts are applicable to things-in-themselves, to the view of the Analogies, that as modes of time-consciousness the categories could never be applied even to a sensuous intuition different from our own.

In the course of expounding the doctrine of real possibility, Kant is led once more to consider the anomalous status of mathematical concepts [A 223–224]. Pure mathematics would seem to be a case of knowledge which is independent of empirical objects. The real possibility of its concepts would therefore be demonstrated without reference to the conditions of a possible experience. To avoid this conclusion, Kant retreats to the position which he takes on several other occasions, that pure mathematics is knowledge only by virtue of its application to empirical intuition.[63] This and other aspects of the Postulates reveal the empiricist side of Kant's thought, which receives its strongest expression in the Analytic rather than the Aesthetic and Dialectic.

The Second Postulate defines the *actual* as "that which is bound up with the material conditions of experience, that is, with sensation" [B 266]. To say that something exists is simply to say that it can be perceived, or can be connected by empirical laws with other things which can be perceived. I infer the existence of a man from his footsteps in the sand, according to empirical laws based on past experience. I infer the existence of atomic particles from the traces in cloud chambers and the readings on meters, again according to empirical laws. The latter case is significantly different because the object whose existence is inferred can never, in any ordinary sense, be itself an object of perception. Nevertheless the assertion of its existence is valid in Kant's theory.[64] Kant states his

[63] A 224. Compare B 147: "Mathematical concepts are not, therefore, by themselves knowledge, except on the supposition that there are things which allow of being presented to us only in accordance with the form of that pure sensible intuition."

[64] What is more to the point, such an assertion is *meaningful*, since it purports to be founded on a connection with perception by way of empirical laws, and is therefore at least in principle verifiable. Needless to say, the thrust of Kant's

view with great force in the Antinomy of Pure Reason, where he emphasizes the transcendentally ideal character of appearances:

The real things of past time are . . . objects for me and real in past time only in so far as I represent to myself (either by the light of history or by the guiding-clues of causes and effects) that a regressive series of possible perceptions in accordance with empirical laws, in a word, that the course of the world, conducts us to a past time-series as condition of the present time — a series which, however, can be represented as actual not in itself but only in the connection of a possible experience. Accordingly, all events which have taken place in the immense periods that have preceded my own existence mean really nothing but the possibility of extending the chain of experience from the present perception back to the conditions which determine this perception in respect of time. [A 495] [65]

In passages such as these Kant reveals the strength of his commitment to the foundation-stone of empiricism, *viz.*, that perception is the limit and sole source of our knowledge of objects.

It would be easy, but I think quite wrong, to interpret these statements as a return to the subjectivist position of the early stages of the Deduction. The central problem for Kant in the later developments of the Analytic is the distinction between subjective association and necessary connection. The postulation of an independent realm of phenomena, separate both from perceptions and things in themselves, is merely an (unsuccessful) attempt to solve this problem; it is not, as Kemp Smith for example supposes, the distinctively Critical doctrine in the light of which all else must be characterized as uncritical. In the Analogies, I have suggested, Kant solved the problem, and nothing in his discussion of the Postulate of Actuality in any way constitutes a giving up of that solution. In fact, the present section, by its uncompromising language, clears away the last vestiges of a reliance upon the unnecessary and contradictory doctrine of double affection. [66]

---

argument is all toward transforming propositions about the limits of the actual into criteria of the meaning and verifiability of material-object statements. However, Kant never fully saw this fact, and inasmuch as the doctrine of the Analytic contains an irreducible psychological component, it seems better not to labor the point.

[65] Compare with Hume's discussion of history, *Treatise*, pp. 145–146.

[66] Kant, of course, returned both to subjectivism and to the theory of double affection, and consequently these comments have a somewhat editorial flavor. In extenuation, I would argue that it is important to demonstrate the logical independence of the Analogies doctrine from the Objective Deduction theory of transcendental synthesis. It should be noted that Kemp Smith adopts, in his transla-

The *necessary*, finally, is "that which in its connection with the actual is determined in accordance with universal conditions of experience" [B 266]. Kant explains that this refers to "material necessity in existence, and not merely formal and logical necessity in the connection of concepts" [A 226]. The distinction, however unclear, is exceedingly important. Logical necessity is a characteristic of propositions, and attaches to them by virtue of their reducibility to some analytically valid mode of reasoning, such as the syllogism.[67] Material necessity, on the other hand, seems to be a property of objects of experience, and as Kant explains, it concerns only the connection of their states. It is, in other words, the conditional necessity of one state, given another — in short, the necessity of causal connection [A 227–228]. We can also view material necessity as a property of propositions, but in this case they would be synthetic propositions. As Kant asserts in the discussion of the proofs for the existence of God, "all existential propositions are synthetic" [B 626]. It follows from the general conclusions of the Analytic that all material necessity derives from the conditions of the possibility of experience, that *third thing* which mediates between the subject and predicate of a synthetic judgment known *a priori*. A further consequence, of course, is that "the character of [material] necessity in existence extends no further than the field of possible experience" [A 227].

From the definitions of actuality and necessity, it is immediately

---

tion of the first paragraph of the discussion of actuality, a variant reading by Valentiner for which there is no justification. The passage should read: "The postulate bearing on the knowledge of things as *actual* demands *perception* (consequently, sensation of which we are conscious), not to be sure immediate perception of the object itself whose existence is to be known, but nevertheless connection of it (the object) with some actual perception, in accordance with the analogies of experience, etc., etc." Kemp Smith reverses a clause, and translates: "The postulate bearing on the knowledge of things as *actual* does not, indeed, demand immediate *perception* (and, therefore, sensation of which we are conscious) of the object whose existence is to be known. What we do, however, require is the connection, etc., etc." This is undoubtedly a sentence which Kant would have been happy to include in the *Critique*, but it is not the sentence he wrote, nor does it convey the precise thought which he had in mind. The aim of the sentence, as originally written, is to emphasize that all knowledge of objects must, directly or indirectly, be tied to a perception of which we are *actually conscious*. As Hume would put it, all knowledge is based upon a present impression. To obscure this point is to obscure the lesson of the entire section.

[67] The basis of the syllogism is the transitivity of identity, or of class inclusion. Both of these relations could reasonably be viewed by Kant as based on analytic connections.

obvious that the two terms are coextensive.[68] All that which is actual must bear a necessary connection to perception, and hence be necessary in the sense of the Third Postulate. Conversely, the necessary is clearly the actual — specifically, that which occupies objective time position. The coincidence of the actual and the materially necessary is, of course, a manifestation of the phenomenal determinism to which Kant is committed. To happen, Kant argues in the Second Analogy, is to occupy an objective position or sequence in time, and this is nothing more nor less than to be causally determined. In the physical realm, Newtonian physics provided the model of determinism, but Kant is less clear about psychological phenomena. Sometimes he thinks they must be susceptible to scientific (i.e., causal) explanation, and this is the view which his theory implies. At other times he treats the matter as an open question, or even gives a negative answer.

In like manner, Kant argues that the realm of real possibility is no larger than that of actuality and necessity [A 230 ff]. For the actual contains all that was, is, or will be, and nothing beyond that could ever conform to the conditions of experience. Otherwise there would be more than one nature, and more than one unity of apperception, which is an empty supposition. Such thoughts are logically consistent, perhaps, but they cannot find an object within experience, and hence lack real possibility.

The Postulates are followed, in the second edition, by a "General Note on the System of the Principles" [B 288–294]. In this very significant short passage, Kant attempts to reinstate space in the Analytic, in keeping with the revisions of the Refutation of Idealism. After the concentration of attention on time-consciousness in the Schematism and Principles, it comes as a surprise to read:

in order to understand the possibility of things in conformity with the categories, and so to demonstrate the *objective reality* of the latter, we

---

[68] In the following discussion, I have deliberately ignored Kant's unclear remarks about the restriction of material necessity to states of substance rather than substance itself. Such a distinction rests on the hopelessly confused doctrine of substance expounded in the First Analogy. Since I do not understand it I cannot comment upon it, though it goes without saying that Kant sets great store by it. Fortunately, Kant is equally attached to the Second Analogy theory of substance, which I think I do understand somewhat, and which I have therefore employed here and elsewhere.

need, not merely intuitions, but intuitions that are in all cases *outer intuitions*. [B 291]

Kant goes on to assert that in order to give objects to the concepts both of substance and causality, we need the intuition of a permanent. This can be obtained only from space (namely, as matter), for "in inner sense no permanent intuition is to be met with" [B 292]. As I have tried to make clear, the implications of this change are far-reaching and profound for the Analytic.

The Refutation of Idealism[69]

The Refutation of Idealism, inserted by Kant into the Postulates in B, is a new and much improved version of the argument which appears as the fourth Paralogism of Pure Reason in the first edition Dialectic [A 367–380]. The significance of the Paralogisms can be inferred from the fact that it and the Deduction were the only sections which Kant completely rewrote for the second edition. When we examine the content of these two passages, we discover that they complement one another as obverse and reverse of the same coin. The *Critique* as a whole can be viewed as a refutation of the philosophical movement begun by Descartes. In the Deduction, Kant takes the Cartesian premise, "I think," and demonstrates the proper conclusions to be deduced from it. In the Paralogisms, he takes the same "I think," and refutes the false conclusions drawn by Descartes.

We now come to . . . the concept or, if the term be preferred, the judgment, "I think." . . . The *rational* doctrine of the soul . . . professes to be a science built upon the single proposition "I *think*." Whether this claim be well or ill grounded, we may, very fittingly, in accordance with the nature of a transcendental philosophy, proceed to investigate. [A 341–342]

The proposition to which Kant attaches the name "Idealism," stated as the conclusion of the Fourth Paralogism, is: "The existence of all objects of the outer senses is doubtful" [A 367]. He thus interprets idealism, after the manner of Descartes, as an agnostic rather than a dogmatic position:

The term *"idealist"* is not, therefore, to be understood as applying to those who deny the existence of external objects of the senses, but only to those who do not admit that their existence is known through immediate per-

[69] For an exhaustive discussion of Kant's various treatments of idealism, see Kemp Smith, pp. 298–321.

ception, and who therefore conclude that we can never, by way of any possible experience, be completely certain as to their reality. [A 368–369]

As a refutation of this scepticism, Kant offers the following argument: "Objects *outside* us" means "*things which are to be found in space*" [A 373]; now we have an outer sense, which has the form of space, as the Aesthetic has shown; and as the Analytic has shown, a real (substance) is given in that space; hence there really are things to be met with in space [A 373–374]. Kant now goes on to make the extraordinary statement that, of course, "space itself, with all its appearances, as representations, is . . . only in me" [A 375]. Over and over again, he says that space "is to be found . . . *in us*" [A 373], that "these external things, namely matter, are in all their configurations and alterations nothing but mere appearances, that is, representations in us" [A 371], that "space itself . . . is nothing but an inner mode of representation" [A 378]. It is not surprising that the first reviewers of the *Critique* interpreted Kant as espousing a Berkeleyan idealism. The fault was in large measure Kant's, for he failed to make full use of the results of the Analytic to distinguish his view from Berkeley's. In the second edition Refutation, this fault is remedied.

Weldon describes the Refutation of Idealism in B as "a condensed restatement of the main contention of the Deduction that consciousness of self depends on knowledge of objects, so that the latter cannot be doubted consistently with the retention of the former." [70] This is close to, but not quite exactly, the truth. Strictly speaking, the Refutation is a somewhat weaker proof which follows as a corollary from the Deduction. Descartes had asserted, as the premise of his philosophy, that he was conscious of himself as a thinking being. But Kant does not believe that this is the proper way to phrase the primary evidence of an introspective analysis of consciousness. Rather, as he says in the Deduction in B, the premise is: "It must be possible for the 'I think' to accompany all my representations" [B 131]. The formal unity of all consciousness, and not the immediate awareness of a thinking being, serves as the starting point for philosophical argument. Mere consciousness without intuition can never yield knowledge of any entity, even of myself. As the Refutation points out, the existence

[70] Weldon, p. 189.

of the self as an object of knowledge is something to be proved, not assumed.

Thus the Deduction begins from the unity of consciousness.[71] The Refutation of Idealism, on the other hand, begins from Descartes' own premise, namely that "I am conscious of my own existence as determined in time" [B 275]. Kant then merely shows that, as a consequence of the Deduction, this experience (= empirical knowledge) of myself presupposes objects independent of me in space. Both the existence of the empirical self and the existence of physical objects are facts which can be deduced from the unity of consciousness, and each is bound up with the other. As Kant says in a footnote to the Preface in B, intended as a commentary on the Refutation:

The reality of outer sense is thus necessarily bound up with inner sense, if experience in general is to be possible at all; that is, I am just as certainly conscious that there are things outside me, which are in relation to my sense, as I am conscious that I myself exist as determined in time. [B xli]

EPILOGUE
KANT'S METAPHYSIC OF NATURE

With the Postulates of Empirical Thought, the task of the Analytic is ended. The System of all Principles of Pure Understanding stands forth in its totality, issuing in orderly fashion from the highest principle of synthetic judgments, that "every object stands under the necessary conditions of synthetic unity of the manifold of intuition in a possible experience" [A 158]. The Axioms, Anticipations, Analogies, and Postulates are "the synthetic judgments which under these conditions [of sensibility, as stated in the Schematism] follow *a priori* from pure concepts of understanding, and which lie *a priori* at the foundation of all other modes of knowledge" [A 136]. There remains for the reader the very difficult problem of determining just what relation exists between this System of Principles and the *corpus* of empirical knowledge which it grounds.

Kant himself offers several different and contradictory accounts

[71] Or more precisely, from the unity of apperception, which is the purely logical fact that the "I think" can always be attached to any representation. Whether it is so attached in a particular case is irrelevant. Cf. A 117 note.

of the status of the System of Principles. The simplest, although as we shall see the most questionable, is that suggested by the "four questions" of the *Prolegomena* and second edition additions to the Introduction of the *Critique*. The second question, which purports to capture the essence of the Analytic, asks: "How is pure science of nature [or pure natural science = *reine Naturwissenschaft*] possible?" [B 20]. In my discussion of this passage,[72] I suggested that in the *Prolegomena* Kant treats the question, Is pure natural science possible? while in the *Critique* he demonstrates that it is actual. In short, the Analytic can be viewed as Kant's proof of the validity of Newtonian physics. The appearance in the Anticipations of the dynamical theory of matter and the demonstration of the laws of conservation of matter and action and reaction in the Analogies lend weight to such a reading.

Nevertheless, the *Critique* offers ample evidence for alternative interpretations. The Aesthetic and Analytic together form a system of transcendental philosophy which, Kant asserts, is "occupied not so much with objects as with the mode of our knowledge of objects in so far as this mode of knowledge is to be possible *a priori*" [B 25]. The knowledge yielded by the Analytic has as its object the cognitive faculty itself rather than the spatial configurations of matter with which physics is concerned. The *Critique* does not present a new exposition of the law of gravitation or the parallelogram of forces; it explains how (or demonstrates that) those and other laws are possible, by analyzing the conditions of a possible experience in general. It leaves to experiment and investigation the precise content of the physical sciences, confining itself to a proof that such a thing as physical science must in principle be attainable. The First Analogy assures us that permanence, in some form or other, will be met with in experience; the Axioms guarantee the applicability to the material world of the theorems of pure mathematics; the Second Analogy justifies the search for necessary connections in the presented patterns of association.

It is also possible, in keeping with many of Kant's utterances, to broaden our conception of the Analytic and view it as a general analysis of the universal and indispensable features of experience and the natural world. In the phrase which H. J. Paton chooses as the title for his commentary, the first half of the *Critique* presents

[72] Cf. p. 47, above.

a "metaphysic of experience." [73] The dependence of the world of phenomena on the *a priori* forms of cognition makes possible a system of immanent metaphysics. Not merely mathematics and physics, but all empirical knowledge at whatever level of scientific precision, is seen to conform to certain general laws which can be read off, as it were, from the innate forms of the mind. Such a metaphysics simultaneously yields positive results in the System of Principles, and negative results in the critique of previous transcendent metaphysical arguments [the Dialectic].

Finally, the *Critique* might be read in a modern vein as an essay in the analytic philosophy of science. The central concepts and modes of inference of the existing sciences are subjected to a dissection which reveals their presuppositions, interpretations, limitations, and proper employment. Such an investigation takes Newtonian physics and Euclidean geometry as givens and attempts to isolate and then to generalize their methodology. Although on occasion it can yield new knowledge and even dictate to the sciences (as when it determines whether a science of the mind is possible), for the most part it is a subservient discipline, dependent upon its subject matter both for content and criteria.

It would be pointless to attempt a decision among these several interpretations, for at least the first three can be supported by many passages from the *Critique*. Rather, it is interesting to see what lines of argument in the Analytic tend to incline Kant in one or the other direction, and how certain unresolved problems of the *Critique* bear upon the status of the System of Principles. The nature of the categories, their relation to empirical concepts, the problem of pure intuition and the Schematism, the significance of the Axioms and its connection with the Aesthetic, and the basic distinction between *a priori* and *a posteriori* knowledge will be seen to come together in this question.

The first explicit statements concerning the nature of the *a priori* knowledge yielded by the Analytic appear in the closing paragraphs of the Objective Deduction. The understanding is "the lawgiver of nature," Kant asserts [A 126], and he then adds:

However exaggerated and absurd it may sound, to say that the understanding is itself the source of the laws of nature, and so of its formal unity,

[73] Cf. Paton, vol. i, p. 72.

such an assertion is none the less correct. . . . Certainly, empirical laws, as such, can never derive their origin from pure understanding. That is as little possible as to understand completely the inexhaustible multiplicity of appearances merely by reference to the pure form of sensible intuition. But all empirical laws are only special determinations of the pure laws of understanding, under which, and according to the norm of which, they first become possible. [A 127–128]

We see here the ambivalence which runs all through the Analytic on this topic. In the opening sentences of the passage, Kant seems quite unequivocally to assert that the laws of nature originate in the mind. But if this were taken to mean that every last detail of the phenomenal world owed its existence to the legislative action of the mind — that the melting points of solids, the anatomical peculiarities of reptiles, the precise number and arrangement of heavenly bodies, could somehow be traced to the Table of Categories — then Kant would find himself committed to an obvious absurdity. What is more, he would have destroyed the careful balance between empiricism and rationalism, sensibility and intelligence, observation and ratiocination, which he wished to substitute for the one-sided philosophies of his predecessors. I have already suggested the origin of Kant's difficulty: so long as he identifies the formal (space, time, categories) with the *a priori* and the material (sensation, empirical concepts) with the *a posteriori*, he will be irresistibly drawn to assimilating all knowledge to *a priori* knowledge. Kant's reply, of course, is that he avoids the extremes of rationalism by means of his formula, "conditions of a possible experience." He makes no pretence at deducing the law of cause and effect from concepts alone. Rather, he draws it and the other principles of pure understanding out of the premise that we have experience [= consciousness].

There still remains the problem, however, of explaining the role in empirical knowledge of observation and experiment. Can one really elicit all of Newtonian physics from the mere fact of consciousness? What relation, if any, do the less formal sciences of chemistry or biology bear to the principles of mathematical physics? The *Critique* offers very little in the way of answers to these questions, and what it does offer is ambiguous or contradictory. In the introduction to the System of Principles, Kant makes the following statement:

Even natural laws, viewed as principles of the empirical employment of understanding, carry with them an expression of necessity, and so contain at least the suggestion of a determination from grounds which are valid *a priori* and antecedently to all experience. The laws of nature, indeed, one and all, without exception, stand under higher principles of understanding. They simply apply the latter to special cases of appearance. These principles alone supply the concept which contains the condition, and as it were the exponent, of a rule in general. What experience gives is the instance which stands under the rule. [A 159]

The language of this passage is too imprecise to allow any confidence in interpretation. Kant seems to be suggesting that particular causal judgments can be viewed as special cases of the causal maxim. Boyle's law relating the temperature and pressure of a volume of gas, for example, would somehow be an "instance which stands under the rule" of the Second Analogy. But what does this mean? We cannot deduce Boyle's Law, indeed we cannot deduce any specific causal connections at all, from the causal maxim.

The phrases "special cases" and "instance" might indicate that Kant has in mind the relation between a class concept and one of its designata. Thus, pure physics asserts that in a collision of two bodies, the sum of the products of their masses and velocities is unchanged throughout [Law of the Conservation of Momentum]. Experience, in the form of my ordinary perception of objects, "gives me the instance which stands under" this law; i.e., it presents me with two beings which I judge to be moving bodies in collision. After ascertaining their masses and velocities *by experience*, I discover that their behavior conforms to the general law.

We may still ask, however, what relation the Law of Conservation of Momentum bears to the causal maxim. Kant shrinks in the *Critique* from asserting even that we can have *a priori* knowledge of the most general laws of mathematical physics. Speaking of the division of the System of Principles into mathematical and dynamical, he says:

It should be noted that we are as little concerned in the one case with the principles of mathematics as in the other with the principles of general physical dynamics. We treat only of the principles of pure understanding in their relation to inner sense. . . . It is through these principles of pure understanding that the special principles of mathematics and of dynamics become possible. [A 162]

So the Analytic demonstrates only the possibility of physics, and not the validity of Newton's laws themselves. What this means, I take it, is that the Analogies and other principles demonstrate the existence of some science of nature or other, conforming to such general criteria as are contained in the principle of permanence and the causal maxim. The existence of a science of nature, i.e., the conformity of experience to laws, is guaranteed by the fact that only through such conformity does experience [= consciousness] become possible. "There are certain laws which first make a nature possible," Kant states in the conclusion to the Analogies, "and these laws are *a priori.*" But empirical laws "can exist and be discovered only through experience, and indeed in consequence of those original laws through which experience itself first becomes possible" [A 216]. The Transcendental Philosophy will not take the place of scientific investigation; its function is to set the limits and define the forms of natural science, and to assure the scientist that the laws which he seeks are there to be found.

Kant's confusion over the nature of the principles of pure understanding can be traced in part to the ambiguities in his theory of the categories. As I pointed out in discussing the Schematism,[74] Kant let himself in for a good deal of trouble by treating the categories as class concepts. As thus conceived, their relation to empirical concepts and to the manifold of sensuous intuition was obscured. Instead of being represented as different in logical type from empirical concepts, they were said merely to differ in the degree of their purity (i.e., freedom from sensuous content). So it might be made to appear plausible that the categories, and the laws derived from them, were the "highest principles" of a homogeneous system whose lower and less pure components were the ordinary laws of physical science.

However, Kant himself undercuts any such interpretation by distinguishing the categories in kind from empirical concepts. I mentioned the two possible ways of characterizing the difference: first, that categories are rules for synthesizing a pure manifold, and empirical concepts are rules for synthesizing an empirical manifold (of perceptions); second, that categories are second-order rules which prescribe the procedures for constructing empirical con-

[74] Cf. pp. 207–208, above.

cepts. The former, I argued, was incapable of being integrated into the argument of the Deduction by reason of the inadequacy of the theory of double affection.[75] The latter seems to me the most defensible alternative for Kant. If it is adopted, then Newtonian physics, which employs empirical concepts (matter, motion, etc.), is divorced from Transcendental Philosophy. The system of principles would have to be viewed in the second of the four ways described above, as a body of *a priori* knowledge concerning the possibility and characteristics of natural science in general.

The clearest and most detailed discussion of these problems in the critical writings appears in the Preface to the *Metaphysical Foundations of Natural Science*, published by Kant in 1786. There he takes pains to make precise the relationship between the doctrine of the Analytic and the principles of physical science. He also advances the substantive portion of his theory by explaining for the first time the exact connection between the mathematics validated by the Aesthetic and the principles of the Analogies.

Kant begins the *Metaphysical Foundations* with an exercise in definition. *Nature*, he states, is "the sum-total of all things, in so far as they can be *objects of our senses*, and therefore of experience; in short, the totality of all phenomena." [76] As there are two forms of sensibility, so any doctrine of Nature is divisible into a *doctrine of body* and a *doctrine of soul*. Any doctrine of Nature, and hence the doctrine of body, has a part based upon empirical principles and a part based upon rational principles. The former is not genuinely natural science, for that term "necessitates a knowledge through reason of its system." [77] Hence it is better called "*historical doctrine of nature*, comprising nothing but systematically-ordered facts respecting natural things." [78] The latter, or rational part of the doctrine of body, is natural science, but only that portion which deals with body "wholly according to principles *a priori*" is natural science properly so-called. In the chart on page 308, I have diagrammed Kant's system of classification. By natural sciences based on empirical principles, Kant means such disciplines as chemistry, whose laws are really only empirical generalizations. In fact, he

[75] Cf. pp. 164–174, above.
[76] *Metaphysical Foundations of Natural Science*, trans. and ed. by Bax, p. 137.
[77] *Ibid.*, p. 138.
[78] *Ibid.*

asserts, "chemistry . . . should be rather termed systematic art than science." [79]

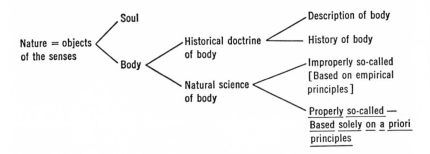

Kant now distinguishes between the material of the *Critique*, particularly of the Analytic, and the theory to be developed in the *Metaphysical Foundations of Natural Science*. The *Critique* presents the cognitions which reason derives from mere concepts, and this can be described as the "metaphysics of nature." [80] It is presupposed by natural science proper, "for laws, i.e., principles of the necessity of that which belongs to the *existence* of a thing, are occupied with a conception which does not admit of construction, because its existence cannot be presented in any *a priori* intuition." [81] The transcendental portion of the metaphysics of nature is entirely neutral as to the nature of its objects. The Analogies apply with equal validity to bodies or to souls.[82]

However, the metaphysics of nature may be specified by introducing the empirical concept of a particular kind of object. The general conclusions of transcendental metaphysics of nature (i.e., the System of Principles) are then applied to that concept. The only two concepts which can possibly form the basis for a particular metaphysical natural science are body, which yields physics, and soul, which yields psychology. In summary, then, the *Critique of Pure Reason* expounds the principles of transcendental metaphysics of nature in general, while the *Metaphysical Foundations*, by adding the empirical concept of matter, develops the particular

[79] *Ibid.*
[80] *Ibid.*, p. 139.
[81] *Ibid.*
[82] *Ibid.* Kant ignores the fact that the First Analogy introduces the concept of matter, and thereby excludes psychology, or the doctrine of soul, from the realm of natural science. The Anticipations have similar implications, although they could more easily be adapted to a doctrine of the soul.

metaphysical natural science of body. This latter, which is the pure *a priori* portion of physics in general, can be termed a "metaphysic of corporeal nature." [83]

Thus far, little has been said that genuinely advances our understanding of the relation between the System of Principles and empirical knowledge in general. Now, however, a wholly new line of argument is introduced which considerably revises the teaching of the *Critique*. According to Kant,

in every special natural doctrine only so much science *proper* is to be met with as mathematics; for, in accordance with the foregoing, science proper, especially of nature, requires a pure portion, lying at the foundation of the empirical, and based upon an *à priori* knowledge of natural things. Now to cognise anything *à priori* is to cognise it from its mere possibility; but the possibility of determinate natural things cannot be known from mere conceptions; for from these the possibility of the thought (that it does not contradict itself) can indeed be known, but not of the object, as natural thing which can be given (as existent) outside the thought. Hence, to the possibility of a determinate natural thing, and therefore to cognise it *à priori*, is further requisite that the *intuition* corresponding *à priori* to the conception should be given; in other words, that the conception should be constructed. But cognition of the reason through construction of conceptions is mathematical. . . . [A]s in every natural doctrine only so much science proper is to be met with therein as there is cognition *à priori*, a doctrine of nature can only contain so much science proper as there is in it of applied mathematics.[84]

From this it follows, says Kant, that neither chemistry nor empirical psychology can ever achieve the status of natural science. Whether the subsequent developments of those disciplines would have made him change his mind, we can never know, but in their striving for mathematization, the less formal sciences seem to have accepted the standard enunciated here by Kant.[85]

For the first time it becomes possible to see the relation between the Aesthetic and the Analytic in the Critical system. Pure mathematics gives us rules for the construction of objects in intuition, while pure metaphysics of nature (the System of Principles) lays down the *a priori* rules for the cognition of those objects through

[83] *Ibid.*, p. 142.
[84] *Ibid.*, pp. 140–141.
[85] Though not for his reasons, needless to say. The striking feature of Kant's theory is its ability to explain *why* mathematics is the measure of genuine science. Kant does not merely urge the other sciences to ape physics on the grounds of its success or prestige.

concepts. The Axioms of Intuition now appear as the mediating element between the two. The real conclusion of the Axioms is that pure mathematics can be applied to the objects of outer intuition. Thereby the possibility of an *a priori* natural science of body is guaranteed.

CHAPTER III

THE GROUND OF THE DISTINCTION
OF ALL OBJECTS IN GENERAL INTO
PHENOMENA AND NOUMENA

When the reader raises his head at the end of the Analytic and looks around him, he discovers that the long and difficult argument which has passed before him is merely one part of a larger undertaking. There remains yet the greater portion of the *Critique*, devoted to a systematic exposure of the contradictions and confusions of all past metaphysics. To prepare the reader for this transition from Analytic to Dialectic, Kant introduces the chapter on Phenomena and Noumena. Since the order of exposition of the *Critique* mirrors the architectonic structure of the Critical Philosophy, the chapter is both a "limiting chapter" marking off the division between the discussions of appearance and reality, and also a chapter about the "limiting concept" (*Grenzbegriff*) which marks off the division between appearance and reality themselves, namely *noumenon*.

The content of the chapter, for the most part, requires no close analysis. Its principal interest lies in Kant's attempts to revise and clarify the concept of the thing in itself so as to make it serviceable for the Critical Philosophy. This involves purging the concept of any positive meaning, for the Analytic has demonstrated the impossibility of giving any content to the concept of the independently real. The second edition revisions, which are considerable, display a subtle shift of emphasis in the direction of a more sceptical and negative conception of the noumenon. The differences are more in tone and expression than in substantive doctrine, but the net effect is to make it more difficult for Kant to adhere to the simple view that the categories have potentially universal application and are limited by sensibility. Rather than analyze the text paragraph by paragraph, I shall make some general comments concerning the subject of the chapter.

Kant's original problem, as stated in the letter to Herz, was to explain how we could have *a priori* knowledge of the independently real. That we had such knowledge was presupposed in the *Dissertation*. The solution of the *Critique* is that *a priori* knowledge can only be accounted for on the assumption that it is knowledge of the real *as it appears* rather than *as it is in itself*. With this realization, the long investigation of the Analytic begins. For knowledge, we must have the *concept* of an object: understanding provides that concept in the form of the pure categories. But to have application, and thereby validity, the concept must be given an *object*. The human mind can be given an object only by being passively affected, thus acquiring a manifold of sensibility. So the conditions for an object being given become the conditions which limit the applicability of the categories, viz., the schemata. The employment of the concept of an object (= the categories) beyond the limits of sensibility is purely problematical. Since no object is given beyond sensibility, we cannot know whether the categories have a legitimate universal employment.

In the course of the development of this theory in the Analytic, one problem is lost sight of: the existence, status, and legitimate description of independent reality, or things in themselves. That Kant never doubts the existence of independently real entities is shown by the following passage from the Preface to the second edition:

All possible speculative knowledge of reason is limited to mere objects of *experience*. But our further contention must also be duly borne in mind, namely, that though we cannot *know* these objects as things in themselves, we must yet be in position at least to *think* them as things in themselves; otherwise we should be landed in the absurd conclusion that there can be appearance without anything that appears [*dass Erscheinung ohne etwas wäre, was da erscheint*]. . . . [O]ur Critique has shown [the distinction] to be necessary, between things as objects of experience and those same things as things in themselves. [B xxvi–xxvii]

The theory of the first half of the *Critique* cannot even be stated without presupposing the existence of the independently real: the manifold of sensibility is the product of an affection of the self by things in themselves; the transcendental activities of synthesis produce, and therefore cannot themselves be located in, phenomenal objects, but instead are attributed to the transcendental ego or self in itself. Thus for Kant it must be possible to talk about the independently real, even if it is impossible to have knowledge of it. In keeping with the principles of the Critical Philosophy, he therefore must submit this concept — *independent reality* — to an analysis and *deduction*. In effect, the chapter on Phenomena and Noumena is such a deduction.

There are at least three different terms which are used in the *Critique* in reference to the realm of things in themselves. An exploration of the relations among them will help to make clear some of the tendencies in Kant's thinking. The terms are (1) the *independently real* or *thing in itself*, (2) the *transcendental object* = x, and (3) *noumenon*.

(1) The concept of the independently real is the concept of an object which is independent of the conditions of knowledge. In the language first adopted in the *Dissertation*, it is the thing as it is rather than as it appears. The object, presumably, is not in the strict sense *unconditioned*, for it is a created substance and has relations of conditionality with other independent realities. However, the concept is that of an object not conditioned by the forms of sensibility and understanding. (Note: the repeated references to the *concept* of the object are indispensable, for otherwise the point of Kant's distinction between appearance and reality is lost. The independent object can perfectly well be *cognized* under conditions — it is then *known* as an appearance — but it is not for that reason any less an independent object in and of itself. The appearance, on the other hand, since it is merely a species of my representations, is *not* distinguishable from the mode in which it is known.) The phrase "thing in itself" is, I think, simply a synonym for "independently real thing."

(2) The concept of the transcendental object = x, or object in general = x, is in its first appearance the concept of a something which corresponds to our knowledge [A 104]. All knowledge must have its object, but as there seems to be no way of going beyond our representations to the locus of their reference, we may form only the bare concept of an x. On some occasions, as the first-edition portions of the chapter on Phenomena and Noumena indicate, Kant identified the object = x with the thing in itself. In

stage I of the Deduction in A, however, he makes a very significant move away from this view. Using Kant's terminology more precisely than he himself was accustomed to do, we may say that he began with the concept of a *transcendent object* = *x*, and then shifted to the concept of a *transcendental object* = *x*. The former is merely the concept of the thing in itself, but the latter is the concept of the ground of the unity of a manifold of representations in one consciousness. It thus serves as a stage in the development of the doctrine of the categories as modes or functions of unity of a manifold.

(3) "Noumenon" taken in its strict sense means "object of intelligence," as "phenomenon" means "object of sensibility." In the *Dissertation*, the realm of the independently real is properly described as "noumenal," for the mind cognizes it by means of the pure concepts of intelligence, uncontaminated by sensibility. However, as Kant holds that all knowledge involves the establishment of a *direct* relation between mind and object, and inasmuch as concepts of any sort relate only *indirectly* to their objects, this sense of "noumenon" merges with another and quite different meaning: object of an intellectual intuition. "Intellectual intuition" can be defined by combining the characteristics of its component terms: it is *intuition*, which is to say a means through which a mode of knowledge is in immediate relation to objects [B 33]; and it is *intellectual*, which is to say active rather than passive. Such an intuition creates the object in the act of intuiting it [B 72], and therefore Kant asserts that only God can be endowed with intellectual intuition.[1]

Finally, in the chapter before us Kant gives to "noumenon" yet a third meaning, of a purely negative sort:

If by "noumenon" we mean a thing so far as it is *not an object of our sensible intuition*, and so abstract from our mode of intuiting it, this is a noumenon in the *negative* sense of the term. But if we understand by it an *object* of a *non-sensible intuition*, we thereby presuppose a special mode of intuition, namely, the intellectual, which is not that which we possess, and of which we cannot comprehend even the possibility. This would be "noumenon" in the *positive* sense of the term.[2] [B 307]

---

[1] Compare Spinoza, who held that in God there was no distinction between conceiving a thing and creating it.

[2] The two are related to "phenomenon" as contradictory and contrary, respectively.

It is this concept of a *limit* to the realm of phenomena toward which Kant is working, and the precise distinction between the positive and negative senses of "noumenon" is much clearer in the second edition. Nevertheless, he continues to use the concepts of the thing in itself, the object in general $= x$, the object of intelligence, and the object of intellectual intuition, and it is quite instructive to examine the reasons for his failure to bring them all into accord with one another.

The root of the trouble is the unfinished character of the development in Kant's thought which I have called the *epistemological turn*. As Kant moved toward the theory of the *Critique*, he progressively subordinated all questions of being to questions of knowing. Thus, an investigation of the object of knowledge was turned into an analysis of the concept of that object, until finally the object became the concept — specifically, the concept for reorganizing a manifold of perceptions. Concomitant with this transformation was the spelling out of the subjective conditions of knowledge. Eventually, Kant concluded that no knowledge, indeed no conception, of an object was possible save under the conditions of such knowledge or conception. But then it is clear that there is a contradiction in the demand for a concept of the independently real, if by this is meant the real, independent of any mode of conceiving it.

Pressed by this consequence of his theory, Kant continually slips from talking about an *independent* object to talking about an object which is *known in a different way*, namely, an object of an intellectual intuition.[3] This in turn raises once again the difficult question of the extension of the categories beyond the limits of sensible intuition. I have already suggested some of the reasons why Kant wishes to preserve a possible transcendent employment for the categories, reasons indeed which are brought to the fore in the portion of the *Critique* following the present chapter. However, the tendency to read "object of intellectual intuition" for

[3] Cf. A 252: "The concept of a *noumenon* . . . is not indeed in any way positive, and is not a determinate knowledge of anything, but signifies only the thought of something in general, in which I abstract from everything that belongs to the form of sensible intuition. But in order that a noumenon may signify a true object, distinguishable from all phenomena, it is not enough that I *free* my thought from all conditions of sensible intuition; I must likewise have ground for *assuming* another kind of intuition, different from the sensible, in which such an object may be given."

"thing in itself" seriously jeopardizes any such employment. The categories are "mode(s) of combining (the) manifold — mode(s) peculiar to our understanding" [B 306]. But an intuitive understanding (or an intellectual intuition — the two seem to be the same) knows its object "not discursively through categories, but intuitively in a non-sensible intuition" [B 311]. That is to say, an intuitive understanding is not compelled to introduce unity into a diversity presented in space and time.[4] Consequently, once the categories are seen to be rules of synthesis rather than ordinary class concepts, it follows that they have not even problematic application to anything other than a sensuous manifold.

It seems, then, that as he prepares to enter upon a discussion of the applicability of pure concepts to things in themselves, Kant has definitively answered the question in the negative. That he draws back from this conclusion is apparent in the Paralogisms and the Antimonies, and of course also in the later ethical writings. His broader interests demand that a meaning, if not an object, be given to the concept of a causal and substantial self in itself. Nevertheless, Kant does not merely ignore the implications of the Analytic as he moves on to the Dialectic. In several passages, he strives to give a new and distinctively epistemological interpretation to the Ideas of Reason, for example in the Appendix on the Regulative Employment of Reason. As the *Third Critique* shows, interpretations within the phenomenal realm can be found for such transcendent concepts as the idea of cosmological purposiveness or the aesthetically sublime. But for the proper explanation of his ethical theory, Kant cannot avoid employing the categories in the manner originally conceived, as universal concepts having a problematic application to things in themselves.

[4] It will be recalled that the manifoldness of our perceptions is due to their being spread out in space and time. See Introduction, the discussion of Hume, above.

Concluding Remarks

NEW AND REVOLUTIONARY DOCTRINES IN THE THEORY OF A PRIORI SYNTHESIS

My aim in the preceding pages has been to demonstrate that the central portion of the *Critique of Pure Reason* constitutes a single connected argument, having the form which Kant claims for it and worthy in its profundity and subtlety of the exalted reputation which it has acquired. If I have met with any success, it has only been by a single-minded concentration on what seemed to me the most promising lines of Kant's thought, to the exclusion of other tendencies and developments which might well have a stronger claim to his allegiance. Viewed thus narrowly, my commentary was completed at the point in the discussion of the Second Analogy where I was able to present the Final Version of the Argument of the Analytic.[1] Needless to say, however, the interest of Kant's philosophy does not end with that proof of the causal maxim. It may therefore be fitting to devote these concluding pages to a more general discussion of the philosophical significance of the new and revolutionary doctrines which come together in the theory of *a priori* synthesis.

Modern philosophy began with Descartes' discovery of the problem of subjective consciousness. The method of doubt, culminating in a bare *cogito*, created for Descartes and succeeding philosophers two apparently insoluble problems. Descartes' criteria of certainty, in accordance with which he bracketed all unprovable belief, are so strict that there seems to be little or nothing save the *cogito* itself which can legitimately be said to be known. The first problem, then, is to demonstrate the possibility of non-trivial knowledge about the world. At the same time, the progression of doubt drives the knowing subject in upon itself until finally it re-

[1] Cf. pp. 278–279, above.

treats to the mere fact of its own self-consciousness. Any subsequent advance to knowledge must thus also bridge the gulf between subject and object, and so the second problem is to reintroduce the knowing subject into the world of objective existence. The close relation between the two problems can be observed most easily in the work of the British empiricists. Their increasing scepticism about the possibility of ever satisfying Descartes' strict criteria of certainty carries them to a progressively more subjective doctrine, until finally Hume allows only a solipsism of the present impression.

Strictly speaking, this brief characterization is quite false. Locke, Berkeley, and Hume do not form a school, and their philosophical theories cannot be fitted into a neat progression. Kant, however, seems to have viewed them in this way. He was wrong to do so, but he was not wrong in believing that scepticism and dogmatism (i.e., rationalism) are the natural alternative outgrowths of the Cartesian philosophy. He simply failed to recognize the extent to which some of his predecessors — in particular, Hume — had anticipated his attempts at discovering a middle way.

Kant's solution to the problem posed by the Cartesian revolution is based on three discoveries or new turns of thought which developed slowly in his writings. These innovations, like all great advances in philosophy, have the effect of completely altering the terms of the discussion. In that sense, Kant does not so much answer Hume or refute Descartes as show them that they have misconceived their problems. The three keys to the Kantian doctrine are: First, the epistemological turn; Second, the recognition of a multiplicity of types of necessity; and Third, the rule-analysis of concepts and the consequent shift from a theory of mental contents to an account of mental functions.

The epistemological turn is the progressive substitution of epistemological for ontological or metaphysical considerations. It is the recognition that the knowing subject can never be ignored, or bracketed out. Since all knowledge is the knowledge by a subject, even the most general investigation of the modes and categories of being will have to begin with an analysis of the limits and preconditions of knowing. We may abstract from the perceptual peculiarities of the individual, from the particular state of scientific advance of his age, and even from the most pervasive social and cultural biases, but we can never abstract from the subject *qua* knowing human being. If there are forms of perception and cognition which are inherent in the fact of consciousness itself, then these will constitute the limits of Being, so far as it can be discussed at all. To extend our investigation beyond those limits will involve us in an empty play of words for which no content can ever be provided. It might be meaningful to ask what the character of experience would be for a creature whose sensory organs were receptive to magnetic fields or radio waves or indeed other physical forces of which we are not now aware. Perhaps we can even consider the possibility of a sensibility whose basic form differs from our three-dimensional space. But it is self-contradictory to inquire what objects are like independently of being perceived and conceived — what they are like to God, for example, or more absurdly still, what they are like *in themselves*.

Descartes' method of doubt is quite obviously the first step in the recognition of the priority of the epistemological. By focussing upon the conscious self as the first known and best known thing, he assures that the subject will not be ignored. But Descartes did not carry through the consequences of his method. He continued to employ the categories of substance and cause to describe the self which he had discovered. Despite his dramatic *conte de fée* of a deceiving devil, he still viewed his problem as that of re-establishing contact between the conscious subject, whose substantial nature he never doubted, and an independent objective world order. The farce of the pineal gland is a fitting memorial to the impossibility of such a task.

Kant realized that the alternatives — either dogmatic assertion of an (undemonstrable) connection between subject and object, or sceptical denial of the possibility of knowledge — were falsely posed. Both presupposed a definition of "object" which abstracted completely from the conditions of knowledge. But suppose that for "object," defined ontologically, we were to substitute "object of knowledge," defined epistemologically. Then it might prove possible to achieve a reconciliation of subject and object, albeit at the price of recognizing that there can be no knowledge of the totally unconditioned.[2]

---

[2] It is clear, I hope, that this impossibility stems from the internal contradictions of such a demand, and not from any postulated limitation of our cognitive ap-

But thus far the epistemological turn seems only a sophisticated surrender to the most extreme forms of subjectivism. If our knowledge does not have independent reality as its object, then it is not knowledge at all. At this point Kant carries his revolution to a second stage, in its significance even more profound than the first. He examines the concept of an object of knowledge, which has replaced the concept of an object *simpliciter,* and discovers that the substantive content of that concept is exhausted by the notion of *objectivity.* The object of knowledge is nothing but a "that which." As Kant puts it in the Deduction, where he is discussing the source of the necessity of our knowledge, "this object is no more than that something, the concept of which expresses such a necessity of synthesis" [A 106]. Universality and necessity of judgment are the defining marks of that objective ground which is demanded to distinguish knowledge from mere fancy.

What Kant has done in this two-stage transformation is to substitute certain logical characteristics of judgments for the illegitimate notion of an independent universe of objects. He has thereby taken the first important step toward solving Descartes' problem, but there are undoubtedly many who will feel that he has not so much redefined it as defined it away. Universality and necessity may indeed be among the marks of knowledge, but there is also the belief in an object "out there" (*ob-ject*), standing over against (*gegen-stand*) the subject. If that has been lost, then the result is scepticism, no matter what one calls it.

This criticism is extremely hard to meet, though I believe it to be totally without force. To some extent it is based on a misunderstanding of Kant's position, a misunderstanding much like that which Dr. Johnson manifested when he kicked the stone. Kant's own statements to the contrary notwithstanding, it is not the teaching of the *Critique* that phenomena are merely in the head, or that in any ordinary sense material objects are not real. But to the more sophisticated objection — that the "ordinary sense" includes and must include the idea of an ontologically independent object — there can be no answer beyond a careful reiteration of all the reasons why such a demand is self-contradictory. Universality and necessity are all you can get, Kant says in effect. Therefore, they

---

paratus. Even God could never know an unconditioned other, for as medieval theologians recognized, that would entail a limitation of His being.

are all it has ever been legitimate to demand. Anyone who persists in asking what the world is *really* like — in other words, who wishes to know what an object is like independently of the conditions of his knowing what it is like — must then simply be dismissed as unserious. In the terminology of a later philosophical school, he needs to be cured, not answered.

Merely to restate Descartes' problem in this way is to take a tremendous step forward, but Kant immediately discovers that another major obstacle stands in his way. The criteria of necessity which Descartes employs, and which now have been substituted for the concept of an object, seem to rule out the possibility of ever finding judgments which can qualify as knowledge. Descartes, like Plato and many other philosophers before him, has erected as his model of cognitive certainty the analytic necessity of logical or mathematical deduction. The consequence, as Hume clearly saw, is to constrict the borders of knowledge until nothing but trivial tautologies fall within. Again Kant must either revise the definition of the key terms or else admit the victory of scepticism. This time it is "necessity" which must be re-examined. What Kant gives us in the *Critique*, and indeed throughout the Critical writings, is an exhaustive analysis of the modes of necessity. The key to the solution of the Analytic, as I have several times indicated, is Kant's new conception of synthetic necessity. The relation of the predicate to the subject in a scientific judgment is neither the analytic inclusion of a tautology, as Leibniz had maintained, nor the mere habitual conjunction of association, *à la* Hume. It is a third, distinctive relation which is characterized as synthetic unity.

But merely to assert the existence of a new mode of connection was insufficient. In order to give content to the notion of synthetic necessity, Kant introduced his third great transformation, the rule-analysis of concepts. All the mental entities which had been described in static terms on the analogy of pictures before the mind, or shapes abstracted from their material, are seen by Kant to be actually mental functions or activities. Knowledge is an activity, not a state, of the mind. Judgment can be understood only if we first analyze judging. The cognitive activities are performed according to innate rules of the mind, and it is in these rules that Kant discovers the new kind of necessity which he seeks. Synthetic necessity is seen to be the necessary order and grouping of a variety of acts or entities which have been performed or produced according to a single connected rule.

With this last development, Descartes' original problem, and the philosophy of the seventeenth and eighteenth centuries, have been irrevocably transmuted. The *Critique* is not the completion and fulfillment of philosophy, as Kant himself considered it, but it may justly be considered the beginning of philosophy, or at least of living philosophy. No one who has mastered the *Critique* can ever view that which precedes it as other than preparation for Kant. Too much of what has followed it can only be viewed as a falling away.

Bibliography

Index

BIBLIOGRAPHY

Adickes, Erich. *Kants Lehre von der Doppelten Affektion Unseres Ich als Schüssel zu Seiner Erkenntnistheorie* (Tübingen: Mohr, 1929).

Alexander, H. G. (ed.). *The Leibniz-Clarke Correspondence* (Manchester: Manchester University Press, 1956).

Aristotle. *Works,* translated under the editorship of W. D. Ross, 12 vols. (Oxford: Clarendon Press, 1908–1952).

Beattie, James. *An Essay on the Nature and Immutability of Truth* (Edinburgh, 1770).

Hume, David. *Enquiries Concerning the Human Understanding and Concerning the Principles of Morals,* ed. by L. A. Selby-Bigge, 2nd edition (Oxford: Clarendon Press, 1902; reprinted 1936).

—————— *A Treatise of Human Nature,* ed. by L. A. Selby-Bigge (Oxford: Clarendon Press, 1888; reprinted 1951).

James, William. *The Principles of Psychology,* 2 vols. (New York: Henry Holt, 1890).

Kant, Immanuel. *Gesammelte Schriften,* Hrsg. von der Koniglich Preussischen Akadamie der Wissenschaften (Berlin: G. Reimer, 1902–   ).

—————— *The Critique of Judgement,* trans. with Analytical Indexes by J. C. Meredith (Oxford: Clarendon Press, 1952).

—————— *Critique of Pure Reason,* trans. by Norman Kemp Smith, 2nd impression with corrections (London: Macmillan, 1933; reprinted 1950).

——————*Kant's Inaugural Dissertation and Early Writings on Space,* trans. by J. Handyside (London: Open Court, 1929).

—————— *Kritik der Reinen Vernunft,* Hrsg. von Raymund Schmidt, 2te Auflage (Hamburg: Felix Meiner Verlag, 1930).

—————— *Prolegomena to any Future Metaphysics,* trans. with Introduction by Lewis White Beck (New York: Liberal Arts Press, 1950).

—————— *Prolegomena, and Metaphysical Foundations of Natural Science,* trans. with a biography and introduction, by Ernest Belfort Bax (London: G. Bell & Sons, 1883).

Leibniz, G. W. *Selections,* ed. by Philip Wiener (New York: Scribner, 1951).

Lewis, Clarence Irving. *An Analysis of Knowledge and Valuation* (La Salle: Open Court, 1947).

Locke, John. *An Essay Concerning Human Understanding,* abridged and ed. by A. S. Pringle-Pattison (Oxford: Clarendon Press, 1924).

Paton, H. J. *Kant's Metaphysic of Experience,* 2 vols. (London: George Allen & Unwin, 1951).

Smith, Norman Kemp. *A Commentary to Kant's 'Critique of Pure Reason',* 2nd edition, revised and enlarged (London: Macmillan, 1923; reprinted by Humanities Press, 1950).

Vaihinger, H. *Commentar zu Kant's Kritik der Reinen Vernunft,* 2 bde. (Stuttgart: W. Spemann, 1881–1892).

Weldon, T. D. *Kant's Critique of Pure Reason,* 2nd edition (Oxford: Clarendon Press, 1958).

Wolff, Robert Paul. "Hume's Theory of Mental Activity," *Philosophical Review,* 49:289–310 (July 1960).

—— "Kant's Debt to Hume via Beattie," *Journal of the History of Ideas,* 21:117–123 (January-March 1960).

in B, 47–48; regressive and progressive in, 44, 46–47
psychology, 298, 309; and philosophy, 100–101, 176–177
pure categories, 216–217
pure concepts: applied to object = x, 146–147; conditions of appearance, 94, 100; deduction of, 38, 67–77, 89; in *Dissertation*, 87, 214; nature of, 76, 204, 208; and real use of intelligence, 15, 41; relation to intuition, 31–32; role in Deduction, 117–118; as rules of synthesis, 32, 33, 71, 125; and schemata, 2–7, 212; and things-in-themselves, 33–34, 64, 70, 85–93 passim, 99–100; validity of, 93, 95
pure intuition: 73–75, 218–223, 230, 272–273; ambiguities in, 72–75, 236; and double affection, 171, 222; and perception, 219, 233; = pure form of intuition, 237
pure manifold, 174, 237–238, 259n; separate, 218–219, 220–221
pure mathematics, 189–190, 221n, 226–227, 295
pure space, 189–190
pure time, 272–273
purposiveness, 38

quality, 234

ratiocinatio polysyllogistica, 53
rationalism, 192, 216
real, 235, 266–267
reality, 15, 313; knowledge of, unconditioned, 88, 92–93
reason, 41; in Critical Philosophy, 36, 203, 204
reciprocity, 285, 287, 288–289
Refutation of Idealism, 43, 167, 289; in A, 300; in B, 254–255, 299–301; and inner sense, 191, 200
regressive method: in Analogies, 252, 266; in Deduction, 112, 139–140, 153; nature of, 44–46, 161; not a proof, 46, 53, 55–56; in *Prolegomena,* 46–47
regularity theory of causation, 282–283
Regulative Employment of Reason, 70–71
regulative principles, 247
relation: categories of, 66–67; of ideas in Hume, 25–27, 28–30
representation: meaning of, 108n, 109; nature of, 105, 263–264; of succession, 267, 268

reproduction: according to a rule, 101–102, 215–216; in imagination, 127–130, 131, 134, 153–154, 200–201, 281
reproductive imagination, 171, 222; in Deduction, 141, 174
reversible succession, 289–292
rule-analysis of concepts, 323–324
rule-directed activities: nature of, 121–125, 212–213; and synthesis, 130–131, 140–141, 178; two types, 124–125
rules: analysis of, 121–125, 133–134; concepts as, 32, 63, 70; first and second order, 124–125; Ideas as, 70–71; and judgment, 205; for synthesis, 32, 178, 208, 210, 217

schemata: and categories, 209, 210, 216–217, 242n, 312; and concepts, 210–214; defined, 211, 247
Schematism, 151, 180, 206–210, 214–218; artificiality of, 43, 207, 208–209; role of, 205–208 passim; rules and concepts in, 70
schematised categories, 216–217, 223
science, 191, 249–250, 306; and Analytic, 181, 302; experiment in, 304–305; must be mathematical, 309; possibility of, 302
Second Analogy, 180, 279–280, 289; analyzed, 260–283; causation in, 280–283; and Deduction, 274–277; flaws in, 200–201, 267–269; nature of objects in, 110–111, 134; principle in A and B, 261; proofs analyzed, 261–276; proof in A, 266–267; proof in B, 275–276
second-order rules, 213
self, 109; how known, 96, 143, 192–193, 198, 200; in Hume, 107–108, 142n; nature of, 143–145, 170, 290n
self-consciousness, 194–195, 199
sensation, 172n, 295; form and matter in, 234; as matter of intuition, 73, 220, 233
sensibility: in *Dissertation,* 12, 14, 87–88; limits intelligence, 21, 31–32, 214; other forms of, 215, 216; relation to understanding, 209, 210, 294–295
simultaneity, 3, 67, 252
simultaneous causation, 280–282, 291–292
Smith, Norman Kemp: on Analogies, 248, 254, 257, 269, 287–289; on *Critique,* 56, 66, 79, 293, 296; on idealism, 299n; on Kant's knowledge of Hume, 142n; on Kant's theory of knowledge,

DATE DUE